15.99

FROM THE GARDEN TO

From the Garden to the Street

An introduction to 300 years of poetry for children

MORAG STYLES

READER IN CHILDREN'S LITERATURE,
HOMERTON COLLEGE, CAMBRIDGE

CASSELL

Cassell
Wellington House
125 Strand, London WC2R 0BB

PO Box 605
Herndon, VA 20172

First published 1998

British Library Cataloguing-in-Publication Data
A catalogue record for this book is available from the British Library.

ISBN 0-304-33224-0 (hardback)
0-304-33222-4 (paperback)

Typeset by Kenneth Burnley in Irby, Wirral, Cheshire.
Printed and bound in Great Britain by Redwood Books, Trowbridge, Wiltshire.

For my mother

Contents

Preface

I began keeping notes on the history of poetry written for children in early 1989 and was dabbling in the field for some years before applying myself seriously to the task of writing this book. I was able to do so by being given research time and study leave from Homerton College where I have worked for the last 20 years. I am grateful to the Principal, Kate Pretty, the Research Directors and my colleagues for providing me with the opportunity to complete this massive undertaking.

As there are not many scholars in this field, it has sometimes felt a lonely occupation. But I owe a debt to a great number of friends and colleagues who have kept me company along the way. First of all, there is Victor Watson with whom I have worked closely for many years and from whom I have learned so much about children's literature. Helen Taylor, collaborator and fellow poetry enthusiast, read some of the chapters in draft and made honest, critical and constructive comments which were most valuable. John Beck commented painstakingly on socio-historical points in many crude drafts and patiently served as a guinea-pig for the non-specialist reader, keeping me steady when I threatened to run up too many blind alleys and attractive-looking paths and by-ways. Sheila Miles provided sociological analysis and a friendly response when I was getting discouraged.

Mary Hamer encouraged me to find and use my own voice in academic as well as personal writing; insofar as I have managed to do so, she deserves the credit. Eve Bearne and David Whitley both offered feedback and were invariably positive and kind, as well as insightful. Clive Wilmer gave excellent advice on a crucial section of the text at a time when he was busy with his own writing. Heather Glen was invariably enouraging and helpful; her outstanding book, *Vision and Disenchantment*, was a source of inspiration.

Margaret Meek/Spencer proved a wise commentator on a couple of chapters. Although I could never hope to equal her scholarship, I tried to keep before me her example of academic study combined with respect for children as readers. Finally, Naomi Roth, my editor, believed in me, waiting out several missed deadlines and 'dead-ends' before she received the final manuscript.

I should also like to mention the librarians in the West Room, Reading Room and Rare Books Room who fetched literally hundreds of books for me over the years from the remotest outposts of the Cambridge University Library. To all of them I offer my sincere thanks; and to my son, Ross, who endured close contact with an obsessed and distracted mother for rather a long time. All the shortcomings are, of course, of my own making.

MORAG STYLES
Cambridge, 1997

Acknowledgements

A few sections from this book have appeared in a slightly modified form in the following publications:

M. Hilton *et al.* (eds), *Opening the Nursery Door*, Routledge, 1997.
P. Hunt (ed.), *Routledge International Companion Encyclopedia of Children's Literature*, Routledge, 1996.
C. Powling and M. Styles (eds), *The Books for Keeps Guide to Poetry*, BFK, 1996.
M. Styles *et al.* (eds), *Voices Off: Texts, Contexts and Readers*, Cassell, 1996.
'Lost From the Nursery', *Signal*, 63, 1990.

The author and publishers are grateful for permission to quote from the following sources:

John Agard, c/o Caroline Sheldon Literary Agency, for 'A Clown's Conclusion' from *Laughter is an Egg*, Penguin Books, 1991, and 'Half-Caste' from *Get Back Pimple*, Penguin Books, 1996.

Random House for extracts from John Agard, 'No Rain, No Rainbow' from *Say It In Granny*.

Allan Ahlberg for four lines from 'Please Mrs Butler' p. 10 and twenty-one lines from 'The Cane' pp. 58–60 from *Please Mrs Butler* copyright © Allan Ahlberg, Kestrel Books, London, 1983. Reproduced by permission of Frederick Warne & Co.

The Estate of Hilaire Belloc and Peters Fraser & Dunlop for sixteen lines from 'Jim and the Lion' and nine lines from 'Tarantella' from *Hilaire Belloc: Complete Verse*, Pimlico, London, 1991.

James Berry for extracts from 'Only One of Me', 'When I Dance', 'Mek Drum Talk, Man', 'I Wohn Get a Complex', Jamaican Toad', Mum Dad and Me', 'Black Kid in a New Place', 'Letter from YOUR SPeCiAL- BiG-pUPPY-DOg' from *When I Dance*, Hamish Hamilton [Penguin Books] 1988, copyright © James Berry; part of 'Playing a Dazzler' from *Playing a Dazzler*, copyright © James Berry, Hamish Hamilton, London, 1996, p. 16. Reproduced by permission of Frederick Warne & Co.

Edward Kamau Brathwaite for an extract from 'Didn't He Ramble', *The Arrivants*, OUP 1973, by permission of Oxford University Press.

Alan Brownjohn for part of 'We are going to see the rabbit' copyright © the Author;

Charles Causley and David Higham Associates for extracts from 'Who?', 'The Jolly Hunter', 'Timothy Winters', 'My Mother saw a Dancing Bear', Tell Me, Sarah Jane' from *Figgie Hobbin,* Macmillan, 1970; 'On St Catherine's Day', 'Tavistock Goose Fair', 'Why?' from *Jack the Treacle Eater ,* Macmillan, 1987; 'Rise Up, Jenny' from *The Young Man of Cury*, Macmillan, 1991.

The Literary Trustees of Walter de la Mare, and the Society of Authors as their representative for parts of 'The Listeners', 'Nicholas Nye', 'Silver', 'The Fly', 'Seeds' and 'Tartary' from *The Complete Poems of Walter de la Mare,* 1969 [USA 1970].

David Higham Associates for parts of 'The Night Will Never Stay', 'It Was a Long Time Ago' from *Something I Remember: Selected Poems for Children by Eleanor Farjeon,* Puffin, 1987; extracts from 'City-Under-Water' and 'Cat!' from *Silver, Sand and Snow,* Michael Joseph by Eleanor Farjeon.

Nikki Giovanni copyright © 1971 for an extract from 'Mattie Lou at twelve' from *Spin a Soft Black Song*, Hill & Wang, USA, 1971.

Carcanet Press Ltd for extracts from 'Warning to Children' and 'The Mirror' by Robert Graves from *Complete Poems: Robert Graves,* Carcanet Press Ltd, 1997.

Phoebe Hesketh and Martin Hesketh for an extract from 'Truant'.

Reprinted by permission of Alfred Knopf Inc. for 'My Old Mule' from Collected Poems by Langston Hughes, copyright © 1994 by the Estate of Langston Hughes.

Ted Hughes and Faber for extracts from 'Sheep', 'Donkey', 'Badger', 'Cows', 'The Fly', 'Foal', 'Lobworms' from *What is the Truth?,* Faber, 1984; 'Snow-shoe Hare', 'Cat', 'Thrush' from *The Iron Wolf,* Faber, 1995.

LKJ Music Publishers for permission to reproduce 'Inglan is a Bitch' by Linton Kwesi Johnson.

Jackie Kay and Penguin Books for extracts from 'Two Carla Johnsons', 'Two Niagaras', 'Carla's Kisses' and the entire poem 'Two of Everything' from *Two's Company,* Blackie, London, 1992, copyright © Jackie Kay. Reproduced by permission of Frederick Warne & Co.

A. P. Watt Ltd on behalf of The National Trust for extracts of poems by Rudyard Kipling; 'The River's Tale' from C LR Fletcher's *History of England ;* four lines about John Bunyan quoted in *Kipling the Poet* by Robert Keating; four lines from 'If' from *Rewards and Fairies*; six lines from 'The Way Through the Woods' from *Puck of Pook's Hill;* four lines from 'The Glory of the Garden'.

The Society of Authors as the Literary Representative of the Estate of John Masefield for part of 'Cargoes'.

Roger McGough for extracts from 'A Poem about Violence', 'The Pet', 'A Good Poem' from *Sky in the Pie*, Viking Kestrel, 1983; 'First Day at School', 'Nooligan' from *You Tell Me*, Viking Kestrel, 1979; 'When I played as a kid' from *Nailing the Shadow*, Viking Kestrel, 1987. Reprinted by permission of the Peters Fraser & Dunlop Group Ltd. On behalf of Roger McGough.

Colin McNaughton for extracts from 'Monday's Child', 'A Fat Lot of Good' and 'Short Sharp Shock' from *There's an Awful Lot of Weirdos in out Neighbourhood* © 1987 Colin McNaughton. Reproduced by permission of the publisher Walker Books Ltd.

Reed International Books for extracts from poems by A.A. Milne as follows: 'The Three Foxes', 'The Doremouse and the Doctor', 'The King's Breakfast', 'Happiness' and 'Hoppity' from *When We Were Very Young*, Methuen, London, 1923; 'Furry Bear', 'Twice Times', 'Solitude', 'In the Dark' from *Now We Are Six*, Methuen, London, 1927.

Adrian Mitchell for an extract from 'The Thirteen Secrets of Poetry' in *The Thirteen Secrets of Poetry*, MacDonald, 1992; extracts from 'Dumb Insolence', 'Nothingmas Day' and the entire poem 'Give Us a Brake' from *Balloon Lagoon*, Orchard Books, 1997; extract from 'Song in Space' from *Adrian Mitchell's Greatest Hits*, Bloodaxe Books, copyright © Adrian Mitchell. Reprinted by permission of The Peters Fraser and Dunlop Group Limited on behalf of Adrian Mitchell.

Educational Health Warning! Adrian Mitchell asks that none of his poems are used in connection with any examinations whatsoever.

Anthea Bell for the translation of Christian Morgenstern's *Lullabies and Lyrics,* North-South Books, 1992.

From *Custard and Company* by Ogden Nash; 1] Copyright 1933 by Ogden Nash; first appeared in THE NEW YORKER; 2] Copyright © 1961 by Ogden Nash. By permission of Little, Brown and Company.

Grace Nichols for extracts from 'Wha Me Mudder Do', 'I Like to Stay Up' and 'Granny' from *Come on into my Tropical Garden* A & C Black, 1988; 'Give Yourself a Hug' from *Give Yourself a Hug,* A & C Black, 1994. Reproduced with permission of Curtis Brown Ltd, London on behalf of Grace Nichols. Copyright © Grace Nichols.

John Murray (Publishers) Ltd for six lines from 'The Highwayman' by Alfred Noyes.

Extracts from *I Saw Esau*. Text © 1992 Iona Opie. Illustrated by Maurice Sendak. Reproduced by permission of the publisher Walker Books Ltd.

Gareth Owen and Harper Collins Publishers for extracts from 'Miss Creedle teaches creative writing' from *Song of the City,* Collins, 1985; 'Salford Road' and 'Empty House' from *Salford Road and other Poems*, Collins, 1988.

Brian Patten for parts of 'Pick-a-Nose Pick's Awful Poem' from *Gargling with Jelly,* Viking Kestrel, 1979. Copyright © Brian Patten.

James Reeves. Extracts from 'Little Fan' and 'The Sea' from *James Reeves: Complete Poems for Children*, 1973. By permission of Laura Cecil, Literary Agent for Children's Books.

Dominic Rieu for part of 'Sir Smashem Uppe' by E. V. Rieu.

Michael Rosen for extracts from 'In the daytime I am Rob Roy', 'I'm alone in the evening', 'If you don't . . .', 'Mum'll be coming home today . . .', 'When we opened the door' and the entire poem 'I've had this shirt' from *Mind Your Own Business*, Andre Deutsch/Scholastic, 1974; 'Old Mother Hubbard' from *Hairy Tales and Nursery Crimes*, Andre Deutsch/Scholastic, 1985; an extract from 'Harrybo' from *The Hypnotiser*, Andre Deutsch/Scholastic, 1988 copyright © Michael Rosen.

Vernon Scannell copyright © for extracts from 'Poem on Bread' and 'Growing Pain'.

Anne Serraillier for extracts from 'Anne and the Field Mouse' and 'The Rescue' by Ian Serraillier.

Shel Silverstein and Harper Collins Publishers New York for 'Listen to the Mustn'ts' from *A Light in the Attic*. Copyright © 1981 by Evil Eye Music, Inc.

Myfanwy Thomas and Oxford University Press for part of 'Adlestrop' from *Edward Thomas: Collected Poems*.

Kit Wright for extracts from 'Horace the Hedgehog', 'Dave Dirt was on the 259', 'All of the Morning', 'Where all the Flowers Went' from *Rabbiting On* (1979), *Hot Dog* (1981), *Cat Among the Pigeons* (1987), Puffin.

A. P. Watt Ltd. on behalf of Michael Yeats for eight lines from 'The Song of Wandering Angus' taken from *The Collected Poems of* W. B. Yeats. Reprinted with permission of Scribner, a Division of Simon & Schuster from *The Collected Works of W. B. Yeats, Volume 1: The Poems*, revised and edited by Richard J. Finneran, New York: Scribner, 1997.

Benjamin Zephaniah for extracts from 'Over De Moon' from *Talking Turkeys*, Viking, 1994; 'Walking Black Home'; 'Natural Anthem' and 'Danny Lives On' from *Funky Chickens*, Viking, 1996 copyright © Benjamin Zephaniah.

Every effort has been made to trace copyright holders. The author and publishers would be interested to hear from any copyright holders not here acknowledged.

Introduction

From the 'garden' of childhood to real life on the street in 300 years of poetry for children

My ambitions in writing this book are many. The first and simplest is to provide an informative account of the history of poetry written for children in Britain and, to a lesser extent, America in the last three centuries. In so doing, I want to show how children's poetry has developed during this period, as well as tracing continuities between the past and present. The task as I have described it so far is straightforward, if laborious. There might be various ways of going about it, but the job to be done is surely to analyse the major poets, branches of poetry, forms, styles and genres across three centuries.

But what do we mean by children's poetry? Can we identify such a thing as a child's poem? The answer is 'not easily', except for the negation; that is to say, I can show you poems that are not for children because they are about things children do not understand or are written in language that is too complex for young readers to take in. Even a statement like that must be qualified since children with a good start in poetry can manage quite sophisticated texts from writers such as Shakespeare, Gerard Manley Hopkins or Emily Dickinson, especially if the verse is musical, lyrical or tells a good tale. W. H. Auden offers the other side of the coin in his much-quoted comment that 'While there are some good poems that are only for adults, because they pre-suppose adult experience in their readers, there are no good poems which are only for children.'[1]

The notion of children's poetry implicit in this book centres on what has been specifically written with young readers in mind (aged between about 5 and 12), but also includes poetry shared with the adult canon which editors have selected for children or which children have found, liked, borrowed and hoarded for themselves. There is a critical debate on this issue and I ought to make my own position clear. Many commentators on children's poetry think that what is written explicitly for the young is generally inferior to poetry, written for adults, that children are able to comprehend. Neil Philip, for example, the influential editor of *A New Treasury of Poetry*, stresses in his introduction the need to be 'cautious with poems written specially for children, preferring on the whole work which makes itself available to a young reader without any sense of talking or writing down.'[2] I take the contrary view that poetry written with children as their major audience should be valued in its own right and not disparaged as 'talking or writing down'. Elsewhere, however, Philip strikes a different note. In his well-informed introduction to *The New Oxford Book of Children's Verse* he says: 'there is a recognizable tradition of children's verse . . . that is at once separate from and intermingled with the larger poetic tradition, but it has its own landmarks and its own rhetoric.' He goes on to show how a poet like Emily Dickinson 'tests any makeshift boundaries between poetry for children and poetry for adults to their limits.'[3]

Yet many adults hold to a somewhat idealized notion of childhood, tending to prefer poetry that confirms this view to that which disturbs it. Although I may unconsciously fall into this habit myself now and again, it is my wish to seek out poetry that is as honest, vigorous and unsentimental as, in my view, children generally are. There is certainly a place in this book for poetry that is tender, light or thoughtful, but I have been ruthless with anything that smacks of being precious or condescending in its treatment of children.

Then there is the issue of the 'canon'. I have given serious attention to all the poets who have loomed large in the history of children's poetry such as Blake, Carroll, Lear, Rossetti, Stevenson and de la Mare. But a large part of what has come to be known as children's poetry was actually written for adults and has either been adopted by children themselves or apparently colonized on their behalf for the juvenile canon. Why? Have generations of anthologists played a role in privileging their own taste for literary poetry rather then acknowledging the preferences of the young? Or have children always been drawn to the narrative and lyric qualities of any poetry that they were able to understand? These questions are explored further in Chapters 9 and 10.

The question of how writing for children is valued by the literary elite of any given era is also raised in Chapter 9. Much recent academic work on children's literature acknowledges the marginalized position of children's texts within literature as a whole. This book is no exception and one of my aims is to challenge the notion that children's literature is not as worthy of serious attention as adult work. Indeed, this book seeks to underline the fact that the young have been well catered for in poetry from Bunyan's homely 'rhimes' to the wit of McGough and others today. Also, running on parallel and intertwining tracks throughout this history is the oral tradition whose robustness and vitality is celebrated, particularly in Chapter 4.

Another important question inevitably raised by this book is whether or not there is an enduring or a changing sense of the child or a notion of childhood that can be analysed through the poetry. And what about all the children who, before the late nineteenth century, could not read or who did not have access to books? Class, gender, race and privilege cannot be ignored. This history is necessarily a partial one and largely middle class in orientation, since there is little evidence about the reading experiences of working-class children, let alone their preferences in poetry. Until the late eighteenth century at the earliest, the cost of books put them out of reach of all but the fairly wealthy. Verse was, however, affordable and accessible to many through chapbooks and broadsheets which circulated widely and cheaply up and down the country. The role of chapbooks in the dissemination of poetry to a wide reading public and their influence on what was being written for children is taken up in Chapter 1.

As for gender, one of the most exciting discoveries of this research has been the number of women who wrote significant poetry for children in their time, but who get very little mention in the critical literature. There are gaping holes in our knowledge about women's writing for children and I suspect that Dorothy Wordsworth, who will be known to most readers, and Jane Johnson, who will not, are just two of many who wrote admirably for the young within the private domain. I attempt to redress the balance a little by restoring some names like those of Ann and Jane Taylor, Charlotte Smith and Christina Rossetti to their rightful place in the history of children's poetry throughout this book and especially in Chapter 7. I also demonstrate that some poetry by women, especially that written for very young children, has distinctive qualities of sensuality and physicality that are otherwise little evident within the genre. Christina Rossetti is the purest exponent of this kind of verse, but it is not widely known.

> My baby has a mottled fist,
> My baby has a neck in creases;
> My baby kisses and is kissed,
> For he's the very thing for kisses.[4]
> (Christina Rossetti)

What began life as a relatively simple scholarly history then, has proved to be much more complicated. One of the difficulties was organizational; it would have been boring and unwieldy to do a straightforward historical trawl through children's poetry. Instead, I have worked rather loosely on a thematic ordering, beginning with early religious poetry for children, moving on to the Romantic period, lingering on the oral tradition, before focusing on humour and the two best-known nonsense writers of the Victorian era, Carroll and Lear. Going back and forward in time I shift the focus to women poets, then turn the spotlight on Rossetti and Stevenson, both of whom I argue produced landmark collections for children. Finally, I deal with popular narrative and lyric poems, mostly of the nineteenth century; consider the range of verse written for children in the twentieth century, featuring de la Mare, Milne, Causley and Hughes; and conclude by showing the quality of contemporary poetry and the nature of its appeal to the young. In the remainder of this Introduction I open up some of the debates that permeate the book.

(I have also paid attention in a small way to illustrations, since they are interesting in their own right and have played a significant part in the appeal of poetry to children.)

Visions of Arcadia

> I dream of a place where I long to live always:
> Green hills, shallow sand dunes, and nearing the sea;[5]
> (Walter de la Mare)

I called this book, *From the Garden to the Street*, because one of the most significant continuities in the otherwise great variety of poetry written for children is its location in the 'natural' world – until the 1970s, that is. In poetry for children written between the seventeenth century and 1970, three emphases predominate: the smallness and prettiness of children; their location in a rural setting, often an idyllic one; and the association of poetry with magic and music. The last is enduring and probably always will be, but is balanced these days by plenty of poetry that aspires to realism. But the view of childhood that seeps out of the pages of many early poetry books associates children with attractive little things such as dolls, toys and puppies. This is a long way from flesh and blood children who are often large, noisy and boisterous; and you only have to think of the real lives of the youthful chimney sweeps Blake describes at the end of the eighteenth century or children of the urban poor in the Victorian period to realize that far from being 'natural', it is an idealized middle-class construct of childhood that is presented in many eighteenth- and, indeed, nineteenth-century poems.

Locating poetry for children in the countryside suggests that in poetry as well as in life it is fresh and healthy for children to be outside in the open air. Unfortunately, this excludes many readers, including children of the labouring poor working alongside their parents in mines and factories or toiling on the land. The countryside experiences of agricultural labourers' children were anything but carefree. But in poetry for children until fairly recently, gardens are places of play where the animals can cavort with the children, where trees change with the seasons and scented flowers bloom; above all, it appears to be a 'natural' setting and by association, children are natural too. The labour that actually sustained these cultivated settings is invisible, as Raymond Williams has repeatedly pointed out.

No preface is more revealing in this respect than Kenneth Grahame's as he confides to his adult readers in his *Cambridge Book of Poetry for Children*, 1916.

In compiling a selection of Poetry for Children, a conscientious Editor is bound to find himself confronted with limitations so numerous as to be almost disheartening . . . His task is to set up a wicket-gate giving admission to that wide domain, with its woodland glades, its pasture and arable, its walled and scented gardens here and there, and so to its sunlit, and sometimes misty, mountain-tops – all to be more fully explored later by those who are tempted on by the first glance. And always he must be proclaiming that there is joy, light and fresh air in that delectable country.[6]

Kipling goes further:

> Our England is a garden that is full of stately views.
> Of borders, beds and shrubberies and lawns and avenues,
> With statues on the terraces and peacocks strutting by;
> But the Glory of the Garden lies in more than meets the eye.[7]

In fact, part of the appeal for this kind of arcadia was that the reality of urban life for large numbers of people was living in polluted cities, often in miserable conditions. Longing for the countryside, or what was often in reality large, landscaped estates, and idealizing it was part of the pastoral idyll so prevalent in the literature of the epoch. Hazlitt[8] wrote an essay 'On the Love of the Country' in 1814 which took account of the developing relationship between childhood and the countryside by suggesting that natural objects have nostalgia value because they can powerfully bring back childhood memories. No wonder poets have taken up this theme with such conviction.

In *Secret Gardens*, Humphrey Carpenter[9] argues that children's writers of the Edwardian period, such as Milne, Barrie and Grahame were searching for arcadia; certainly their books glorify the natural world in distinctive ways. Before them, the poetry of the Romantics was largely situated in the outside world and populated by those visualized as at one with nature, including children who came 'trailing clouds of glory' with access to a visionary simplicity that was denied to adults. But poetry for children had been doing that since well before the Romantics. In the earlier period the rural settings of poetry tended to be communal places, whereas post-Romantics were more likely to choose private, 'secret' gardens. I address these issues in Chapters 2 and 3. While I realize that I am clustering rather different entities together – the wild, untamed, natural world at one extreme and formal, fenced-in, cultivated gardens at the other – my argument about the location of children's poetry in a 'rural' setting applies to both.

Keith Thomas[10] offers a historical perspective on what he calls 'this feeling for the countryside, real or imagined'. Reminding us of the gentry's love affair with the countryside that exists to the present day, he explores the profound shift in sensibilities that happened in Britain between 1500 and 1800. The desirability of close ties with nature became widespread for a wider social group than just the upper classes. 'It was these centuries which generated both an intense interest in the natural world and those doubts and anxieties about man's [sic] relationship to it which we have inherited in magnified form.'[11] Using Pepys's *Diary* and other evidence of the period, Thomas tells us that one of the reasons why the fire of London did such damage in 1666 is that it broke out on a Sunday morning when most of the chief merchants were away, as usual, in the country!

Thomas asserts that by 1800 there was widespread concern for animal welfare and 'an increasing number of people had begun to plant trees and to cultivate flowers for emotional satisfaction. These developments were but aspects of a much wider reversal in the relationship of the English to the natural world.'[12] The countryside idyll, so common in the poetry of the period, was a far cry from the reality of life in the countryside which, for the labouring poor, was as 'solitary, poor, nasty, brutish and short'[13] as in the towns; the genuine renewal found in the countryside could only be enjoyed by those with the wealth and leisure to do so. As Thomas put it: 'the social inequality of the English countryside meant that arcadia had vanished [if it had ever existed] . . . The cult of the countryside was, therefore, in many ways a mystification and an evasion of reality.'[14]

In terms of poetry for children, 'the garden' motif became predominant during the nineteenth century. The tame, domestic, fragrant gardens created by many poets and anthologists as reflections of their own preoccupations, which were often at odds with the rather different realities faced by many children, are highlighted in Chapters 3 and 13.

> To house and garden, field and lawn,
> The meadow gates we swang upon,
> To pump and stable, tree and swing,
> Good-bye, good-bye, to everything![15]
> (Robert Louis Stevenson)

Raymond Williams touches on the same themes in his outstanding book, *The Country and the City*. He writes of how the country has been construed as 'a natural way of life: of peace, innocence, and simple virtue', all of which are potent ideas in children's poetry. Williams goes on to review the history of the pastoral idyll within literature which he traces back to Virgil. Most importantly, Williams shows how the country and the city were equated with moral values so that: 'an ordered and happier past [is] set against the disturbance and disorder of the present. An idealization . . . served to cover and to evade the actual and bitter contradiction of the time.'[16] And this same idealization of the country was reflected in poetry for children – until recently.

Poetry of the late twentieth century is a different matter. Much of it is firmly positioned in the city street, bedroom or school playground where children, often neither little nor pretty, are depicted as individuals with strengths and faults; whereas parents, teachers and other significant adults, far from embodying wisdom, are often presented in a critical, though still largely affectionate light. Placing children's poetry in an urban setting is more than a move out of arcadia; with it comes a 'street-wise' outlook, plus the language, mores and characters of the ordinary street. Sometimes it is suburban, sometimes cosmopolitan or multi-ethnic, but basically it reflects the everyday life of most children as they know it. Instead of a politely expressed subject matter which excluded the experience of some readers, this is poetry that offers an open invitation to all by drawing on 'real-life' situations, using the appeal of boisterous humour and writing in a style that is lively and engaging, but not difficult to penetrate. At best, this is cleverly crafted, realistic poetry with bite and relevance, though it also has a thoughtful and tender side often ignored by critics. As for the countryside, poets like Ted Hughes have largely displaced idyllic rural imagery with realism about the natural world as an elemental but harsh environment, while many other poets tackle 'green' issues head on. Kit Wright's amusing parody of 'Where have all the flowers gone' is a typical example of the current treatment of nature.

> Where have all the flowers gone,
> The flowers that were standing on
> The grave beside the churchyard wall?
>   My little brother grabbed them
>
> And stuffed them in an old tin can
> And took them home to give my Gran.[17]
>   (Kit Wright)

The 'street-wise' school of contemporary children's poetry is predominant in the late 1990s, but it is not the only significant trend in poetry publishing. There are still immensely popular poets like Charles Causley writing out of a different tradition – that of the balladeer and storyteller, as well as a number of others who favour verse with more obvious connections with the past. Modern poetry for children is, in fact, in a healthy state with a great variety of voices being heard and plenty of choice for discriminating readers. If there is also some mediocre material getting into print on the wave of more talented exponents, it was ever thus and they will soon fall by the wayside, like the flowers.

Constructions of childhood

> . . . blest the Babe,
> Nursed in his Mother's arms, who sinks to sleep,
> Rocked on his Mother's breast; who with his soul
> Drinks in the feelings of his Mother's eye![18]
>   (William Wordsworth)

In *Constructing and Reconstructing Childhood*, Allison James and Alan Prout[19] talk about the 'way in which the immaturity of children is conceived and articulated in particular societies into culturally specific sets of ideas and philosophies, attitudes and practices that combine to define "the nature of childhood"'. They underline the fact that we take childhood as a given category, whereas it actually varies from social group to social group, from culture to culture, from one time to another. Yet many poets writing about or for children hold an implicit view of childhood that they take to be 'natural', but which is actually largely a white, middle-class, Western construction. This naturalizing of the categories of class, race and gender affects the reading of children's poetry: when a poem makes an assumption about a child living in a nursery, or having a nanny, or there being plenty to eat all the time, or little boys behaving this way or that, we need to treat it as an expression of a particular and probably privileged point of view; an expression of the historical or cultural context in which the poem was written.

In a similar vein, Marx Wartofsky in *The Child and Other Cultural Inventions*[20] talks of the historically changing construction of childhood:

> The world's construction of the child is no homogenous model even within a given society, for differences in social class, race and sex, often entail differences in opportunity, freedom and expectations . . . The child comes to be socialized as the child of that particular historical world.

He goes on to suggest that 'traditional, mythic models of childhood are nervous attempts to conceive childhood in terms of what we can contain and control'. That is only too evident in the early history of children's poetry, particularly when it is associated with Romanticism. These ideas are developed in Chapter 2.

If 'the child' is essentially a cultural invention, then different human cultures have invented different children. The most popular current model of childhood, espoused by influential educationalists and, indeed, most middle-class people in Britain and America, gives primacy to certain psychological explanations of child development, including the importance of play and creativity, especially in the early years of life. As these constructions are 'humane', and as many of us are deeply embedded within these belief systems ourselves, it is all too easy to assume that that is the way things are or always were, rather than going to the trouble of problematizing these assumptions.

Poetry for children, then, tends to naturalize childhood along the lines of the dominant ideologies of the time. When E. V. Lucas[21] says that Stevenson has 'recaptured in maturity the thoughts, ambitions, purposes, hopes, fears, the philosophy of the child', he assumes he knows what children hope, feel etc. In an insightful article about Ted Hughes's masterpiece, *What is the Truth?*, Neil Philip offers up a familiar essentialist view of 'great' poetry and of childhood. Philip[22] is also sure he can recognize when poetry itself is the 'real thing':

It is for me a statement of faith in the importance of poetry: faith that it is too important to be debased for the young, and faith that the young, when they meet the real coin, can redeem its full value.

Historians and literary critics provide some of the answers about how childhood has been constructed over the centuries. Zachary Leader, for example, in *Reading Blake's Songs*[23] discusses the climate for children's literature in the late eighteenth century. This was an age:

in which artists, intellectuals, social reformers, teachers, and parents were passionately and sharply divided in their attitudes towards childhood and education.

Leader comments on the new seriousness shown and importance given to discussion of the sorts of books children should read. The more humane philosophy of Locke and others towards children, their education and their reading was converted into an obsessive neo-Puritanism in the late eighteenth century, partly brought about through fear of revolution. Referring to the influential intellectuals, social reformers, educationalists and writers of this era, Leader points out that:

the passion and industry it brought to its campaigns for the abolition of slavery . . . was no less marked in its attempts to provide suitable reading matter for the young, or to create day or Sunday schools for the children of the poor . . . and the children's books they inspired . . . strengthened old-fashioned Calvinist attitudes.[24]

This relentless campaign against playfulness and fancy was more pronounced in fiction than in poetry with many children's writers decrying the dangers of fantasy in any form, including fairy tales. Lucy Aikin recognizes this trend in the preface to *Poetry for Children*[25] in 1801:

Since dragons and fairies, giants and witches, have vanished from our nurseries before the wand of reason, it has become a prevailing maxim that the young mind should be fed on mere prose and simple fact.

And since she was a wise young woman:

It may well be questioned whether the novel-like tales now written for the amusement of youth, may not be productive of more injury to the mind, by giving a false picture of the real world, than the fairy fictions of the last generation, which only wandered over the region of shadows.

If we go further back in time, debates centre on whether the separate existence of childhood was recognized at all. Keith Thomas[26] writing about the early modern period, disputes Philippe Aries's well-known claim that in medieval society 'the idea of childhood did not exist; that is not to suggest that children were neglected, foresaken or despised. The idea of childhood is not to be confused with affection for children: it corresponds to an awareness of the particular nature of childhood that distinguishes the child from the adult.'[27] Thomas also disagrees with J. H. Plumb[28] in his assertion that relationships between parents and children were often callous before the eighteenth century: 'although the methods of early modern parents may have been different from ours, their affection and concern for their children were no less great . . . '[29] Thomas emphasizes the fact that historians mostly write about adult attitudes to children and the real history of children is largely excluded from official records.

Plumb and Aries offer a rather depressing picture of children as victims, whereas Thomas suggests that children were more subversive and less inclined to meekly obey adult dictates than other historians have led us to believe. This is not, of course, to say that many children did not lead hard and oppressed lives or that some were not cruelly treated; it is just that diarists and others living before the eighteenth century have told another version of this story. Thomas provides an encouraging catalogue of the misdemeanours, high spirits and generally anarchic behaviour of the young from the upper, middle and working classes, alike. It is reassuring to find that some children seem always to have resisted constraints put upon them and resourcefully found some space to play, however much adults tried to limit their freedom. 'In the early modern period . . . there were periodic collisions between children and grown-ups because many children had their own values and priorities to which adults were either indifferent or positively hostile.'[30]

Ivy Pinchbeck and Alan MacFarlane also cite examples of a less repressive picture of childhood in documentary evidence. MacFarlane's study of *The Family Life of Ralph Josselin, a Seventeenth Century Clergyman* shows that his children were just as unmanageable and as well loved as they are today. 'If Josselin is typical, Puritan fathers were less austere and less able to exert control over their children than some historians would have us believe.'[31] Pinchbeck notes that 'enlightened' notions of childhood have always been prevalent in parts of British society.

Constructions of childhood are, then, varied, contradictory and subject to change. As Wartofsky puts it: 'the child is constructed from the whole range of practices, interactions and institutions that comprise the social and historical life-world . . . Children are what school architects, playgrounds, child labour laws and living spaces in the current ecology and ecology of families constitute the life-world of childhood as.'[32] In reading the poetry of childhood, we need to look critically at the unintentional prejudices and implicit value judgements that permeate verse written for and about children, even though poets, anthologists and critics often fail to do just that.

Defining children's poetry

I have made no attempt to provide a definition of poetry. As no two poets or teachers or critics seem able to agree on even a working definition, I am not going to enter or prolong what seems to me an unproductive debate.

James Mackay Shaw makes the same point in his massive work, *Childhood in Poetry*: 'the compiler . . . cannot take refuge in a universally accepted definition of poetry, for no such definition exists'. Nor does children's verse 'fit neatly into the category of poetry for or about children. The answer is that children have a way of breaking into the sacred preserves of adult literature and staking out corners as peculiarly their own.'[33] Quite so.

In this book, however, I mean to include anything and everything that could possibly be classed as poetry – hymns, songs, playground rhymes, raps, verse forms and free verse, trivial or profound. I subscribe to the widest possible definition of poetry, embracing everything from Auden's 'memorable speech'[34] to Heaney's defence of everyday language that somehow 'summons up the energies of words' and poetry that is 'one of the ordinary rituals of life'.[35] Some of these ideas are explored more fully in Chapter 13.

Like Auden, I want to distance myself from Matthew Arnold's notion of 'touchstones' by which one could somehow measure the quality of a poem and, by implication, notions of what is good poetry for children. I try (and doubtless fail) to take as much account of children's preferences[36] in poetry as to that which I find substantial and well written; the two sometimes coincide, but not invariably. We certainly need to acknowledge that there is some poetry, which is often funny or rude or close to doggerel that children enjoy, but in which adults can see little value.

Victor Watson, for example, one of the most original contemporary writers on children's literature, selected an undistinguished and highly sentimental poem in a recent book of poetry devoted to childhood favourites. This modest little verse – the first poem that he loved as a child – presumably served the purpose of initiating him into some of the satisfactions that poetry offers.

> I'm sittin' on the doorstep,
>   And I'm eating bread an' jam,
> And I aren't a-cryin' really,
>   Though I speks you think I am.
>
> I'm feelin' rather lonely,
>   And I don't know what to do,
> 'Cos there's no one here to play with,
>   And I've broke my hoop in two.[37]
>   (Marion St John Webb)

Most children, some of whom appreciate challenging poetry of the past and present, are keen on scurrilous verse. A typical example is this scrap from the oral tradition happily lisped by children just out of infant school:

> Ooh! Ah! I've lost me bra
> I've left me knickers in me boyfriend's car!

And it gets updated with every new generation – *Ooh! Ah! Cantona!* [*sic*] is among the latest as I write. These days it might be a television jingle or a football chant:

> I'm Popeye the sailor man
> I live in a pot of jam
> The jam is so sticky
> it sticks to my willy
> I'm Popeye the sailor man.
>
>   *   *   *
>
> Man. United are short-sighted
> Tra la la la la
> They wear glasses
> On their arses
> Tra la la la la. [38]
>   (Anon)

Popeye goes on to 'piddle on the middle', while Man. United wear 'rubies on their boobies' and so on, demonstrating the pleasure children appear to take in crafting the rude rhyme, particularly when they think adults will disapprove of it. Whatever the content, one of my intentions in this book is to extend the boundaries of the conventional canon of children's poetry and to consider any verse that has made a strong impact on children. I give some attention to these ideas in Chapters 4 and 5.

However impartial I may have tried to be, my own enthusiasms and prejudices will be all too evident. It seems sensible, therefore, to be explicit about the qualities I value in children's poetry. My taste is fairly catholic – on the one hand, like most readers, I am drawn to musical language and to poets who are skilled and rigorous in their employment of metre, rhyme and form, and to poetry with universal appeal. Ezra Pound's remark about poetry being language pared down to its essentials has always struck me as sound. On the other hand, I also favour the robustness and vitality so evident in the oral tradition and in so much of the free verse and dialect poetry of the late twentieth century. I admire poems that speak to children with immediacy and directness, if they are well written, as well as those that are moving, tender, profound or substantial. I like poetry that takes risks, speaks out against injustice and, above all, respects its audience.

In this Introduction, I have attempted to outline something of the scope of this book and anticipated some of the arguments to be addressed. I certainly want to question the 'common sense, taken for granted' well-aired notions about children's poetry. My ideal reader is one who is willing to take an open-minded attitude to what is *children's* poetry, who it is for, how childhood is represented in it and which poets have made a significant contribution to its development. Whether the reader will be convinced remains to be seen. I believe, at any rate, that the story is worth telling.

On a practical note

In this history, my intention is to consider most of the poets who have written for children up to the end of the 1980s, including those who wrote for adults but whose poetry was or is regularly anthologized for the young. I try to mention most of the significant poetry collections, except in the case of prolific writers. Because there are so many talented poets writing for children today, I have been forced to concentrate on a handful and have reluctantly excluded many worthy of attention. It goes without saying that I will have neglected some poets and ignored others who deserve a place in a book such as this. The scope of the subject is so wide that omissions are, I suspect, inevitable.

I have included the dates of birth and death for poets who were born before this century on the first occasion when the poet is encountered or in the chapter in which they feature most prominently. The same is true for dates of books of poetry. Although I have tried to write about individual poets principally within the chapter where their work best fits, this has proved impossible in several cases, particularly when a poet crosses several genres. For example, however hard I tried to confine them, the Taylor sisters have strayed into several different chapters!

After scrutinizing an early draft, my editor pointed out that the book was reading rather like an encyclopedia. This version would have been uncontroversial, but that *From the Garden to the Street* would have been an altogether duller enterprise. Though I now clearly express my own judgement, I have attempted to be fair and do justice to each poet; I have also tried not to be swayed too much by my own tastes and prejudices. In many cases, familiarizing myself with the poetry and learning more about the poet has led to greater regard and appreciation. At any rate, I look forward to lively arguments with those who will want to question some of the views and ideas in this book.

To research 300 years of poetry for children has been a challenging undertaking and a labour of love. I have made new friends with many poets of the past and come to know them as intimately as time would allow. I have spent days and days in the Bodleian Library copying (in pencil) poems out of tiny, exquisite books decorated with black and white woodcuts published two or three hundred years ago. My own 'local', Cambridge University Library has been my second home for weeks on end every summer for the past seven years. The pleasure of anticipation with which I approached the latest pile of fragile, little books waiting for me in the Rare Books Room, some of which contained poems that have rarely seen the light of day, was more than worth the effort of poring through many that had to be discarded. Countless biographies and innumerable critical books have failed to blunt my passion for the subject. As for contemporary children's poetry, I had already spent a working lifetime immersed in its study.

Finally, the reader will notice that the sub-title of this book is 'An introduction to 300 years of poetry for children'. I have long ago given up the idea that I will ever feel that this book is finished. The challenges are endless and there is still so much work to be done in this field. I hope others will take up the debates and carry on the scholarship in this deeply fascinating area of study. If this book helps anyone to embark on that journey, I will be satisfied.

Notes

1   W. H. Auden, *The Dyer's Hand*, Faber, London.
2   Neil Philip, ed. *A New Treasury of Poetry*, Blackie, London, 1990, p. 15.
3   Neil Philip, ed. *The New Oxford Book of Children's Verse*, Oxford University Press, Oxford, 1996, pp. xxv-xxvi.
4   Christina Rossetti, *Sing-Song*, Routledge, London, 1872.
5   Walter de la Mare, from 'I Dream of a Place', *Collected Rhymes and Verses*, Faber, London, 1944.
6   Kenneth Grahame, ed. *Cambridge Book of Poetry for Children*, 1916, p. v.
7   Rudyard Kipling, from 'The Glory of the Garden', quoted in *I Remember: Famous People's Favourite Childhood Poems*, Bodley Head, London, 1993.
8   William Hazlitt, *Selected Essays*, ed. Geoffrey Keynes, London, 1946, pp. 3-8.
9   Humphrey Carpenter, *Secret Gardens: a Study of the Golden Age of Children's Literature*, George Allen & Unwin, London, 1987, p. 7.
10 Keith Thomas, *Man and the Natural World: Changing Attitudes in England*, 1500-1890, Penguin, 1983, p. 13.
11 *Ibid.*, p. 15.
12 *Ibid.*, p. 243.
13 Thomas Hobbes, *Leviathan*, orig., 1651, ed. Michael Oakeshott, Basil Blackwell, Oxford, 1946.
14 Thomas, *op. cit.*, p. 251.
15 Robert Louis Stevenson, from 'Farewell to the Farm', *A Child's Garden of Verses*, London, 1885.
16 Raymond Williams, *The Country and the City*, Chatto and Windus, London, 1973, p. 60.
17 Kit Wright, from 'Where all the Flowers Went', *Hot Dog*, Kestrel, London, 1981.
18 William Wordsworth, from 'The Prelude' Book Second, *William Wordsworth's Selected Poems*, ed. John Hayden, Penguin, London, 1994, p. 330.
19 Allison James and Alan Prout, eds *Constructing and Reconstructing Childhood: Contemporary Issues in the Sociological Study of Childhood*, Falmer, London, 1990, p. 1.

20   Marx Wartofsky, 'The Child's Construction of the World and the World's Construction of the Child' in Frank S. Kessel and A. W. Siegal (eds), *The Child and other Cultural Inventions*, Houston Symposium 4, Praeger Publications, New York, 1983, pp. 188–215.

21   E. V. Lucas, 'Some Notes on Poetry for Children', *Fortnightly Review*, Vol. LX, London, 1986.

22   Neil Philip, The Signal Poetry Award, *Signal*, 47, May 1985, p. 76.

23   Zachary Leader, *Reading Blake's Songs*, Routledge, London, 1981, p. 5.

24   *Ibid.*, p. 9.

25   Lucy Aikin, *Poetry for Children*, London, 1801, beginning of Preface.

26   Keith Thomas, 'Children in Early Modern England' in *Children and their Books*, eds Gillian Avery and Julia Briggs, Oxford University Press, Oxford, 1989, p. 45.

27   Philippe Aries, *Centuries of Childhood*, trans. Robert Baldick, London, 1962, p. 128.

28   J. H. Plumb, 'The New World of Children', *Past and Present*, 67, 1975.

29   Thomas, *op. cit.*, p. 47.

30   Thomas, *op. cit.*, p. 57.

31   Alan MacFarlane, *The Family Life of Ralph Josselin, a Seventeenth Century Clergyman*, Cambridge University Press, Cambridge, 1970, p. 125.

32   M. Wartofsky in Kessel, *op. cit.*

33   James Mackay Shaw, *Childhood in Poetry*, Vol. 1, Gale Research Company, Detroit, 1966, p. 6.

34   W. H. Auden and J. Garrett, *The Poet's Tongue*, G. Bell and Sons, London, 1936, p. v.

35   Seamus Heaney, *Preoccupations: Selected Prose 1968–1978*, Faber, London, 1980, p. 45.

36   In my opinion, there is too much purely literary discussion of what is suitable poetry for children with little account being taken of what young readers choose to read, buy and share with friends. I have tried throughout this book to make explicit whatever evidence is available of children's preferences in poetry, even when it is at odds with my own taste.

37   'The Littlest One', Marion St John Webb, quoted in *Through the Windows of this Book*, Homerton College Centenary Anthology, ed. Morag Styles, Homerton College, Cambridge, 1994.

38   Children's playground rhymes collected by teachers on the Advanced Diploma in Language and Literature at Homerton College, Cambridge, 1994.

CHAPTER 1

Devotions and Didacticism

Religious verse for children

In books, or works, or healthful play,
Let my first years be past;
That I may give for ev'ry day
Some good account at last.[1]

Before 'Alice'

F. J. Harvey Darton claimed in his ground-breaking text, *Children's Books in England* (1932), that Lewis Carroll's *Alice* (1865) was 'the spiritual volcano', the first real liberty of thought in children's books.[2] It wasn't quite that, but here was a fictional child telling adults how ridiculous they were and proving much more intelligent and resourceful than the outrageous characters she encounters. Until 'Alice', children's literature was dominated by controlling, authoritarian and often stringently religious adult voices. Before the nineteenth century most authors wrote for children to teach, improve, counsel, admonish and direct them, particularly in matters of religion. In this book I will linger over the exceptions to that rule – the moments when poets tried to look at the world from the child's point of view or imagine what it might be like to be small and vulnerable or just to observe, acknowledge and enjoy the way that young people behave and think.

Apart from the work of a handful of humorists, it was not until Stevenson's *A Child's Garden of Verses* in 1885 that a collection of poetry for children appeared that was entirely free of moralizing or mention of religion. Children's verse was still weighed down by adults' determination to instill a code of good manners, conventional behaviour and religious observance in the young until well into the Victorian period. The changing social and religious climates of the seventeenth, eighteenth and nineteenth centuries are, of course, reflected in the poetry which, with one or two back-trackings along the way, becomes more sympathetic, funnier and fanciful over time.

It is not chance, therefore, that the first chapter of this book is devoted to religious verse. As William Sloane put it: 'Nothing in our more diffuse civilisation quite holds the pivotal position, the centrality, which religion held in 17th century England and

America.'[3] When Sloane investigated books for children written before 1710, he found that only a handful were not religious – and those referred to sport, manners, riddles, moral exhortation or courtesy. What must be understood about these 'good, Godly books' for children was their devotion to the concept of 'truth'; lies were considered akin to heresy and most kinds of fantasy or fiction constituted lying. Distrust of leisure, desire for material advantage and an emphasis on the practical were also prevalent in that period. Apart from chapbooks, which are discussed later, children looking for light relief in published form (and these texts were frowned upon by many adults) found them in the stories of Robin Hood, Aesop's fables, ballads, history/folklore such as Guy of Warwick fighting the dragon, or Foxe's Book of Martyrs with their gruesome tortures and deaths. We know from diaries and letters of the period that children were particularly devoted to Foxe's Martyrs for their gory illustrations as well as gripping text. Children's interest in such material seems to be historically constant, with horror fiction and videos roughly equivalent today. I suspect the young will always be drawn to the sensational and gruesome and that their elders will always deplore this trend and try to protect them from it.

In her book *Vision and Disenchantment*, Heather Glen[4] takes account of writing for children before and during the late eighteenth century, describing it thus: 'This conflict between the desire to appeal to the child's sensibility . . . and the need to instruct and direct can be traced in most of the poetry written for children . . . At best, such verse has an imaginative vitality . . . which *is always pressed into the service of a larger didactic purpose . . .*' (my emphasis). It is arguable whether purely didactic intentions can ever produce outstanding poetry, except where the writer combines religious belief with a feeling for poetic language and tenderness towards children. Fortunately, some poets, the best of whom were often writers of hymns which were not necessarily meant for congregational singing, did achieve this mix and to them I devote most attention in this chapter where I trace the progress of devotional verse for children, didacticism running like a thread through this little history.

Puritanism and poetry

Until the beginning of the nineteenth century then, most poetry for children was either devotional or didactic or, more likely, both. The Puritan tradition had a lasting influence on children's literature until the nineteenth century and, as Gillian Avery[5] pointed out, 'children's books have always been particularly vulnerable to the ideologies of the age'. Puritan belief was founded on the concept of original sin; indeed, the whole of creation was considered depraved and corrupt and the only way to become one of the elect was by religious conversion and devout observance. Some of the earliest texts for children were, therefore, those which focused on pious, saintly behaviour with threats of everlasting damnation for any errors or misdemeanours. James Janeway's infamous *A Token for Children*[6] is such a text, '*being an Exact Account of the Conversion, Holy and Exemplary Lives, and Joyful Deaths, of several young Children'*, published in 1671. Here is a snatch of Janeway: a pauper child is brought to live in the house of a good, Christian gentleman, even though the child was 'so filthy and nasty, that he would even have turned one's stomach to have looked on him'; the child was 'a very Monster of wickedness and a thousand times more miserable and vile by his sin, than by his poverty . . . He would call filthy Names, take God's name in vain, curse and swear, and do almost all kinds of mischief.'

I can imagine the youth of the seventeenth century finding this material fascinating, but not necessarily for the reasons Janeway would have approved! The 'true' stories (Janeway is keen to stress the authenticity of his sources and how the words were taken verbatim from 'the dying lips of Christian children') always end the same way with the redemption of these young sinners after religious conversion and their consequently happy deaths, as they drift off to the certainty of a heavenly after-life. Avery[7] suggests that *A Token* is 'probably the most influential children's book ever written' and praises its poignant, direct and artless simplicity. It certainly sold in large numbers and throws illuminating light on this period. When life is short and uncertain, it puts an emphasis on what happens after death and this is reflected as much in the juvenile as the adult literature of the period.

It is all too easy, however, to go along with the conventional view of Puritanism as a harsh, humourless, even cruel set of beliefs and practices which involved rigid disciplining of children and which produced a literature lacking in any charm or light relief. John Somerville reminds us in *The Discovery of Childhood in Puritan England* that:

> sustained interest in children in England began with the Puritans, who were the first to puzzle over their nature and their place in society . . . to write books exclusively for children and to show an awareness of the differences involved in communicating with them.[8]

Somerville's impressive study and the work of MacFarlane, Pollock, Thomas and others throws a more sympathetic light on Puritanism, particularly in terms of their attitude to children. It is also worth remembering that Puritanism began life as a radical movement with worthy principles such as rejection of licentiousness and concern for the family. Dissenters in general were responsible for a significant proportion of children's literature until the end of the nineteenth century. Somerville:

> Not only did Puritans and Dissenters write a greater number of works for children, they were also more imaginative than the Anglican authors, who simply adapted the traditional courtesy manuals to a younger audience.[9]

Constructions of childhood

The primary purpose behind writing religious poetry for the young before the nineteenth century was to save their souls at worst, and help them glorify God and take pleasure and consolation from devotional belief at best, with admonishments about the need for good behaviour and regular worship as a constant. Children, then, in the extreme Puritan tradition are born in original sin and have to be rescued from Satan's clutches: wise and devout parents, teachers and clergymen treat them harshly in order that they may be redeemed. Here is John Calvin: 'For though they [infants] have not yet produced the fruits of their iniquity, yet they have the seeds of it within them; even their whole nature is as it were a seed of sin . . .'[10] There was no space in such a philosophy for the young person's particular inclinations, no deviation from what was accepted as the correct line of action. As Ivy Pinchbeck put it:

> It is not surprising that they [Puritan parents] devoted as much thought to the spiritual upbringing of their children as conscientious parents spend today on health and general personality development.[11]

The well-known social historian, Keith Thomas,[12] reassures us that the true history of Puritanism is not quite so bleak as it might seem in his fascinating article on children in the early modern period. There are plenty of accounts of naughty, noisy, grubby, badly behaved children in the sixteenth and seventeenth centuries to suggest that the young were certainly not universally cowed and constrained by their elders and that they have probably always been a subversive sub-group within society.

> We have already seen that the essential attributes of juvenile subculture included a casual attitude to private property, an addiction to mischief, and a predilection for what most adults regarded as noise and dirt . . . But in no way did they more obviously reverse adult priorities than in the value they set on play . . . Of course, when we say that children preferred play to work we mean only that they liked doing serious things which adults regarded as trivial and frivolous.[13]

'Some easy pleasant book'

As a greater awareness of the benefits of gentler treatment for children and the value of playfulness were better understood, kinder though usually still devout messages began to emerge in the poetry of the late eighteenth and early nineteenth century. Such ambitions were aided by new printing techniques, publishers willing to provide for such desires, and parents with the time, money and inclination to fulfil them. Recreational books for children began to emerge in the middle of the eighteenth century, particularly through the good offices of the successful children's publisher, printer and bookseller, John Newbery (1713-1767)[14] and later in the century by John Marshall, Joseph Johnson, William Darton, John Harris and Benjamin Tabart, all of whom prospered from the sale of children's books. Newbery was a remarkably energetic writer/printer/publisher with a good eye for business. As John Rowe Townsend put it in his recent book about Newbery:

> The new middle class was interested in self-improvement and in the education of its children, if only as a means of advancement. This was the opportunity that Newbery saw and seized . . . But the idea that the book should amuse as well as improve its reader was the distinguishing characteristic of eighteenth century books for Little Masters and Misses of which John Newbery's are the prime examples.[15]

Rousseau's writing, particularly *Emile*, was also influential at the end of the eighteenth century. Although John Locke wrote *Some Thoughts Concerning Education* as early as 1693, it took some time to become part of mainstream thinking. Once it took hold, Locke's text provided an important steer in the humanization of education and literature for children and was reprinted regularly throughout the eighteenth century. Most important in this context are Locke's views about children as the products of their education; the advantages of uniting amusement with instruction which makes playfulness acceptable in the young; children's natural curiosity being something to cherish; and that '*some easy, pleasant Book suited to his Capacity, should be put into his Hands*'[16] (my emphasis).

However, there is still a yawning gap in the history of poetry written for children until the present century – those who were too poor to buy books and those who were not able to read, come first to mind. Because of the brutal exploitation of working-class people, the pernicious labour laws their children were subject to, and the harsh conditions suffered by agricultural labourers, the children of the poor had very little leisure in which to read, let alone access to books and learning. But there were broadsheets, ballads and chapbooks. These works of popular literature contained rhymes, poems, stories, cut-down versions of histories and romances, songs, tales, pictures and gossip. Crudely printed little books did a flourishing trade in this period and were sold by travelling pedlars up and down the country. They were considered barely respectable and potentially dangerous by many, but it is likely that they made their way into the hands of a great number of children. By the end of the eighteenth century, chapbooks were specifically designed for children, focusing on nursery rhymes, fairy tales, alphabet books, doggerel verse, riddles and the like.

In *Small Books and Pleasant Histories*, Margaret Spufford suggests that many more poor people could read before the nineteenth century than had previously been thought was the case, though they generally could not write. And what they read were the chapbooks and other lively broadsheets. She shows, for example, that significant numbers of agricultural labourers in the seventeenth century read printed pamphlets containing a fascinating mix of religious tracts, news, political propaganda, almanacs, songs, astrological predictions and, as ever, sex and sensation.[17] Although this popular literature was much frowned upon, a well-to-do 'civil servant' like Samuel Pepys[18] (1633–1703) collected it assiduously all his life. When you read the opening of a version of Robin Hood (1686) in Pepys' collection, the appeal is obvious.

> Both Gentlemen & Yoemen bold
> or whatsoever you are,
> To have a stately story told
> attention now prepare:
> It is a Tale of Robin Hood,
> that I to you will tell,
> Which being rightly understood,
> I know will please you well.[19]

John Rowe Townsend suggests that the 'ancient romances, ballads and folk tales, surviving from the days before print but out of favour among educated adults, [were] either spurned as peasant crudities or detested as immoral or dangerous to youth'.[20] Glen takes a similar line:

> Children's books had originally been produced by the Puritans in an attempt to counteract what they saw as the pernicious influence of popular chapbooks. Throughout the history of eighteenth century publishing one can trace the pressure of that competition: material from the chapbooks – especially nursery rhymes and riddles – is often to be found enlivening the more expensively produced little books of the polite publishing firms . . .[21]

Popular literature apart, the standard critical line[22] on writing for children before the Victorian period was that its main impulse was instructional and that it was inflexible, harsh and lacking in literary merit. Consequently, it offered little in the way of diversion or appeal to the young. I take a slightly wayward view and will attempt to convince the reader that some of this verse was far more interesting than we have been led to believe. Furthermore, in order to appreciate children's poetry in this period, we need to understand the social and religious context in which it was written. In the seventeenth century, for example, many poets suffered great hardship for their beliefs and wrote for children out of genuine conviction and some tenderness. And as Somerville put it:

Chear, Keach and Bunyan [three of the most notable Puritan writers, two of whom we meet later in this chapter] all had the enforced leisure of prison in which to indulge the poetic impulse.[23]

Most religious poets realized that in order to succeed with their audience, they had to amuse them too. The obligation to entertain young readers as well as teach them is evident in a close reading of prefaces as well as in the poetry itself. It is also worth mentioning that most of the poetry books discussed in this chapter contained illustrations to tempt their readership, usually simple woodcuts, until better printing techniques in the latter part of the eighteenth century provided scope for more elaborate and ambitious embellishments.

'When at the first I took my pen in hand' – the poetry of John Bunyan

> A tinker out of Bedford,
>   A vagrant oft in quod,
> A private under Fairfax,
>   A minister of God . . .[24]
>   (Rudyard Kipling)

John Milton is one of the earliest religious poets to have been anthologized for children; his hymns, such as Let Us With a Gladsome Mind, have been sung by them for many centuries. But it was earnest, severe, unswervingly God-fearing John Bunyan (1628–1688), described by A. P. Davis as a 'sectarian mechanick preacher with a considerable class antipathy and hatred of wealth'[25] who was one of the first writers to attempt verse specifically for children. To understand Bunyan one must recognize that this artisan/preacher of humble birth was writing to save lives (or souls at least) and, at a time of persecution for his religion was attempting literally to hang on to his own, while never straying from his deeply held beliefs. He uses, therefore, allegory, myth, parable and metaphor in his writing in order to get his message across, while simultaneously trying to avoid direct heresy and inevitable prosecution. In the event, Bunyan spent a third of his adult life in prison, where he wrote his impressive literature, including The Pilgrim's Progress and Country Rhimes for Children. He was a man in Nelson Mandela's mould of steadfastness and principle, refusing to give an assurance he would not preach if he was released from prison and consequently spending eleven extra years behind bars. As a poor man much published and read in his own lifetime and still appreciated 300 years later, he is a rare phenomenon. In the words of Bunyan scholar, N. H. Keeble:

The Pilgrim's Progress holds a unique place in the history of our literature. No other seventeenth century text save the King James Bible, nothing from the pen of a writer from Bunyan's social class in any other period . . . has ever enjoyed such an extensive readership.[26]

There is not, at first sight, much light relief in Bunyan's influential single book of poetry for children, except the charming woodcuts. *Country Rhimes for Children*,[27] 1686, was variously titled *Divine Emblems, Temporal Things Spiritualised* or, as it was first known, *A Book for Boys and Girls*. Despite generations of critics slighting it, *Country Rhimes for Children* has much to recommend it. Graham Midgley tells us that it was popular for generations, and reprinted more often than any of his poetic volumes.[28] Glen also recognizes its importance:

[it is] . . . a volume which illustrates very clearly that ambivalence of aim which was to inform books for children throughout the eighteenth century. Its effort to compete with the chap-books is apparent in its crude little wood-cuts; and there is a vivid colloquial life about much of the poetry – an imaginative effort to enter the child's way of seeing the world – which must have been very attractive to young readers.[29]

Look, for example, at the language of Bunyan's address to the Courteous Reader and his willingness to go in for a bit of clowning.

> Wherefore good Reader, that I save them may,
> I now with them, the very Dottrill play.
> And since at Gravity they make a Tush
> My very Beard I cast behind the Bush.
> And like a Fool stand fing'ring of their Toys,
> And all to show them they are Girls and Boys.
> Nor do I blush, although I think some may
> Call me a Baby, cause I with them play:
> I do't to show them how each Fingle-fangle,
> On which they doating are, their souls entangle,

And before that:

> To have a better Judgement of themselves,
> Than wise Men have of Babies on the Shelves.
> Their antrick Tricks, fantastick Modes, and Way,
> Shew they like very Boys and Girls do play
> With all the frantick Fopp'ries of this Age,

And that in open view, as on a Stage;
Our bearded Men do act like beardless Boys,
Our Women please themselves with childish Toys.[30]

Despite the serious message and the heavy moralizing tone, there are many references to toys in this extract and some indication that Bunyan understood children's need for play, though he is severe with adults who act like children, as he sees it. Bunyan knows he must enter into a playful relationship with young readers, disguising his 'beard' (adult status, moral advice) by getting in touch with a child's world. The reference to 'Fingle-fangle' for passing crazes and pretty things is apt and charming. The poems may not show the same originality and power of *Pilgrim's Progress*, but they do have a rough and homely appeal. Bunyan also included an alphabet, lists of popular names of boys and girls broken into syllables, a list of numerals and written numbers, separate lists of vowels, consonants, digraphs and tips for spelling, before embarking on the poems. (It was quite common at that time to give a spelling lesson or two in a book intended for children; it might be the nearest to teaching some children got.)

Midgely writes persuasively that Bunyan 'was a developing poet discovering and exploring, through a long career, the resources of language and the rhythms of poetry'.[31] Here is Bunyan's refreshing defence of his authorship of *The Pilgrim's Progress*. Although it was not composed with children in mind, it takes the form of simple verse which they would be able to understand.

When at the first I took my pen in hand,
Thus for to write, I did not understand
That I at all should make a little book
In such a mode;

*   *   *

Thus I set pen to paper with delight,
And quickly had my thoughts in black and white.[32]

*   *   *

It came from mine own heart, so to my head,
And thence into my fingers trickled,
Then to my Pen, from whence immediately
On paper I did dribble it daintily.[33]

There is plenty to applaud in *Country Rhimes*. The following extract from 'Of the Boy and Butter-Fly' is delightful, showing Bunyan's facility for the lyrical use of language, even when he is making a moral point. He paints the little boy realistically as so besotted with chasing butterflies that he hardly notices he is getting scratched to pieces by thorns and nettles. The way that children can throw themselves into enthusiasms is convincingly described and sometimes Bunyan strikes a real poetic note as in 'When all her all is lighter than a Feather'.

> Behold how eager this our little Boy
> Is of this Butter-Fly, as if all Joy,
> All Profits, Honours, yea and lasting Pleasures,
> Were wrapt up in her, or the richest Treasures,
> Found in her, would be bundled up together,
> When all her all is lighter than a Feather.
>
> His running thorough Nettles, Thorns and Bryers,
> To gratify his Boyish fond Desires;
> His tumbling over Mole-hills to attain
> His end, namely his Butter-Fly to gain;
> Doth plainly shew, what Hazzards some Men run,
> To get what will be lost as soon as won . . .[34]

In *English Children's Books* Percy Muir, the distinguished historian of children's literature, complains about a hen's egg reminding Bunyan of decay and death, rotten eggs of hypocrites, bees of stings and butterflies of 'false toys'.[35] But Muir is too harsh. Bunyan was merely reflecting the fashion of his day in using emblems to symbolize moral and spiritual themes. Here are two typical Bunyan morals: the first, 'Upon a Snail', makes its point quite gently; 'Upon a Penny Loaf' tells a simple truth and relates its message to poverty and hardship.

> And tho' she doth but very softly go,
> However 'tis not fast, nor slow, but sure;
> And certainly they that do Travel so,
> The prize they do aim at they do procure.
>
> *   *   *
>
> Thy Price one Penny is, in time of Plenty;
> In famine doubled 'tis from one to twenty.
> Yea, no Man knows what Price on thee to set,
> When there is but one Penny Loaf to get.[36]

Muir fails to see, as Christopher Hill the historian does, that 'In Bunyan's emblem poems the description of unexpectedly familiar natural objects is invariably far livelier and in better verse than the moral drawn.'[37] In fact, Bunyan was ahead of his time in drawing children's attention to all sorts of everyday items (candles, eggs, bells, a whipping-top, a penny loaf, spectacles, a hobby-horse, a sheet of white paper, musical instruments played with talent and without . . .), as well as features of the natural world (a frog, a swallow, a cuckoo, a mole, blow-flies, a snail, a bee, the sun, rising or setting . . .) and only a few purely devotional emblems. The following extracts demonstrate that Bunyan had a fine eye for what children might enjoy and that he employed some skill in bringing his 'emblems' to life.

> The frog by nature is both damp and cold,
> Her mouth is large, her belly much will hold.
>> ('Upon the Frog')

or

> About the yard she cackling now doth go,
> To tell what 'twas she at her nest did do.
>> ('On the Cackling of a Hen')

or

> So many birds, so many various things,
> Tumbling i'th'element upon their wings.
>> ('Of Fowls flying the the Air')

or

> This pretty bird, O! how she flies and sings,
> But could she do so if she had not wings?
> Her wings bespeak my faith, her songs my peace;
> When I believe and sing my doubtings cease.[38]
>> ('Upon the Swallow')

Bunyan is unusual for his time in using domestic objects that children would be familiar with as subject matter for his poetry. However, Darton is severe:

> to describe them with a rugged simplicity, and then say what lesson could be drawn from such emblems . . . the greatest and most direct of all allegory-writers had used complete simplicity, here almost tortures his mind to find a moral.

But Darton, rightly, goes on to defend the 'touches of homeliness', 'queer gentleness' and 'in the halting lines a soul at once violent and tender . . . trying to speak to those whose unformed minds it hardly believes it can understand'.[39] It may not reach the heights of *The Pilgrim's Progress*, one of the most translated and well-known books ever written, but *Country Rhimes for Children* is certainly an interesting and innovative piece of work by an important writer who had, according to Midgley,

> This gentleness, this ability to speak in a voice children would understand and find attractive, is a quality which above all distinguishes Bunyan from . . . the tradition of the Baptist poets and writers, among whom were many who produced books of poems and prose for the guidance and edification of children in the sevententh century.[40]

Country Rhimes had run to nine editions by 1724 – an extraordinary publishing success at that time. Reluctantly, we take our leave of Bunyan with the words of his rousing hymn from *Pilgrim's Progress* ringing in our ears. An earnest message, steadfast faith, unswerving integrity and memorable imagery underline Bunyan's determination 'to be a pilgrim'.

No lion can him fright,
He'll with a giant fight,
But he will have the right
To be a pilgrim.[41]

Youth's divine pastime

Abraham Chear (d. 1668) writing a few years earlier than Bunyan, also cared for
children as the openings to many poems testify: 'Sweet John, I send you here', 'My
pretty Child', 'Sweet Child' all begin kindly enough in *A Looking-Glass for Children*,
published posthumously in 1672, 'Being a Narrative of God's gracious Dealings with
little Children . . . together with sundry seasonable Lessons and Instructions to
Youth'.[42] But Chear is true to his period and, characteristically, this promising start is
followed by a severe lesson.

> My pretty Child, remember well,
>   You must your wayes amend;
> For wicked Children go to Hell,
>   That way their courses tend.

Of course, such a message would have been commonplace to Puritan children and
would not have carried the charge it does today. Like Bunyan, Chear was a Dissenter,
who spent time in prison for his religious beliefs where he wrote *A Looking-Glass*. He
does occasionally find a gentler voice: some of his verse was good and was certainly
popular in its day, despite its insistent tone of piety and awful warnings of retribution.
Somerville offers a more sympathetic stance than most commentators, suggesting
that Chear and others like him:

> were trying to speak children's language rather than making them speak theirs
> [adults] . . . [and that] children were being entertained and would come to
> think of themselves as being worthy of such treatment.[43]

> Sweet Child, Wisdom you invites,
>   To hearken to her Voice;
> She offers to you rare Delights,
>   Most worthy of your Choice.
> Eternal Blessings in his Wayes,
>   You shall be sure to find;
> Oh! therefore in your youthful Dayes,
>   Your great Creator mind.[44]

Unlike Bunyan and Chear, Nathaniel Crouch (1632–1725) made a good living out of regurgitating in simple form other people's writing. Using the pseudonym of Richard Burton or R. B., Crouch rewrote stories from history or the Bible, plus riddles, fables and other amusements, including *The Young Man's Calling*, 1678, and *Delightful Fables in Prose and Verse*, 1691. Percy Muir describes him as one of the earliest writers to offer children pleasure and excitement in their reading. *Youth's Divine Pastime*, 1691, included 'The Tower of Babel', which was very popular for at least two decades. Despite considering Crouch an 'industrious hackney scribbler', Muir suggests that his texts 'mark the first real effort to provide children with reading-matter . . . to which they would look forward with pleasure and excitement in their leisure time'.[45]

> After the dreadful Flood was past,
>   And Mankind did abound,
> A Tower they built, for fear the earth
>   Should once again be drowned.
>
> And that they to posterity
>   Might leave a lasting name.
> The Almighty saw it and was much
>   Displeased with the same.[46]

Divine songs

By the early eighteenth century some branches of children's literature slowly, almost imperceptibly, began to soften. It is fitting, therefore, to introduce one of the most popular poets for children of all time, Isaac Watts (1674–1748). Watts is still fairly well known as a writer of hymns regularly sung in church today, such as 'O God our help in ages past' and 'Jesus shall reign where'er the sun'. In *Hymns Unbidden*, Martha England suggests that 'The English hymn as a literary form may almost be said to have come into being with the lyrics of Watts.'[47] His contribution to children's verse is at least as significant. Watts's humane approach to childhood, as well as his religious intentions, are set out in the title of his famous book, *Divine Songs Attempted in Easy Language for the Use of Children*,[48] 1715, where the dedication quotes Matthew, Chapter XXI: 'Out of the Mouths of Babes and Sucklings thou hast perfected Praise'.[49]

As well as addressing the daughters of his beloved patron, Sir Thomas Abney, in the preface, Watts also speaks earnestly

> To all that are concerned in the Education of Children: 'It is an awful and important Charge that is committed to you. The Wisdom and Welfare of the succeeding Generation are instrusted with you beforehand, and depend much on your Conduct . . .'

This conventional opening becomes more interesting when Watts shows insightful understanding of poetry:

What is learnt in Verse is longer retained in Memory, and sooner recollected
. . . there is something so amusing and entertaining in Rhymes and Metre, that
will incline Children to make this part of their Business a Diversion . . . This
will be a constant Furniture, for the Minds of Children, that they may have
something to think about when alone . . .[50]

The maxim that to put a text into verse aids memory is aptly demonstrated in an
extract from 'The Ten Commandments':

Thou shalt have no more Gods but me.
Before no Idol bow thy knee.

Take not the Name of God in vain,
Nor dare the Sabbath Day profane.[51]

Zachary Leader describes Watts as a 'typical rich man's minister'[52] in contrast to
Bunyan. While that is true, it should not detract from Watts's achievement as a
children's writer and a maker of hymns. Indeed, Watts had much to thank his patron
for – a brief visit to Sir Thomas Abney of Theobalds, Hertfordshire, to recover his
health, actually lasted until his death, 36 years later! The family looked after their
fragile chaplain tenderly and in the comfort of this position Watts wrote his hymns,
pursuing what for the time were quite liberal ideas about education, urging kindness
in instructing children, 'the Bible, Protestantism, patriotism and obedience'. Like
many of his contemporaries he warned against the evil influence of:

silly tales and senseless rhymes. . . [which] terrify tender minds with dismal
stories of witches or ghosts . . . shocking and bloody histories, wanton songs or
amorous romances . . .[53]

He also held the common eighteenth century belief that making children literate
would also make them good and that poetry was a means of teaching virtue. In
Reading Blake's Songs, Leader describes Watts as holding together the seemingly
incompatible visions of childhood disseminated by Calvin and Locke causing
inevitable tensions between what he should feel and did feel – 'the old Puritanism of
the age of Cromwell and the new humanism of the age of Addison'.[54] Even so, his
writing emphasized the tenderness of the young and concentrated on keeping them
on a straight path to Heaven rather than focusing on the miseries of Hell as many of
his contemporaries and precursors did.

Part of the appeal of Watts's *Divine Songs* lies in his lyric gift, mostly favouring four-line verses of eight and six syllables alternatively, the usual metre for psalm tunes. Watts's evident affection for children softens the didactic elements which are also there.

> Hush! my dear, lie still and slumber,
>   Holy angels guard thy bed!
> Hea'nly blessings without number
>   Gently falling on thy head.

> *   *   *

> How many children in the Street
>   Half naked I behold?
> While I am clothed from Head to Feet,
>   And cover'd from the Cold.[55]

His poetry would not have continued to sell in great numbers until the beginning of the present century, if there wasn't a lasting quality to the verse. Darton's assessment of *Divine Songs* states:

> They must ever be a landmark, early but clear, in the intimate family history of the English child, who was at last beginning to be seen to be a little adventurous, independent pilgrim, worth watching with love and care, and even with some regard for possible differences of character within his own category.[56]

Although Lewis Carroll turned Watts's songs into nonsense in the Alice books, parody is a form of tribute that is worthless if the original is not well known. Carroll's parodies can be taken as evidence both of the continuing popularity of *Divine Songs* nearly 150 years after they were published and, of course, of a climate where it had become possible to make fun of moral verse.

> How doth the little busy Bee
>   Improve each shining Hour,
> And gather honey all the day
>   From every opening Flower!

> How skilfully she builds her Cell!
>   How neat she spreads the Wax!
> And labours hard to store it well
>   With the sweet food she makes.[57]
>   (Watts)

How doth the little crocodile
Improve his shining tail,
And pour the waters of the Nile
On every golden scale!

How cheerfully he seems to grin,
How neatly spreads his claws,
And welcomes little fishes in
With gently smiling jaws![58]
                    (Carroll)

Visions in verse

Divine Songs has a distinguished publishing history and poems from it are still occasionally anthologized today. Watts certainly influenced many who turned their pens to writing for children in the eighteenth century, probably including John Marchant who wrote *Puerilia: Amusements for the Young*, and Nathaniel Cotton (1705–1788) who produced *Visions in Verse* – 'for the Entertainment and Instruction of Younger Minds' in the same year, 1751. Cotton also ran a lunatic asylum and was the caring doctor of another poet, William Cowper. *Visions* was very popular in Cotton's own lifetime and it was printed in many different editions, but it was rather adult in subject matter – health, marriage, happiness, friendship, death – and there isn't much that is distinctive or worth close scrutiny in the poetry.

Childhood and Youth engage my Pen,
'Tis Labour lost to talk to Men.
Youth may, perhaps, reform, when Wrong,
Age will not listen to my Song.
He who at Fifty is a Fool,
Is far too stubborn grown for School.[59]

Marchant had more open views on what was suitable for children – feasts, dance, country scenes, toys, music, drinking and 'Occurrences that happen within [children's] own little Sphere of Action'. He must be one of the earliest writers to follow Locke's precept that 'the mind of a child is aptly compared to a sheet of white paper on which we write what we please'. However, he also showed genuine concern for the happiness of children: 'It is important . . . that the first notions instilled into its tender mind, be such that are most consonant to reason, truth and virtue . . . Children must have something to amuse and divert them in their reading . . . I have composed every song in as pleasant and humorous a stile as I could.'[60] But the poetry itself was weak and did not sell particularly well.

This little Ball
Against the Wall
Or up and down I toss;
It mounts aloft,
And down as oft,
It nimbly comes and goes.

So now I've done,
Away I'll run,
My Work demands me hence;
A little Play
Is no Delay
But whets my Diligence.[61]

'Gentle Jesus, Meek and Mild'

A gifted writer of this period whose work is available to children through his hymns is Charles Wesley (1707–1788), described by Iona Opie as 'one of the most inspired and prolific hymn-writers of all time'.[62] Among those hymns are 'Hark! the Herald-Angels Sing' and 'Gentle, Jesus, Meek and Mild' which appeared in *Hymns for Children*, 1763, and included works by his equally famous brother, John, who was the more severe of the two: '[When children] do understand them [Hymns] they will be children no longer, only in years and stature.'[63]

Martha England talks of Wesley as a tolerant, but strenuous evangelist who was 'the finest hymn writer of any century':

As a man and as a poet, Wesley's confidence was in the power of myth to act upon the imagination, and thus to educate, to accomplish didactic, exemplary and energizing functions in mind and heart and soul . . . Wesley, like Blake, spoke his whole mind to a child and his entire view of life is present in his children's songs.[64]

England also pointed out the debt Blake owed to Wesley. Look at the similarities, for example, in Wesley's 'Gentle Jesus' and Blake's 'The Lamb':

Gentle Jesus, meek and mild,
Look upon a little child

Jesus, gentle loving Lamb,
Let me call Thee by Thy name.
                    (Wesley)

> He is meek & he is mild;
> He became a little child.
> I a child & thou a lamb,
> We are called by his name.[65]
> 　　　　　(Blake)

Generations of children and adults have sung Wesley's exquisitely musical hymns. He could be stern; more often he was tender. England convinces us that Wesley's special talent lay in his ability to make a child important in her or his own eyes:

> Wesley abounds in moral instruction . . . but his songs open out on a world where some tremendous experience is going to take place . . . He held a sacramental sense of the beauty of holiness . . . There is no parallel in hymnody.[66]

> The arms within whose soft embrace,
> 　My sleeping babes I see;
> They comprehend unbounded space,
> 　And grasp infinity.[67]

The amusement of children

It is worth noting the use of terms like 'amusement' and 'entertainment' creeping into poetry titles for 'younger minds' during the eighteenth century, indicating a more liberal climate in reading and publishing for children. Even so, Leader reminds us that 'the latter half of the century, with the rise of Methodism and the Anglican Evangelical movement, the Puritan spirit returned in force, accompanied by a species of juvenile literature much like that of the previous century'.[68] *Hymns for the Amusement of Children*, 1772, by Christopher Smart (1722–1771) were in the same vein as Marchant and Cotton but by a much finer poet. Smart is famous among other things for *Jubilate Agno* which includes the brilliantly original 'My Cat Jeoffry'.

Stepson-in-law of John Newbery, who tried to help him with money problems, Smart is one of a surprisingly large number of poets who suffered bouts of madness. He also went to prison for debt on more than one occasion. *Hymns for the Amusement of Children* was, indeed, written during incarceration in Dublin Jail. Smart, who also translated fables and wrote versions of Jesus's parables for children, was working in the same tradition as Bunyan and Watts, but his is a more tolerant and less exacting Christian ethic. The form of his verse is looser and more experimental and in some respects anticipates William Blake with whom he had a lot in common. They both lived and worked in London, struggled with money, were deeply, but unconventionally religious, favoured tenderness towards children and, most significantly perhaps, were tormented by a cast of mind inclined to be extreme and exacting on themselves and others. Consequently, both men found life excessively difficult.

The hymns that follow give some idea of Smart's voice.

> If you are merry sing away,
>   And touch the organs sweet;
> This is the Lord's triumphant day
> Ye children in the Gall'ries gay,
>   Shout from each Godly seat.
>
> It shall be May tomorrow's morn,
>   A field then let us run,
> And deck us in the blooming thorn,
> Soon as the cock begins to warn,
>   And long before the sun.
>
> *　　　　*　　　　*
>
> With white and crimson laughs the sky,
>   With birds the hedge-rows ring;
> To give the praise to God most high,
> And all the sulky friends defy
>   Is a most joyful thing.[69]
>
> *　　　　*　　　　*
>
> David has said and sung it sweet,
> That God with mercy is replete;
> And thus I'll say, and thus I'll sing,
> In rapture unto Christ my King.
>
> King of my heart and my desires,
> Which all my gratitude inspires,
> Bids me be great and glorious still,
> And so I must, and so I will . . .[69]

The first has a sweetness of touch, depicting children gaily enjoying themselves in the countryside, full of natural sport in the lushness of May. Smart's world is not severe or threatening: the children are urged to deck themselves with flowers, run about the fields and shout their praise of God. The adjectives and verbs are positive – 'merry, sweet, triumphant, gay, blooming, joyful . . . sing, shout, deck, laughs, ring' . . . Those who can't enjoy such things –'sulky friends' – are to be *defied*. The second shares the same characteristics and resounds with the musical final line, 'And so I must, and so I will'. If Smart moves religious verse for children on in terms of his gentle tone and welcoming playfulness as attributes with which to praise God, there are echoes of what was to come in the poetry of Blake who does something decidedly more radical. His poetry is considered in the following chapter.

'The cursed Barbauld crew'

Not all children's versifiers were of the calibre of Smart. A much more limited world is presented for children by the rather grim and mundane Lady Eleanor Fenn (d. 1813), aka Nurse Lovechild, whom Darton records as a 'professional moralist' and a hack, but whose writing he admitted showed some good observation and humour.[70] Although her pseudonym suggests she loved children, her verse offered little in the way of diversion. Her most famous book, *The Golden Present*, 1780,[71] states that it is for 'all little Masters and Misses of Europe, Asia, Africa and America', but then follows the usual dogmatic advice.

> My little children pray attend
> The admonition of a Friend
> Who places here before your view,
> The Boon of Vice and Virtue too;
> All who are good the Orange share,
> The Rod no naughty boy shall spare.

She goes on to enquire whether the

> ... little Ladies and Gentlemen have paid such Attention to my Endeavours as I would wish, I shall therefore insist upon your giving me a Proof of your Docility by letting me see whether you can repeat the Alphabet without the Assistance of these little Devises which the Engraver has charged me so much money for ...[72]

This is pedestrian fare, but it surely does not deserve Percy Muir's castigation of Fenn as a member of a 'monstrous regiment' – women writers for children known for their severity and relentlessly 'addicted to moralizing'.[73] Muir is drawing on Charles Lamb's famous remark to Coleridge about 'the cursed Barbauld Crew, those Blights and Blasts of all that is human in man and child'.[74]

Lamb is typical of the early Romantic period in his condemnation of writers of moral tales, some of which were in verse and most of which were written by women. It is doubly ironic when Lamb's own poetry for children is examined, as it combines lack of originality with half-hearted moralizing (see Chapter 3). Closer examination of the 'Barbauld Crew' shows that such a rude grouping of women does not bear scrutiny, as it contained writers working in different styles at different times in different genres. To lump together in a disparaging way writers as disparate as Sarah

Trimmer, Maria Edgeworth, Hannah More, Priscilla Wakefield, Dorothy Kilner, Ann and Jane Taylor, Charlotte Smith and Anna Barbauld is simply unfair. Unfortunately, the mud stuck. Readers can judge for themselves, as the work of the latter five poets is discussed in this book.

What Muir, Lamb and others thought these women had in common was 'indefatigable' toil to produce moral texts for children with 'no preconceptions beyond turning out persuasive didacticisms of the sort that publishers could sell'.[75] But the work of these women was by no means homogeneous; nor were they narrow-minded moralists inspired to make a bit of easy 'pin money' and it is wrong to categorize them in this way. Muir is also unjust in depicting these writers as unrelievedly punitive. Some held puritanical views about what should be provided for young readers but, like the Puritans, the positive side is the serious attention they were willing to give to children and their reading. Norma Clarke goes further: 'it can be argued that women who wrote rational literature for children were consciously . . . offering those children, and the adults they would grow into, tools for re-appraising their social and political situations'.[76] Nicholas Tucker also mounts a spirited defence of some of these writers in relation to their views on fairy tales in *Opening the Nursery Door*.[77] A re-evaluation of the 'monstrous regiment' is taking place at last.

Hymns in prose

One member of that meanly titled 'crew' who needs further attention is Anna Barbauld (1743–1825). To include her in Muir's unkind list is a misrepresentation of her significance as a writer. Darton writes admiringly of her *Hymns in Prose for Children*, 1781, as language 'so simple, yet so majestic, [they are] worth giving to children'.[78] A child prodigy – she could read fluently at three – Barbauld was the aunt of Lucy Aikin, the children's writer and anthologist, and sister of John Aikin with whom she produced a popular magazine, *Evenings at Home* (1792–6). Barbauld's own poetry was highly regarded in the late eighteenth century with Coleridge famously walking 40 miles to meet her. A person of immense industry, married to a Dissenting minister of fragile mental and physical strength with whom she later ran a school, Barbauld also wrote an influential series of *Lessons for Children*, edited six volumes of Samuel Richardson's letters, produced *The British Novelists* in 50 volumes and, as Norma Clarke tells us 'engaged in political pamphleteering on the slave trade . . . [she was] one of the most humane, enlightened, rational and sensitive women writers of the period . . .'[79]

Barbauld can be uncompromising. Her stance on children's poetry promulgated in the preface of *Hymns in Prose* is depressingly rigid. 'It may well be doubted whether poetry *ought* to be lowered to the capacities of children, or whether they should not rather be kept from reading verse; for the very essence of poetry is an elevation in thought and style above the common standard'.[80] Fortunately, Barbauld appears to deviate from such views in her actual writing. She believed that by getting in touch with nature, children would get closer to God and it is the references to the natural world in the hymns, where she is most poetic.

> The golden orb of the sun is sunk behind the hills, the colours fade away from the western sky, and the shades of evening fall fast around me.

> Come, let us go forth into the fields, let us see how the flowers spring, let us listen to the warbling of the birds, and sport ourselves upon the new grass.

> The winter is over and gone, the buds come out upon the trees, the crimson blossoms of the peach and the nectarine are seen, and the green leaves sprout.

> The hedges are bordered with tufts of primroses, and yellow cowslips that hang down their heads; and the blue violet lies hid beneath the shade.[81]

Hymns for infant minds

Religious poetry continued to be regularly composed for children in the nineteenth century. Ann and Jane Taylor (who are discussed more fully in Chapter 7) were central in developing a more affectionate school of poetry for the young. Their most famous collection *Original Poems for Infant Minds*, was followed by other volumes, one of which was entitled *Hymns for Infant Minds*, 1810.[82] The sisters who lived on a modest income were able to publish *Hymns* at their own expense, and made the not inconsiderable sum of £150 profit in its first year. This gives some indication of the popularity of these two writers and the buoyancy of the market for children's books.

Hymns for Infant Minds contain somes warm-hearted poems about angels, the promise of heaven and praises for Christian virtues, but there are also warnings against weaknesses such as pride, impatience, anger or 'a wicked heart'; preparation for a 'good' death; exhortations about virtuous behaviour and references to stories from the Bible. Mostly, children are presented with a loving Jesus whose care for little children is likened to an affectionate father. If we ever doubted it, the Taylors would convince us that kind and loving relationships between middle-class parents and children were the norm by 1810, though obedience, 'duty', devout behaviour and religious observance on behalf of the latter were certainly expected. The worst excesses of the Puritan era have been left behind and we have moved to the comparative gentleness of the New Testament.

> Kind angels guard me every night,
>   As round my bed they stay:
> Nor am I absent from thy sight
>   In darkness or by day.[83]
>   ('Praise for Daily Mercies')

> Jesus Christ, my Lord and Saviour,
>   Once became a child like me;
> O that in my whole behaviour,
>   He my pattern still might be.[84]
>   ('The Example of Christ')

The angels are kind and tend the child by day and night in the first hymn; Jesus's own connections with childhood are emphasized in the second. But we have not completely left Puritanism behind: note the tendency to savour physical sufferings more reminiscent of the previous two centuries in other hymns by the Taylors.

> Nailed upon the cross, behold
>   How his tender limbs are torn!
> For a royal crown of gold
>   They have made him one of thorn!
>
> See! the blood is falling fast
>   From his forehead and his side!
> Hark! he now has breathed his last!
>   With a mighty groan he died![85]

As the anonymous editor of the composite version of the Taylors' best-known poems wrote in the preface to the 1876 edition:

> It is no easy task to write for children in a manner that shall at once entertain and instruct them . . . Many authors, content with being instructive, entirely forget that children should be amused and interested if they are to read, or rather to remember children have a perfect horror of dry pieces of morality, unrelieved by incident or fancy . . .[86]

We have come a long way from the severity of the seventeenth century, though Bunyan would, I think, have recognized the point the editor is making. It had taken nearly two centuries for the social and religious climate to change sufficiently for such liberal comments to be acceptable. It is, however, worth remembering that the Taylors, writing in the first decade of the nineteenth century, were still living at a time when fairy tales and nursery rhymes were considered harmful to the young and where imagination and fantasy were frowned on. As late as 1840, Samuel Griswold Goodrich, American writer of the popular Peter Parley tales, wrote that 'much of the vice and crime in the world can be imputed to these atrocious books i.e. fairy tales'.[87] The special gift of the Taylor sisters was to be able to write acceptably for their time and manage to amuse so many young readers.

Little words of love

The American writer, Eliza Follen's (1787–1860) object in *New Nursery Songs for all Good Children*[88] of 1832 was 'to endeavour to catch something of that good-humoured pleasantry, that musical nonsense, which makes Mother Goose so attractive to children of all ages . . .' Her foreword stresses the lack of 'capacity, taste and moral sense of children', so she attempts to avoid the defects of Mother Goose. 'If children love to lisp my rhymes, while the parents find no fault in them I ask no higher praise.'[89] Note the somewhat precious tone of the editorial and the fact that the songs are only for good children; but nursery rhymes are respectable at last and can be placed side by side with hymns. In fact, although Follen is somewhat sentimental, she writes with a delicate touch and there is little that is didactic in this book. Like many of her counterparts in Britain, she worked tirelessly for the abolition of slavery, and was editor of *The Child's Friend* between 1843 and 1850. One of her hymns, still sung by children today, focuses on kind deeds and the diminutive to which the Victorians were so partial.

> Little deeds of kindness,
>   Little words of love,
> Make our earth an Eden,
>   Like the heaven above.[90]

Around the same time, 1833, Felicia Hemans (1793–1835) produced her *Hymns for Childhood*.[91] A poet of great range, Hemans could turn her pen to most genres. 'The Skylark', one of the finest hymns written for children in the nineteenth century, is indicative of the qualities of Hemans's adult poetry: uplifting sentiments, detailed observations of nature, a harmonious ear. The devotional side of the hymn equates belief and religious observance with a joy and 'rapture' which were to be the distinctive qualities of a later poet, Christina Rossetti. (Hemans is discussed more fully in Chapter 7.)

> The sky-lark, when the dews of morn
> Hang tremulous on flower and thorn,
> And violets round his nest exhale
> Their fragrance on the early gale,
> To the first sunbeam spreads his wings,
> Buoyant with joy, and soars and sings.
>
> Thus my Creator! thus the more
> My spirits wing to Thee can soar,
> The more she triumphs to behold

Thy love in all thy works unfold,
And bids her hymns of rapture be
Most glad, when rising most to Thee![92]

'All things bright and beautiful'

Cecil Frances Alexander (1818–1895) is the last religious poet I want to consider in detail. She was writing in the 1830s when other concerns had taken over from the central religious impulse in poetry for children by most other writers. Married to the Archbishop of Armagh in Ireland (who fondly believed her to be a genius), Alexander was very hardworking – an affectionate wife and mother, tireless in her work for the poor in her community, a keen gardener and an enthusiastic hostess. She was conscientious in the composition of hymns, but was more concerned to celebrate her faith than aspire to great poetry. Her husband tells us in a memoir that:

> no apparent claim of rhythm or language or imagery could plead effectually with her for retention when her clear and severe judgement told her that its continued existence would impair the precision and accuracy of the conveyance of her thought.

The rule she was invariably guided by was this – 'It must be *sung;* it must be *praise;* it must be *to God.*'[93] Consequently, the poetry is modest in its merits, but many of her hymns are still sung heartily in schools and churches today. 'Once in Royal David's City', 'There is a green hill far away', 'Do no sinful action' and 'All things bright and beautiful' are all by her. Like Leonardo's Mona Lisa, in one respect only, 'All things bright' has become a cliché through overfamiliarity and few bother to give the original the consideration it deserves. It is worth lingering over this hymn, if only to see how childhood is being conceived in devotional verse by the mid-nineteenth century.

All things bright and beautiful,
   All creatures great and small,
All things wise and wonderful,
   The Lord God made them all.

Each little flower that opens,
   Each little bird that sings,
He made their glowing colours,
   He made their tiny wings.

Alexander draws the reader's attention positively to the diminutive nature of certain of the creatures in God's kingdom (birds, flowers, 'tiny', 'little', 'small'), an allusion perhaps to the vulnerability of children and the fact that small things and people can be 'wise and wonderful'. She also creates an appealing image of 'bright', 'beautiful' creatures with 'glowing colours' and reminds the reader that all these glorious things are made by God. It is a happy, colourful universe with a loving God that is emphasized here.

> The rich man in his castle,
> The poor man at his gate,
> God made them, high or lowly,
> And ordered their estate.

No radical voice, of course, but the conventional view of most of the early Victorian middle class that people should accept whatever station they were placed in and look forward to the comfort of life after death. However, Alexander does not mention the after-life as the place where good children achieve their just rewards which is a clear change from Puritan verse; nor does she labour her point.

> The purple-headed mountain,
> The river running by,
> The sunset and the morning,
> That brightens up the sky.
>
> The cold wind in the winter,
> The pleasant summer sun,
> The ripe fruits in the garden,
> He made them every one.[94]

She returns to the natural world – mountains, rivers, sunsets and the sky above – simply but evocatively described and tells young readers that they must accept the good and the bad; the bitter winter wind, as well as the warmth and abundance of the summer. The benevolence of Christianity is stressed with children likened to tender plants to be nurtured and requiring some teaching in order to praise God. Alexander's gift was to write for children with simplicity and directness in approachable language: her success cannot be doubted in the hymns that are chosen in assemblies and Sunday Schools, week after week, 150 years later.

Hymns for Little Children appeared in 1848, and ran to many editions. It was followed by several other books of verse, including *Moral Songs*, 1849 and *Sunday School Book of Poetry*, from which the following extract is taken. It shows she was able to empathize with a child with its kind, motherly tone, not unlike some of Rossetti's rhymes for babies which are discussed in Chapter 7.

In the room corners I watch the dark shadows,
Deepening, and lengthening, as evening comes on,
Soon will the mowers return from the meadows;
Far to the westward the red sun is gone.
By the green hedgerow, I see her now coming,
Where the last sunbeam is just on her track.
Still I sit by you, love, drowsily humming,
Sleep, little baby, till mother comes back.[95]

Morning has broken

By the middle of the nineteenth century Eliza Follen could write in *The Lark and the Linnet: Hymns, Songs and Fables*[96] that:

> Most of the poems were written with no other hope than that they would instruct or please some child . . . It may be objected to the book, that gay and serious pieces are bound up together; but so it is in human life and human nature . . .

Devotional verse could now be considered alongside songs, fables and other 'gay pieces'. Christina Rossetti, who was deeply religious, does just that in *Sing-Song* and many poets for children continued to include some religious verse in their collections until around the early part of this century. By then, nature poetry had become the primary theme.

One of the few poets of the twentieth century to write a significant number of popular religious poems for children is Eleanor Farjeon whose work is considered in Chapter 11. The best known is 'Morning has Broken' which captures something of Farjeon's enthusiasm and optimism for life. Although this is a devotional poem, references to religion have become indirect.

To bring us to the end of the twentieth century one of the finest anthologists of them all, Charles Causley, who has written some exquisite carols himself, compiled a book of Christian verse, *The Sun, Dancing*,[97] in 1982. Causley selected quite a few of the poets discussed in this chapter, plus William Blake, who leads us to the next. Blake and Causley share a view of Christian poetry that is open rather than narrow, humane rather than severe, passionate rather than pious; that seems as good a place as any to close this account of religious verse for children.

A dog starved at his master's gate
Predicts the ruin of the State.

A horse misused upon the road
Cries to heaven for human blood.

Each outcry of the hunted hare
A fibre from the brain does tear.

Kill not the moth nor butterfly;
For the Last Judgement draweth nigh.[98]

Notes

1 Isaac Watts, *Divine Songs attempted in easy language for the use of children*, M. Lawrence, London, 1715.

2 F. J. Harvey Darton, *Children's Books in England*, Cambridge, 1932. I make frequent references to this text, not just because Darton is a fount of information, but because his judgement is invariably sound.

3 William Sloane, *Children's Books in England and America in the Seventeenth Century*, New York, 1955, p. 11.

4 Heather Glen, *Vision and Disenchantment*, C.U.P. Cambridge, 1983, p. 12.

5 Gillian Avery, 'The Puritans and their Heirs' in *Children and their Books*, eds. G. Avery & J. Briggs, Clarendon Press, Oxford, p. 95.

6 James Janeway, *A Token for Children, being an Exact Account of the Conversion, Holy and Exemplary Lives, and Joyful Deaths, of several Young Children*, Example VII, London, 1671, pp. 671–2.

7 Avery, *op. cit.*, p. 113.

8 C. John Somerville, *The Discovery of Childhood in Puritan England*, University of Georgia Press, London, 1992, pp. 3, 23.

9 *Ibid.*, p. 25.

10 John Calvin, 'Institutes, Book Two', quoted in Zachary Leader's *Reading Blake's Songs*, Routledge, London, 1981, p. 6.

11 Ivy Pinchbeck, quoted in Leader, *ibid.*, p. 8.

12 Keith Thomas, 'Children in Early Modern England' in *Children and their Books, op. cit.*,

13 *Ibid.*, p. 57–8.

14 For further information on the life and works of John Newbery, see John Rowe Townsend below.

15 John Rowe Townsend, *Trade and Plumb-cake for ever, Huzza!*, Colt Books, Cambridge, 1994, pp. 1,3.

16 John Locke, *Some Thoughts Concerning Education*, 1693, eds John & Jean Yolton, Clarendon Press, Oxford, 1989, p. 212.

17 Margaret Spufford, *Small Books and Pleasant Histories*, Methuen, London, 1981.

18 See *The Diary of Samuel Pepys*, this edition *The Shorter Pepys*, edited Robert Latham, Penguin London, 1985.

19 Anon, part of Samuel Pepys Library of 'Penny Merriments' housed in Magdalene College, Cambridge and quoted in Roger Thompson, ed. *Samuel Pepys' Penny Merriments*, Constable, London, 1976, p. 57.

20 Townsend, *op. cit.*, p. 2.

21 Glen, *op. cit.*, p. 8.

22 See for example Darton (Note 2) Chapter 4, Muir (Note 35) Chapters 1,3.

23 Somerville, *op. cit.*, p. 129.

24 Rudyard Kipling, quoted in *Kipling the Poet*, Peter Keating, Secker & Warburg, London, 1994, p. 205.

25 Quoted in Zachary Leader, *Reading Blake's Songs*, Routledge, London, 1981, p. 22.

26 N. H. Keeble, ed. *The Pilgrim's Progress* by John Bunyan, Oxford, 1984, p. xi.

27 John Bunyan, *Country Rhimes for Children*, 1686. Also entitled *A Book for Boys and Girls* and *Divine Emblems*. An edition with modernised spellings is available for children, published by Ina Books, Oakhill, 1987.

28 Graham Midgley, *The Miscellaneous Works of John Bunyan*, Volume VI, *The Poems*, Oxford, 1980, p. xxvii

29 Glen, *op. cit.*, pp. 10–11.

30 Bunyan, *op. cit.*,

31 Midgely, *op. cit.*, p. xxvii.

32 Roger Sharrock in *John Bunyan: Conventicle and Parnussus, Tercentenary Essays*, ed. N. H. Keeble, Clarendon Press, Oxford, 1988, p. 71.

33 John Bunyan, *The Holy War*, p. 251, quoted by Roger Pooley in Keeble, *ibid.*, p. 91.

34 Bunyan, *Country Rhimes, op. cit.*,

35 Percy Muir, *English Children's Books 1600–1900*, Batsford, 1954–1985, p. 29.

36 Bunyan, from 'Upon a Snail' and 'Upon a Penny Loaf', *Country Rhimes, op. cit.*

37 Christopher Hill, *A turbulent, seditious and factious people: John Bunyan and his church, 1828–1688*, Oxford, 1989, p. 270.

38 Bunyan, *Country Rhimes, op. cit.*

39 Darton, *op. cit.*, pp. 64/5.

40 Midgley, *op. cit.*, p. xliii.

41 John Bunyan, *The Pilgrim's Progress*,1678, this edition, ed. Roger Sharrock, Penguin, London, 1985.

42 Abraham Chear, *A Looking Glass for Children*, London, 1672.

43 Somerville *op. cit.*, p. 129.

44 Chear *op. cit.*

45 Muir *op. cit.*, p. 35.

46 Nathaniel Crouch, *Youth's Divine Pastime*, London, 1691.

47 Martha England & John Sparrow, *Hymns Unbidden*, The New York Public Library, 1966, p. 44.

48 Isaac Watts, *op. cit.*

49 *Ibid.*

50 Watts, *op. cit.*, ed. J. H. P. Pafford, Oxford, 1971, pp. 144–6.

51 *Ibid.*

52 Leader, *op. cit.*, p. 22.

53 Isaac Watts, *Essay towards the encouragement of Charity Schools*, 1728, quoted in Pafford, *op. cit.*, p. 26/7.

54 Vivian de Sola Pinto quoted in Leader, *op. cit.*, p. 15.

55 Watts, *Divine Songs, op. cit.*

56 Darton, *op. cit.*, p. 111.

57 Watts, from 'How Doth the Little Busy Bee' and 'How Doth the Little Crocodile', *Divine Songs, op. cit.*

58 Lewis Carroll, *Alice's Adventures in Wonderland*, 1865.

59 Nathaniel Cotton, *Visions in Verse*, London, 1751.

60 John Marchant, *Puerilia: Amusements for the Young*, London, 1751.

61 *Ibid.*

62 Iona & Peter Opie, *The Oxford Book of Children's Verse*, Oxford, 1973–93, p. 386.

63 John Wesley, quoted in Leader, *op. cit.*, p. 9.

64 Martha England & John Sparrow, *op. cit.*, p. 46.
65 Wesley & Blake, quoted in England, *ibid.*, p. 44.
66 *Ibid.*, pp. 46, 54.
67 Wesley, quoted in England, *ibid.*, p. 57.
68 Leader, *op. cit.*, p. 8.
69 Christopher Smart, from 'Mirth' and 'Plenteous Redemption', *Hymns for the Amusement of Children*, London, 1772.
70 Darton, *op. cit.*, p. 163.
71 Eleanor Fenn (Nurse Lovechild), *The Golden Present*, London, 1780.
72 *Ibid.*
73 Muir, *op. cit.*, p. 82.
74 Charles Lamb, quoted in Darton, *op. cit.*, p. 129.
75 Muir, *op. cit.*, p. 82.
76 Norma Clarke, 'The Cursed Barbauld Crew: Women writers and writing for children in the late eighteenth century', in Hilton, Styles, Watson, eds, *Opening the Nursery Door: Reading, Writing and Childhood, 1600-1900*, Routledge, London, 1997, p. 93.
77 Nicholas Tucker, 'Fairy Tales and their Early Opponents: in defence of Mrs Trimmer', 1997, ibid.
78 Darton, *op. cit.*, p. 153.
79 Clarke, *op. cit.*, p. 94.
80 Anna Barbauld, *Hymns in Prose*, London, 1781.
81 *Ibid.*, Hymn 1, pp. 11-13.
82 Ann and Jane Taylor, *Hymns for Infant Minds*, Darton, London, 1810.
83 From 'Praise for Daily Mercies', *ibid.*
84 From 'The Example of Christ', *ibid.*
85 *Ibid.*
86 *Poetry for Children: the complete works of Ann & Jane Taylor*, Ward Lock & Tyler, London, 1876.
87 Samuel Griswold Goodrich, 1840, quoted in Darton, *op. cit.*, p. 222.
88 Eliza Follen, *New Nursery Songs for all Good Children*, Blackwood & Sons, London, 1832, p. iv.
89 *Ibid.*
90 *Ibid.*
91 Felicia Hemans, from 'The Skylark', *Hymns for Childhood*, 1834, in *Poetical Works of Mrs Hemans*, Blackwood, Edinburgh, 1839.
92 *Ibid.*
93 William Alexander, ed. *Mrs Alexander's Poems*, London, 1896.
94 Cecil Frances Alexander, 'All Things Bright and Beautiful', *Hymns for Little Children*, London, 1848.
95 Cecil Frances Alexander, *Sunday School Book of Poetry*, 1865.
96 Eliza Follen, *The Lark and the Linnet: Hymns, Songs and Fables*.
97 Charles Causley, ed. *The Sun, Dancing*, Puffin, Harmondsworth, 1982.
98 William Blake, from 'Auguries of Innocence'. *The Poems of William Blake*, ed. W. H. Stevenson, London, 1971.

CHAPTER 2

Romantic Visions

The influence of Romanticism
on children's verse

Thou little Child, yet glorious in the might
Of heaven-born freedom on thy being's height.[1]

In the first chapter I showed how Puritan ideas were predominant in writing for children during the seventeenth and eighteenth century. This chapter focuses on the development of Romanticism and its influence on children's poetry ever since. Why have Romantic notions been so central in children's poetry? The simple answer, of course, is that the Romantics produced some of the best poetry ever written in English which still appeals widely 200 years after it was first published. Some Romantic poetry is easily accessible to the young, both in terms of subject matter and language. Indeed, one of the criticisms of early Romantic poetry was its apparent simplicity and naivity in form and language as well as content. Childhood itself was of great interest to the Romantics, as it was to the Puritans, but the views of childhood which stood at the heart of the Romantic ideal were completely at odds with Puritan thinking. Wordsworth, in particular, spoke of childhood in quasi-mystical terms, writing in one of his most quoted poems that 'The Child is father of the Man'.[2]

The 'new dawn' of Romanticism

The Romantic movement grew up in an age when, as Harold Bloom put it, the French Revolution was 'the most important external factor . . . Out of the ferment that failed to produce a national renewal [or revolution] there came instead the major English contribution to world literature since the Renaissance, the startling phenomenon of six major poets appearing in just two generations.'[3] Out of this 'new dawn' came 'apocalyptic longings, themselves expressions of a radical Protestant temperament, that most clearly distinguishes Romantic poetry from most of the English poetry that had been written since the Renaissance.'[4] Romanticism heralded in a more liberal era which touched children's literature as it did most aspects of life at that time of social, political, intellectual and artistic change, though Roger Lonsdale reminds us this was not so quick to follow as some commentators have suggested: 'The "revolution" announced by the *Lyrical Ballads* has always been retrospectively exaggerated and its impact was far from immediate.'[5]

Space does not permit me to attempt any serious study of the major Romantic figures who wrote for an adult audience. Despite their importance in the history of poetry, Percy Bysshe Shelley and George Gordon Noel, Lord Byron are neglected in this volume, while Coleridge gets scant mention. (All three make a small appearance in Chapter 10.) I do give some attention to William Wordsworth, because of his pivotal role in redescribing childhood. John Keats is also touched on, as he is the Romantic with whom so many young people of early adolescence fall metaphorically in love. Romantic precursors – Cowper, Burns and Scott – who have featured strongly in children's anthologies over the years are considered briefly and I conclude with John Clare whose poetry has so many connections with childhood. None of these poets was seriously engaged in writing for children, though their work has had a strong impact on children's literature. Our interest is threefold: why has their poetry been selected for children? how did these poets deal with childhood? and how did they influence poetry for children? William Blake is the only major figure in this period who wrote for children and it is his poetry that merits substantial appraisal in this chapter. Even in his case, the intended audience for his poetry is still in dispute, as we shall see.

Romantic poetry explores a wide range of themes in language and forms that are distinctive to individual poets. However, there are some ideas which all the Romantic poets held more or less in common. In *English Poetry of the Romantic Period*, J. R. Watson describes Romanticism thus:

> subjective rather than objective, fragmentary rather than complete, organic rather than preconceived in form, interested in nature, the self, the wonderful, and the supernatural; interested, too, in confusion, fluidity, indeterminacy. These matters . . . [form] part of an astonishing change of sensibility, under the influence of which we are still living: our ideas about the nature of the individual, the society in which he lives, the natural world which surrounds him, and the role of art in society, all of these are inherited from the Romantic period.[6]

Before we engage with those beliefs, which were to overturn the cool, orderly and what Glen calls 'polite' nature of mainstream thought and manners of the late eighteenth century, I want to begin by tracing four poets who anticipate in various ways features of the Romantic movement.

Rural walks – the poetry of William Cowper

William Cowper (1731–1800) was a man of nervous and delicate disposition who never fully recovered from his mother's early death, after which he spent a wretched time at boarding school. He trained for the Bar and became a Clerk in the House of Lords, later suffering bouts of madness. He moved to Olney in 1767 with a Mrs Unwin with whom he formed a close (but chaste) relationship and who took care of him for many years through several bouts of mental illness. In Olney he was part of a liberal, evangelical community which campaigned against slavery and his poetry often reflected his social concerns. Lucy Aikin includes Cowper in *Poetry for Children*, 1801, one of the earliest anthologies for young readers. 'Against Slavery' is one of the most moving poems on the subject ever written.

> I would not have a slave to till my ground,
> To carry me, to fan me while I sleep,
> And tremble when I wake, for all the wealth
> That sinews bought and sold have ever earn'd.
> No: dear as freedom is,
> I had much rather be myself the slave,
> And wear the bonds, than fasten them on him.[7]

Cowper had a nice sense of humour shown to good effect in his delightful letters, in poems like 'John Gilpin' (see Chapter 10) and 'The Task'. Although the latter begins in mock-heroic style, before long Cowper flexes his pen as a poet of nature.

> For I have lov'd the rural walk through lanes
> Of grassy swarth, close cropt by nibbling sheep,
> And skirted thick with intertexture firm
> Of thorny boughs; have lov'd the rural walk
> O'er hills, through valleys, and by rovers' brink,
> E'er since a truant boy I pass'd my bounds
> T'enjoy a ramble on the banks of Thames:[8]

There is a pleasant informality to Cowper's poem, a sense of the poet's genuine pleasure in his walks, a mood of tranquility, an authentic description of nature. In *The Loved Haunts of Cowper*, Thomas Wright describes him as spending his childhood 'attached to every tree, gate, and stile in his neighbourhood [of Berkhamstead] . . . '[9] Mary Jacobus argues that there were significant similarities between Wordsworth and Cowper in their nature poetry; for example the 'transference of sensation to inner life, its merging of natural and internal landscapes'.[10]

> Mighty winds
> That sweep the skirt of some far-spreading wood
> Of ancient growth, make music not unlike
> The dash of ocean on his winding shore,
> And lull the spirit while they fill the mind . . .[11]

Cowper was keen to turn his back on the artificiality typical of Augustan poetry at that time, but Romantic he is not. His treatment of nature, for example, is still more ornamental than elemental; and poor people in his poems, though treated with sympathy, know their place in society and act from reason rather than inspiration and imagination. Heather Glen points out that in 'Truth', for example, his 'happy peasant' is sentimentalized, and her 'humble' place is seen as ordained by 'nature'. 'But he does attempt to portray some actual details of her life and to suggest the challenge she offers the values of the polite world . . .'[12]

> Yon cottager, who weaves at her own door,
> Pillow and bobbins all her little store;
> Content, though mean; and cheerful, if not gay;
> Shuffling her threads about the live-long day,
> Just earns a scanty pittance; and at night
> Lies down secure, her heart and pocket light . . .[13]

'The Poplar-Field' has been repeatedly chosen for children. Here are the two opening stanzas with their pleasant sing-song rhythm:

> The poplars are felled, farewell to the shade
> And the whispering sound of the cool colonnade,
> The winds play no longer, and sing in the leaves,
> Nor Ouse on his bosom their image receives.
>
> Twelve years have elapsed since I last took a view
> Of my favourite field and the bank where they grew,
> And now in the grass behold they are laid,
> And the tree is my seat that once lent me a shade.[14]

Fanny Price thrilled to Edmund's reading of Cowper's poetry in *Mansfield Park*. Popular in children's anthologies until at least the middle of the nineteenth century, Cowper was Jane Austen's favourite poet and deserves to be better known today.

'Of Mice and Men' – the poetry of Robert Burns

> Wee Willie Gray, and his leather wallet,
> Peel a willow wand to be him boots and jacket;
> The rose upon the brier will be him trouse an' doublet,
> The rose upon the brier will be him trouse an' doublet.

Wee Willie Gray, and his leather wallet,
Twice a lily-flower will be him sark and cravat;
Feathers of a flee wad feather up his bonnet,
Feathers of a flee wad feather up his bonnet.[15]

It has often struck me as interesting that in the period running up to the publication of *Lyrical Ballads* in 1798, two poets, both of them working men, living at opposite ends of the country were producing work which had many similarities with Romantic poetry, although they were totally different writers from each other and had quite distinctive voices. We will examine William Blake later, a poet of the city of London, but I should like to turn now to Robert Burns (1759–1796) who immortalized a quieter, less familiar place – rural Ayrshire, where most of his life was spent as a small, largely unsuccessful landowner who eked out a living from the land. Like Shakespeare in England, Burns has become an icon, or worse still, a cliché of everything Scottish; he is used as an emblem of Scottish nationalism and romantic idolatry, as well as the subject of proper academic regard and popular affection. Just the same, one of the delights of a Scottish childhood is that you cannot ignore Burns's poetry and most natives can quote and sing quite a bit of the Bard, and do so with pride.

Although Burns is one of the most translated poets in the world, he is not always given proper attention in England. The excuse the English make for ignoring Burns is that they cannot understand the language, yet there is nothing difficult about many of his poems – 'A Red, Red Rose' or 'Ae Fond Kiss', for example. His name is also omitted from most studies of Romantic poetry, despite Burns's claim as a precursor.

Apart from the single ditty reproduced above, Burns did not write for children, yet his poetry has featured regularly in anthologies since the beginning of the nineteenth century. The appeal of Burns to the young must surely lie in his warmth, his lyric gift, directness of expression and a wicked sense of fun. Editors usually select his songs – 'Green Grow the Rashes O' [*sic*], 'John Barleycorn', 'The Banks of Doon', though poems like 'To a Mouse', 'To a Mountain Daisy' and extracts from 'Tam O'Shanter' are also popular. Although most are in Scots dialect, Burns's poems chosen for children are usually short, tuneful and easy to understand. Burns loved nature, particularly the streams and rivers of his birthplace, and enchantingly set numerous songs of love in a rural landscape. Like the Romantics who were to follow, he often used the beauty of the natural world in his longer poems as a starting-point for introspection about the human condition. A poet who could make a masterpiece out of addressing a mouse which he nearly kills by accident while ploughing, could write about profound as well as simple things in a language children could understand.

Wee, sleekit, cowrin, tim'rous beastie,
O what a panic's in thy breastie!
Thou need na start awa sae hasty,
    Wi' bickering brattle!
I wad be laith to rin an' chase thee,
    Wi' murdering pattle!

I'm truly sorry Man's dominion
Has broken Nature's social union,
An' justifies that ill opinion,
    Which makes thee startle,
At me, thy poor, earth-born companion,
    An' fellow-mortal![16]

Children can empathize with the small creature's terror, its life or death dependent on the whim of a large human; and the way the poet calls the mouse a 'fellow-mortal'. They also tend to enjoy Burns's descriptive language – who cannot sympathize with a 'Wee, sleekit, cowrin, tim'rous beastie' or feel tenderly towards the 'panic in thy breastie'? Even young readers can understand something of the humanity in Burns's attitude to the 'wee' mouse; they probably also have some inkling of what 'Nature's social union' is supposed to be and some sense the melancholy at the heart of the poem which ends like this:

The best-laid schemes o' mice an' men
    Gang aft a-gley,
An' lea'e us nought but grief an' pain
    For promis'd joy!

Still thou art blest, compar'd wi' me!
The present only toucheth thee:
But, och! I backward cast my e'e
    On prospects drear!
An' forward, tho' I canna see,
    I guess an' fear![17]

This is a truly multilayered text; the reader brings new understandings to the poem at different stages of life. The conclusion certainly hits sharply in middle age, yet the little boy who recited the poem with such vigour during a 1996 television programme was clearly deeply engaged with it aged only 11.[18] Any child can enjoy Kate's angry litany of her drink-sodden husband's misdemeanors in 'Tam O'Shanter': 'She tauld thee weel thou was a skellum, /A blethering, blustering, a drunken blellum'; the same wife who sits 'Gathering her brows like gathering storm, / Nursing her wrath to keep it warm.' Children of the late eighteenth century might also have revelled in the delicious list of gory details recounted in Tam's famous journey:

> By this time he was cross the ford,
> Whare, in the snaw, the chapman smoor'd;
> And past the birks and meikle stane,
> Whare drunken Charlie brak's neck-bane;
> And thro' the whins, and by the cairn,
> Whare hunters fand the murder'd bairn;
> And near the thorn, aboon the well,
> Whare Mungo's mither hang'd hersel . . .[19]

Burns, of course, told a good tale well and was very funny too, as is evident in 'Tam O'Shanter'. Young readers are also amused by the poet's tongue-in-cheek admonition in 'To a Louse' to avoid 'Sae fine a lady! / Gae somewhere else and seek your dinner, / On some poor body.' The amusing but truthful ending to the poem is now part of the culture.

> O wad some Pow'r the giftie gie us
> To see oursels as ithers see us!
> It wad frae monie a blunder free us
>   An' foolish notion:
> What airs in dress an' gait wad lea'e us,
>   An' ev'n Devotion![20]

This most original poet, who never travelled outside Scotland, led an eventful life, achieving some fame in his lifetime, but dying in poverty and neglect. Burns was the son of poor but respectable people. He may have run about barefoot, but his father scraped the money together to employ a tutor. Burns had a reasonable education and was an avid reader all his life. A natural radical, he had to break free of the social, educational and religious constraints of his time, class and community to express himself in poetry. Living when he did, always struggling to support his family which included a few 'bairns' born out of wedlock, Burns was forced to compromise his beliefs in different ways. Despite mixing with rich and titled people, he remained true to the ordinary folk he lived among in his beloved Ayrshire. 'A Man's a Man for A' That' displays many of Burns's talents and themes: it is witty, it is written in authentic Scots, it sneers contemptuously at indolence, wealth, hypocrisy and vanity and it gives a rousing cheer to the 'man o' independent mind'.

> Ye see yon birkie ca'd 'a lord',
>   Wha struts, an' stares, an' a' that;
> Tho' hundreds worship at his word,
>   He's but a coof for a' that:
> For a' that, an' a' that,
>   His ribband, star, an' a' that:
> The man o' independent mind
>   He looks an' laughs at a' that.[21]

His story is sympathetically and vividly told by Catherine Carswell in 1930, still the best biography to date. She recognizes the weaknesses of his character – waywardness, sexual licentiousness, tendency to depression – but also the energy, generosity and vitality of the man.

> That circumstances have so often warped and destroyed men [*sic*] of genius is a sad fact of human history; that the man of genius does not merely defy circumstances, but draws from them all the nourishment his genius demands for its flowering, is of all facts the most consoling. Robert's spine had been bent by excessive labour and insufficient food at a tender age; his instincts had been thwarted by a crippling moral code, and his mind had been misled by a spurious culture. Yet, as much by the futility as by the violence of his struggle, as much by his defeat as his mastery of untoward surroundings, as much by his lapses as by his aspiration, he extracted the vital elements from a forbidding soil.[22]

Perhaps we learn most about Burns as a man and a poet in the preface to the original volume of his poems, 600 copies of which were published in Kilmarnock, 1786, at three shillings a head. He was about to set off for the West Indies to escape financial ruin and moral infamy – he had fathered another illegitimate child – but the success of the poems made him change his mind.

> Although a Rhymer from his earliest years, at least from the earliest impulses of the softer passions, it was not till very lately that the applause . . . wakened his vanity so far as to make make him think anything of his was worth showing; and none of the following works were ever composed with a view to the press. To amuse himself with the little creations of his own fancy, amid the toil and fatigues of a laborious life; to transcribe the various feelings, the loves, the griefs, the hopes, the fears, in his own breast; to find some sort of counterpoise to the struggles of a world, always an alien scene, a task uncouth to the poetical mind; these were his motives for courting the Muses, and in these he found Poetry to be its own reward.[23]

Like Blake, Burns was a radical and his poems often pour scorn on wealth and privilege and speak up for ordinary folk. He was forced on occasion to compromise his beliefs as a poor man living in dangerous times. Nor was working as an exciseman (which he did in the last few years of his life) the perfect job for a poet with socialist leanings, but it gave him what his poetry had failed to provide – enough cash to feed his growing family. Through his many personal difficulties, he kept faith with the culture and the people of his origins. Working hard and living hard, his songs capture rural Ayrshire of the late eighteenth century and celebrate the oral tradition of Scotland which he collected assiduously all his life. The fact that Burns borrowed and improved many popular lyrics was not unproblematic, as the authorship of many traditional songs was left in doubt. However, the songs assured him wide and lasting appeal; in Scotland children still learn them at school. Burns may have been neglected by scholars of English poetry, the same is not true of children's literature which has faithfully included him in anthologies up to and including the present day.

'Pibroch of Donuil' – the ballads of Sir Walter Scott

> O, Young Lochinvar is come out of the west,
> Through all the wide Border his steed was the best;[24]

Another Scottish poet whose work has connections with Romanticism is Sir Walter Scott (1771–1832), author of *Minstrelsy of the Scottish Border*, who was also a great collector of old Scottish songs and ballads. As an aristocratic and devoted Tory, Scott could not have been less like Burns, but they shared a passion for Scotland's authentic lyrical voice. Scott also probably did more than any other writer to popularize Scottish history in novels and poems. He was one of the most revered poets in Britain in his own life-time and is arguably the most cited poet in nineteenth-century novels.

Unfortunately, ballads like 'Pibroch of Donuil Dhu' and 'Young Lochinvar' are now regarded as too difficult for children by many contemporary publishers and editors, who exclude them from anthologies. Certainly their counterparts in the nineteenth and earlier twentieth century appeared not to have any such problem. Andrew Lang quoted both poems in *The Blue Poetry Book* in 1892 where he takes distinguished anthologists such as Palgrave to task for failing to include 'more than a tenth of the number . . . born north of the Tweed'. (Unfortunately, he falls down himself on at least two counts by contemporary standards – for failing to include more than four poems by women out of 150, and only one by a poet who actually wrote for children!)

Lang explains his inclusion of Scott (and Burns) in his poetry book 'intended for lads and lassies' . . . not to 'exorbitant local patriotism', but because 'singers of the North, for some reason or other, do excel in poems of action and adventure . . . ' As for Scott, Lang praises that 'Homeric quality . . . no man has [since] displayed in the same degree . . . In the development of a love of poetry it is probable that simple, natural, and adventurous poetry like Scott's comes first . . . '[25] In my own schooldays in Edinburgh, many of us used to declaim verses such as this short extract from 'Pibroch of Donuil Dhu' which trip so satisfyingly off the tongue.

> Pibroch of Donuil Dhu,
> Pibroch of Donuil
> Wake thy wild voice anew,
> Summon Clan Conuil.
> Come away, come away,
> Hark to the summons!
> Come in your war array,
> Gentles and commons.
>
> Come from deep glen, and
> From mountain so rocky,
> The war-pipe and pennon
> Are at Inverlochy.
> Come every hill-plaid, and
> True heart that wears one,
> Come every steel blade, and
> Strong hand that bears one.[26]

R. J. Watson suggests that Scott's poetry is Romantic,

in that it treats of a world remote from the concerns and constraints of the day in a manner that indicates Scott's love of imaginative freedom. His poems have affinities with the world of legend and folk-tale: they are associated with an ideal world, with history seen as excitement, tragedy and romance . . . Scott's verse is flexible, daring and often exotic . . . and in his largeness of sympathy and wide humanity Scott resembles Byron more than he does any of the major Romantic poets.[27]

Like the Romantics, Scott turns to nature as a grand theme, though for him it is inextricably associated with Scottishness:

> . . . Caledonia! stern and wild,
> Meet nurse for a poetic child![28]

Scott was well represented in poetry anthologies for children until the latter half of this century where his verse, like his novels, has fallen out of favour. There are genuine difficulties with unfamiliar language and convoluted writing in some of the prose, but Scott's ability to weave high romance and adventure into melodic poetry ought to ensure him a niche with young readers today, as this extract from 'Madge Wildfire's Song' demonstrates:

> Proud Maisie is in the wood,
>   Walking so early;
> Sweet Robin sits on the bush,
>   Singing so rarely.
>
> 'Tell me, thou bonny bird,
>   When shall I marry me?'
> – 'When six braw gentlemen
>   Kirkward shall carry ye.'[29]

Eternity's sunrise – the poetry of William Blake

> He who binds to himself a Joy
> Doth the winged life destroy;
> But he who kisses the Joy as it flies
> Lives in Eternity's sunrise.[30]

The most significant figure in this history is William Blake (1757–1827), the great poet of childhood from this period, indeed of any period, who wrote, illustrated, designed and printed *Songs of Innocence* in 1789, reissued in 1794 with *Songs of Experience* as part of a larger collection. Blake, who famously declared that 'every thing that lives is holy' and that you could '. . . see a World in a Grain of Sand And a Heaven in a Wild Flower, Hold Infinity in the palm of your hand And Eternity in an hour . . .'[31] was an original, out on his own, a visionary genius, a true radical, a man of passion and compassion. As Darton movingly put it: 'a great imaginative writer had . . . broken into the narrow library that others were toiling so laboriously to fill for children . . . they never dreamt of knocking at the gate of heaven or playing among the tangled stars.'[32] Darton is an appreciative critic of Blake's poetry for children, catching something of Blake's notes of pure joy in his desire to communicate this poet's extraordinary talent to others. Peter Ackroyd, a recent biographer, takes a similar position on *Songs of Innocence*: 'they seem to us now to express all the energy and confidence of a poet who has at last found the way forward . . .'[33]

What then was this struggling engraver doing in *Songs of Innocence* that was so extraordinary? In some respects it was quite conventional. As Victor Watson suggests:

Some [of the poems] are expressions of a young child's developing sense of goodness; some are poems for bed-time; one is a nonsense poem; in others, children take on the language of adults to address creatures smaller than themselves.[34]

Ackroyd points out that Blake 'borrowed the movement of the ballads, hymns and nursery rhymes that were all in the air around him . . . '[35] Blake's *Songs* were certainly influenced by the English hymn tradition – Watts and Wesley in particular. Martha England describes how Blake takes his pastoral imagery directly from Wesley and employs similar 'stanza forms, rhyme words, variety of measure and tone, and subtle representation of sound . . . Blake's songs were in that area where the hymn, the pastoral, and children's literature unite.'[36]

There is still controversy about whether or not Blake was writing solely with children in mind. Ackroyd thinks he did and also suggests that Blake tried to capitalize on the growing market for children's literature in that period. If that is so, this son of a small shopkeeper (his father was a hosier) lacked any business sense at all, as he priced himself out of the market[37] and went to extraordinary lengths to fulfil his vision by an elaborate process of printing which meant that every copy was unique and expensive. Added to that, the poems in *Innocence* are often argumentative or satirical and there is 'a suggestion of distance and even parody within the most apparently "naive" lyrics . . .'[38] Glen also takes up this point, suggesting that Blake sought to initiate a debate about morality with the adults of his day, as well as wishing to please children.

Zachary Leader is most persuasive on this point and I will quote him at some length.

. . . Neither work [*Innocence* nor *Experience*] seems to have been intended primarily for juvenile readers . . . [Blake] knew, through personal acquaintance and professional experience, a great deal about juvenile literature; lived in a world which took children's books seriously; disagreed with the theories and assumptions upon which most of them were based; and saw all too clearly that their ultimate effect was to deny children what he felt were their most valuable qualities. Furthermore, since most juvenile literature was illustrated, a children's book for adults would provide Blake with a perfect opportunity to extend his recent experiments . . . in illuminated printing. The deceptively simple and reassuring rhythms of nursery rhyme, folk-song, jingle, lullaby, ballad, and hymn, when combined with an equally child-like pictorial style . . . would lull the reader into expecting conventional themes – laziness, for instance, or disobedience – to be conventionally treated. When expectations were then subtly undermined, the larger implications of the themes and conventions of traditional children's books would be thrown into relief . . . It was, in effect, *a children's book for adults* [my emphasis].[39]

Blake held strong views about childhood and education. As Leader put it:

> If anyone is to be educated, therefore, it is the adult. And the child should be his teacher . . . Children, to the extent that they are untouched by adult 'experienced' habits of mind, express or realise their divine humanity instinctively . . . Those qualities it invites us to admire in the innocents who sing and people its *Songs* are the very ones we need when reading: unselfconsciousness, emotional and imaginative daring, a refusal to abstract and generalize. *Innocence* . . . teaches us to approach the world as a child would.[40]

Glen agrees and speculates as to why Blake chose to express his ideas in a genre (i.e. the children's book) in which:

> . . . real imaginative life . . . was consistently being subordinated to instructive purposes . . . they did not rouse the children's capacities for wonder: they told them how to think.

She argues that Blake worked 'to frustrate the notion that there should be an unequivocal moral point'. His poems range from howls of anger at injustice to poems without any argument in them at all; from 'disconcerting inconclusiveness' to an alternative vision of a harmonious, peaceful, loving and almost heavenly state of being. Glen suggests that Blake is attacking eighteenth-century notions of rationality as well as doing something even more radical.

> In choosing to present his vision in the form of a book for children he was choosing to engage directly with the coercive strategies of its dominant culture – strategies which the children's book, with its rationalistic simplification of unambiguous subject-matter, its assumption that its readers should passively accept instructions clearly embodied . . . by refusing to conform to these assumptions, by frustrating those expectations . . . he exposed their crippling and destructive implications . . .[41]

Even so, *Songs of Innocence* certainly *included* children within their intended audience, since the introductory poem concludes with the words – 'And I wrote my happy songs / Every child may joy to hear.'[42] Blake is unequivocally on the side of the weak, poor and vulnerable, presenting his vision in memorable language that is sometimes apparently simple, sometimes deeply melodious, and often powerful and disturbing. Blake's songs take place in an imagined natural world which is both benign and beautiful. Cruelty is committed by people who should know better – 'aged men', 'guardians of the poor', 'Knaves and Hypocrites', 'Priests' and 'Kings'. And children are some of the most deeply oppressed in Blake's universe. Take 'Holy Thursday':[43]

> Twas on a Holy Thursday, their innocent faces clean,
> The children walking two & two in red & blue & green;
> Grey headed beadles walk'd before with wands as white as snow,
> Till into the high dome of Paul's they like Thames' waters flow.
>
> O what a multitude they seem'd, these flowers of London town!
> Seated in companies they sit with radiance all their own.
> The hum of multitudes was there, but multitudes of lambs,
> Thousands of little boys & girls raising their innocent hands.

'Holy Thursday' is based on a real event of the time, when thousands of orphans paraded in pairs along the banks of the Thames to St Paul's Cathedral for a service of Thanksgiving. The ritualistic procession is emphasized by details such as the bright colours of the children's clothing, contrasted with the colourless, grey-haired beadles. The relentless 'flow' of the multitudes echoes the movement of the river. Blake presents the reader with a striking image – 'innocent faces' walking the streets of London under the tutelage of so-called older and wiser 'guardians'. His deprecation of such a charade is underlined by stirring metaphors, as children are likened to 'flowers of London town' or 'multitudes of lambs'. Blake heightens the tension by repetition ('multitudes', for example, is used three times in one stanza), contrasts, and the use of irony, such as the adults who sit *beneath* the children (see below). It is the poor and the young who provoke a heavenly vision conjured up by the presence of angels, songs raised to heaven and the pure 'radiance' of the children.

A quick reading of the poem would not suggest that it is out of place with typical children's literature of the period: conventions such as clean faces, concepts like innocence, demure marching children overlooked by beadles with wands (which could be used for beatings?) all seem predictable enough imagery. It is when this poem is probed more deeply that the uncertainties begin and Blake's alternative vision is unlocked. His awful warning in the final stanza is deeply moving now. To contemporaries living in an age of revolution the 'mighty wind they raise to heaven' and 'thunderings' might have caused disquiet of a different kind.

> Now like a mighty wind they raise to heaven the voice of song,
> Or like harmonious thunderings the seats of heaven among.
> Beneath them sit the aged men, wise guardians of the poor.
> Then cherish pity, lest you drive an angel from your door.

Even bleaker is the poem of the same title in *Songs of Experience*.[44] Blake opens with an 'appalling' question for those in positions of power and responsibility :

> Is this a holy thing to see
> In a rich and fruitful land,
> Babes reduced to misery,
> Fed with cold and usurous hand?

He goes on to attack the horrors of poverty:

> Is that trembling cry a song?
> Can it be a song of joy?
> And so many children poor?
> It is a land of poverty!

> And their sun does never shine,
> And their fields are bleak and bare,
> And their ways are fill'd with thorns:
> It is eternal winter there.

The poem ends on a baffled, inconclusive note :

> For where'er the sun does shine,
> And where'er the rain does fall,
> Babe can never hunger there,
> Nor poverty the mind appall.

Conventional wisdom suggests that *Songs of Experience* deals with similar subject matter to *Songs of Innocence*, but from an angrier and more disenchanted point of view. Leader disagrees:

> *Innocence* is a book of visionary as opposed to moral instruction . . . If we think of *Innocence* as an 'alphabet' or 'guide' to vision, one which teaches us how to read, *Experience* functions as a kind of exercise book or 'reader' . . . its ultimate purpose is to strengthen rather than weaken visionary habits.[45]

Blake's *Songs* which he produced by hand, no two copies exactly the same, were published in small quantities to a mixed reception. Benjamin Heath Malkin, for example, wrote in 'A Father's Memoirs of his Child', 1806, that ' . . . if Watts seldom rose above the level of a mere versifier, in what class must we place Mr Blake, who is certainly inferior to Dr Watts?'[46] Malkin is right in seeing the debt Blake owed to Watts's *Divine Songs*, but otherwise he fails to appreciate the poetry or recognize the substance of Blake's writing. Indeed, *Innocence* was too radical for many and what was then regarded as Blake's eccentric behaviour meant that he could be discounted as unbalanced or even mad, though Harold Bloom takes an entirely opposing view, calling Blake 'the sanest of all poets, who by the dubious irony of literary history was considered mad by some of his contemporaries . . .'[47]

Certainly, the nature of the verse was not what most readers would have expected or, perhaps, wanted to think about. For example, Victor Watson[48] suggests that:

> 'The Chimney Sweeper', while offering a simple reassuring message to a very young child, simultaneously challenges the adult reader into a different reading about the exploitation of children. Other contemporary moral issues are treated in a similar way, comforting for the child-reader, troubling for the adult.

Glen makes a similar point:

> The underprivileged . . . have their own distinctive voices. They are not the objects of sympathy or protesting comment.[49]

In Blake's moral landscape it is the sheep who lead the shepherd; the 'little ones', not the nurse, decide when it is time for bed; and it is a child in the 'Introduction' who tells the piper what to do.

> Piper, sit thee down and write
> In a book that all may read.
> So he vanish'd from my sight,
> And I pluck'd a hollow reed,
>
> And I made a rural pen,
> And I stain'd the water clear,
> And I wrote my happy songs
> Every child may joy to hear.[50]

Blake often draws an analogy between children, birds, animals and Christ. The tender, all-embracing love of God, expressed through the metaphor of Christ as a lamb, is depicted as benevolently caring for animals and small human beings alike, their natural affinities emphasized.

> And thus I say to little English boy:
> When I from black and he from white cloud free
> And round the tent of God like lambs we joy . . .

*　　　*　　　*

Little Lamb, I'll tell thee:
He is called by thy name,
For he calls himself a Lamb.
He is meek & he is mild,
He became a little child:
I a child & thou a lamb,
We are called by his name.

       *   *   *

'No, no, let us play, for it is yet day
And we cannot go to sleep;
Besides, in the sky the little birds fly
And the hills are all cover'd with sheep.[51]

In this universe Blake presents nature as a kind of garden where childish pleasure can be played out by its occupants. Blake was one of the first poets to emphasize the strong connection between nature and childhood, a 'naturalness' most earlier writers sought to curb. Do some of the stereotyped images we are now so familiar with, courtesy of Disney and others, where children and animals exist in happy union together, actually stem from Blake's imagery? Did the originality of Blake's vision get distorted during the late Victorian period producing a sentimentalized travesty of Blake's message in poetry and art?

In both collections, but especially *Songs of Experience*, we also see an angry Blake creating uncompromising images of injustice, cruelty and greed with which to admonish, not children, but adults. Blake makes us imagine the plight of the little chimney sweeper all too clearly:

When my mother died I was very young,
And my father sold me while yet my tongue
Could scarcely cry ''weep! 'weep! 'weep! 'weep!'
So your chimneys I sweep & in soot I sleep.

And by came an Angel who had a bright key,
And he open'd the coffins & set them all free;
Then down a green plain leaping, laughing, they run,
And wash in a river, and shine in the sun.[52]

One hundred and fifty years after the abolition of child labour in Britain, only a hardened reader could escape being deeply moved by those words. Ackroyd underlines the truthfulness of Blake's account by quoting a social reformer of the period's description of chimney sweeps: 'He is now twelve years of age, a cripple on crutches hardly three feet seven inches in stature . . . His hair felt like a hog's bristles, and his head like a warm cinder . . .'[53] But the world Blake shows us in the *Songs* is full of harrowing images. 'Break this heavy chain / That does freeze my bones around', wails the poet who goes on to castigate the iniquities of schooling, having refused to go to school as a child himself.

In *The Little Vagabond*, Blake understands the boy's preference for the warmth and forgetfulness of the ale-house while the cold church can only offer prayers for his soul, but nothing for his physical needs. Why can't the church provide both, Blake demands in this poem, a point of view which might be considered radical in these more compassionate times.

> And God, like a father rejoicing to see
> His children as pleasant and happy as he,
> Would have no more quarrel with the Devil or the barrel,
> But kiss him & give him both drink and apparel.[54]

Who could ignore the lamentations of the unfortunate in the streets of London after Blake's exposure of human misery, exploitation and decay? Phrases like 'charter'd street' and 'mind-forg'd manacles' are so powerful that they have become part of the vernacular 200 years on.

> I wander thro' each charter'd street
> Near where the charter'd Thames does flow,
> And mark in every face I meet
> Marks of weakness, marks of woe.
>
> In every cry of every man,
> In every Infant's cry of fear,
> In every voice, in every ban,
> The mind-forg'd manacles I hear . . .[55]

But Blake could also be unbelievably tender. Poems like 'The Lamb', 'The Blossom' and 'Spring' have a nursery rhyme quality – 'Little Lamb / Here I am; / Come and lick / My white neck, / Let me pull / Your soft Wool . . . ' The best compliment I can pay 'A Cradle Song', that gentle lullaby written by a childless man, is that it might have been composed by a woman and, indeed, foreshadows what women were about to publish for children. Victor Watson agrees:

> Early critics believed that this extreme simplicity of style was an oddity arising
> from his being socially isolated, possibly even unbalanced; but it is more likely
> that he was the first great poet to draw on the oral traditions of the eighteenth-

century nursery, capturing the gentle child-centred rhetoric of mothers singing and talking to their children.[56]

> Sweet smiles, in the night
> Hover over my delight;
> Sweet smiles, Mother's smiles,
> All the livelong night beguiles.
>
> Sweet moans, dovelike sighs,
> Chase not slumber from thy eyes.
> Sweet moans, sweeter smiles,
> All the dovelike moans beguiles.[57]

The cover illustration of *Innocence* shows a woman sharing a book with two children set in a landscape of Blake's imagination beside a tree of knowledge which bends around them as if for protection, peopled by spirits and birds, bursting with fruit and fronds. The words, 'Songs of Innocence', are coloured gold and blaze like flames, as apparitions float, curl, lean and balance on the individual letters. It is at once harmonious, enchanting and portentous. In the songs, Blake integrates the poems with the pictures: there are many illustrations where vine-like tendrils spread themselves around the page, curling in and out of words; in others, adult figures bend tenderly over children or hold their hands, and little ones are depicted laughing, singing, dancing, sitting close by lambs or even riding tigers. 'These are discrete works of art in which the words are only one element in a unified design', comments Ackroyd.[58] Blake was an outstanding and innovative craftsman who showed what could be achieved in the symbiosis of words and pictures. It is an interesting observation that, so far as I am aware, no one has attempted to illustrate the complete *Songs of Innocence* in the twentieth century, whereas virtually every significant poet of the past for children has been re-interpreted by modern artists. Perhaps illustrators simply recognize Blake's masterpiece as a work of art that stands alone.

Largely unrecognized in his own time, *Songs of Innocence* was not published in a conventional edition until 1839. Once that happened, it was not long before Blake's poetry became a consistent feature in anthologies of poetry for children. Small children do not always understand the ideas behind the poems and find the language strange. Yet in a poem like 'The Tyger', most children respond powerfully to the aspects they can comprehend – the melody, the images, the powerful words and, of course, the passion.

> And when the stars threw down their spears
> And water'd heaven with their tears,
> Did he smile his work to see?
> Did he who made the Lamb make thee?

Tyger! Tyger! burning bright
In the forests of the night,
What immortal hand or eye
Dare frame thy fearful symmetry?'[59]

Blake is a great landmark in poetry for children: his moral and imaginative vision towers above that of other writers and illustrators of his period. Ackroyd sums up the impact of the *Songs*: they were 'a complete and coherent statement . . . in an extraordinarily condensed and almost ritualistic way; the visual completeness, the insistent metres, the impersonal skill of calligraphy, turn these poems into achieved works of art that seem to resist conventional interpretation . . .'[60]

'The language really used by men' – William Wordsworth and *Lyrical Ballads*

As we reach the end of the eighteenth century, Romantic ideas began to filter into the social, political, educational and literary landscape of Britain. The influential ideas of Jean-Jacques Rousseau's *Emile* (1762), Thomas Paine's *The Rights of Man* (1791) and Mary Wollstonecraft's *A Vindication of the Rights of Women* (1792) were in the air. Revolutions in Europe and America and the war with France had done much to shift opinion, and the growing poverty and homelessness in huge industrial cities could no longer be ignored. Wordsworth published *Lyrical Ballads* in 1798 when England was largely a rural society; by 1830 it had become an industrial country, where peasants and aristocrats were outnumbered by the urban working class and rapidly expanding bourgeoisie. For many people, particularly poets committed to the creative power of the artist, it felt like an apocalyptic new age.

It is instructive, therefore, to pause at 1798 with the publication of *Lyrical Ballads*, a defining moment for the history of poetry. The anonymous poems by Wordsworth and Coleridge, who were firm friends during this period, were accompanied by a short 'advertisement'[61] which had things to say of a radical and challenging nature to the readership of its time. It suggested, for example, that one should look to poets rather than critics for the 'honourable characteristics' of poetry; that poetry can be made out of every subject 'which can interest the human mind'; that the poems in *Lyrical Ballads* were to be considered 'as experiments'; that the 'author' sought to get away from 'the gaudiness and inane phraseology of many modern writers'. Wordsworth and Coleridge were clearly intending to open up a debate with their readers, describing poetry as 'a word of very disputed meaning' and reminding them that taste in poetry could only be acquired by 'a long continued intercourse with the best models of composition'.[62]

They went on to warn readers that the language of the poetry might seem 'too low', anticipating the famous statement in Wordsworth's preface to the 1805 edition, almost as well known now as the poems themselves: 'the principal object which I proposed to myself in these Poems was to choose incidents and situations from common life, and to relate or describe them . . . in a selection of language really used by men . . .'[63] As Bloom put it, Wordsworth's vision found its 'highest honorific words in "simple" and "common" . . . hallowing the commonplace . . .'[64]

Glen shows us that this was more than the humane voice of the Enlightenment. In his poetry Wordsworth 'actively refuses to confirm some of its readers' most basic expectations' and offers instead 'a fundamental poetic questioning of some of the most deep-rooted of polite eighteenth century assumptions.'[65] She cites the often irregular metre, the awkward rhyme-scheme, the apparent naiveté and inconclusiveness of some of the verse, reflecting the complexity and untidiness of actual experience.

'The child is father to the man' – Romantic poetry and childhood

Lyrical Ballads also contains poems that show the way Wordsworth's thinking about childhood was developing. Many of the poems make reference to children or mothers. 'We Are Seven', for example, centres on the determined voice of a little girl who asserts that although two of her brothers and sisters lie dead in the graveyard, her family still consists of the original seven. In the poem (of which there is at least one chapbook version) the narrator tries to persuade the little girl that her reasoning or at least her mathematics is wrong. Wordsworth, however, allows the child to have the last word:

> Twas throwing words away; for still
> The little maid would have her will,
> And said, 'Nay, we are seven!'[66]

In 'Anecdote for Fathers', Wordsworth turns conventional thinking on its head as the adult learns from his son, while the mother in 'The Mad Mother' is comforted by love for her infant.

> Oh dearest, dearest boy! my heart
> For better lore would seldom yearn,
> Could I but teach the hundredth part
> Of what from thee I learn[67]
> ('Anecdote for Fathers')

> The babe I carry on my arm
> He saves for me my precious soul.[68]
> ('The Mad Mother')

But it was not until 1804 that Wordsworth wrote the lines about childhood which are now so famous that the Ode, like its title, has indeed become 'immortal' – 'Intimations of Immortality from Recollections of Early Childhood'. The first stanza begins:

> There was a time when meadow, grove, and stream,
>   The earth, and every common sight,
>   To me did seem
>   Apparelled in celestial light,
> The glory and the freshness of a dream.
> It is not now as it hath been of yore; –
>   Turn whereso'er I may,
>   By night and day,
> The things which I have seen I now can see no more.[69]

Freshness of vision and joy in being alive are equated with childhood. Wordsworth mourns the loss of the child's vision that comes with adulthood; later in the poem he tells us that 'the glory and the freshness of the dream' can only be recaptured by remembering the ecstasy of that freedom and communion with nature, and learning from it.

> Heaven lies about us in our infancy
> Shades of the prison-house begin to close
> Upon the growing Boy,
> But he beholds the light, and whence it flows,
> He sees it in his joy;[70]

In the Ode, Wordsworth emphasizes the symbiotic union between the mother and the child: 'Behold the Child among his new-born blisses, / A six years' Darling of a pigmy size!' He develops this theme in 'The Prelude' where he presents the infant learning about love in his mother's arms.

> . . . blest the Babe,
> Nursed in his Mother's arms, who sinks to sleep,
> Rocked on his Mother's breast; who with his soul
> Drinks in the feelings of his Mother's eye![71]

Lionel Trilling writes that 'The safety, warmth, and good feeling of his mother's conscious benevolence is a circumstance of his first learning . . . [the Babe] sees things through his mother's eyes . . .'[72] In his poetry, Wordsworth equates childhood with innocence, freedom and love; he asserts that childhood holds the key to spiritual and imaginative life in adulthood. He tells the reader to try to recapture what was as natural as breathing when we were children – a joy in physical closeness with another human being, a sensual oneness with and appreciation of the natural world based on instinct and intuition rather than rational knowledge and learning. He warns that a loss of 'vision' is inevitable as we grow older, but hopes for a compensatory wisdom in maturity. Wordsworth's message takes us a long way from the moral code of Puritanism, the Protestant ethic and eighteenth-century rationality. Indeed, as Bloom tells us, his central desire 'was to find a final good in human existence itself'[73] though he shares with the Puritans a sense of the unique value of each individual.

'O'er vales and hills' – Romantic poetry and nature

For the Romantic poets, appreciation of nature was one of its most significant themes. In 'Lines composed above Tintern Abbey', Wordsworth writes that he was

> . . . well pleased to recognise
> In nature and the language of the sense
> The anchor of my purest thoughts, the nurse,
> The guide, the guardian of my heart, and soul
> Of all my moral being.[74]

There was, first of all, the healthy physical and spiritual delight to be found in the natural world and the appreciation of its beauty which the poets wrote about in realistic detail. The health-giving aspect of nature was, in part, a reaction against industrialization, the polluted towns with grim working conditions for their inhabitants. In 'Frost at Midnight', Coleridge reminds the reader:

> For I was reared
> In the great city, pent 'mid cloisters dim,
> And saw nought lovely but the sky and stars.

and invokes a spiritual prayer for his baby whose growing up, he hopes, will be in nature's tender care. Coleridge's loving murmur to his infant son is one of the most moving passages in Romantic poetry.

> Dear Babe, that sleepest cradled by my side,
> Whose gentle breathings, heard in this deep calm,
> Fill up the interspersed vacancies
> And momentary pauses of the thought!
> . . .
> But *thou,* my babe! shalt wander like a breeze
> By lakes and sandy shores, beneath the crags:
> . . .

Therefore all seasons shall be sweet to thee,
Whether the summer clothe the general earth
With greenness, or the redbreast sit and sing
Betwixt the tufts of snow on the bare branch
Of mossy apple-tree, while the nighthatch
Smokes in the sun-thaw . . .[75]

Writing of *Lyrical Ballads*, Richard Holmes describes the 'almost pedagogic importance given to nature as a moral and educative force . . . the human ideal of the collection'.[76] In frequent poems of this period, nature is seen as a better teacher than those of the academic sort. When Coleridge wrote of his infant son, Hartley: 'I deem it wise / To make him Nature's play-mate'[77] in 'The Nightingale', he focuses on 'nature's powers of healing and enchantment'.[78] The Romantics believed in 'the power of natural landscape in childhood [hence "the child of nature" motif] to give strength and stability . . . no longer a background [for poetry] . . . but a source of vital and mysterious power, and an object and an inspirer of love'.[79] Look at the force and solidity of Wordsworth's nouns in the extract from 'Tintern Abbey' above: nature is 'anchor', 'nurse', 'guide', 'guardian' and 'soul'.

The Romantics distanced themselves from the conventional, and often ornamental, tributes to nature of the eighteenth century. Their praise was much more passionate, vivid, charged with feeling, both sensual and intellectual, and based on genuine familiarity and experience. But Wordsworth went further than that. J. R. Watson writes: 'no longer is the external world a source of pleasure: it is a moral force, a source of inspiration, a support in time of trouble, a blessing and a joy . . . the landscape affects the mind, and the mind reciprocally affects the landscape'.[80] Nature also provides a means of externalizing emotion, what Watson calls a 'creative relationship between the internal mind and the external world', put at its simplest, he says, by Byron:

Are not the mountains, waves, and skies, a part
Of me and of my soul, as I of them?[81]

Finally, the Romantics associated nature with a visionary influence which went beyond human endeavours and understanding. Watson:

The encounter between the poetic mind and this magnificence in and beyond nature is one of the most heroic features of Romantic poetry . . . It is at the moment of being lost [crossing the Alps] that Wordsworth discovers the full power of the imagination rising before him, finding his central self at the moment of greatest confusion . . . the great questions arise, pushing themselves forward insistently: 'Who am I?' 'What is my relationship to the world?'[82]

'Do I wake or sleep?' – the poetry of John Keats

No poet has ever appreciated the natural world in sweeter verse than John Keats (1795–1820). Keats demands a small place in this chapter because of the impact his poetry has had on readers from the early nineteenth century, right up to the present day. Because all his poetry was written when he was young (Keats died aged 25), his voice has a freshness and idealism that is very appealing to teenage readers. His life story is romantic, too, and his poetry alludes to emergent sexual feelings which, perhaps, strikes a chord with this age group. As biographer Stephen Coote put it 'Keats was unselfconsciously explicit about associating the imaginitive pleasures of poetry with the imagined pleasures of sex.'[83] Losing his parents at an early age, Keats put great tenderness into his relationships with his brothers and little sister, Fanny. The brotherly concern and affection for his siblings, movingly conveyed in his letters, may have developed an unusual sympathy for children from one so young himself. But perhaps the primary appeal of Keats's poetry lies in the rapture of his language. His evocation of autumn, for example, is so vivid that you have to draw on most of your senses to do justice to the poem.

> While barred clouds bloom the soft-dying day,
> And touch the stubble-plains with rosy hue;
> Then in a wailful choir the small gnats mourn
> Among the river sallows, borne aloft
> Or sinking as the light wind lives or dies;
> And full-grown lambs loud bleat from hilly bourn;
> Hedge-crickets sing; and now with treble soft
> The redbreast whistles from a garden-croft;
> And gathering swallows twitter in the skies.[84]

And before the reader hears that famous nightingale, she is drunk on Keats's opening lines:

> My heart aches, and a drowsy numbness pains
> My sense, as though of hemlock I had drunk . . .[85]

Barely suppressed pain seeps out of the poem which goes on to describe the nightingale's song making the poet sensible of 'The coming musk-rose, full of dewy wine, / The murmurous haunt of flies on summer eves.' Both Shelley and Keats use nightingales and skylarks as the metaphorical wings for poetry that soars into realms beyond mere appreciation of nature. In the case of Keats, 'Ode to a Nightingale' is about the human condition, the transient nature of happiness and 'the precarious life of the imagination'.[86] It is also about the twin Keatsian themes of truth and beauty:

'What the imagination seizes as Beauty must be truth . . . with a great poet the sense of Beauty overcomes every other consideration . . . ';[87] to appreciate great beauty and all the joy it brings, there is a price to pay – suffering and pain.

Keats delves into the classical world and the Old Testament, going beyond historical time in his search to understand the human condition. In the end, J. R. Watson describes the poet as 'left with the local landscape, himself under the tree in the Hampstead garden, the bird's song getting fainter . . . The syllables sound like bird song, and the surroundings are sketched with a beautiful economy – the meadows, the stream, the hillside, the next valley . . . ' How, asks Keats in a haunting question, can human beings face up to the conflicting needs and demands of the imagination and the natural world in its mixture of misery and pleasure, escapism and reality?

> Was it a vision, or a waking dream?
> Fled is that music – Do I wake or sleep?[88]

Romanticism and children's verse

As we have seen, Wordsworth held attitudes towards childhood which fundamentally challenged the dominant ideology of his day and which helped to shape writing for and about children for a long time to come. His views, though radical for their time, have to be understood as part of the shift in perceptions about the nature of children and their role within the family and society itself which was already taking place in the second half of the eighteenth century. The historian J. H. Plumb argues that:

> This gentle and more sensitive approach to children was but part of a wider change in social attitudes; a part of that belief that nature was inherently good, not evil and what evil there was derived from man and his institutions; an attitude which was also reflected among a growing elite in a greater sensitivity towards women, slaves and animals [sic].
>
> Children, in a sense, had become luxury objects upon which their mothers and fathers were willing to spend larger and larger sums of money, not only for their education, but also for their entertainment and amusement.[89]

It is no surprise in this climate that Romantic poetry should begin to be selected for children in the first half of the nineteenth century, but it was quite slow to become fashionable to do so. The first editor, as far as I am aware, to include a Romantic poet in an anthology for children is Lucy Aikin in 1825. Lucy's father, John Aikin, was the editor of the *Monthly Magazine*, a radical journal for which Wordsworth wrote; as Lucy was a young woman with a literary bent, she was likely to be familiar with Wordsworth's poetry before the publication of *Lyrical Ballads* in 1798. Yet the first edition of Lucy Aikin's *Poetry for Children*[90] in 1801 is conventional for the time in its choice of subject matter and poets – Pope, Cowper, Homer, Virgil, Shakespeare, Barbauld, Dryden, Scott. Nor did W. F. Mylius include any Romantic poetry in the 1820 edition of his *First Book of Poetry for Children*[91] which features Watts, Addison, Gay, Hannah More, Goldsmith, Charlotte Smith and Robert Burns's 'To a Mountain Daisy'.

If *Lyrical Ballads* was as innovative as Wordsworth intended, it might have seemed too great a break with tradition to include his work in a children's anthology at the turn of the century. This was also a period of intense anxiety about popular uprisings, where potential revolutionaries were rounded up to be transported or even executed. A special agent (a sort of eighteenth-century version of Special Branch) was sent to the Quantocks, where Wordsworth and Coleridge were living in 1797, to keep an eye on their activities. It seems reasonable that a woman writer whose living depended on her pen might have had to wait for the calmer waters of the 1820s to select Romantic poetry for the young. Indeed, Wordsworth and Coleridge's poetry took some time to be well known, let alone popular and respected, within the literary community of the early nineteenth century.

It is salutary to remember that new literature of most kinds is treated with suspicion at first. In the event, it seems to have taken 30 years or so for Romantic poetry to become widely respectable and, perhaps, acceptable for children. By the 1825 volume of *Poetry for Children*,[92] Lucy Aikin had decided to include four poems by Wordsworth – 'To a Butterfly', 'The Pet Lamb', 'Hailstones' and 'The Redbreast and the Butterfly'. But as far as I can judge, she was ahead of her time in so doing, as it took longer still for other Romantic poets to gain a place in the children's canon. *Child Life*,[93] for example, a prestigious anthology edited by the American, John Greenleaf Whittier in 1874, includes Wordsworth as the only exemplar of Romantic poetry. By 1883 the anonymous editor of *Poetry for the Young*,[94] chose Wordsworth, Byron, Burns and Blake; and Andrew Lang's *Blue Poetry Book*[95] of 1891 features a number of poems by each of the above mentioned, plus two poems apiece by Shelley and Keats. None of them selected Coleridge, though he is just as likely as the others to be selected for children today.

A shepherd's calendar – the poetry of John Clare

I have left John Clare (1793–1864) until last. Like Blake he was born into a poor family, self-educated, suffering poverty and mental anguish in later life, deeply attached to the woman he married. Born in Northamptonshire, this son of a labourer started work as an under-gardener at the tender age of seven. Although he lived a hard life, he never lost his love of nature or his ability to describe it vividly in emotionally charged, melodic verse. Clare did not write specifically for children, but his poetry is often chosen for them and there have been several editions of his work specifically for a young audience. Although his poetry is comparatively simple, at times Clare can be as visionary as Blake.

Hill-tops like hot iron glitter bright in the sun,
And the rivers we're eying burn to gold as they run;
Burning hot is the ground, liquid gold is the air;
Whoever looks round sees Eternity there.[96]

Clare's chosen subject matter is the rural world about him, his feelings and sympathies for the poor, weak and lonely, which he sometimes expresses in a childlike way. His poetry also constitutes a shift in the way childhood was perceived and longed for. Clare achieved some literary success with *Poems Descriptive of Rural Life* (1820) and *The Village Minstrel* (1821). Later books, like *The Shepherd's Calendar* (1827), were a disappointment at the time. Eventually Clare suffered a complete mental breakdown and tragically spent the last 23 years of his life in an asylum for the insane.

In a poem about a ladybird Clare uses homely language ('topt wi' flowers), reminiscent of Burns, emphasizing the fragility of life, apparently in the insect's voice. It is a poem full of delicacy and one that any child could read.

My home it shakes in wind and showers
Pale green pillar topt wi' flowers
Bending at the wild winds breath
Till I touch the grass beneath
Here still I live lone clock a clay
Watching for the time of day[97]

'February' is similarly accessible showing off Clare's pictorial eye for detail. There is a note of caution and some frigid, wintry imagery towards the end of the poem, which begins on a positive upbeat note.

The snow has left the cottage top;
    The thatch moss grows in brighter green;
And eaves in quick succession drop,
    Where grinning icicles have been,
Pit-patting with a pleasant noise
    In tubs set by the cottage-door;
While ducks and geese, with happy joys,
    Plunge in the yard-pond brimming o'er.

The sun peeps through the window-pane;
    Which children mark with laughing eye,
And in the wet street steal again
    To tell each other spring is nigh.[98]

Some evocations of childhood focus on happier times and vividly convey the joy of being alive to all the senses.

> When jumping time away on old Crossberry Way,
> And eating haws like sugarplums ere they had lost the may,
> And skipping like a leveret before the peep of day
> On the roly-poly up and downs of pleasant Swordy Well,
> When in Round Oak's narrow lane as the south got black again
> We sought the hollow ash that was shelter from the rain,
> With our pockets full of peas we had stolen from the grain;
> How delicious was the dinner-time on such a showery day!
> Oh, words are poor receipts for what time hath stole away,
> The ancient pulpit trees and the play.[99]

Clare's vivid description of his mother telling tales at the fireside brings alive the pleasures of storytelling.

> Oh, spirit of the days gone by –
> Sweet childhood's fearful ecstasy!
> The witching spells of winter nights,
> Where are they fled with their delights?
> When list'ning on the corner seat,
> The winter evening's length to cheat,
> I heard my mother's memory tell
> Tales superstition loves so well:
> Things said or sung a thousand times,
> In simple prose or simpler rhymes.[100]

Clare's memories of childhood are as strong as those of Wordworth, but suffused with despair as the poet recognizes the huge contrast between the freedom of his 'boyish hours' and the burdens and constraints of adulthood. No idealized notion of childhood here.

> Now this sweet vision of my boyish hours
> Free as spring clouds and wild as summer flowers
> Is faded all – a hope that blossomed free
> And hath been once no more shall ever be.[101]

Towards the end of his life, Clare's poetry becomes sadder and more anguished: 'yet what I am, none cares or knows; / My friends forsake me like a memory lost; / I am the self-consumer of my woes . . .'[102] The last is a lament by a tortured soul who longs for the comfort of childhood memory and closeness with his God; Clare locates himself lying in a grassy place beneath 'the vaulted sky'.

> I long for scenes where man hath never trod
> A place where woman never smiled or wept
> There to abide with my creator God,
> And sleep as I in childhood sweetly slept,
> Untroubling and untroubled where I lie
> The grass below, above, the vaulted sky.[103]

Clare pulls together three strands of Romanticism – nature, childhood and religion. These were the same themes that many of those writing nature poetry for children sought to pursue, as we shall see.

By the middle of the nineteenth century Romantic poetry was extensively published and well known. Though it still unsettled some members of polite society, it was a force to be reckoned with, having many admirers as well as exponents. The simplest and most tuneful examples of Romantic poetry, particularly those relating to nature or childhood, or those which told a lively tale, have been been a consistent feature in anthologies for children chosen by generations of editors ever since. One of their great themes was the natural world, the favoured location for children's poetry until very recently. In the next chapter we take a closer look at nature poetry, concentrating this time on poets who wrote with children in mind.

Notes

1   William Wordsworth, 'Ode on Intimations of Immortality from Recollections of Early Childhood' (1807). *A Choice of Wordsworth's Verse*, ed. R. S. Thomas, Faber, London 1971.

2   *Ibid.*

3   Harold Bloom, *Poetics of Influence*, ed. J. Hollander, Henry Schwab, New York, 1988, pp. 3,4.

4   *Ibid.*, p. 11.

5   Roger Lonsdale, *Eighteenth Century Women Poets*, Oxford, 1990, p. xli.

6   J. R. Watson, *English Poetry of the Romantic Period*, Longman, 1985, p. 1.

7   William Cowper quotation, Lucy Aikin, ed. *Poetry for Children*, London, 1801.

8   William Cowper, from 'The Task', *William Cowper: Poetical Works*, ed. H. S. Milford, Oxford, 1967.

9   Thomas Wright, *The Loved Haunts of Cowper*, Fisher Unwin, London, 1894, p. 10.

10 Mary Jacobus, *Romanticism, Writing and Sexual Difference: Essays on The Prelude*, Oxford, 1989, p. 48.

11 Cowper, *op. cit.*

12 Heather Glen, *Vision and Disenchantment, Blake's Songs and Wordsworth's Lyrical Ballads*, Cambridge, 1983, p. 3

13 William Cowper, from 'Truth', *William Cowper: Poetical Works,* ed. H. S. Milford, Oxford, 1967.

14 William Cowper, from 'The Poplar Field', *ibid.*

15 Robert Burns, 'Wee Willie Gray', *Scots Musical Museum,* ed. James Johnson, 6 volumes (1787–1803).

16 Robert Burns, from 'To a Mouse', *Poems Chiefly in the Scottish Dialect,* orig. John Wilson, Kilmarnock, 1786, *The Poetry of Robert Burns,* Centenary Edition, ed. W. E. Healey and T. F. Henderson, Vol. 1, Caxton, London, 1896.

17 *Ibid.*

18 22 January 1996, *Omnibus: The Ploughboy of the Western World,* BBC television.

19 Robert Burns, from 'Tam O'Shanter', *Poems,* Edinburgh, 1793 edition.

20 Burns, from 'To a House', *ibid.,* 1786.

21 Burns, from 'A Man's a Man for A' That', *op. cit.,* 1793.

22 Catherine Carswell, *The Life of Robert Burns,* Canongate Classic, Edinburgh, 1930/96. p. 126.

23 Burns, 1786, *op. cit.,* in Henley and Henderson, pp. 1–2.

24 Sir Walter Scott, from 'Young Lochinvar', *The Poetical Works of Scott,* ed. J. L. Robertson, Oxford 1894.

25 Andrew Lang, ed. *The Blue Poetry Book,* London, 1891, p. vii.

26 Scott, from 'Pibroch of Donuil Dhu' in Robertson *op. cit.*

27 Watson, *op. cit.,* pp 101, 105.

28 Scott, from 'Patriotism' in Robertson, *op. cit.*

29 Scott, from 'Madge Wildfire's Song' in Robertson, *ibid.*

30 William Blake, 'Eternity', *The Poems of William Blake,* ed. W. H. Stevenson, London, 1971.

31 William Blake, from 'Auguries of Innocence' in Stevenson, *ibid.*

32 F. J. Harvey Darton, *Children's Books in England,* ed. B. Alderson, Cambridge, 1932/82, p. 179.

33 Peter Ackroyd, *Blake,* Sinclair Stevenson, London, p. 122.

34 Victor Watson unpublished manuscript, *Cambridge Guide to Children's Books,* forthcoming.

35 Ackroyd, *op. cit.,* p. 122.

36 Martha England, *Hymns Unbidden,* The New York Public Library, 1966, pp 47–8.

37 *Songs of Innocence* started out at around five shillings, a lot of money at that time, and cost three guineas in 1818.

38 Ackroyd, *op. cit.,* p. 122.

39 Zachary Leader, *Reading Blake's Songs,* Routledge, London, 1981, pp. 32, 33.

40 Leader, *op. cit.,* pp. 30,35.

41 Glen, *op. cit.,* pp. 31/32.

42 William Blake, from 'Introduction', *Songs of Innocence,* facsimile of 1789 edition, Dover, London, 1971.

43 Blake, from 'Holy Thursday', *ibid.*

44 William Blake, from 'Holy Thursday', *Songs of Experience,* 1794, ed. Stevenson, 1971, *op. cit.*

45 Leader, *op. cit.,* p. 36.

46 Benjamin Heath Malkin, 'A Father's Memoirs of his Child', *Literary Journal,* 1806, pp. 34–5. Quoted in G. E. Bentley jnr., *William Blake, The Critical Heritage,* London, 1975, p. 45.

47 Bloom, *op. cit.,* p. 13.

48 Watson, *op. cit.*

49 Glen, *op. cit.,* p. 31. I suppose a good analogy for today might be the critical voices of many disabled people about charities in their name; there is all the difference in the world between handouts to unfortunates and equality of opportunity for the able-bodied and the disabled.

50 *Songs of Innocence, op. cit.*

51 Blake, from 'The Little Black Boy', 'The Lamb', 'Nurse's Song', *ibid.*
52 Blake, from 'The Chimney Sweeper', *ibid.*
53 Quoted in Ackroyd, *op. cit.*, p. 125.
54 Blake, from 'The Little Vagabond'.
55 Blake, from 'London', *Songs of Experience, op. cit.*
56 Victor Watson, *op. cit.*
57 Blake, from 'A Cradle Song', *Songs of Experience, op. cit.*
58 Ackroyd, *op. cit.*, p. 122.
59 Blake, from 'The Tyger', *Songs of Experience, op. cit.*
60 Ackroyd, *op. cit.*, p. 122.
61 *Lyrical Ballads*, London, 1798, reprinted in 1898, ed. Thomas Hutchinson, London, 1910.
62 *Ibid.*, pp i-iii.
63 William Wordsworth, Preface to *Lyrical Ballads*, London, 1805.
64 Harold Bloom, *op. cit.*, p. 16.
65 Glen, *op. cit.*, p. 7.
66 William Wordsworth, from 'We are Seven', 1798, *op. cit.*
67 Wordsworth, from 'Anecdote for Fathers', *ibid.*
68 Wordsworth, from 'The Mad Mother', *ibid.*
69 William Wordsworth, from 'Ode on Intimations of Immortality from Recollections of Early Childhood', 1804, in *A Choice of Wordsworth's Verse, op. cit.*
70 Wordsworth, *ibid.*
71 William Wordsworth, 'The Prelude', London, 1850.
72 Lionel Trilling, *The Liberal Imagination*, Oxford, 1981, p. 139.
73 Bloom, *op. cit.*, p. 16.
74 William Wordsworth, from 'Lines Composed above Tintern Abbey', *Lyrical Ballads*, 1798, *op. cit.*
75 Samuel Taylor Coleridge, from 'Frost at Midnight', 1798, *S. T. Coleridge: Poems* ed. John Beer, Everyman, London, 1974.
76 Richard Holmes, *Coleridge: Early Visions*, Hodder, London, 1989, p. 190.
77 Coleridge, from 'The Nightingale'.
78 Holmes, *op. cit.*, p. 193.
79 J. R. Watson, *op. cit.*, p. 56.
80 *Ibid.*, p. 58.
81 George Gordon, Lord Byron, from 'Childe Harold's Pilgrimage', III st. 75, *The Complete Poetical Works*, Oxford, 1980.
82 Watson, *op. cit.*, p. 63.
83 Stephen Coote, *John Keats: a Life*, Hodder, London, 1995, p. 20.
84 John Keats, from 'To Autumn', 1819, *John Keats: The Complete Poems*, ed. J. Barnard, Penguin, Harmondsworth, 1973.
85 John Keats, from 'Ode to a Nightingale', originally published in *Annals of the Fine Arts*, July 1819, in Barnard *ibid.*
86 J. R. Watson, *op. cit.*, p. 363.
87 John Keats in a letter to Benjamin Bailey, Nov. 1817, p. 37, and a letter to George and Tom Keats, Dec. 1817, p. 43, quoted in Robert Gittings, ed. *Letters of John Keats*, Oxford, 1970.
88 Watson, *op. cit.*, p. 366.
89 J. H. Plumb, 'New World of Children; in *The Birth of a Consumer Society*, Neil McKendrick, John Brewer and J. H. Plumb, Europa Publications Ltd, London, 1982, pp. 291, 310.
90 Lucy Aikin ed. *Poetry for Children*, London, 1801.

91 W. F. Mylius, *First Book of Poetry for Children*, London, 1820.
92 Lucy Aikin, ed. *Poetry for Children*, 1825.
93 John Greenleaf Whittier, ed. *Child Life*, London, 1874.
94 *Poetry for the Young*, London, 1883.
95 Andrew Lang, *op. cit.*
96 John Clare, 'from Autumn', *John Clare: Poems and Prose*, eds E. Robinson and D. Powell, Oxford, 1984.
97 Clare, from 'Clock-a-Clay', *ibid.*
98 Clare, from 'February', *ibid.*
99 Clare, from 'Remembrances', *ibid.*
100 Clare, from 'January', *ibid.*
101 Clare, from 'The Mores', *ibid.*
102 Clare, from 'I am', *ibid.*
103 *Ibid.*

CHAPTER 3

'Sweet Flowers I Bring'

Nineteenth-century nature poetry for children

Sweet Violets! from your humble beds
Among the moss, beneath the thorn,
You rear your unprotected heads,
A:.d brave the cold and cheerless morn
Of early March;[1]

The most consistent feature in poetry for children over 300 years is the centrality of nature as a theme.[2] The association of childhood with a rural location and gardens is reflected in the title and is one of the central tenets of this book. Since Bunyan penned his *Country Rhimes* in 1686, large numbers of poets have written for children about every aspect of animal life, the elements, the countryside and the seashore. Nature is, of course, one of the great themes for poetry at any time in any culture regardless of the audience. But it is not the main engine firing contemporary children's poetry, as we shall see in the concluding chapters, though nature remains and will, I think, always remain a strong impulse in writing for the young. The association of some nature poetry with idealized images of childhood has already been explored in the Introduction.

In this chapter I want to trace the history of nature poetry written specifically for the young. I shall give some prominence to the work of poets who deserve a wider audience such as Charlotte Smith and Dorothy Wordsworth, as well as introduce some forgotten voices from the nineteenth century.

'To read in nature's book' (the poetry of Charlotte Smith)

Charlotte Smith (1749–1806) dedicated her most elaborate poem, 'The Emigrants', to William Cowper who described her as 'Chain'ed to her desk like a slave to his oar, with no other means of subsistence for herself and her numerous children, with a broken constitution . . .'[3] The broken constitution, in an emotional sense, may have been the result of Charlotte's appalling marriage to Benjamin Smith who was womanizer, debtor and profligate rolled into one. Her physical constitution was wrecked by bearing 12 children (whom she loved dearly; three died in childhood) and struggling to support them financially by her publications throughout her life.

Hers is a sad story which began well enough with a happy childhood spent in comfort and ease in London. In a Memoir, her sister, Catherine Ann Dorset, painted a picture of the young Charlotte as cheerful, gay, funny, fond of acting and an avid reader. Although she was famous for writing mournful verse, you can see her sense of humour at work in a poem like 'Thirty-Eight', 1791, which begins:

> In early youth's unclouded scene,
> The brilliant morning of eighteen,
> With health and sprightly joy elate,
> We gazed on youth's enchanting spring,
> Nor thought how quickly time would bring
> The mournful period – thirty-eight![4]

The mature Charlotte (she was married at barely 16) was an unhappy woman as her writing shows all too plainly. In a letter to her sister she confides:

No disadvantage could equal those I sustained; the more my mind expanded, the more I became sensible of personal slavery; the more I improved and cultivated my understanding, the further I was removed from those with whom I was condemned to pass my life; the more closely I saw by these newly acquired lights the horror of the abyss into which I had unconsciously plunged.[5]

Despite her miseries, Smith stuck by her husband for many years, until she separated from him legally in 1787. Before that she went to heroic efforts on his behalf, taking her large brood of children to join him in enforced exile in France (to avoid his debtors) while she was pregnant with her twelfth child and making great efforts to repay his debts on more than one occasion. She nobly (but perhaps misguidedly) joined him in the Debtors' Prison in 1784 where she wrote one of her finest works, 'Elegiac Sonnets', which sold well and was highly regarded by poets like Burns, Coleridge and Wordsworth, as their tributes to her, and Dorothy Wordsworth's journal, all testify. Roger Lonsdale, who has done such a fine job of bringing many previously neglected poets to public attention, reminds us that a contributor to the *Gentleman's Magazine* in 1786 thought 'her sonnets superior to those of Shakespeare and Milton'.[6] A sixth edition saw the light of day in 1792, some indication of the popularity of Smith's poetry over a decade.

Poor melancholy bird – that all night long
Tell'st to the Moon, thy tale of tender woe;
From what sad cause can such sweet sorrow flow,
And whence this mournful melody of song?
Thy poet's musing fancy would translate
What mean the sounds that swell thy little breast,
When still at dewy eve thou leav'st thy nest,
Thus to the listening night to sing thy fate.
Pale sorrow's victims wert thou once among,
Tho' now releas'd in woodlands wild to rove,
Say – hast thou felt from friends some cruel wrong,
Or diedst thou martyr of disastrous love?
Ah! songstress sad! – that such my lot might be,
To sigh and sing at liberty – like thee![7]

This beautifully written poem, 'To a Nightingale', is moving in its melancholy, world-weary tones and uses the bird's songs of 'sweet sorrow' to express human aspirations and disappointments, as other Romantic poets were to do later. But subsequent critical opinion has been hard on Smith. The Opies called her verse only 'warm-hearted'[8] and complain that it lacked polish; in *The Oxford Companion to Children's Literature*, she only merits a few lines as a 'minor poet'.[9] Smith's poetry is rarely cited in books about Romanticism.[10] J. R. Watson, for example, does not mention her at all despite devoting a large part of his book on Romantic poetry to its precursors. The current interest in what women were writing in the Romantic period has led to the beginnings of a reappraisal of Smith's significance. Jennifer Breen, for example, in *Women Romantic Poets* suggests that Smith 'helped to re-establish the use of the sonnet form in English poetry'[11] which had been effectively out of use for about 100 years.

Fortunately, Smith has found a real champion in the scholarship of Stuart Curran who edited *The Poems of Charlotte Smith* in 1993. He writes:

> Charlotte Smith was the first poet in England whom in retrospect we would call Romantic . . . she established enduring patterns of thought and conventions of style that became norms for the period. Her most direct beneficiary among the more canonical male poets was William Wordsworth, who seems to have felt her impact from the first.'[12]

This is true as Wordsworth wrote with percipience that Smith was 'a lady to whom English verse is under greater obligations than are likely to be either acknowledged or remembered'.[13] Curran sums up her place in the history of Romanticism:

Smith's singular achievement is to free established poetic discourse from its reliance on polished couplets, formal diction, and public utterances, and through centering on internal states of mind to realize an expressive and conversational intensity.[14]

Curran considers the poem she was writing when she died in 1806, 'Beachy Head', her masterpiece. In what may be an overstatement of the case, Curran suggests that 'no poem of the period can one find so powerful an impulse to resolve the self into nature'.[15]

> On thy stupendous summit, rock sublime!
> That o'er the channel rear'd, halfway at sea
> The mariner at early morning hails,
> I would recline . . .
>
> . . .
>
> . . . and rent the solid hills,
> Biding the impetuous main flood rush between
> The rifted shores, and from the continent
> Eternally divided this green isle.[16]

Charlotte Smith wrote one of the earliest books of its kind, *Conversations Introducing Poetry for the Use of Children Chiefly on the Topic of Natural History*. It was a collaboration with her sister, Catherine Ann Dorset, where a fictional mother and two children discuss manners, morality, nature and poetry. It included poems like this one, 'Invitation to the Bee':

> Child of patient industry,
> Little active busy bee,
> Thou art out at early morn,
> Just as the opening flowers are born,
> Among the green and grassy meads
> Where the cowslips hang their heads;
> Or by the hedge-rows, while the dew
> Glitters on the harebell blue.[17]

The anonymous editor wrote in the preface to a later edition of *Conversations*:

> She was a close observer of nature . . . few writers have given more truthful and lifelike pictures of the creatures whose habits and ways she has studied, and even the lightest touch in her description is correct.[18]

This can clearly be seen in *Invitation*, which gives a radiant account of early morning in a meadow, already the site of bees at work. Her book also had a didactic purpose; as Curran put it, 'Smith's efforts are very much directed to a child's needs and level of comprehension, with the poems serving as mnemonic devices for retaining information and as instruments of moral and ecological information.'[19] Take the first and last verses of 'A Walk by the Water':

> Let us walk where reeds are growing,
>   By the alders in the mead,
> Where the crystal streams are flowing,
>   In whose waves the fishes feed.
>
> . . .
>
> Do not dread us, timid fishes,
>   We have neither net nor hook;
> Wand'rers we, whose only wishes
>   Are to read in nature's book . . .[20]

Smith's invitation for a waterside walk is very appealing and concludes with a delightful image of 'wand'rers we' who seek to 'read in nature's book'.[21]

With so many dependants, Smith was forced to be assertive on their behalf, wrangling with her publishers for decent advances and assiduously promoting her subscription list. Smith made a living from her fiction; she wrote poetry for only the best reasons – because she loved it and felt a compulsion to do so. Smith was, like Wordsworth, a moderate radical in her time; she was an early supporter of the French Revolution, but grew disillusioned with it like so many others. Her personal struggles were of a more domestic sort – to keep a roof over the family's head and a bid for personal freedom were momentous enough to make her a fighter all her life. She was a distinguished early feminist showing, as Curran put it, 'a seasoned professionalism that made her one of the exemplary writers of her age'.[22]

'You may love a screaming owl' – the writing of Dorothy Wordsworth

Dorothy Wordsworth was a contemporary of Charlotte Smith. She wrote journals, letters and a handful of poems with authenticity and passion about daily life, gardening, walks, her family and the people she encountered, including children to whom she related well. Dorothy Wordsworth's writing is often assumed only to be of interest as background material for readers of her famous brother's poetry. In fact, her writing indicates that she, too, was talented in this sphere with a special gift for describing nature and domestic life.

We know from her Grasmere journal how attuned she was to the landscape of the Lakes and how much she loved growing things. 'She gives me eyes, she gives me ears'

wrote William Wordsworth in 'The Sparrow's Nest'. In 'Tintern Abbey' he
documents how his sister's feeling for nature provided inspiration for his poetry:

> My dear, dear Friend, and in thy voice I catch
> The language of my former heart, and read
> My former pleasures in the shooting lights
> Of thy wild eyes. Oh! yet a little while
> May I behold in thee what I was once,
> My dear, dear Sister![23]

Coleridge also praised her response to nature as 'simple, ardent, impressive –

> In every motion her most innocent soul
> Outbeams so brightly . . .

her eye watchful in minutest observation of nature – and her taste a perfect
electrometer . . .'[24] Thomas de Quincey was another neighbour during part of the
period when the Wordsworths lived at Dove Cottage in the Lake District. He
described Dorothy as 'the wildest person that I have ever known'[25] and went on to
praise her quickness, alertness, 'unique delicacy and grace'[26] and her radiant response
to the beauty around her. An enthusiastic walker and gardener, Dorothy Wordsworth
sported a 'Gypsy Tan' as she was always out of doors. In her famous journals, which
her brother mined for inspiration, she writes of nature with a poet's eye.

On a less happy note, de Quincey speculates as to whether the condition
(something like what is now described as senile dementia) which Dorothy suffered for
the last 20 years of her life, came about because she was 'a woman divided against
herself'. He thought that Dorothy's writer self was permanently compromised by this
absorption of her talents into her brother's poetic estate.[27] Dorothy Wordsworth was
certainly not alone among women in that period in suppressing her literary gifts or in
thinking that what she did write was of little value.

In *Women in Romanticism*, Meena Alexander writes admiringly of Dorothy's
journal:

> The domestic details of her ordinary life, the chores of cooking and cleaning
> house, washing, ironing, baking, digging in the garden, 'sticking' peas are
> juxtaposed with notations of work with William on his poems, copying them
> out, listening to him recite them. They are juxtaposed too with those delicate
> descriptions of nature so highly prized by Wordsworth and Coleridge in which
> Dorothy . . . sets out her sense of reality, the ordinary objects of perception,
> grass, insects, tree trunks, clouds, skirmishing . . . with an almost visionary edge
> to perception.[28]

> 4 February 1802 . . . Midges or small flies spinning in the sunshine; the songs of the lark and redbreast; daisies upon the turf; the hazels in blossom; honeysuckles budding. I saw one solitary strawberry flower under a hedge. The furze gày with blossom . . .

> 16 March 1802 . . . The moon was a good height above the mountains. She seemed far and distant in the sky there were two stars beside her, that twinkled in and out, and seemed almost like butterflies in motion and lightness.[29]

> 15 April 1802 . . . I never saw daffodils so beautiful. They grew among the mossy stones about and about them; some rested their heads upon these stones as on a pillow for weariness; and the rest tossed and reeled and danced, and seemed as if they verily laughed with the wind, that blew over the lake; they looked so gay, ever glancing, ever changing . . .[30]

William's poem has become one of the best known in the world, but it was Dorothy who taught him how to see the daffodils. As Mary Moorman put it – 'Her prose is as lively and natural, as inevitable in its movement as a mountain stream, its language as transparently clear.'[31] Dorothy Wordsworth's verse for children naturally drew on this passion for nature and on her educational ideas which were strongly influenced by Rousseau's *Emile*. When the neglected little three year old, Basil Montagu, came to board for a while at Dove Cottage, Dorothy commented: 'We teach him nothing but what he learns from his senses. He has an insatiable curiosity which we are always careful to satisfy to the best of our ability.'[32] The method seemed to work as Basil grew into a 'lusty, blooming, fearless boy'.[33] There is that same directness, common sense and domesticity evident in her poems. In 'Address to a Child during a Boisterous Winter Evening' (written for her brother's children), she explains artlessly that 'how he [the wind] will come, and whither he goes, / There's never a scholar in England knows.' There are descriptions of the havoc the wind is likely to make in the garden, followed by a cosy ending emphasizing the indoor warmth against the freezing windswept outdoors.

> He may knock at the door – we'll not let him in;
> May drive at the windows – we'll laugh at his din.
> Let him seek his own home, wherever it be:
> Here's a cosy warm house for Edward and me.[34]

In the poem that follows, Dorothy wanted to teach children a lesson in discrimination. She offers a firm but gentle admonishment to a child about the differences between enjoying a chicken dinner and the uniqueness and beauty of animals. She understood that to make children take notice you do not preach.

There's more in words than I can teach:
Yet listen, child! – I would not preach;
But only give some plain directions
To guide your speech and your affections.
Say not you *love* a roasted fowl,
But you may love a screaming owl,
And, if you can, the unwieldy toad
That crawls from his secure abode
Within the mossy garden wall
When evening dews begin to fall.[35]

Dorothy Wordsworth's insights into nature were for the private rather than public domain.[36] Even though her writing is now published, she continues to suffer critical injustice. 1863 saw the publication of a beautifully illustrated volume of *William Wordsworth's Poems for the Young*[37] with a vignette by Millais, containing at least one uncredited poem by Dorothy. The Penguin edition of Dorothy's journal, *Home at Grasmere*[38] appends William's poems, but none of Dorothy's. So it is illuminating to read Hyman Eigerman's *The Poetry of Dorothy Wordsworth*, where he puts some of her poetic prose into verse. Although this is a somewhat dubious activity, it is interesting to see what her nature poems for adults might have looked like:

A sweet evening,
As it had been a sweet day,
And I walked quietly
Along the side of Rydale lake
With quiet thoughts.
The hills and the lake were still –
The owls had not begun to hoot,
And the little birds had given over singing.[39]

'The lark is warbling' – nature poetry for the young

Jane and Ann Taylor's *Original Poems for Infant Minds*, 1804, was the most influential poetry book for children of the first half of the nineteenth century. The Taylors set many of their poems in a rural landscape amidst flowers, fields, trees and animals, but their nature poetry is of a rather domestic kind. Not for them the wild, untamed countryside, but they did want to encourage young readers to appreciate the natural world.

Awake, little girl, it is time to arise,
Come shake drowsy sleep from your eye;

> The lark is now warbling his notes to the skies,
> And the sun is far mounted on high.
>
> O come, for the fields with gay flowers abound,
> The dewdrop is quivering still,
> The lowing herds graze in the pastures around,
> And the sheep-bell is heard from the hill.[40]

There is a kindly tone to this typical poem by Jane Taylor and though it addresses the child gently enough, it is a poem of its time with a slightly moralistic edge ('it is time to arise'). The presentation of nature may appear somewhat gushy (quivering dewdrops, gay flowers etc.) to contemporary readers. Looked at more positively, Jane paints an attractive and peaceful pastoral scene and invites children to look closely at some of the inviting features of the world about them. Its small-scale, harmonious description of rural beauty and lilting rhyme and metre with a little girl at the centre of the picture combine to make it an appealing child-centred poem.

Writing just before the Taylors is Lucy Aikin who included several of her own nature poems in her anthology, *Poetry for Children*, 1801.

> See, mamma, what a sweet little prize I have found!
> A robin that lay half-benumb'd on the ground.
> I caught him, and fed him, and warm'd in my breast,
> And now he's as nimble and blithe as the best.
> Look, look, how he flutters! – He'll slip from my hold:
> Ah, rogue! you've forgotten both hunger and cold!
> But indeed 'tis in vain, for I shan't set you free,
> For all your whole life you're a prisoner with me.
> Well housed and well fed, in your cage you will sing,
> And make our dull winter as gay as the spring.
> But stay, – sure 'tis cruel, with wings made to soar,
> To be shut up in prison, and never fly more!
> And I, who so often have long'd for a flight,
> Shall I keep you prisoner? – Mamma, is it right?
> No, come pretty Robin, I must set you free –
> For your whistle, though sweet, would sound sadly to me.[41]

Lucy Aikin's accomplishments as a nature poet are modest enough, but her work is interesting in the light it throws on her time, remembering that she came from a fairly progressive, though not particularly affluent, literary family. In many respects the sentiments of this undistinguished little poem are in line with many others of the late eighteenth century: it is wrong to cage wild things; children should be kind to animals and so on. Lucy Aikin also *empathizes* with the bird, but she does so from the imagined viewpoint and voice of a child. The message of this poem is more to do with liberty than with the good behaviour of children and very little to do with robins. It is not surprising to learn that Lucy Aikin was a campaigner against slavery all her life.

Bees, butterflies and peacocks

Good morrow, gentle Humble-bee,
You are abroad betimes, I see,
And sportive fly from tree to tree,
        To take the air;

And visit each gay flower that blows;
While every bell and bud that glows,
Quite from the daisy to the rose,
        Your visits share.

Saluting now the pied carnation,
Now on the aster taking station,
Murmuring your ardent admiration;
        Then off you frisk,

Where poppies hang their heavy heads,
Or where the gorgeous sun-flower spreads
For you her luscious golden beds,
        On her broad disc.

To live on pleasure's painted wing
To feed on all the sweets of spring
Must be a mighty pleasant thing,
        If it would last.

But you, no doubt, have wisely thought,
These joys may be too dearly bought,
And will not unprepared be caught,
        When summer's past.[42]

In language that is as lush as its subject matter, Catherine Ann Dorset (1750?–1817?) conjures up a sultry summer garden with bees gathering honey from 'gorgeous sun-flowers' in a poem that is formal, tasteful and beautifully composed. Dorset's (and Smith's) knowledge of natural history cannot be doubted, as the prose dicussion which precedes the poem bears out:

The *apis terrestis* or earth bee, and the *apis nemorum* or wood bee . . . those two are the commonest sorts, and the first is what you saw go into his subterraneous house. As they appear as busy as the common honey bee, and to collect the nectar and the pollen of flowers in the same manner, it is probable that their habits are nearly the same; yet I never recollect having heard that their hoards of honey had been discovered in digging into banks, or those places they are known to frequent. And it was on the supposition that they were not equally provident with their congeners the honey bee, that, as a lesson of industry and forecast, the verses were composed . . .[43]

We have now had examples of nature poetry that seek to look at the world with a child's eyes and understanding. Smith, Wordsworth, Taylor and Dorset all make some attempt to imagine their insects and animals as a child might. They also want to provide knowledge, but in each case didactic intention is tempered with a desire to match beautiful nature with beautiful poetry.

Some poets for children engage with the emotions evoked by such scenes just as the Romantics did. Dorset's 'The Humble Bee' is in many respects a poem of adult sensibilities with a world-weariness of spirit and a sense of disappointment that all joys must come to an end. But in the best-selling *The Peacock At Home*, 1807,[44] she was much more child-centred and though she was also keen to inject some realistic natural history as well as fun, it is entirely free of moralizing.

> Description must fail, and the pen is unable
> To recount all the lux'ries that covered the table.
> Each delicate viand that taste could denote,
> Wasps a la sauce piquante, and flies en compote;
> Worms and frogs en friture for the web-footed fowl,
> And a barbecued mouse was prepared for the owl;
> Nuts, grain, fruit, and fish, to regale every palate,
> And grounsel and chickweed served up in a sallad.[45]

The litany of amusing dishes is reminiscent of Edward Lear writing 40 years later. Isn't the 'web-footed fowl' rather like some of the extravagant creatures who crop up in 'The Quangle Wangle Quee'? Dorset's poem is quite delightful and contains a wise and amiable preface: 'the Poem was written expressly for the amusement of very young readers'. Instead of nature-study lessons, 'it was rather my wish to excite them to satisfy curiosity by inducing them to apply to other books for that information . . .'[46] She then directs the reader to Bewick's *British Birds* and other such texts, adding that the references to birds in the poem are consistent with their biology.

There were other poets trying in quiet ways to soften the harsh lessons for children which had so dominated their literature until the first decade of the nineteenth century. William Roscoe (1753–1831), Member of Parliament for Liverpool, was a liberal, compassionate, public-spirited man. It was his poem, 'The Butterfly's Ball and the Grasshopper's Feast' of 1807 which set off a craze for narrative poems about insects, birds and tiny animals which contained a fair amount of authentic natural history. Dorset produced the best of the sequels, but 'The Butterfly's Ball' has great charm, too.

> Then the grasshopper came, with a jerk and a spring,
> Very long was his leg, though but short was his wing;
> He took but three leaps, and was soon out of sight,
> Then chirp'd his own praises the rest of the night.
>
> With Step so majestic the Snail did advance,
> And promis'd the Gazers a Minuet to dance.
> But they all laugh'd so loud that he pull'd in his Head,
> And went in his own little Chamber to Bed.
> Then as Evening gave way to the shadows of Night,
> Their Watchman, the Glowworm, came out with a light.[47]

Within the year 'The Peacock at Home' and 'The Butterfly's Ball' had sold 40,000 copies between them. That would still be considered a good sales record today. Children were clearly hungry for the combination of amusement and natural history in verse.

Charles Lamb (1775–1834), the well-known essayist, man about town and friend of many of the leading writers of his day, was highly critical of poetry written for children at this time and of the Taylors in particular, finding their work much too harsh and didactic. It was with some disappointment, therefore, that I first read *Poetry for Children*, 1809, of which he was author of a third, his sister Mary Lamb (1764-1847) supplying the rest. It is inferior to the Taylors in craft, content, appeal to children and sense of humour. Darton describes the poems as lacking in originality or fresh viewpoint and 'well within the Moral Tale ring-fence'.[48] Here are extracts from the Lambs' depictions of bees and butterflies; it is hard to believe they knew, as they certainly did, Wordsworth's 'To a Butterfly'.

> Your dancing, spangled, powder'd beau,
> Look, through the air I've let him go:
>   And now we're friends again.
> As sure as he is in the air,
> From this time, Ann, I will take care,
>   And try to be humane.[49]

     *   *   *

His aching limbs while sick he lay
Made him learn the crush'd bees' pain;
Oft would he to his mother say,
'I ne'er will kill a bee again.'

In 1811 *The Monthly Review* opined:

Nothing can be either more natural or more engaging than the subjects of these little Poems; and they will teach children to be happy by making them reflect on their own comforts, and by exciting them to promote the happiness of others.[50]

In reality, posterity's neglect of *Poetry for Children* suggests that the Lambs wrote pedestrian verse!

The main trends in the nature poetry I have provided so far appear to be references to children's experiences set within a rural landscape, sometimes with a moral edge, and amusing narrative fantasies which drew on knowledge of natural history. Later, poets became more interested in exploring nature in its own right, though a lot of it was sentimental or idealized and much of it undistinguished. Nature poetry for children had not changed dramatically by the final decade of the nineteeth century and we can run through some of the key players quite quickly.

'Sweeter blossoms'

Mary Elliott's (1794–1870) nature poetry, for example, was truly abysmal; she was better known in her day as the author of moral tales such as *The Orphan Boy*, 1812, and *The Adventures of Thomas Two-Shoes*, 1818, a sequel to *Goody Two-Shoes*. This is the best I could find – 'The Rose', popular at the time it was written (1824) speaks for itself.

Lightly climb yon garden wall,
Where laburnum branches fall;
Move their yellow flowers aside,
Sweeter blossoms far they hide,

No loud boisterous boys we see,
Yet there seems no lack of glee;
Groups of merry girls appear –
We shall glean some pleasure here.[51]

Another prolific author, Mary Howitt (1799–1888) wrote several poetry books that focused on nature, in titles such as *Sketches of Natural History*, 1834, and *Fireside*

Verses, 1839. She sometimes collaborated with her equally prolific writer-husband, William, but was the better poet of the two. 'Corn Fields' is from *Fireside Verses*.

> In the young merry time of spring
>   When clover 'gins to burst;
> When blue-bells nod within the wood,
>   And sweet May whitens first;
> When Merle and Mavis sing their fill,
> Green is the young corn on the hill.[52]

A poet who scarcely features in histories of children's literature is our third Mary – Mary Claude. A religious poet, in her best work there is just a hint of what Christina Rossetti would do much more brilliantly in *Sing-Song*.

> When every singing-bird has hid
>   Its head beneath its wing,
> Except the little nightingale
>   That stays awake to sing;
>
> When owls and bats come out for food,
>   And in the meadows fly,
> The silver moon, so beautiful,
>   Is gliding through the sky.[53]

Two young women who put in an appearance in most reviews of nineteenth-century children's poetry are Elizabeth Hart (1822–1888) and Menella Bute Smedley (1820–1877) who wrote a banal book entitled *Poems Written for a Child*[54] in 1868. Though it was well liked in its day, I consider it doggerel by any other name. We have reached the period when Lear and Carroll were writing; the latter apparently used to present copies of *Poems Written for a Child* to his little girl friends. It reminds me of Bottom in *A Midsummer Night's Dream*.

> O Moon – said the children – O Moon, that shineth fair,
> Why do you stay so far away, so high above us there?
> O Moon, you must be very cold from shining on the sea;
> If you would come and play with us, how happy we would be!

Another popular writer of this period was Juliana Ewing (1841–1885), daughter of Margaret Gatty of *Aunt Judy's Magazine* fame, to which she was a regular contributor. A major writer of fiction (including *The Brownies and Other Tales*, 1870; *Jackanapes*, 1879; and *Six to Sixteen*, 1875, a favourite of Kipling's), part of her strength as a story-writer lay in her unwillingness to write 'down' to children. Unfortunately, the same cannot be said about her poetry, the best known of which is 'The Doll's Wash', 1874. In 'The Burial of the Linnet', Ewing's condescension to her audience is apparent; so, unfortunately, is the appeal. Auden's famous lament may owe a debt to Ewing's final line?

> Found in the garden – dead in his beauty.
>   Ah, that a linnet should die in the spring!
> Bury him, comrades, in pitiful duty,
>   Muffle the dinner bell, solemnly ring.[55]

Marigold Garden

The Opies do not include Kate Greenaway (1846–1901) in *The Oxford Book of Children's Verse*, but she seems to keep good company with some of the poets cited so far in the mid period of the nineteenth century. She is much better known, of course, for her distinctive illustrations, usually featuring cute, well dressed, pretty little children somewhat lacking in animation. Greenaway was one of the key artists of the Victorian period and a friend of John Ruskin who took an interest in her career and with whom she collaborated on a number of occasions. Ruskin's influence was not particularly constructive; his excessive praise of her work was treated with contempt by many, but she remained devoted to him. Among the poems whose work Greenaway illustrated were those of Ann and Jane Taylor and Robert Browning's *The Pied Piper of Hamelin*. Two of Greenaway's books that feature her own poems are *Under the Window*, 1879 and *Marigold Garden*, 1885; indeed her illustrations of children are often presented amidst the setting of formal gardens. Despite the titles, this is not really nature poetry; more of manners and games. Here is a snippet from 'On the Bridge':

> I think I'll get some stones to throw,
> And watch the pretty circles show.
> Or shall we sail a flower-boat,
> And watch it slowly – slowly float?[56]

Greenaway was better at writing rhymes for very young children like this one:

> Little wind, blow on the hill-top,
>   Little wind, blow down the plain;
> Little wind, blow up the sunshine,
>   Little wind, blow off the rain.[57]

This brings us neatly to the close of the nineteenth century where a famous novelist for children also wrote poetry which has since been largely forgotten, Edith (Bland) Nesbit (1858–1924). Her masterpiece was *The Railway Children*, 1904, which, like *The Wouldbegoods*, *The Story of the Treasure Seekers*, *The Phoenix and the Carpet* are classics of fiction and still admired today. Her poetry always focused on nature – *Songs of Two Seasons*, 1891, *Flowers I Bring and Songs I Sing*, 1893, *Bright Wings* (in the shape of a butterfly), 1890, and *A Pomander of Verse*, 1895. 'Lullaby' is faintly reminiscent of Rossetti.

> Sleep, sleep, my treasure,
> The long day's pleasure
> Has tired the birds, to their nests they creep;
> The garden still is
> Alight with lilies,
> But all the daisies are fast asleep.
>
> Sleep, sleep, my darling,
> Dawn wakes the starling,
> The sparrow stirs when he sees day break;
> But all the meadow
> Is wrapped in shadow,
> And you must sleep till the daisies wake![58]

I have missed out Christina Rossetti's nature poetry in *Sing-Song*, as she is discussed in detail in Chapter 7. Once we reach the twentieth century, Walter de la Mare and others continue to write fine nature poetry in the same tradition. Since the 1970s, however, nature has had to give way as the primary theme in children's poetry, though many poets refer to 'green' issues in their work. The most distinguished living nature poet is Ted Hughes (considered in Chapter 12) who divides his attention between older and younger readers. Hughes has brought a new toughness and honesty to the subject matter of animals and landscapes which owes little to nature poetry of the past. His work also charts a revolution in perception about his intended audience. He respects young readers enough to write the truth – even when it is disturbing. Nature poetry for children has come of age.

Notes

1 Charlotte Smith, *Conversations Introducing Poetry to Children Chiefly on the Topic of Natural History*, London, 1804.

2 I take the natural world to include plants, habitats, animals, the weather and the seasons, the sea as well as the land.

3 William Cowper in a letter to William Hayley, Tuesday 29 January, 1793, *The Letters and*

Prose Writings of William Cowper, Volume IV, 1792–1799, ed. James King et al., Oxford, 1984, p. 281.

4   From 'Thirty-Eight', *The Poems of Charlotte Smith*, ed. Stuart Curran, Oxford, 1993.

5   Charlotte Smith in a letter to Catherine Ann Dorset, quoted in Stuart Curran, *op. cit.*, p. xx

6   Roger Lonsdale, *Eighteenth Century Women Poets*, Oxford, 1990, p. 366.

7   Charlotte Smith, 'To a Nightingale', *Elegaic Sonnets*, London, 1794.

8   Iona and Peter Opie, eds, *The Oxford Book of Children's Verse*, 1973, p. 381.

9   Humphrey Carpenter and Mari Pritchard, eds, *The Oxford Companion to Children's Literature*, 1984, p. 488.

10 Happily this is changing as academics have become more interested in women's writing in general and female Romantic poets in particular.

11 Jennifer Breen, *Women Romantic Poets*, J. M. Dent, London, 1992, p. 165.

12 Curran, *op. cit.*, p. xix.

13 William Wordsworth, quoted in *Poetic Form and British Romanticism*, Stuart Curran, Oxford, 1989, p. 30.

14 *Ibid.*

15 Curran, 1993, p. xxvii.

16 Charlotte Smith, from 'Beachy Head', in Curran, *ibid.*

17 Smith, from 'Invitation to the Bee', 1804, *op. cit.*

18 Smith, London, p. v.

19 Curran, *op. cit.*, p. xxviii.

20 Smith, from 'A Walk by the Water', Curran, *op. cit.*, p. 21.

21 *Ibid.*

22 Curran, *op. cit.*, p. xxxviii.

23 William Wordsworth, from 'Lines Composed above Tintern Abbey', *Lyrical Ballads*, London, 1798.

24 Samuel Taylor Coleridge, *The Poetical Works*, ed. E. H. Coleridge, Oxford, 1912, p. 168.

25 Thomas De Quincey, *Recollections of the Lakes and Lake Poets*, ed. David Wright, Penguin, London, 1980, p. 205.

26 *Ibid.*, p.2 01.

27 *Ibid.*, p. 201.

28 Meena Alexander, *Women in Romanticism*, Macmillan, London, 1989, p. 80.

29 Dorothy Wordsworth quoted in Mary Moorman, ed., *The Journals of Dorothy Wordsworth*, Oxford, 1971, pp. 4,5.

30 Dorothy Wordsworth, *Home at Grasmere*, ed Colette Clark, Penguin, 1978, p. 192.

31 Moorman, *op. cit.*, p. xvii.

32 Robert Gittings and Jo Manton, *Dorothy Wordsworth*, Oxford, 1988, p. 53.

33 Dorothy Wordsworth quoted in *Women in Romanticism*, ed. Meena Alexander, Macmillan, 1989, p. 16.

34 Dorothy Wordsworth, from 'Address to a Child During a Boisterous Winter Evening', quoted in *William Wordsworth's Poems*, Vol. 1, ed. John Hayden, Penguin.

35 Dorothy Wordsworth from 'Loving and Liking', quoted in Iona and Peter Opie, eds, *The Oxford Book of Children's Verse*, 1973.

36 In the event, some of Dorothy's poems were published in William Wordsworth's own collections.

37 *Wordsworth's Poems for the Young*, Alexander Strahant Co., London, 1863.

38 Dorothy Wordsworth, *Home at Grasmere*, *op. cit.*

39   Hyman Eigerman, *The Poetry of Dorothy Wordsworth*, Columbia University Press, New York, p. 24.

40   Ann and Jane Taylor from 'Morning', *Original Poems for Infant Minds*, Darton, London, 1804.

41   Lucy Aikin, *Poetry for Children*, London, 1801.

42   Catherine Ann Dorset in *Charlotte Smith, Conversations Introducing Poetry to Children Chiefly on the Topic of Natural History*, London, 1804. I have previously attributed 'The Humble Bee' to Charlotte Smith. She was the principle author of *Conversations* and indeed, the poem seemed typically Smith in style and tone. However, in *The Poems of Charlotte Smith*, Stuart Curran appears to attribute 'The Humble Bee' to Dorset.

43   *Ibid.*, p. 76.

44   'The Butterfly's Ball' was so popular that about a dozen writers tried their hands at similar poems in the next year or so.

45   Catherine Ann Dorset, from *The Peacock at Home*, London, 1809.

46   *Ibid.*

47   William Roscoe, from *'The Butterfly's Ball and The Grasshopper's Feast'*, London, 1807.

48   F. J. Harvey Darton, *Children's Books in England*, Cambridge, 1932, p. 190.

49   Charles and Mary Lamb, *Poetry for Children*, London, 1809.

50   'Poetry for Children', *The Monthly Review*, 1811 (Charles and Mary Lamb, London, 1809).

51   Mary Elliott, from *The Rose*, Darton, London, 1824.

52   Mary Howitt, from 'Corn Fields', *Fireside Verses*, Darton and Clark, London, 1844.

53   Mary Claude, from 'Song', *Little Poems for Little People*, London, 1847.

54   Elizabeth Hart and Menella Bute Smedley, from 'The Moon', *Poems Written for a Child*, London, 1868.

55   Juliana Ewing from 'The Burial of the Linnet', quoted in Opie, *op. cit.*, p. 254.

56   Kate Greenaway, from 'On the Bridge', *Marigold Garden*, London, 1885.

57   Kate Greenaway, *Under the Window*, London, 1879.

58   Edith Nesbit, from 'Lullaby', *A Pomander of Verse*, Bodley Head, London, 1895.

CHAPTER 4

Old Mother Hubbard

And other nursery rhymes, old and new

Old Mother Hubbard
Went to the Cupboard
To fetch her poor dog a bone;
When she got there
The cupboard was bare
And so the poor dog had a moan.[1]

I am told that when I was a small child, as soon as I mastered speech, I would perform endless recitations of nursery rhymes to an appreciative family audience. I learned early how to achieve centre stage, captivate listeners and, no doubt, stay up later than I might otherwise have done. The point is that nursery rhymes entranced me, aged two and a half, *and* the grown-ups I had dealings with. 'What kind of verses are they to have become the best known in the world?' ask the Opies in *The Oxford Dictionary of Nursery Rhymes*[2] and to have become 'so constant an ingredient of children's literature that they have been published in almost every shape and style of book that has been manufactured'.[3]

Faced with a present to buy for a friend's baby, a new niece or grandson, it is now traditional to select a book of nursery rhymes. The choice before the purchaser will be lavish with a wide assortment of well-illustrated books of Mother Goose on display in any decent bookshop. Flicking through the anthologies, the buyer often finds a long-forgotten favourite from the past which might be shared, in turn, with the child for whom it is intended. And that sharing is often active as the rhymes can be accompanied by hand movements and clapping or lend themselves to rhythmic rocking. So the bond between one childhood and another is established with mutual satisfaction, regardless of class, gender or race.

As babies grow up, they encounter the rhymes at nursery, play group and infant school, in oral and written form, sometimes sung or with a musical accompaniment, as well as at home in playful encounters with brothers, sisters, parents, grandparents; through tape, video, television and visits to the supermarket, as well as books. Little Bo Peep and Little Jack Horner may be decorated on their plates, bibs and mugs, perhaps, on the wallpaper in their bedrooms, the T-shirts they are wearing, on their packets of felt tip pens, on the covers of colouring books, breakfast cereals and tubs of yogurt. In *The Natural History of Make-Believe*, John Goldthwaite suggests that nursery rhymes are 'our most common currency after the Bible'.[4]

'The infant scholar's reading'

So 'Jack and Jill', 'Mary, Mary, Quite Contrary' and 'Tom, Tom, the Piper's Son' have become an established part of Western culture in the late twentieth century. Variations on these rhymes are widespread and not just in Britain and America – collectors of vernacular literature have shown the similarities between nursery verse coming out of different parts of Europe and Scandinavia, and the fact that in some form or other, it exists in most parts of the world. Goldthwaite again: 'As a literature Mother Goose is an invention of the English, but nursery rhymes, needless to say, are universal.'[5] I want to trace how the popularity of nursery rhymes came about and to look at the derivations for, and children's responses to, this eternally popular literature – 'the novel and light reading of the infant scholar', as James Orchard Halliwell engagingly put it in 1842.[6]

In a single chapter, I can provide only a bare outline of the terrain; for a full and scholarly account of nursery rhymes and their derivations, readers need look no further than the Opies, cited in the bibliography. I have, however, examined most of the texts I mention in original editions and scrutinized the rhymes in some detail in order to select a small sample of scraps and fragments from this antique literature for the reader to enjoy. The chapter closes with some attention to recent rhymes for newer nurseries from a range of cultures.

The Opies tell us that the term 'nursery rhyme' was not coined until the third decade of the nineteenth century. Otherwise they were known as songs or ditties in Britain and Mother Goose rhymes in America. Definitions of nursery rhymes are notoriously hard to come by, because the essence of these rhymes is so difficult to pin down. In *The Poetry of Nonsense*, Emile Cammaerts suggests they are 'essentially poetical because [they are] essentially musical'[7] which is true, but not just of nursery rhymes. He asserts that the topsy-turvy, upside-down, irresponsible, absurd and playful nature of these rhymes reflects children's hostility to the well-ordered world of adults. That may be right, though it is worth remembering that many rhymes began life as creations of adult interest in religion, love or politics which lost their charge over time, but were saved from extinction by retaining a place in the nursery. And the claims made for Mother Goose are not humble. 'The best of the older ones are nearer to poetry than the greater part of *The Oxford Book of English Verse*', Robert Graves[8] declaims extravagantly. John Goldthwaite:

> Mother Goose is numberless, a steady-state universe with no big bang, no closure, no definitive edition. New songs are piping into existence in odd corners of the planet every day.[9]

The history of nursery rhymes

Harvey Darton's appreciative comments on the substance and form of nursery rhymes are almost as delicious as the texts themselves:

> They are of parentage as uncertain as a piebald kitten. They overlap into the baby talk and the ancestral singing games of children themselves . . . They vary from one mother to another, one child to another, one street or village to another. They belong to all epochs and all nations, and there is [thank Heaven] no hope of ever identifying the true source of more than a handful of them . . .[10]

The Opies' research into the oral tradition is impressive and they have gone a long way towards providing us with histories of many of the rhymes; even so, the thrust of Darton's argument is valid. He goes on to consider children's games and rhymes:

> Heaven knows what broken pride, what good cheer, what devious politics and baby prattle, fears, hopes, eternities of the human mind, are jumbled in this flotsam of the most private of all worlds, child's play.[11]

Before the Opies, two of the greatest collectors of the English oral tradition were Joseph Ritson and James Orchard Halliwell who edited *Gammer Gurton's Garland* and *The Nursery Rhymes of England,* in 1784 and 1842 respectively. Ritson is described by Goldthwaite as the 'nursery's first scholar'[12] He also published a *Collection of English Songs* in 1783 and *The Life and Ballads of Robin Hood* in 1795. Halliwell was another early scholar to recognize the value of nursery rhymes. So was Sir Walter Scott:

> [I am] firmly convinced of the 'imagination-nourishing' power of the wild and fanciful lore of the old nursery.[13]

Halliwell tries to get to the heart of the genre by suggesting that they contain 'a meaning and a romance, possibly intelligible only to very young minds, that exercise an influence on the fancy of children'.[14] Perhaps Nicholas Tucker's definition is the vaguest and the best of all: nursery rhymes are 'smooth stones from the brook of time, worn round by constant friction of tongues long silent'.[15] In this chapter, the definition of nursery rhymes is similarly all-embracing and strays without apology into the territory of playground rhymes and other by-ways of the oral tradition.

The Opies offer a tantalizing list of the many varieties of the nursery rhyme: '. . . infant jingles, riddles, catches, tongue-trippers, baby games, toe names, maxims, alphabets, counting rhymes, prayers and lullabies with which generation after generation of mothers and nurses have attempted to please the youngest, as well as proverbs, sayings, customs, superstitions, seasonal chants, rude gests [*sic*] and romantic lyrics.'[16] They come from everywhere and anywhere, pinched from popular ballads, street cries, plays, stage productions, folk-songs, political jingles and the like.

This lively vernacular development runs as a subversive current alongside so-called 'respectable society'. In the eighteenth century the content of nursery rhymes was conventionally seen as the 'imbecilities of the peasantry', part of the general disapproval of fancy and fantasy in any shape. Disapproval was even stronger, of course, in the seventeenth century, when any fictional form, let alone the fairy tale or nursery rhyme, was considered trivial and even dangerous in a religious, educational and literary climate still largely driven by the Puritan ethic. Even John Locke, so liberal in outlook on childhood, castigated rhymes and stories which would 'fill his Head with perfectly useless trumpery . . .'[17] Locke went on to recommend Aesop's fables, the livelier stories from the Bible and Reynard the Fox – pretty good advice. Anyway, it seems that no amount of deprecation could keep Little Boy Blue and friends down for long.

Halliwell traces many rhymes back to the seventeenth century. For example, 'Thirty days hath September', 'Three Blind Mice' and 'Little Tommy Tucker' are dated 1606, 1609 and 1607 respectively. The Opies think the former may be as early as the thirteenth century. 'There was a lady loved a hogge; / Hony, quoth shee' goes back to the time of Charles 1 and 'Archdeacon Pratt could eat no fat, / His wife would eat no lean' to 1659. Before the Grand Old Duke of York put in an appearance, there was:

> The King of France, and four thousand men,
> They drew their swords, and put them up again. (1489)

and

> The King of France went up the hill,
> With twenty thousand men:
> The King of France came down the hill,
> And ne'er went up again. (1588)[18]

The Opies reckon that ten per cent of the rhymes in *The Oxford Dictionary of Nursery Rhymes* date back to 1650 or earlier and a quarter to a half to be at least 200 years old. Bringing us up to the nineteenth century, they cite dozens of examples of popular theatre productions in London based on nursery rhymes: 'Old Mother Hubbard' was at Covent Garden in 1833, 'Tom Tucker' at Queens in 1845, 'Ladybird Ladybird' at the Pavilion in 1853, and so on.

ABCs in verse

Tommy Thumb's Pretty Song Book, 1744, is usually regarded as the earliest full-blooded collection of nursery rhymes by 'Nurse Lovechild, Mother Goose, Jacky Nory,

Tommy Thumb, and other eminent Authors',[19] containing nine rhymes still familiar today. These include 'Sing a Song of Sixpence', 'Ladybird, Ladybird', 'Little Robin Red Breast', 'London Bridge is broken down', 'Hickere, Dickere, Dock' [*sic*], 'Oranges and Lemons' and 'There was an old Woman lived under a Hill'. It was published by John Newbery who opened his bookshop in the same year, moving to his better-known address, the Bible and Sun, near the Chapter House in St Paul's Churchyard, in 1745. The landmark date of 1744 sees the birth of *A Little Pretty Pocket Book*, also by Newbery, which is widely regarded as the first published item of genuine children's literature. Here's a nice bit of nonsense from it.

> Great A, B, and C,
>   And tumble-down D
> The Cat's a blind Buff,
>   And she cannot see.[20]

Before that a certain T. W. published *A Little Book for Little Children* in 1712,[21] including 'A was an Archer' and 'I saw a Peacock with a fiery tail' which still regularly make an appearance in poetry anthologies for children. ABC books have a special place in the history of reading pedagogy, as well as poetry. A large number of working-class children learned to read using ABCs, horn-books, battledores and primers mostly provided by chapbook peddlars. There was no special literature for the young until the religious books of the mid-seventeenth century – before that children shared what was available for adults. Margaret Spufford and others have demonstrated that there was quite a flourishing cheap print culture, even in rural parts of Britain (which means there must have been poor people who could read) as early as the seventeenth century.[22] And this is where they began:

> A was an Archer, and shot at a Frog;
> B was a Blind-man, and led by a Dog:
>
> Y was a Yeoman, and work'd for his bread;
> Z was Zeno the great, but he's dead.[23]

A nursery library has recently been discovered in Indiana, USA, which Jane Johnson,[24] a middle-class English woman living in Olney between 1737 and 1752, created for her children. Apart from the light this material throws on domestic literacy and its own intrinsic appeal, one of its gems is a delightful 'A was a' which, as far as I have been able to trace, is Jane Johnson's original.

> A was an Alderman, in a fine Gown.
> B was a Barber, that shaved his Crown.
> C was a Cobbler, and liv'd in a Stall.
> D was a Drawer, Pray Sir do you Call?
> E was an Empress, enrobed in black.
> F was a Fox with a Goose at his back.[25]

Some of the social comment is interesting. 'L was a lady whose beauty was frail.' and 'N was a naughty boy in his dish' are predictable. 'P was a Pirate and rob'd on the Seas' shows her understanding of a child's taste for adventure, while 'Q was a Quaker as stiff as you please' is a typically Anglican view of Dissent in the early part of the eighteenth century. 'R was a Robber and dy'd by the Rope' is a grisly reminder of how felons were punished then.

Mother Goose's Melody

The next published collection of note after *Tommy Thumb's Pretty Song-Book* was *Mother Goose's Melody*, 1760. Its author is widely suspected to be the poet Oliver Goldsmith who worked with Newbery at that time and who was known to revel in children's rhymes and games. At any rate, in a rare admission of the key role of women in promoting, if not making, nursery verse for children, its anonymous editor offers these words of wisdom:

> . . . singing these songs and lullabies to children is of great antiquity . . . the custom of making Nonsense Verses in our schools was borrowed from the practice among the old British nurses; they have indeed, been always the first preceptors of the youth of this kingdom, and from them the rudiments of taste and learning are naturally derived. Let none speak irreverently of this ancient maternity . . . as they may be considered as the great grandmothers of science and knowledge . . .[26]

This exquisite anthology is a treasure trove of nursery rhymes from the oral tradition and poems by 'that sweet Songster and Nurse of Wit and Humour, Master William Shakespeare'.[27] (This is the earliest reference to Shakespeare for children that I have come across. It is interesting that Shakespeare should make his debut in children's literature in the genre of nursery rhyme/nonsense.) *Mother Goose's Melody* is full of old, familiar rhymes and maxims, some which have fallen out of usage, with a picture on every page. Two of the rhymes are not well known today, but their tongue-in-cheek perkiness is very appealing.

Then replied the little maid,
Little Sir, you've little said
To induce a little maid for to wed, wed, wed;
You must say a little more,
And produce a little ore,
Ere I make a little print in your bed, bed, bed.
(Verse 2 of 'A Love Song')

Trip upon trenchers,
And dance upon dishes,
My mother sent me for some bawm, bawm, bawm,
She bid me tread lightly,
And come back quickly,
For fear the young men should do me some harm, harm, harm.
Yet didn't you see,
Yet didn't you see,
What naughty tricks they put upon me;
They broke my pitcher,
And spilt my water,
And huff'd my mother,
And chid her daughter,
And kissed my sister instead of me.[28]
('Melancholy Song')

Slightly suggestive rhymes were commonplace in this period, such as the anonymous 'Harry Come Parry' of 1805.

Harry Come Parry, when will you marry?
When apples and pears are ripe.
I'll come to your wedding without any bidding,
And stay with the bride all night.[29]

No one is exactly sure when in the 1770s Newbery published *A Collection of Pretty Poems* 'for the amusement of children three feet high by a Mr Tommy Tagg Esq' which opens with a cheeky address to his readers to whom 'he has nothing to say to those gentlemen, but to his critics he presents his compliments and wishes them a merry Christmas'.[30] These were not what we usually think of as nursery rhymes, rather a mixture of nonsense, moral verse and short, funny poems, such as this one.

> Nature a thousand ways complains,
> A thousand words express her pains:
> But for her laughter has but three,
> And very small ones, ha, ha, he.

Ritsons's *Gammer Gurton's Garland*[31] came out in 1784, dedicated to 'the amusement of all good little children who can neither read nor run'.[32] 'There was an old woman who lived in a shoe', 'Hark, Hark the Dogs do Bark', 'Goosey, Goosey Gander' and 'A diller, a doller' all made an early appearance.

The first decade of the nineteenth century saw a flurry in the publishing of nursery verse. 'Cobbler, Cobbler', 'Little Polly Flinders' and 'Tweedledum and Tweedledee' joined the fray in *Original Ditties for the Nursery*, 1805.[33] Tabart's *Songs for the Nursery*[34] the same year, had the sub-title 'collected from the works of the most renowned poets', but this excellent anthology actually contains mainly rhymes and songs – 'Hush-a-by baby', 'Bye Baby Bunting', 'This Little Pig', 'Ride a Cock Horse' and such like including, what seems to me, a version of Burns's 'Up in the Morning Early', unless it is the original which Burns adapted, as he was, of course, a great collector of Scottish songs.

> Cold and raw the north wind doth blow
> > Bleak in the morning early,
> All the hills are cover'd with snow,
> > And winter's now come fairly.

It also includes a misogynous early version of Solomon Grundy – 'Tom, Tom of Islington' who:

> Married a wife on Sunday,
> Brought her home on Monday,
> Bought a stick on Tuesday,
> Beat her well on Wednesday

and so on.

Pretty Tales for Children[35] 1806, contains 'Little Tom Tucker', 'Hey Diddle Diddle', 'Boys and Girls come out to Play' and 'Sing a Song of Sixpence', as well as at least one song by Shakespeare. It was followed the next year by Tabart's rather insipid and moralistic *Jingles* or *Original Rhymes for Children*[36] and Harris's more interesting *Original Ditties for the Nursery*[37] which were 'so wonderfully contrived that they may be either sung or said by Nurse or Baby'. It has a mixture of nursery rhymes, cautionary tales and moral verse, such as this one.

Come hither, little piggy wiggy, come and learn your letters,
And you shall have a knife and fork to eat with like your betters,
No, no, the little pig replied, my trough will do as well,
I'd rather eat my victuals there, than go and learn to spell.[38]

Old Mother Hubbard and other old Dames

Nursery rhymes exist in different versions with recognizable variations of dialect and form in different parts of Britain, in different languages in other parts of the world and change from one generation to another. Sometimes one particular version may gain prominence and get more or less fixed over time, because a writer creates a definitive version. Sarah Catherine Martin (1768–1826) is such an author, though she goes unmentioned in many guides to children's literature. An early love of William IV, this lively, chatty young woman wrote and illustrated *The Comic Adventures of Old Mother Hubbard and her Dog*[39] in 1805. Published by Harris, Newbery's successor, the book was immediately popular and had sold in its thousands within a few months. There is some controversy over the origins of this early nursery rhyme, but whether or not the character was invented by Sarah Martin does not really matter very much. What *does* matter is that Sarah Martin is recognized as the person who gave us the rhyme as we know it today. Unfortunately, Sarah Martin is just one of several women poets who either composed original rhymes or brought old ones to fruition, yet whose names are not widely known. If the authorship of nursery verse is considered unimportant, some of the rhymes appear to be anonymous when they are not.[40]

The Opies are never casual about attribution and include a detailed publishing history of 'Old Mother Hubbard' in *The Oxford Dictionary of Nursery Rhymes*. They inform us that there are 26 titles under Sarah Martin's name in the British Museum catalogue, so she is a writer who certainly deserves attention and credit for producing one of the first, best-seller nursery rhymes. In fact, it seems quite likely that Sarah Martin based Mother Hubbard very closely on 'Old Dame Trot' by T. Evans published the year before; if so, she deserves full marks for commercial acumen. Certainly, Mother Hubbard was a character well known as early as the the sixteenth century. It is not originality for which Sarah Martin deserves recognition, but for her ability to adapt the rhyme suitably for the juvenile publishing market of her day.

> She went to the hosier's
> To buy him some hose;
> But when she came back
> He was dressed in her clothes.
>
> The dame made a curtsy,
> The dog made a bow;
> The dame said, Your servant,
> The dog said, Bow-wow.[41]

The 13 verses all feature the resourceful canine hero outwitting his indulgent mistress. Sarah Martin had a better sense of fun than the likely precursor of the rhyme. 'Dame Trot' is a duller creation.

> Old Dame Trot,
> Some cold fish had got,
> Which for pussy,
> She kept in Store,
> When she looked there was none
> The cold fish had gone,
> For puss had been there before.[42]

Old Mother Hubbard was preceded by Dame Trot and followed by Old Mother Twitchett, Old Mother Shuttle, Old Mother Niddity Nod, Dame Wiggins of Lee and others. If Sarah Martin is rarely credited with Mother Hubbard, neither is the Mrs Pearson who is thought to have written 'Dame Wiggins Of Lee'[43] in 1823. Ruskin admired this poem and wrote some extra verses which were published in 1885 with Kate Greenaway illustrations. He confessed in the preface 'my rhymes do not ring like the real ones'.[44] Here is a chance for the reader to decide.

> To give them a treat,
> She ran out for some rice;
> When she came back,
> They were skating on ice.
> 'I shall soon see one down,
> Aye, perhaps, two or three.
> I'll bet half-a-crown,'
> Said Dame Wiggins of Lee.
>   (Mrs Pearson, 1823)

> When spring-time came back
> They had breakfast of curds;
> And were greatly afraid
> Of disturbing the birds.
> 'If you sit, like good cats,
> All the seven in a tree,
> They will teach you to sing!'
> Said Dame Wiggins of Lee.
>   (John Ruskin, 1885)

The Scottish song, 'You Canna Kick Your Granny aff a Bus', may have the same parentage and so may the eccentric Old Lady in the works of Edward Lear (though there are many more Old Men and Old Persons).

> There was an Old Lady of France,
> Who taught little Ducklings to dance;
>   When she said, 'Tick-a-tack!'
>   They only said, 'Quack!'
> Which grieved that Old Lady of France.[45]

Rhymes about old women include the one who sat spinning and that's just the beginning; the one whose name was Peg and wore a cork-leg; the one who lived in a shoe and had so many children she didn't know what to do; and the one who had hot pies and cold pies to sell, wherever she goes you may follow the smell! Alice Gomme[46] cites a Yorkshire version of an Old Dame rhyme.

> I'll away to t'beck to wash my neck,
> When I get there, I'll ask t'ould dame what o'clock it is?
> It's one, and you'll be hanged at two.
>
> I'll away to t'beck to wash my neck,
> When I get there, I'll ask t'ould dame what o'clock it is?
> It's two, and you'll be hanged at three.

And so on until it's 11 o'clock and 'you'll be hanged at twelve'! Halliwell's version from another part of the country is less extreme.

> To Beccles; to Beccles!
> To buy a bunch of nettles!
> Pray, Old Dame, whats o'clock?[47]

Mary's Lamb

We don't know who wrote the words of that game, but we do know that the American, Sara Hale (1788–1879) was the author of 'Mary's Lamb' in 1830 which E. V. Lucas described as the best-known four-line verses in the English language. Sara Hale, a widow with five children to support, was editor of the Boston *Lady's Magazine* (1828–1837) and *The Juvenile Miscellany* (1834–1836) and also wrote novels and short stories for children.

> Why does the lamb love Mary so?
>   The eager children cry;
> Why, Mary loves the lamb, you know,
>   The teacher did reply.[48]

I have also come across an anonymous and tamer sequel called *The Mountain Lamb* in a publication of 1894, with the first verse of 'Mary's Lamb' on the cover, which may or may not be by Sara Hale.

> With one knee on the grass
> Did the little maiden kneel,
> While to that mountain lamb
> She gave its evening meal.[49]

'Twinkle Twinkle Little Star'

'The Star' was written by Jane Taylor in 1806 in *Rhymes for the Nursery*[50] although it is credited as 'Nursery Rhymes' in an anthology called *Easy Rhymes and Simple Poems*,[51] 1864. In a later anthology, *Poems Every Child Should* Know,[52] 100 years after it was written, 'The Star' had become 'anonymous'. It is rather like a nursery rhyme in its well-honed simplicity and remains a nursery classic. The whole poem is worth scutiny (not just the familiar first verse), as I believe it to be a landmark in poetry for children.

> Twinkle, twinkle, little star,
> How I wonder what you are!
> Up above the world so high,
> Like a diamond in the sky.
>
> When the blazing sun is gone,
> When he nothing shines upon,
> Then you show your little light,
> Twinkle, twinkle, all the night.
>
> Then the traveller in the dark,
> Thanks you for the tiny spark!
> He could not see which way to go,
> If you did not twinkle so.
>
> In the dark blue sky you keep,
> And often through my curtains peep,
> For you never shut your eye
> Till the sun is in the sky.
>
> As your bright and tiny spark
> Lights the traveller in the dark,
> Though I know not what you are,
> Twinkle, twinkle, little star.[53]

This is a flawless piece of nursery verse. There isn't a spare word in this poem which rings like a bell. Such a simple idea to explore (as Stevenson did 80 years later in 'Escape at Bedtime') the wonder of the night sky by focusing on a single star helping travellers find their way in the dark. The poem works through a harmonious balance of repetition and contrast – night and day, sun and stars, dark and light, wonder/know not 'what you are' (verses 1 and 5) . . . and through child-centred imagery – 'little star', 'tiny spark', 'diamond/sky'. It also contains appealing details like the star peeping through the curtains; the lonely traveller on the darkened road relieved to find a glimmer of light; the glittering jewel in the black sky; the star keeping its eye open till the sun comes up. Jane Taylor leaves the young reader *wondering*: 'I know not what you are'.

John Goldthwaite castigates the Taylor sisters for taking Mother Goose out of the chapbook and making her over:

> . . . into the classic, quaint old bird in a bonnet that we all know, surrounded by milkmaids and dimpled tots in a generically lovely, preindustrial land of make-believe.[54]

He really cannot lay the blame on the Taylors for the sentamentalizing of Mother Goose which happened during the Victorian period. What he fails to recognize is that he is discussing two quite separate traditions: the nursery rhyme which elsewhere he admits comes 'out of apparent chaos'[55] from the disorderly, casual, robust world of the oral tradition; and poetry consciously composed with children in mind by writers who wish to communicate with young readers. Both traditions should be valued for the different things they offer.

Lost from the nursery

The world deserved to know that 'The Star' was written by a modest young woman who lived quietly and industriously in Lavenham, Suffolk, doing most of her writing for children in the first decade of the nineteenth century. Yet it is still uncredited in *A Puffin Book of Hymns*[56] published in 1992. The same fate befell whichever Taylor sister wrote 'The Baby's Dance' which Halliwell fails to credit in *Nursery Rhymes of England*, published in 1842. It took only 36 years for this poem to become anonymous, even for a scholarly collector of the oral tradition and while Ann Taylor was still alive! Sara Coleridge's best poem, 'The Months of the Year', was described as 'an old song' in *Poems Every Child Should Know* and 'an old rhyme' in *A Book of Verses for Children*, 1897. The latter was edited by E. V. Lucas who was very knowledgeable about children's poetry and should, perhaps, have known better, but it is again the quality of the poem which makes it seem like something from the oral tradition. In *Poetry For The Young*, 1883, Charlotte Smith's exquisite 'To The Ladybird', published in her sister, Catherine Dorset's *The Peacock at Home*, 1807, is also uncredited. 'The

Ladybird' rhyme has a longer derivation, but it was Charlotte Smith who polished it to perfection.

> Oh! Lady-bird, Lady-bird, why dost thou roam
> So far from thy comrades, so distant from home?
> Why dost thou, who canst revel all day in the air,
> Who the sweets of the grove and the garden canst share;
> In a fold of a leaf, who canst form thee a bower,
> And a palace enjoy in the tube of a flower;
> Ah, why, simple Lady-bird, why dost thou venture,
> The dwellings of man so familiar to enter?[57]

Few are aware today that it was Mary Howitt who penned the ever popular 'The Spider and the Fly' in 1834 in a book called *Sketches from Natural History*. It appears to be completely original.

> 'Will you walk into my parlour' said the Spider to the Fly,
> 'Tis the prettiest little parlour that ever did you spy;
> The way into my parlour is up a winding stair,
> And I have many curious things to shew when you are there.'
> . . .
> With buzzing wings she hung aloft, then near and nearer drew,
> Thinking only of her brilliant eyes, and green and purple hue -
> Thinking only of her crested head – poor foolish thing! At last,
> Up jumped the cunning Spider, and fiercely held her fast.
> He dragged her up his winding stair, into his dismal den,
> Within his little parlour – but she ne'er came out again![58]

In the same period, the American Eliza Follen produced another winner, 'The Three Little Kittens' in a collection entitled, *Little Songs for Little Boys and Girls*.

> Three little kittens lost their mittens;
>   And they began to cry,
>   'Oh, mother dear,
>   We very much fear
>   That we have lost our mittens.'
>   'Lost your mittens!
>   You naughty kittens!
>   Then you shall have no pie!'
>   'Mee-ow, mee-ow, mee-ow.'
>   'No, you shall have no pie.'[59]

I could cite many more examples. These poems did not get 'lost from the nursery'[60] by any deliberate or malicious intention. In an age of casual attribution, such losses inevitably occur. Some might argue that it is a compliment that the poems seem worthy of 'nursery rhyme' status. The other side of that argument is that poems credited to the oral tradition mean invisibility for their authors who were often likely to be less privileged people including, of course, women.

Victorian nursery verse

Nursery rhymes were a well-established feature of middle-class childhood culture by the Victorian period, though there were still voices raised in opprobrium against all kinds of fantasy for some time to come. Christina Rossetti, whose sub-title for *Sing-Song*, 1872, is a *Nursery Rhyme Book*, is considered in detail in Chapter 7. This was the period when nursery rhymes merged into nursery verse.

Three poets, more or less contemporary with Rossetti, who wrote popular nursery verse were William Allingham (1824–1889), Aunt Effie (1811–1898) and William Brighty Rands (1823–1882). Aunt Effie, pseudonym of Jane Euphemia Browne, daughter of a well-to-do landowner in Cumberland, wrote books of verse such as *Aunt Effie's Rhymes for Little Children*, 1852, and *Aunt Effie's Gift for the Nursery*, 1854, which were much loved at the time. 'A Cobweb Made to Order' is typical of her poetry; so is 'The Turtle Dove's Nest'. Although I now find the latter nauseatingly twee, I remember singing it lustily as a little girl!

> A hungry spider made a web,
>   Of thread so very fine,
> Your tiny fingers scarce could feel
>   The little slender line.
>   Round-about, and round-about,
>   And round-about it spun,
> Straight across and back again,
>   Until the web was done.
>   ('A Cobweb Made to Order')

> Very high in the pine-tree,
>   The little Turtle-dove
> Made a pretty little nursery
>   To please her little love.

> She was gentle, she was soft,
>   And her large dark eye
> Often turned to her mate,
>   Who was sitting close by.
>   ('The Turtle Dove's Nest')[61]

William Allingham was an Anglo-Irish poet who published *The Fairies* in 1850, *In Fairyland* in 1870 and *Rhymes for the Young Folk* in 1887. He spent most of his working life as a government customs officer, writing his poems in his spare time, friendly with many in the Pre-Raphaelite circle. The Opies point out that the poem which follows is based on an old Highland ditty adapted as a Jacobite song.

> Tis up the rocky mountain and down the mossy glen,
> We darena gang a milking for Charlie and his men.[62]

became

> Up the airy mountain,
>   Down the rushy glen,
> We daren't go a-hunting
>   For fear of little men;
> Wee folk, good folk,
>   Trooping all together;
> Green jacket, red cap,
>   And white owl's feather.[63]

William Brighty Rands, a parliamentary reporter, was the author of *Lilliput Levee*, 1864, and *Lilliput Lyrics*, as well as often contributing to magazines like *Good Words for the Young*. The poems range from near doggerel to amusing verse for young children. *The Dictionary of National Biography* describes his private life as 'somewhat irregular' and there are certainly too many references to kissing pretty little girls for this author's taste. But he had a good nose for the ridiculous.

> If the butterfly courted the bee,
> And the owl the porcupine;
> If churches were built in the sea,
> And three times one was nine;
>
> If the pony rode his master;
> If the buttercups ate the cows;
> If the cat had the dire disaster
> To be worried, sir, by the mouse.[64]

Olive Wadsworth's 'Over in the Meadow' was included in John Greenleaf Whittier's fine anthology, *Child Life*[65] of 1874; it has frequently been collected for children ever since and was issued in picture book form a few years ago.

> Over in the meadow,
>   In the sand, in the sun,
> Lived an old mother-toad
>   And her little toadie one.
>
> 'Wink!' said the mother;
>   'I wink', said the one;
> So she winked and she blinked
>   In the sand, in the sun.

Whittier was popular in his native USA in the second half of the nineteenth century and his poems were standard fare in schools. Lucy Larcom (1824–1893) collaborated on some of Whittier's anthologies and was editor of *Our Young Forest Folks* in her own right. 'In the Tree-Top' appears in her collection, *Childhood Songs*.

> 'Rock-a-by, baby, up in the tree-top!'
> Mother his blanket is spinning;
> And a light little rustle that never will stop,
> Breezes and boughs are beginning.
> Rock-a-by, baby, swinging so high!
> Rock-a-by![66]

The Scottish writer, George MacDonald (1842–1905) also featured in *Child Life*. He is much better known for his fiction (which often included verse) especially *At the Back of the North Wind*. MacDonald was friendly with Lewis Carroll and was instrumental in urging him to publish *Alice in Wonderland*. Here is a taste of 'Little White Lily'[67] which is pitched at very young children.

> Little white Lily
> Sat by a stone,
> Drooping and waiting
> Till the sun shone.
> Little white Lily
> Sunshine has fed;
> Little white Lily
> Is lifting her head.

'There are fairies at the bottom of the garden'

By the late Victorian period nursery verse got mixed up with cloyingly sweet fairy poems for children. This trend continued into the early decades of this century and

Rose Fyleman (1877–1957) was the best-known author of this unappetizing verse which was extremely popular in its day. Her many fairy books include *Fairies and Chimneys,* 1918, and *The Fairy Flute*, 1921. Fyleman has her champions, but her verse is too coy and sickly for many.

> There are fairies at the bottom of our garden!
>   It's not so very, very far away;
> You pass the gardener's shed and you just keep straight ahead –
>   I do so hope they've really come to stay.[68]

Writing in a similar vein, but a much better poet was the Chicago literary columnist, Eugene Field (1850–1895), who produced some very popular nursery nonsense, including *With Trumpet and Drum*, 1892, and *Love Songs of Childhood*, 1896.

> Wynken, Blynken, and Nod one night,
>   Sailed off in a wooden shoe –
> Sailed on a river of crystal light,
>   Into a sea of dew.
>
> 'Where are you going, and what do you wish?'
>   The old moon asked the three.
> 'We have come to fish for the herring fish
>   That live in this beautiful sea;'[69]

Newer nurseries

A recent trend is the playful reworking of nursery rhymes and fairy tales into updated versions made into picture books, stories, animations and other media texts. Of course, such parodies only work because the original rhymes are known and loved. In terms of poetry, Roald Dahl produced his *Revolting Rhymes* in 1982 and Michael Rosen published *Hairy Tales and Nursery Crimes* in 1985. Rosen gives a contemporary flavour to 'This Little Piggie' by making the protagonist wet his pants, guaranteeing to bring the house down in infant classrooms!

> This little pig went to market,
> This little pig ate some ants,
> This little pig went to Sainsbury's
> This little pig went up in a lift,
> And this little pig
> Went wee wee wee wee wee wee,
> Oh no, I've wet my pants.[70]

Staying with 'This Little Piggy', let's have a look at some recent versions. Louise Bennett, the distinguished Jamaican poet, edited a version of 'Maddah Goose', which includes the aforesaid young porker. As well as transforming the English characteristics to Jamaican culture (roast beef to curried goat, for example), it demonstrates the appeal of Creole as a language. Who can resist the holler of that poor little pig squealing 'Wahi, wahi, wahi, wahi / All de way a im yaad.'

> Dis lickle pig go a markit,
> Dis lickle pig tan a yaad,
> Dis lickle pig nyam curry goat,
> Dis lickle pig got nun,
> Dis lickle pig holla, 'Wahi, wahi, wahi'
>   All de way a im yaad.[71]

'The Tale of a Bold Piglet' celebrates dialect closer to home – Somerset in this instance.

> There was a liddle piglet, he wadn't very old
> He runned away from whoame, he did, he was so very bold.[72]

On a recent visit to Waterstone's Bookshop in Newcastle, visiting children collaborated to give the old rhyme a local twist *and* played inventively with the 'wee, wee, wee' of the final line after hearing the other versions.

> This little piggy went to Newcastle,
> And this little piggy went to France,
> This little piggy got giggly,
> And this little pig did a dance,
> And this little piggy went oui oui oui oui oui
>   all the way to Paris![73]

The original rhyme provides a 'coathanger' for new wit and experimentation. Nursery rhymes are truly multilayered with dual appeal to young and old alike. Modern and contrived these new versions may be, but their roots are in the oral tradition.

'Monday's child is fair of face' will be familiar to many readers, but perhaps not Colin McNaughton's sassy version. You have to read it alongside the author's capricious and engaging illustrations to get the full impact.

> Monday's child is red and spotty,
> Tuesday's child won't use the potty.
> Wednesday's child won't go to bed,

Thursday's child will not be fed.
Friday's child breaks all his toys,
Saturday's child makes an awful noise,
And the child that's born on the seventh day
Is a pain in the neck like the rest, OK![74]

The Canadian poet, Dennis Lee wrote some original nursery rhymes in 1983 in *Jelly Belly* which includes another version of 'Old Mother Hubbard'.

The fridge was soon bulging,
    And so was the shelf.
So she sent for a hot dog
    And ate it herself.[75]

By the 1980s the Caribbean writers who were either born in Britain or who came here to live had began to make an impact on publishing for children in fiction and poetry. Among the interesting things about Caribbean poetry are its links with the oral tradition and its inclusion of nursery rhymes. For example, *When I Dance* by James Berry has a vibrant section of Jamaican proverbs, riddles and songs, and John Agard's second collection for children featured Guyanese proverbs such as this one:

Suppose today
you're feeling down
your face propping a frown.

Suppose today
you're one streak of a shadow
the sky giving you a headache.

Tomorrow
you never know
you might wake up
in the peak of a glow.

If you don't get the rain
how can you get the rainbow?

Say it again, Granny,
No rain, no rainbow.

Say it again, Granny,
No rain, no rainbow.[76]

No Hickory No Dickory No Dock, edited by John Agard and Grace Nichols is a mixture of original nursery rhymes, variations on the old, like the title poem, and traditional Guyanese verse like 'Pussy in de Moonlight'.

> Pussy in de moonlight
> Pussy in de zoo
> Pussy never come home
> Till half past two.[77]

Nursery rhymes from other cultures

Forms of nursery rhymes, musical poems and chants to please or appease small children are universal. Christian Morgenstern (1871–1914), a poet and journalist who lived in Munich, wrote a book of *Kindergedichte und Galgenlieder*, lullabies, lyrics and gallows songs which has recently been reissued in Britain. His *Kindergedichte* have many connections with English nursery rhymes. In this poem a snail talks to himself:

> Might as well be out of my shell,
> Out of my shell might not be as well?
> Little way out?
> Howabout
> inandout
> roundabout
> woundabout
> layabouthereabout
> whereabout thereabout . . .[78]

Here are two examples from farther afield – Native American nonsense and an early Japanese lullaby; both feature little rabbits. It is a tiny dip into a huge pool of fascinating verse for very young children, so varied and yet with so much in common with English nursery rhymes. No doubt much is lost in translation, but you can still see the appeal in the first for its simple, repetitive language and the lovely nonsense word 'leggies'.

> Baby swimming down the river,
> Driftwood leggies, rabbit leggies,
>   Little rabbit leggies.[79]

In the next, the image of the sleepy baby with long ears is most appealing. It is common to call babies 'rabbits' as a term of endearment in late twentieth-century Britain and comforting to think that cultures as wide apart as Native America and early Japan do the same.

Sleep, little one, sleep.
Why are his ears so long?
Baby rabbit of Sleepy Hill.
When his mother carried him
She ate acorns, mulberries.
That is why his ears
have grown so very long.[80]

One of the most delightful examples of nursery verse to be produced in the last few years is a new edition of *I Saw Esau: the Schoolchild's Pocket Book*, illustrated with brilliant virtuosity by Maurice Sendak.

Oh, the grey cat piddled in the white cat's eye,
The white cat said, Cor Blimey!
'I'm sorry, Sir, I piddled in your eye,
I didn't know you was behind me.'[81]

Originally published in 1947, this collection of the oral tradition of childhood was the first offspring of the partnership between Iona and Peter Opie and a lively one it was too. Iona Opie writes that these were the rhymes with 'oomph and zoom', that they:

. . . pack a punch . . . a stinging reply when verbally attacked; the need for comic complaints in the face of persecution or the grinding drudgery of school work . . . a declaration of a child's brave defiance in the face of daunting odds.[82]

It seems fitting to close this chapter with children's voices and playground rhymes ringing in our ears. Not only does it remind us of the vibrancy of vernacular language and children's defiance of adult rules and strictures, but it also gives the last word to the young who are the real guardians of nursery rhymes.

Tommy Johnson is no good,
Chop him up for firewood;
When he's dead, boil his head,
Make it into gingerbread.

*   *   *

Donkey walks on four legs
    And I walk on two;
The last one I saw
    Was very like you.[83]

Notes

1   Michael Rosen, 'Old Mother Hubbard', *Hairy Tales and Nursery Crimes*, Andre Deutsch, London, 1985.

2   Iona and Peter Opie, *The Oxford Dictionary of Nursery Rhymes*, Oxford, 1951, p. 1.

3   Iona and Peter Opie, *Three Centuries of Nursery Rhymes and Poetry*, Introduction, Oxford, 1977, p. xiv.

4   John Goldthwaite, *The Natural History of Make-Believe*, Oxford, 1996, p. 15.

5   *Ibid.*, p. 14.

6   J. O. Halliwell, *The Nursery Rhymes of England*, London, 1842, p. vii.

7   Emile Cammaerts, *The Poetry of Nonsense*, Routledge, London, 1926, p. 37.

8   Robert Graves, quoted in Opie, 1951, *op. cit.*, p. 2.

9   Goldthwaite, *op. cit.*, p. 14.

10 F.J. Harvey Darton, *Children's Books in England*, Cambridge, 1932/82, pp. 99–100.

11 Darton, *ibid.*

12 Goldthwaite, *op. cit.*, pp. 23, 24.

13 Sir Walter Scott, quoted in J.R. Halliwell's *Popular Rhymes and Nursery Tales*, London, 1849, p. ix.

14 J. Halliwell, *op. cit.*, 1842, p. vi.

15 Nicholas Tucker, *Why Nursery Rhymes?* in Virginia Haviland, ed. *Children and Literature: Views and Reviews*, Bodley Head, London, 1973, p. 258.

16 Iona and Peter Opie, *The Oxford Nursery Rhyme Book*, London, 1955, p. 5.

17 John Locke, *Some Thoughts Concerning Education*, London, 1693, this edition John and Jean Yolton, eds, Clarendon Press, Oxford, p. 212.

18 Halliwell, 'The King of France', *op. cit.*, p. 9.

19 *Tommy Thumb's Pretty Song Book*, Newbery, London, 1744.

20 *A Little Pretty Pocket Book*, Newbery, London, 1744.

21 *A Little Book for Little Children*, 1712, though exact date uncertain.

22 Margaret Spufford, *Small Books and Pleasant Histories*, Cambridge, 1981.

23 From *A Was an Archer*, London, 1703.

24 Jane Johnson lived in England, 1706–59; she was a well-to-do vicar's wife living mostly in Olney and Lincolnshire. Her nursery library, poems, letters and stories, mostly composed for her children, have recently come to light, showing one woman's writing in the private domain. *A Very Pretty Story to Tell Children* was written in the same year as *A Little Pretty Pocket Book*, 1744, widely regarded as the first piece of pure children's literature to be published. The nursery library is housed in the Lilly Library, University of Indiana. *A Very Pretty Story* is housed at the Bodleian Library, Oxford.

25 Jane Johnson, unpublished manuscript, now in Bodleian Library.

26 *Mother Goose's Melody*, Preface, Marshall, London, 1760.

27 *Ibid.*

28 From 'A Love Song' and 'Melancholy Song', *ibid.*

29 From 'Harry Come Parry', *Songs for the Nursery collected from the Works of the Most Renowned Poets*, Tabart, London, 1805.

30 *A Collection of Pretty Poems*, Newbery, London, 177? exact date uncertain.

31 *Gammer Gurton's Garland*, London, 1784.

32 Joseph Ritson quoted in Goldthwaite, *op. cit.*, p. 24.

33 *Original Ditties for the Nursery*, Harris, London, 1805.

34 From 'Old and New' and 'Tom, Tom of Islington', *Songs for the Nursery*, Tabart, London, 1805.

35 *Pretty Tales for Children*, London, 1806.

36 *Original Rhymes for Children*, Tabart, London, 1807.

37 From 'Little Piggy Wiggy', *Original Ditties for the Nursery*, Harris, London, 1807.

38 *Ibid.*

39 Sarah Catherine Martin, *The Comic Adventures of Old Mother Hubbard and her Dog*, Harris, London, 1805.

40 For a fuller account, see Morag Styles, *Lost from the Nursery: Women writing poetry for children*, 1800–1850, Signal 63, pp. 177–205.

41 From 'The Comic Adventures of Old Mother Hubbard and her Dog', Martin, *op. cit.*

42 From 'Old Dame Trot', Opie, 1951, *op. cit.*

43 Mrs Pearson, from *Dame Wiggins of Lee*, London, 1823.

44 John Ruskin, from *Dame Wiggins of Lee*, London, 1885.

45 Edward Lear, from *The Book of Nonsense*, 1846 in *Complete Nonsense*, Wordsworth Classics, London, 1994.

46 Alice Gomme, *The Traditional Games of England, Scotland and Ireland*, orig. 1894–98, Thames and Hudson, London, 1984.

47 Halliwell, *op. cit.*, p. 120.

48 Sara Hale, from *Mary's Lamb*, Boston, 1894.

49 From *The Mountain Lamb*, Boston, 1894.

50 Ann and Jane Taylor, *Rhymes for the Nursery*, Darton, London, 1806.

51 *Easy Rhymes and Simple Poems*, London, 1864.

52 *Poems Every Child Should Know*, ed Mary Burt, London, 1904.

53 'The Star', Jane Taylor, 1806, *op. cit.*

54 Goldthwaite, *op. cit.*, p. 25.

55 *Ibid.*, p. 15.

56 Chris Meade, ed. *A Puffin Book of Hymns*, Penguin, London, 1992.

57 Charlotte Smith, from 'Ladybird, Ladybird', in Catherine Ann Dorset, *The Peacock at Home*, Harris, London, 1807.

58 Mary Howitt, from 'The Spider and the Fly', *Sketches from Natural History*, London, 1834.

59 Eliza Follen, from 'The Three Little Kittens', *Little Songs for Little Boys and Girls*, London, 1832.

60 Morag Styles, *op. cit.*

61 Jane E. Browne, from 'A Cobweb made to Order' and 'The Turtle Dove's Nest', *Aunt Effie's Rhymes for Little Children*, Addey and Co., London, 1852.

62 An old Jacobite song quoted in Iona and Peter Opie, eds *The Oxford Book of Children's Verse*, p. 254.

63 William Allingham, from 'The Fairies', *Rhymes for the Young Folk*, Cassell, London, 1887.

64 William Brighty Rands, from 'Topsy-Turvy World' in *Child Life*, ed. John Greenleaf Whittier, Nisbet & Co., London, 1874, p. 146.

65 Olive Wadsworth, from 'Over in the Meadow', *ibid.*

66 Lucy Larcom, from 'In the Tree-Top', quoted in Donald Hall, *The Oxford Book of Children's Verse in America*, New York, 1985.

67 George MacDonald, from 'Little White Lily', in *Child Life*, ed. John Greenleaf Whittier, *op. cit.*

68 Rose Fyleman, from 'Fairies', *Fairies and Chimneys*, London, 1918.

69 Eugene Field, this version from *Wynken, Blynken, and Nod*, Hodder, London, 1912.

70   Michael Rosen, 'This Little Pig', 1985, *op. cit.*

71   Louise Bennett, ed. *Jamaica Maddah Goose*, Jamaica School of Art, Kingston, 1981.

72   'The Tale of a Bold Piglet', traditional.

73   A class of children from a Newcastle primary school ages 9–10 made up this poem with me. All the ideas were theirs.

74   Colin McNaughton, 'Monday's Child is Red and Spotty': *There's an awful lot of Weirdos in Our Neighbourhood*, Walker Books, London, 1987.

75   Dennis Lee, from 'Old Mother Hubbard', *Jelly Belly*, Blackie, London, 1983.

76   John Agard, 'No Rain, No Rainbow', *Say It Again, Granny*, Bodley Head, London, 1986.

77   John Agard and Grace Nichols, 'Pussy in de Moonlight', *No Hickory, No Dickory, No Dock*.

78   Christian Morgenstern, from 'A Snail Talks to Itself', *Lullabies, Lyrics and Gallows Songs*, translated Anthea Bell, selected Lisbeth Zwerger, North-South Books, New York, 1995, originally 1922.

79   An example of the Native American oral tradition translated N. Curtis, *The Indians Book*, Harper and Row, 1950.

80   Traditional Japan, translated by G. Bownas and A. Thwaite, eds, *The Penguin Book of Japanese Verse*, Penguin, Harmondsworth, 1963.

81   Iona and Peter Opie, I *Saw Esau: the Schoolchild's Pocket Book*, Walker Books, London, 1992.

82   *Ibid.*

83   *Ibid.*

CHAPTER 5

The Capacity to Amuse

The history of humour in poetry for children

And always keep a-hold of nurse
For fear of finding something worse.[1]

In *The Oxford Book of Comic Verse*, John Gross suggests that:

> . . . comic verse is verse that is designed to amuse – and perhaps that is as far as any attempt at a definition ought to go . . . it's the realm of the casual and informal, the quirky and the miscellaneous.[2]

Gross is probably right, but I will make some attempt to analyse comic poetry in this chapter just the same. Of all the genres it is, perhaps, through humour that the greatest continuity with the past is apparent. Of course, there have been many changes over the centuries in what is considered amusing for a young audience, particularly in terms of taste. It is now possible in poetry to joke about just about anything; and cheeky children enjoying themselves at the expense of adults is commonplace; so is using language which would once have been considered slang. Here is a typical snatch of contemporary comic verse from Brian Patten, circa 1985:

> You can slip on it in the dark,
> And spread it on bread for a lark.
> Snot! Snot! Green slimy snot!
> I like it a lot![3]

This would have horrified many writers and readers after the Second World War, let alone those who lived two centuries ago. Patten's humour bypasses most adults, and many commentators suggest that he panders to what is perceived to be the worst aspects of childhood culture in poetry like this. They know children enjoy sniggering over such things, but it doesn't do to encourage them, does it? In fact, Patten was simply putting into verse what Roald Dahl had been doing so successfully in his fiction – tapping into what most adults consider the muckier recesses of children's humour. In both cases the authors are talented at what they do and this sort of writing is only one facet of their work.

Inevitably, there are weaker bards with little wit or craft who latch on to anything that makes children laugh. There is quite a surfeit of this undistinguished verse at the moment, but it is harmless and will fall by the wayside in the fullness of time. And adults have to remember, whether they like it or not, that children have a great appetite for vulgarity, as Iona Opie demonstrates so tellingly in *The People in the Playground*.[4] Can we ignore the relish with which it is greeted by children who go on to read more conventional comic verse from Patten's pen and other humorists? Surely it is incumbent on those interested in children's literature to understand the appeal rather than tut-tut from the sidelines. We will return to this debate.

But some things about comic verse have not changed much over time, as it has always existed to some extent as a genre in its own right with a life outside of mainstream poetry. Contemporary cautionary verse, for example, is little different from Hilaire Belloc at the turn of the century. And if you read one of Thomas Hood's witty poems without knowing his dates (1799–1845), you might imagine it was written yesterday.

> Ben Battle was a soldier bold
> And used to war's alarms
> A cannon ball shot off his legs
> So he laid down his arms![5]

The nature of comic verse

There are so many different ways that humour works and it is tantalizingly hard to pin it down. It might be worth distinguishing between verse that is simply lighthearted, and serious poetry with a touch of the comic in it – the difference, if you like, between tickling and horseplay. Some poets are known mainly for their comedy, Edward Lear, Lewis Carroll (who are considered in detail in Chapter 6), Spike Milligan, Colin McNaughton, to take but four; others use a bit of fun, now and again. Most contemporary poets for children choose to write in a humorous vein, some of the time at least. Many of their earlier counterparts did so too, though not as much and not as regularly as today. But the connnection between poetry for the young and the desire to make them laugh is long established.

There is not much difference between comic verse for adults and children except in reference to things a younger audience do not (or should not!) understand, like sexual explicitness. Some branches are less appropriate for the young: satirical verse, for example, because it presupposes a sophistication of reading and life that children do not have access to.

Comic poetry of any age includes subversive verse and that which seeks to poke fun at the po-faced, prudish, pedantic and prejudiced of a particular society. As for the humorists themselves, there does seem to be a link in quite a few between depression and comedy; indeed, there can be a dark side to comic verse. Sometimes humour in poetry can be used to say something deadly serious.

Humorous verse ranges from what is mildly amusing, raising a smile, to the witty but savage message which carries a punch; from side-splitting hilarity, to cleverness with words; from rude and risky language to unconventional, anti-establishment points of view; from an essentially funny story in verse to an amusing description of a person, place or situation. Some humour works through the sparkling use of language; some relates to forms, like limericks; some to the choice of subject matter. Regular features of comic verse include:

- playful language – puns, nonsense words;
- incongruities and surprises;
- comic people and situations;
- flouting conventions;
- confusions – upside-downness;
- exaggeration;
- oddity – the reversal of the expected;
- absurd premises combined with logical conclusions;
- burlesque and slapstick;
- parody.

Parody

As long as there has been printed text, parody has flourished. The desire to make fun of someone else's writing seems instinctive and is often based on affection for the original. The wicked Thomas Hood, for example, could not resist sending up one of Ann Taylor's most popular children's poems, 'My Mother'.[6] Here is an extract from Hood's 'A Lay of Real Life'[7] plus the original which he makes sport with. The sentimentality of the first makes the callousness of the second even funnier. Hood amuses young and old alike by being facetious about a very serious subject – mother love. The gin-sodden slattern is safely remote from middle-class readers' experience and Hood takes the joke further by reversing expectations when he relies, not on his mother, but himself at the end of the poem. The fact that he keeps tightly to the metre and rhyme-scheme of the original adds to the satisfaction.

> Who fed me from her gentle breast,
> And hushed me in her arms to rest,
> And on my cheek sweet kisses prest?
>   My Mother.

> When pain and sickness made me cry,
> Who gazed upon my heavy eye,
> And wept for fear that I would die?
>   My Mother.
>   (Taylor)

> Who let me starve, to buy her gin,
> Till all my bones came through my skin,
> Then called me 'ugly little sin'?
>   My Mother.
>   . . .
> Through all this weary world in brief,
> Who ever sympathised with grief,
> Or shared my joy – my sole relief?
>   Myself.
>   (Hood)

Some of the best-loved parodies are by Lewis Carroll in the Alice books. He, too, makes fun of a Taylor,[8] creating as he does so one of the most unlikely and amusing similes ever written.

> Twinkle, twinkle little star,
> How I wonder what you are!
> Up above the world so high,
> Like a diamond in the sky.
>   (Taylor)

> Twinkle twinkle little bat,
> How I wonder what you're at.
> Up above the world so high
> Like a tea-tray in the sky![9]
>   (Carroll)

Crossing cultures

As well as comic verse being timeless, it crosses cultures in many respects too. What we now call nursery rhymes and cradle songs are found in virtually every part of the world; the instinct to make others laugh in verse (it might be free verse) is similarly all-pervasive. In an African rhyme from the oral tradition, in the first of the examples which follow, the humour is conveyed through insults which are contradictory, because the person is described as being pathetically thin and enormously fat at the same time! The language is bold and crude ('backside', 'belly') and the analogies are witty.

> You!
> Your hands are like drum-sticks.
> You!
> Your belly is like a pot of bad water.
> You!
> Your legs are like wooden posts.
> You!
> Your backside is like a mountain-top.[10]

In the second extract from 'Me Memba Wen' by Frederick Williams[11] from Jamaica, the fun comes partly from the vivid use of the vernacular and partly from the amusing account of the kind of japes children everywhere seem to get up to.

> We a look after de bees, so we tek out
> Som honey fe eat,
> One a dem bwoy no mek sure im
> Smoke off all de bees,
> Im bite de honey comb wid bees pon da
> De bees bite im ina in mout
> Im bawl out WOH, WOH, mi mout, mi mout
> An spit out de whole a it.

The last example is from China and uses humour in a different way – the art of understatement through the languid comment of a detached observer. The powerful creature who can kill anything he likes is smirked at by the small and weak in his hour of difficulty. We have laughed at things like that since Aesop first penned his fables.

> A dragon stranded in shallow water
> furnishes amusement for the shrimps.[12]

Contemporary comic verse is often aided by illustration: this is not new, as many humorists of the past such as Lear and Carroll illustrated their own work or had outstanding artists like Tenniel to do it for them. Nowadays, most publishers would consider illustrations to be essential in a book of funny verse for children. As Quentin Blake,[13] one of the best current comic illustrators, tells us: 'there seems to be some natural affinity between nonsense in words and nonsense in pictures'. And Albert Uderzo,[14] one of the creators of the Asterix stories famous for their visual and verbal wit, says this: 'I think humour is universal, anyway. It doesn't need to be too intellectual or too simple, it's just got to be good. In the end, either it's funny or it isn't. There are no other rules.'

In this chapter I want both to look out for continuities with the past and to examine some of the changes in the history of comic poetry for children. The two main branches of humorous poetry are considered in some detail – nonsense and cautionary verse – and I conclude with some recent humorists in verse. Lewis Carroll and Edward Lear feature in Chapter 6.

Nonsense verse

Quentin Blake:[15]

> There is one respect in which nonsense poetry isn't the least bit crazy: it is the way the poems are made. The rhymes, the metre, the verse-forms are just as regular as, and in many cases identical with, those of more serious poems. Indeed, it's the fact that nonsense poems preserve this decorum that makes them so effective.

In *The Poetry of Nonsense*, Emile Cammaerts[16] states that:

> . . . its impression [nonsense poetry] is produced not by ignoring the general laws of good poetry, but by upsetting them purposefully and by making them, so to speak, stand on their heads . . . there must be perfect harmony between the matter and the form . . . nonsense is practically the only type of poetry which remains in touch with the great mass of people . . . it is first of all the best way, almost the only way, by which we are able to evoke the spirit of the nursery . . . and to enjoy its careless irresponsibility . . .

Edward Strachey,[17] in an introduction to the 1894 edition of Lear's poetry, tried to define nonsense: [it] 'sets itself to discover and bring forward the incongruities of all things within us and without us . . . through its contradictions'. Elsewhere he spoke of nonsense as a true work of the imagination and not as 'a commonplace negative of Sense, not a mere putting forward of incongruities and absurdities, but the bringing out a new and deeper harmony of life in and through its contradictions'.[18]

In *The Natural History of Make-Believe*, one of the most refreshing appraisals of children's literature of the late twentieth century, John Goldthwaite describes nonsense as 'a flirtation with disorder, a turning upside down of the world for the pleasure of seeing it come right up again'.[19]

Goldthwaite, Blake, Strachey and Cammaerts are separated by 100 years, but they are all agreed that nonsense poetry follows rules; they are just a little different from those of serious poetry. They also cite its universality and its wide audience as one of the reasons for its enduring appeal. There has always been plenty of nonsense in the oral tradition – nursery rhymes (which are considered in Chapter 4), riddles, sayings, ballads . . . and the chapbooks provided plenty of printed examples. Shakespeare, of course, had a leaning towards nonsense, particularly evident in some of his songs, many of which have been chosen for children's anthologies, such as this one:

> When that I was and a little tiny boy,
>   With hey, ho, the wind and the rain;
> A foolish thing was but a toy,
>   For the rain it raineth every day.[20]

It goes without saying that some of the best-known, loved and memorable examples of nonsense have already been presented in the previous chapter which chronicled the history of nursery rhymes. John Goldthwaite writes of Polly, Tom, Jack, Jill, Willie and all the others: 'This is our family album. These are the gathered citizens whose names and follies we have passed along over the years like items of backyard gossip . . . It is Mother Goose who first introduces us to who we are in the world, and, it is she who brings us our first make-believe.'[21]

Hood's own

Before Lear and Carroll, there are no particular nonsense poets of note except for Thomas Hood (1799–1845) whom Auden includes in his book of *Nineteenth Century Minor Poets*, although he says that he personally considers Hood: 'a major poet . . . when he is writing as a comic poet he is like nobody but himself and serious in the true sense of the word'.[22]

Indeed, Hood's range as a poet was wide – he was deeply influenced by Keats and *Lyrical Ballads*, but it was as a comic writer that he excelled. Beginning life as an engraver in London (like Blake before him) Hood eventually made his living as a journalist, writing and editing for popular magazines – *The Atheneum*, *The London Magazine*, *The New Monthly Magazine* and others. Suffering from poor health all his life, Hood also was a typical humorist in that he was depressive too. A real Londoner and popular with his contemporaries, Hood counted as friends many of the literary people of his day, including Lamb, Hazlitt and Coleridge. Sharing to an extent the Gothic imagination of some of the Romantic poets, Hood had a taste for the macabre and uses black humour in many of his poems. Take this verse from 'A Waterloo Ballad':

> This very night a merry dance
>   At Brussels was to be;
> Instead of opening a ball,
>   A ball has open'd me.[23]

Struggling all his life to make ends meet, Hood had a social conscience about the underprivileged of early Victorian society. 'I hate the weeping-willow set, who will cry over their pug dogs and canaries, till they have no tears to spare for the real children of misfortune and misery'[24] of whom there were plenty in the London of his day. His poems of social injustice and satires on the rich and callous, though mostly comic in vein, had a strong impact on other writers, most notably Dickens for whom Hood could be said to be a precursor in terms of theme and outlook. In the introduction to his *Selected Poems*, Joy Flint gives a pen portrait of the man:

> At heart Hood is a serious and moral poet – the shadow of the hawk always darkened his sky . . . but he never forgot the value of pantomime, toy theatre and magic lantern, recognising the need for fantasy in the face of harsh reality . . . he remains a hybrid creature: half-clown, half-preacher; light-hearted but gravely haunted; Romantic and Victorian; terse one moment, garrulous the next; illustrator, journalist, poet.[25]

A much-loved father of his own family, and not to be confused with his son, Tom Hood, who was also a writer, Hood had a special feeling for children. I would not be surprised if texts such as *Whims and Oddities*, 1826, or *The Comic Annual* (1830–1839) found their way into many nurseries. Lewis Carroll, for one, was deeply influenced by Hood. When I came to research his poetry, it was a surprise to find how many well-known witty scraps of, as I thought, anonymous verse actually came from Hood's clever pen. Here are a few that have regularly appeared in children's anthologies, such as the final verse of 'Faithless Sally Brown':[26]

> His death, which happen'd in his berth,
> At forty-odd befell:
> They went and told the sexton, and
> The sexton toll'd the bell.

I am not sure if 'November' would be classified as pure nonsense, but it is certainly Hood at his droll best: here is the beginning and ending.

> No sun – no moon!
> No morn – no noon –
> No dawn – no dusk – no proper time of day –
> No sky – no earthly view –
> No distance looking blue –
> No road – no street – no 't'other side the way'
> . . .

No warmth, no cheerfulness, no healthful ease,
  No comfortable feel in any member –
No shades, no shine, no butterflies, no bees,
  No fruits, no flowers, no leaves, no birds, –
November![27]

'Her Moral' is neatly ironical; the rhyme, rhythm, alliteration and overall pace of the poem conspire to make it trip easily off the tongue.

Gold! Gold! Gold! Gold!
Bright and yellow, hard and cold,
Molten, graven, hammered, and roll'd;
Heavy to get, and light to hold;
Hoarded, barter'd, bought, and sold,
Stolen, borrow'd, squander'd, doled:
Spurn'd by the young, but hugg'd by the old
Source of many a crime untold . . .

Hood is in affectionate mode in 'A Parental Ode to my Son' [aged three years five months]; although it is Victorian in style, the sentiments are perfectly familiar today.

Thou pretty opening rose!
(Go to your mother, child, and wipe your nose!)
Balmy and breathing music like the South,
(He really brings my heart into my mouth!)
Fresh as the morn, and brilliant as its star,
(I wish the window had an iron bar!)
Bold as the hawk, yet gentle as the dove –
(I'll tell you what, my love,
I cannot write, unless he's sent above!)[28]

'On the Death of the Giraffe'[29] is classic Hood at his punning best.

They say, God wot!
She died upon the spot;
But then in spots she was so rich,
I wonder which?

Hardly known today, it is high time Hood made a come-back in poetry for children and adults alike. Lewis Carroll and Edward Lear, however, have never been forgotten. As John Mackay Shaw[30] put it:

> The entire course of juvenile poetry was altered by two bachelor writers who had little in common except an elfin lightsomeness and a love of other people's children.

Lear and Carroll are not only the outstanding humorists in verse of the Victorian period, but of all time. To do justice to their poetry, Chapter 6 is devoted to their work.

New nonsense

Carroll and Lear still dominate nonsense verse in anthologies for children, but many others have developed this genre since then. In the twentieth century, Mervyn Peake, Spike Milligan, Shel Silverstein and Colin McNaughton could be said to have inherited Lear's mantle, as they write (or wrote) popular nonsense for the young *and* illustrate it themselves. Mervyn Peake suffered from mental illness after disturbing war-time experiences and his weird and original nonsense poetry may reflect his mental instability to some effect. Peake is better known today for his Gormenghast fiction; he was also was an outstanding illustrator, producing memorable versions of *The Rime of the Ancient Mariner*, *The Hunting of the Snark* and *Treasure Island*. *Rhymes without Reason*[31] was first published in 1944.

> A langorous life I lead, I do
> Lead such a langorous life.
> I lead it Here, I lead it There,
> Together with my wife.
>
> Sometimes we lead it Round-and-round,
> And sometimes Through-and-through;
> It is a life we recommend
> To anyone like You.

Peake may not have been particularly concerned with addressing children, but the images of his creative and troubled mind and his playful language certainly amused young readers. Like Carroll, the sea features in several of the poems. There are Greenland whales, the 'shores of the Arrogant Isles', 'Sensitive, Seldom and Sad are we / As we wend our way to the sneezing sea' and the tiger who lies:

> Upon my golden backbone
> I float like any cork,
> That hasn't yet been washed ashore
> or swallowed by a shark . . .[32]

Peake has a wonderful sense of the ridiculous.

> I waxes, and I wanes, sir;
> I ebbs's and I flows;
> Some say it be my Brains, sir,
> Some says it be my Nose.
>
> It isn't as I'm slow, sir,
> (To cut a story long),
> It's just I'd love to know, sir,
> Which one of them is wrong.[33]

Uncle Paul of Pimlico [who] 'Has seven cats as white as snow' might have influenced Ted Hughes who created some equally outrageous relations in *Meet My Folks*, 1961. It is Hughes at his lightest and has echoes of Peake – 'My Sister Jane', for example.

> At meals whatever she sees she'll stab it –
> Because she's a crow and that's a crow habit.
> My mother says 'Jane! Your manners! Please!'
> Then she'll sit quietly on the cheese,
> Or play the piano nicely by dancing on the keys –
> Oh it never would do to let folks know
> My sister's nothing but a great big crow.[34]

Writing comic verse in a rather different vein is Spike Milligan of 'The Goons' fame, whose first collection, *Silly Verse for Kids*[35] was published in 1968. Milligan has written many books of nonsense of one kind or another since then for children and adults. His books sell well, but have some problems for the classroom, as Milligan sometimes uses racial stereotypes in his verse and pokes fun at other nationalities. It is surprising that publishers who are normally scrupulous about offensive texts for children let him get away with it. Perhaps his status as a much-loved English humorist and 'personality' gives Milligan more leeway.

Milligan lacks an ear for rhythm and his 'Land of the Bumbley Boo' and 'On the Ning Nang Nong', generalized parodies of Lear's nonsense songs, demonstrate the wide gulf between the two poets. But young children do not notice such subtleties and are attracted by the inventiveness of his imagination and his absurd language – monkeys who show their bums and say 'Boo', attacks by wild bananas, ditties about the Queen (hiding Marks and Spencers knickers / With Norman Hartnell dress) and children who live for ever 'Ying tong iddle i Po!'

A compassionate man at heart, Milligan is one of many humorists who regularly suffers from melancholia. He has written honestly and movingly about what it is like to be manic-depressive, describing laughing at the jokes he is making while the tears run down his cheeks. Milligan introduces many young readers to the delights of poetry.

Shel Silverstein, another comic poet, is deeply involved in a child's view of the world. In the work of this inventive American humorist, words and pictures (black and white line drawings) are meshed together; so much so that when his poems are anthologized, he does not allow other artists to illustrate them. His nonsense is difficult to describe, but a kind of crazy, contorted, irrepressible energy seems to spring from Silverstein's pen. There is also a feeling for the 'underdog' and those who are weak, troubled or eccentric; once again, there is the faintest trace of darkness. *Where the Sidewalk Ends* and *A Light in the Attic* were published in 1974. The former begins with an invitation few children want to reject:

> If you are a dreamer, come in . . .[36]

There is an element of the cautionary in some of Silverstein's verse, such as in 'Someone Ate the Baby'.[37] Another poem begins with some unfortunate being eaten by a boa constrictor![38] There is often a serious point of view lurking beneath the zany fun in Silverstein's verse, as in this wise bit of advice to the young.

> Listen to the MUSTN'TS, child,
> Listen to the DON'TS
> Listen to the SHOULDN'TS
> The IMPOSSIBLES, the WON'TS
> Listen to the NEVER HAVES
> Then listen close to me –
> Anything can happen, child,
> ANYTHING can be.[39]

The British nonsense poet who is most popular with children as I write is Colin McNaughton. Like Silverstein, he is a highly gifted comic illustrator whose verse and pictures are similarly symbiotic. McNaughton works in colour and features extreme and exaggerated monsters and 'weirdos' of various kinds who turn out to be less harmful than the resourceful kids with whom they interact. *There's An Awful Lot Of Weirdos In Our Neighbourhood* came out in 1987 and McNaughton has been on the 'bestseller list' ever since. The sub-title reads – 'A book of rather silly verse and pictures', and that is what it is; the pictures are quite ingenious and the verse is as rude as any child could wish. It is hard to do justice to his work without the illustrations:

Our vicar is kind,
But eats more than he should.
I suppose we could call him,
'A fat lot of good.'[40]

and

If your children are ever unruly
(Of course this might never happen),
Just tell them to kindly behave themselves,
Then reach over quickly and slap 'em![41]

Cautionary verse

Cautionary verse reached its apex in 1896 when Hilaire Belloc published *The Bad Child's Book of Beasts*. The feature of the cautionary which stands out most strongly is extreme retribution meted out (usually to children) for smallish misdemeanors which are funny because they are so exaggerated. Some of it can be quite dark or even sick, but at best it is winningly extravagant, witty and totally 'over the top'. Cautionary verse began life quite seriously as the moral tale in verse where the central intention was to control children's behaviour, not to make them laugh. An early precursor with a hint of the cautionary is Dorothy Kilner,[42] who wrote *Poems On Various Subjects For The Amusement Of Youth* in 1785. Although Dorothy Kilner specialized in didactic literature for children, she also had a sense of fun, as this extract from 'The Retort to Master Richard' makes clear:

One evening when Richard return'd from his school,
He was summon'd to sup up some gooseberry fool.
Young Harriot with smiling good humour stood by
And remark'd with what grace he the spoon did apply.
How he graspd it, as fearful t'would drop from his hand,
And e'en held by the bowl to have better command.
And with smacks he each mouthful seemed eager to taste
And the last precious drip was unwilling to waste.
But ye Graces! how can I the sequel relate?
Or tell you, ye powers, that he lifted his plate?
And what must have made a Lord Chesterfield sick,
Why his tongue he applied the remainder to lick.

Apart from being an amusing picture of greedy Richard and his refined sister, it has a jaunty metre and rhyme-scheme which makes it easy to read. The cautionary element lies in Kilner's exaggeration of Richard's table manners and his sister's reactions to them. Kilner had no pretensions about her verse, nor a very rarefied view of her audience:

> . . . its design was to please those minds which were incapable of admiring the beauties of superior composition; and the jingle of the rhyme, it was imagined, would be an agreeable exercise to the memory.[43]

Moral tales in verse

Twenty years later the Taylor sisters who have already been mentioned in the preceding chapters gave the moral tale in verse a new lease of life with the publication of *Original Poems*. Even the gentle Taylors sometimes echoed the brutality of their age in these poems, such as this harsh lesson about the cruelty of fishing.

> But as he jumped to reach a dish,
>   To put his fishes in,
> A large meat-hook, that hung close by,
>   Did catch him by the chin.
>
> Poor Harry kicked, and called aloud,
>   And screamed, and cried, and roared,
> While from his wound the crimson blood
>   In dreadful torrents poured.
>
> 'And oh!' said he, 'poor little fish,
>   What torture they have borne:
> While I, well pleased, have stood to see
>   Their tender bodies torn!'[44]

One of the 'several young persons' who contributed to *Original Poems* in 1804 was Adelaide O'Keefe (1776–1855) who wrote better 'cautionary' tales than the Taylor sisters; they excelled at a different kind of poetry. By underplaying something serious (a major fire) with a casual comment (a bit like 'oops!' in a comic), O'Keefe sets up the classic cautionary situation – an extreme event which provokes a totally inadequate reaction, or vice versa.

The roof and wall, the stairs and all,
And rafters tumble in:
Red flames and blaze, now all amaze,
And make a dreadful din!

And each one screams, when bricks and beams
Come tumbling on their heads;
And some are smashed, and some are dashed;
Some leap on feather-beds.

Some burn, some choke with fire and smoke;
But ah! what was the cause?
My heart's dismayed – last night I played
With Thomas, lighting straws![45]

Another good writer of the moral tale in verse in this period was Elizabeth Turner (1775–1846) who wrote *The Daisy* in 1807, followed by other books of the same type.

Miss Helen was always too giddy to heed
What her mother had told her to shun;
For frequently over the street in full speed,
She would cross where the carriages run.

One morning, intending to take but a peep,
Her foot slipt away from the ground.
Unhappy misfortune the water was deep
And giddy Miss Helen was drown'd![46]

Struwwelpeter

We have to wait until 1845 for the moral tale to move into a higher gear and closer to cautionary verse when Heinrich Hoffmann (1809–1894) wrote *Struwwelpeter*, whose gruesome images still occasionally haunt this author's nightmares. Interestingly, Hoffmann was a doctor in a Frankfurt lunatic asylum who wrote the book for his small son. Many adults who have forgotten most childhood books remember this one for the pure terror they experienced from the illustrations as much as the verse. Who can forget that 'reg-legged scissor-man' who grabs hold of small thumb-suckers:

And cuts their thumbs clean off, – and then,
You know, they never grow again.[47]

The book has long oscillated between being accepted as 'harmless hilarity and being condemned as excessively horrifying, morbid, and even a source of trauma to the sensitive child' writes Humphrey Carpenter[48] in *The Oxford Companion to Children's Literature*. Indeed, the debate about the suitability of *Struwwelpeter* for children still surfaces occasionally. Perhaps the most frightening of all is 'Shock-Headed Peter'[49] which is actually quite mild in the written version, but those terrible claw-like nails and great bush of hair were terrifying enough.

> Just look at him! There he stands,
> With his nasty hair and hands.
> See! his nails are never cut;
> They are grim'd as black as soot;
> And the sloven, I declare,
> Never once has combed his hair;
> Anything to me is sweeter
> Than to see Shock-headed Peter.

Otherwise, there is cruel Frederick who was so ghastly he got bitten by his own dog, Harriet who played with matches and got burnt to death, the man who went out shooting and got shot himself and Johnny Head-in-Air who never looked where he was going and fell in the river. There is also 'The Story of the Inky Boys' where nasty little rascals shout racist comments at a 'woolly-headed black-a-moor':

> And kept on singing, – only think! –
> 'Oh! Blacky, you're as black as ink.'

They get their come-uppance by being dipped in ink themselves and ending as black as the 'harmless black-a-moor'.[50] Although this would not be acceptable today, at least Hoffmann takes the protagonists to task for their cruelty. Hoffmann's illustration of the black boy wielding an umbrella is reminiscent of Helen Bannerman's *Little Black Sambo* which was published at the end of the century.

The Bad Child's Book of Beasts

Hoffmann is the closest to the sort of cautionary verse which Hilaire Belloc (1870–1953) made famous nearly 50 years later. *The Bad Child's Book of Beasts* was published in 1896 and was so popular it sold out within a couple of days. Unlike Hoffmann, Belloc always kept his tongue firmly in his cheek, so the reader is more amused than frightened. Here is an extract about that dastardly lion who made a dinner of poor Jim.[51]

The lion made a sudden stop,
He let the dainty morsel drop,
And slunk reluctant to his cage,
Snarling with disappointed rage.
But when he bent him over Jim,
The honest keeper's eyes were dim.
The lion having reached his head,
The miserable boy was dead!

. . .

His Mother, as she dried her eyes,
Said, 'Well – it gives me no surprise,
He would not do as he was told!'
His Father, who was self-controlled,
Bade all the children round attend
To James's miserable end,
And always keep a-hold of Nurse
For fear of finding something worse.

What has changed? Any desire to be didactic has completely disappeared and left an outrageous tale of dark humour in verse. Belloc is also having a joke at the expense of earlier writers of moral tales. With his sense of fun, his genius for understatement, his well-crafted verse and an instinct for what would appeal to children, the Liberal Member of Parliament for South Salford was on to a winner. Marriott Edgar (1880–1951) turned the poem into a Yorkshire Music Hall version, The Lion and Albert[52] in 1933. Here is Edgar's amusing conclusion which is even funnier when performed by a Yorkshire speaker.

The Magistrate gave his opinion
    That no one was really to blame,
And he said that he hoped the Ramsbottoms
    Would have further sons to their name.

At that Mother got proper blazing,
    'And thank you, sir, kindly,' said she.
'What, waste all our lives rearing children
    To feed ruddy Lions? Not me!'

Belloc was well served by two illustrators – B. T. B. (Basil Blackwood) and Nicolas Bentley. Blackwood illustrated Belloc's books of verse including More Beasts For Worse Children, 1897, and Cautionary Tales, 1907, until he was killed in the First World War. He worked in the then popular style of German expressionism and his caricatures of portly gentlemen, grim policemen and well-dressed young ruffians are both highly amusing and the perfect foil for Belloc's sardonic tongue. Unfortunately, both author and illustrator shared anti-Semitic leanings which are evident in some of the pictures. Bentley made a great success of *New Cautionary Tales* in 1930 and *Ladies and Gentlemen* in 1932. He went on to illustrate T. S. Eliot's *Practical Cats* (discussed in Chapter 10) in 1940.

Harry Graham (1874–1936), writing around the same time as Belloc, is sharper and less focused on the young. His background was in the Coldstream Guards with whom he served in the Boer War. *Ruthless Rhymes for Heartless Homes*[53] was the apt title of his book of cautionary verse published in 1899, examples of which have often been anthologized for children.

> I never shall forget my shame
> To find my son had forged my name.
> If he had any thought for others
> He might at least have forged his mother's.
>
>   *   *   *
>
> Father heard his Children scream,
> So he threw them in the stream,
> Saying as he drowned the third,
> 'Children should be seen, *not* heard!'

After Belloc and Graham, there seems to be a gap in the composition of cautionary verse. Perhaps two world wars blunted the taste for macabre humour? At any rate, it is back in favour and Belloc still has collections in print and is still regularly anthologized today.

Roald Dahl's *Revolting Rhymes*, 1982, and *Dirty Beasts*, 1984 are much enjoyed by children today; but it is Dahl's sauciness that they find so delectable, like the moment when Little Red Riding Hood 'whips a pistol from her knickers'.[54] Michael Rosen is more playful than cautionary in *Hairy Tales and Nursery Crimes,* 1985.[55] Books of comic poetry with a strong representation of cautionary verse, such as *Beastly Boys and Ghastly Girls*[56] still sell well.

Eletephony

I want to close this chapter with some poets who straddle aspects of cautionary and nonsense verse. Laura Richards's (1850–1943) verse has such a freshness that one is surprised to discover that she actually published some of her books for children in the late nineteenth century and predates Mervyn Peake. The Boston-born mother of seven was daughter of Julia Ward Howe who wrote 'The Battle Hymn of the Republic'. As well as composing several volumes of popular children's poetry,

Richards also wrote fables, stories and biography. *Tirra Lirra*,[57] 1932, draws on her many collections and contains some of her most popular poems:

> Once there was an elephant,
> Who tried to use the telephant –
> No! No! I mean an elephone
> Who tried to use the telephone –

> *   *   *

> My uncle Jehoshaphat had a pig,
>   A pig of high degree;
> And he always wore a brown scratch wig,
>   Most beautiful for to see.

Another American, the witty writer and popular columnist, Ogden Nash, wrote a single book for children, *Parents Keep Out*[58] in 1951, but many of the poems he wrote for adults also appeal to the young. Quentin Blake drew from various Nash collections in *Custard and Company*, 1979. Nash has the knack of finding the perfect word (often a pun) to fit the rhyme and exploit the humour. Like most comic writers, he had a serious side; in the *Oxford Book of Children's Verse in America*, Donald Hall describes Nash as the 'Homer, Shakespeare, and Dante of the outrageous rhyme.'[59] Two brief extracts from poems show something of his range. The opening to 'Winter Morning' is masterful, while the mock-lecturely stance taken in 'The Pig' serves to underline the joke.

> Winter is the king of showmen,
> Turning tree stumps into snowmen.

> *   *   *

> The pig, if I am not mistaken,
>   Supplies us with sausage, ham and bacon.
> Let others say his heart is big –
>   I call it stupid of the pig.[60]

Contemporary comic verse

Contemporary comic verse for children is thriving. Well-known humorists like Wendy Cope, Adrian Henri, Roger McGough, Gareth Owen, Brian Patten and Kit Wright regularly write for children as well as adults. Space does not permit a proper consideration of all these talented poets who exhibit distinctive styles, themes and forms. For example, Cope, whose range includes amusing rhymes for the very young, is probably the best living parodist. Henri's exuberant, sometimes bitter-sweet, adult poetry is toned down a little for younger readers, while Patten favours anarchic, child-centred rude verse. What they all have in common, besides wit, is the willingness to be provocative or thoughtful, sad as well as amusing, sometimes making a profound statement in an apparently light poem. So do Jack Prelutsky, Frank Asch, Mary Ann Hoberman and other US comic poets whom I have reluctantly ignored. I conclude this chapter by exploring the work of Roger McGough, Kit Wright and Gareth Owen as representative of comic verse at its best.

'I'm a Nooligan' – the poetry of Roger McGough

Roger McGough is the best punner in the business and the master of word play. He is an acrobat with language, showing off his skill, precocity and verbal athleticism in poem after poem.

> I'm a nooligan
> don't give a toss
> in our class
> I'm the boss
> (well one of them).
>
> I'm a nooligan
> got a nard 'ead
> step out of line
> and you're dead
> (well, bleedin).[61]

As a youngster McGough 'loved the language part of English, doodling with words on the page . . . If you look after the words, the poems look after themselves.'[62] With his Liverpudlian friends, Henri and Patten, McGough formed a popular group called The Scaffold in the 1960s, promoting 'Beat Poetry' with songs and music. Gifted performers, all three still work together on occasion; they are equally known (or better known) in adult poetry circles as for their work with children.

Sometimes McGough takes a word or an idea and plays with it from every conceivable angle. In 'Sky in the Pie' which won the Signal Award in 1984, he rounds on violence and poetry:

> I do not have a licence
> For carrying guns in my poems.
> Nevertheless there is plenty of
> Screaming and swearing. Horrible.
> Blood soaks through the page
> Like an amazing image.[63]

McGough is perhaps more interested in exploring what language can do and pushing logic to its extremities than in looking at childhood itself. He is prepared to be much sharper than most other children's poets, admitting there is a 'shadow round the corner'[64] in his work. In fact, McGough brings to his children's poetry the same characteristics much admired in his adult work: a sense of the absurd, a flair for noting people's eccentricities, the witty aside, terseness, vigour, plus a taste of sadness and despair. He points up the frailties of human nature in poems which sometimes make the reader want to laugh and weep at the same time, like 'The Pet'.[65]

> For now I've a pet
> To put inside
> Something belonging
> To someone who died
>
> He keeps me company
> When I feel sad
> He's my pet slipper
> And I call him 'Dad'.

'A Good Poem' was the opener in McGough's first collection for children (shared with Michael Rosen), *You Tell Me*, 1979. It challenges previously accepted notions of poetry for children, dipping straight into popular culture instead. 'A Good Poem' is the antithesis of romantic writing, suggesting that if you want children to take to poetry, then poetry must take account of children's concerns.

> I like a good poem
> one with lots of fighting
> in it. Blood, and the
> clanging of armour. Poems
>
> against Scotland are good,
> and poems that defeat
> the French with crossbows.
> I don't like poems that
>
> aren't about anything.
> Sonnets are wet and
> a waste of time.
> Also poems that don't
>
> know how to rhyme.
> If I was a poem
> I'd play football and
> get picked for England.[66]

McGough's compassionate side is never far away. For all its exaggeration, 'First Day at School' gets closer than most poems in acknowledging a small child's anxiety and confusion on starting school. While other poets might write with care and kindness about this subject, McGough reveals the misery some children feel. The skill lies in keeping the poem light enough which McGough achieves by writing simultaneously with a child's voice and an adult's understanding, and reflecting the humour in the situation too.

> A millionbillionwillion miles from home
> Waiting for the bell to go. (To go where?)
> Why are they all so big, other children?
> So noisy? So much at home they
> must have been born in uniform
> Lived all their lives in playgrounds
> Spent the years inventing games
> that don't let me in. Games
> that are rough, that swallow you up.
>
> And the railings.
> All around the railings.
> Are they to keep out wolves and monsters?[67]

A recent collection, *Nailing the Shadow*, casts sharp, dark metaphors over childhood. McGough conveys the pain of those little disappointments, an inevitable part of growing up, in his inimitable word play.

> When I played as a kid
> How I longed to be caught
> But whenever I hid
> Nobody sought.[68]

Rabbiting On – the poetry of Kit Wright

Wright is a popular performer and a regular visitor to classrooms and poetry festivals with many strong collections to his credit. Animals always feature in his titles; *Rabbiting On*, 1979, was followed by *Hot Dog, Cat Among the Pigeons* and *Great Snakes*. Wright uses regular metre and rhyme in a variety of forms and is highly regarded for his technical ability. Like McGough, Wright's poetry for children has a lot in common with his work for adults. A sparkling comic ability is what one thinks of first, but he also moves into serious vein in his children's poetry with poems such as 'The Frozen Man', 'Grandad' or 'The Song of the Whale', where he deals movingly with issues as troubling as homelessness, death and hunting species to near extinction. In other poems, Wright subverts the reader's expectations:

> The moon was a luminous toenail,
> Far ingrown,
> When poor old Horace the Hedgehog
> Wandered alone,
>
> Humping his heavy hackles
> Over the lawn,
> Weary as all the time
> Before he was born . . . [69]

Wright's poetry has been wonderfully mirrored by Posy Simmonds as his regular illustrator who is excellent at the fun, but just as good with the sensitive side of his work. Wright describes himself as 'a bit of a kid'[70] and there is an authentic flavour of the naughty boy (a sort of updated *Just William*) in many of his poems. Though Wright's child characters are often troublesome scamps, like Dave Dirt, they are never cruel; they just delight in making grown-ups' lives a misery as they jostle and quip with each other.

> Dave Dirt was on the 259
> (Down Seven Sisters Road it goes),
> And since he'd nothing else to do
> He stuck his ticket up his nose,
>
> He shoved his pen-top in his ear,
> He pulled three hairs out of his head,
> He ate a page out of his book,
> He held his breath till he went red,
>
> He stuck a piece of bubblegum
> Inside a dear old lady's bonnet.
> If you should catch the 259,
> Make sure that Dave Dirt isn't on it![71]

This is classic 'urchin verse' territory (see Chapter 13) and you can see why so many children like it. It is also very well crafted. A writer of genuine kindness, with sympathy for the underdog, a flair for comedy and strong technical skill, Wright's good humoured poetry has a distinctively thoughtful side.

I've been staring
all of the morning
out at the endlessly
falling rain

that drowns the garden
in tank after tank full
of see-through tears without
anger or pain . . .[72]

'My Granny is a Sumo Wrestler' – the poetry of Gareth Owen

Owen is the author of many excellent books of poetry for children. His writing was ahead of his time: *Salford Road*, his first collection, was actually written in the 1960s, but he could not find a publisher willing to take it on until 1979. *Salford Road* was followed by other successful volumes, including *Song of the City* which won the Signal Award in 1986. Owen once worked as a tutor in a College of Education and you can find the amused, teacher-observer in many of his hilarious poems. The major influence on Owen's writing was Keith Waterhouse's *There is a Happy Land*, which helped him find his own authentic, funny, working-class voice. Recently presenter of the BBC Radio 4 *Poetry Please!*, Owen has the 'common touch' and is good at making a wide range of poetry available to listeners from different backgrounds.

A gifted performer, Owen has a splendid sense of the ridiculous and his forte is the comic narrative, shown off to wonderful effect in his account of Blenkinsop, a teacher's nightmare, the pupil with an answer for everything; or the sister who tries to skate like Torville and Dean in her bedroom with dusters on her feet; or Uncle Arthur whose favourite game was 'Are you there, Moriarty?'; or the awful but well-intentioned Miss Creedle in a doomed attempt to teach creative writing:

Are you imagining a time before you were born?
What does it look like? Is it dark?
(Embryo is a good word you might use.)[73]

Owen writes in rhyme and regular metre, yearning 'towards the condition of music'[74] in his poetry. He, too, has a serious side and often looks at the hurts and sensitivities of the young, such as this reflection written in the voice of a 'latch-key' child.

The coals have crumbled to ash;
The fire is out.
I lie, my feet on a chair,
Reading my comic,
Wishing my mother could be home
To tell me not to put them there.[75]

Owen talks about the importance of remembering his own childhood:

Always in the further recesses of my mind I have a hope that there's another soul out there who will say, 'That's how it is . . . or was . . . for me.' Writing is much more to do with memory and recognition than with mere invention.[76]

Owen is also an exponent of that theme most poets for children find their way to some time or another – the loss of childhood – which links him with an earlier humorist whom we have already encountered in this chapter, Thomas Hood. In the closing stanzas of 'Salford Road' and 'I Remember', both poets regret that they cannot hold on to childhood.

> And when I stand in Salford Road
> And think of the boy who was me
> I feel that from one of the windows
> Someone is looking at me.
>
> My friends walked out one Summer day,
> Walked singing down the lane,
> My friends walked into a wood called Time
> And never came out again.
>   ('Salford Road')
>
> I remember, I remember,
> The fir trees dark and high;
> I used to think their slender tops
> Were close against the sky:
> It was a childish ignorance,
> But now 'tis little joy
> To know I'm farther off from heaven
> Than when I was a boy.[77]
>   ('I Remember')

So we end this chapter on humour with a hint of wistfulness which so often forms the under-belly of comic verse. The best of it endures to amuse future generations, as the poetry of Lewis Carroll and Edward Lear demonstrates in the next chapter.

Notes

1   Hilaire Belloc, from 'Jim', *The Bad Child's Book of Beasts*, London, 1896.
2   John Gross, *The Oxford Book of Comic Verse*, Oxford, 1994, p. xxxi.
3   Brian Patten, from 'Pick-a-Nose Pick's Awful Poem', *Gargling with Jelly*, Viking Kestrel, London, 1985.
4   Iona Opie, *The People in the Playground*, Oxford University Press, Oxford, 1990.
5   Thomas Hood, from 'Faithless Nelly Gray', *Whims and Oddities*, London, 1826.
6   Ann Taylor, from 'My Mother', *Original Poems for Infant Minds*, Darton, London, 1804.
7   Thomas Hood, from 'A Lay of Real Life', *Thomas Hood: Selected Poems* ed. Joy Flint, Carcanet, Manchester, 1992.
8   Jane Taylor, from 'The Star', *Rhymes for the Nursery*, Darton, London, 1806.
9   Lewis Carroll, 'Twinkle Twinkle Little Bat', *Alice's Adventures in Wonderland*, London, 1865.
10 From 'You', traditional Igbo poem, quoted in *I like that Stuff*, ed. M. Styles, Cambridge, 1984.
11 Frederick Williams, from *Me Memba Wen*, Broadsheet Press, Nottingham, 1981.
12 Traditional, China.
13 Quentin Blake, *The Puffin Book of Nonsense Verse*, London, 1994.
14 Albert Uderzo, quoted by Colin McNaughton, 'Per Ardua ad Asterix', *Books for Keeps*, No. 87, July 1994.
15 Quentin Blake, *op. cit.*, 1994.
16 Emile Cammaerts, *The Poetry of Nonsense*, Routledge, London, 1926, p. 37.
17 Edward Strachey, Introduction to *Complete Nonsense of Edward Lear*, 1894, reprinted Wordsworth, London, 1994, pp. 7–8.
18 Edward Strachey, quoted in John Goldthwaite, *The Natural History of Make-Believe*, Oxford, 1996, p. 15.
19 John Goldthwaite, ibid., p. 15.
20 William Shakespeare, *Twelfth Night*, Act V, I, 401.
21 Goldthwaite, *op. cit.*, pp. 14, 15.
22 W. H. Auden, *Nineteenth Century Minor Poets*, Faber, London, 1966, p. 19.
23 Hood, from 'A Waterloo Ballad', Joy Flint, 1992, *op. cit.*
24 Flint, Introduction, *ibid.*, p. 16.
25 *Ibid.*, p. 25.
26 Hood, from 'Faithless Nelly Brown', *The London Magazine*, 1822, and Flint, *ibid.*
27 Hood, from 'November', *ibid.*
28 Hood, from 'Her Moral' and 'A Parental Ode to My Son', *New Monthly Magazine*, 1840, and Flint, *ibid.*
29 Hood, *Forget-me-Not*, 1828, and Flint, *ibid.*
30 John Mackay Shaw, *Childhood in Poetry*, Gale Research Co., Detroit, USA, 1966.
31 Mervyn Peake, from 'A Langorous Life', *Rhymes without Reason*, 1944, Methuen, London, 1974.
32 Peake, from 'My Golden Backbone', *ibid.*
33 Peake, from 'I Wakes and I Wanes', *ibid.*
34 Ted Hughes, from 'My Sister Jane', *Meet My Folks*, Faber, London, 1961.
35 Spike Milligan, *Silly Verse for Kids*, Puffin, 1968.
36 Shel Silverstein, *Where the Sidewalk Ends*, Harper and Row, New York, 1974.

37 *Ibid.*

38 *Ibid.*

39 Silverstein, 'Listen to the Mustn'ts', *ibid.*

40 Colin McNaughton, *There's an awful lot of Weirdos in our Neighbourhood*, Walker Books, London, 1987.

41 *Ibid.*

42 Dorothy Kilner, 'The Retort to Master Richard', *Poems On Various Subjects for the Amusement of Youth*, London, 1785.

43 *Ibid.*

44 Ann and Jane Taylor, *Original Poems for Infant Minds*, Darton, London, 1804.

45 Adelaide O'Keefe, *ibid.*

46 Elizabeth Turner, *The Daisy*, London, 1807.

47 Heinrich Hoffman, *Struwwelpter*, 1845, Routledge & Kegan Paul, London.

48 Humphrey Carpenter and Mari Pritchard, eds *The Oxford Companion to Children's Literature*, Oxford, 1984.

49 Hoffman, from 'Shock-Headed Peter', *op. cit.*

50 Hoffman, from 'The Story of the Inky Boys', *ibid.*

51 Hilaire Belloc, from 'Jim', *op. cit.*

52 Marriott Edgar, from *The Lion and Albert*, Methuen, London, 1933.

53 Harry Graham, *Ruthless Rhymes for Heartless Homes*, London, 1899.

54 Roald Dahl, *Revolting Rhymes*, Jonathan Cape, London, 1982.

55 Michael Rosen, *Hairy Tales and Nursery Crimes*, Andre Deutsch, London, 1985.

56 William Cole, ed. *Beastly Boys and Ghastly Girls*, Methuen, London, 1970.

57 Laura Richards, from 'Eletelephony', 'My Uncle Jehoshaphat', *Tirra Lirra,* 1932.

58 Ogden Nash, from 'Winter Morning' and 'The Pig', *Parents Keep Out*, 1951.

59 Donald Hall, *The Oxford Book of Children's Verse in America*, Oxford University Press, New York, 985, p. 306.

60 Ogden Nash, *Custard and Company*, ed. Quentin Blake, Kestrel, London, 1979.

61 Roger McGough, from 'Nooligan', *You Tell Me*, Kestrel, London, 1979.

62 Roger McGough quoted in *The Books for Keeps Guide to Poetry 0-16,* eds Morag Styles and Pat Triggs, London, 1988, p. 41.

63 Roger McGough, from 'A Poem about Violence', *Sky in the Pie*, Viking Kestrel, London, 1983.

64 McGough, in *Books for Keeps, op. cit.*, p. 41.

65 McGough, from 'The Pet', 1983, *op. cit.*

66 McGough, 'A Good Poem', 1979, *op. cit.*

67 McGough, from 'First Day at School', 1979, *op. cit.*

68 McGough, *Nailing the Shadow*, Viking Kestrel, London, 1987.

69 Kit Wright, from 'Horace', *Cat Among the Pigeons*, Viking Kestrel, London, 1987.

70 Wright, quoted in *Books for Keeps, op. cit.,* p. 31.

71 Wright, from 'Dave Dirt was on the 259', 1987, *op. cit.*

72 Wright, from 'All of the Morning', *Rabbiting On*, Collins, London, 1978.

73 Gareth Owen, from 'Miss Creedle teaches Creative Writing', *Song of the City*, Collins, London, 1985.

74 Owen, quoted in *Books for Keeps*, 1988, *op. cit.*, p. 89.

75 Owen, from 'Empty House', *Salford Road and Other Poems*, Collins, 1988.

76 Owen, in *Books for Keeps*, 1988, p. 89.

77 Hood, from 'I Remember, I Remember', Flint, *op. cit.;* Owen, from 'Salford Road, *op. cit.*

CHAPTER 6

Jumblies and Jabberwockies

The nonsense verse of Lewis Carroll and Edward Lear

Will you, won't you, will you, won't you, will you join the dance?
Will you, won't you, will you, won't you, won't you join the dance?[1]

There are several reasons for considering the work of Edward Lear and Lewis Carroll together. They were writing during the same period, publishing for children, in Lear's case, *The Book of Nonsense* in 1846 and concluding with *Laughable Lyrics* in 1877. Carroll's output began with *Alice in Wonderland*, 1865, and his last substantial book was *The Hunting of the Snark*, 1876, though *Sylvie and Bruno* came later. Between them these writers composed the finest nonsense verse that has ever seen the light of day. And as John Lehmann pointed out in his Nottingham Byron lecture of 1972, nonsense is 'a curiously English phenomenon . . . there seems to be a need [for it] in the human soul, as there is for art, or for religion'.[2] This may account in part for why Carroll is probably the best-known English writer for children of all time.

Lear and Carroll both had a tendency towards depression: Jean Kenward's description of nonsense fits both men: 'Underneath the made-up words, the ridiculous romances, and the deft and lilting rhythm lies the deep sadness that is the basis of laughter.'[3] They both came from enormous families, but were awkward in adult society and much more comfortable with children. If they were both loners whose lives were quite unhappy, this may account for their gravitation towards the young with whom they were not self-conscious and one reason why their writing was so exceptionally in tune with children. Neither Lear nor Carroll married and both developed friendships with children which were important to them. Both were also copious letter writers who often included amusingly illustrated nonsense elements within their correspondence. Both were what would now be descibed as somewhat obsessive collectors of trivia (hotel bills, tickets, train times in the case of Lear) with an overdeveloped eye for detail in their daily lives.

But if there was much in common, there were also many differences between these two Victorians. The resolutely conservative Carroll lived in England all his life, only venturing abroad once; Lear spent much of his adult life travelling from country to country, living for long periods in Greece, France and Italy. He died in San Remo where he made his final home in a house called the Villa Tennyson. Indeed, Vivien Noakes subtitled her excellent biography of Lear, 'the life of a wanderer'.[4]

Lear was primarily an artist, while Carroll was a mathematician; though both did some teaching of their subjects, Carroll was a lecturer by profession, apparently rather a dreary one. Lear struggled with poverty all his life and did not go to school until he was 11, whereas Carroll came from a comfortable background, went to public school and spent his professional life with security of tenure and all the privileges accorded to an Oxford tutor. Lear was a *bon viveur* with a great capacity for pleasure whereas Carroll was prim, prudish and abstemious. Carroll was careful; Lear constantly took risks. I could go on. But both men shared something highly significant – extravagant and extrovert sides to their personalities and wonderfully inventive imaginations evident in their books for children which have deservedly achieved classic status. Now it is time to introduce the reader to each writer in turn and demonstrate the justice of my claims for these humorists in verse.

'How pleasant to know Mr Lear!'

Edward Lear (1812–1888) was the 21st child in his family. John Goldthwaite calls him 'the affectionate runt of an enormous litter . . . [who] saw himself as a sport of nature, a Dong with a luminous nose . . .'[5] Because of financial problems with the massive family to support, the short-sighted little boy was virtually abandoned by his parents, though his much older sister, Ann, played her part well as a surrogate mother throughout her life. The early loss of his parents may help to account for the deep lack of confidence Lear suffered from and the feeling of being an outsider, despite having a gift for friendship. This wounded self-esteem also sprang from what Lear felt was his unprepossessing appearance (particularly the family nose); another great trial to him was his struggle to keep secret from most of his acquaintances the fact that he had epilepsy.

Brian Alderson describes Lear as 'something of a poor relation at enormous dinner parties'.[6] Certainly Lear was familiar with many of 'the great and the good' of his day: for example, he was at one time drawing master to Queen Victoria; Tennyson, then Poet Laureate, was a lifelong friend; and Lord Northbrook invited him to India at his own expense while he was Viceroy there. This multi-talented man was capable of setting some of Tennyson's poems to music and (at another time) producing a book of paintings to accompany poems relating to particular places, jokingly calling the latter a *Collection of Poetical Topographical Tennysoniana*.[7] Marianne North remembered Lear:

. . . wandering into our sitting-room through the windows at dusk when his work was over, sit down to the piano, and sing Tennyson's songs for hours, composing as he went on, and picking out the acompaniments by ear, putting the greatest expression and passion into the most sentimental words. He would often set me laughing; then he would say I was not worthy of them, and would continue the intense pathos of expression and gravity of face, while he substituted Hey Diddle Diddle, the Cat and the Fiddle, or some other nonsensical words to the same air.[8]

Tennyson in turn wrote appreciatively of Lear's landscapes, which he produced from his travels all over the world – in this case, Greece:

> – all things fair
> With such a pencil such a pen
> You shadow'd forth to distant men
> I read and felt that I was there:[9]

Lear was prone to extreme melancholy which he jokingly called the 'Morbids'. Even the Tennysons to whom Lear was devoted (especially Emily Tennyson) eventually disappointed him. During a visit in 1860 he wrote in his journal:

> After all, it is perhaps better now, never to feel happy & quiet: so one gradually cares less for life . . . We come no more to the golden shore, where we danced in days of old.[10]

It is sad to learn of Lear's unhappiness, particularly as it is so easy to picture him composing his nonsense alphabets, happily chatting to his many child-acquaintances with the sketch pad ever ready to capture a landscape, a bird or draw a hilarious caricature of himself.

A man of prodigious ability, Lear is now recognized as a gifted if eccentric painter, as well as being a musician, inveterate and amusing letter writer, witty conversationalist, humorist and loyal friend to many. According to Peter Levi what acquaintances remembered most about Lear was his fantastic thirst for fun: 'in spite of all the ups and downs, Edward Lear's spirit was unquenchable, and his zest for life, in his barest watercolour sketches, his most expansive finished paintings, his most casual passing jokes and cartoons and self-caricature, was more alive than most people's'.[11]

Lear's sense of fun and his self-consciousness can be gleaned from the revealing poem, 'By Way of Preface'. Kingsley Amis is rude about Lear's verse in general and this poem in particular in *The New Oxford Book of Light Verse*.[12] It did not seem to occur to Amis that the very thing he disliked about the poems – the whimsy, as he called it – was precisely what people, especially children, enjoyed most.

'How pleasant to know Mr Lear!'
   Who has written such volumes of stuff!
Some think him ill-tempered and queer,
   But a few find him pleasant enough.

His mind is concrete and fastidious,
   His nose is remarkably big;
His visage is more or less hideous,
   His beard it resembles a wig.

He has ears, and two eyes, and ten fingers,
   Leastways if you reckon two thumbs;
Long ago he was one of the singers,
   But now he is one of the dumb.

He sits in a beautiful parlour,
   With hundreds of books on the wall;
He drinks a great deal of Marsala,
   But never gets tipsy at all.

. . .

He weeps by the side of the ocean,
   He weeps on the top of the hill;
He purchases pancakes and lotion,
   And chocolate shrimps from the mill.

He reads but he cannot speak Spanish,
   He cannot abide ginger-beer:
Ere the days of his pilgrimage vanish,
   How pleasant to know Mr. Lear![13]

The depressiveness evident in this poem can be traced throughout Lear's writing which steadily got more gloomy as he aged. Edward Strachey[14] confirmed it:

Mr Lear was by temperament melancholy . . . a gentle sadness through which his humour shone . . . this melancholy never soured his mind nor stopped his matchless flow of humour and bad puns; but it coloured them all.

It is plain to see in 'The Nutcrackers and the Sugar-Tongs':[15]

Must we drag on this stupid existence for ever,
So idle and weary so full of remorse, —
While every one else takes his pleasure . . .

and in 'The Dong with a Luminous Nose'. I could cite numerous other examples.[16]

> When awful darkness and silence reign
>   Over the great Gromboolian plain,
>   Through the long, long wintry nights, –
> When the angry breakers roar
> As they beat on the rocky shore; –
>   . . .
> And now each night, and all night long,
> Over the plains still roams the Dong;
> And above the wail of the Chimp and Snipe
> You may hear the squeak of his plaintive pipe
> While ever he seeks, but seeks in vain . . .

By 1875 Lear was subjecting himself to isolation by rejecting invitations which he would later regret:

> . . . for this lonely life is by no means good for me: & at times the depression from wh. I suffer, is almost intolerable.[17]

It is equally evident in the poetry. Levi points out that there are only two really happy endings in Lear's nonsense songs, though Goldthwaite noticed the defiance of some (for example, 'the nutcrackers and the sugar-tongs . . . never came back'). When poems do end on an upbeat note, it is always in an impossible never-never land of escapism. So the Owl and the Pussycat 'danced by the light of the moon', the Duck and the Kangaroo 'hopped the whole world three times round'; the Daddy Long-legs and the Fly 'play for evermore / At battlecock and shuttledore', and that melee of wierd and wonderful creatures were 'as happy as happy could be, / With the Quangle Wangle Quee.'[18]

But the sadness that pervades Lear's verse is not what children notice. They read him for the nonsense songs which are deliciously melodious, hosting a fantastic cornucopia of characters. Once heard, 'The Owl and the Pussy-Cat went to sea / In a beautiful pea-green boat' . . . or 'They went to sea in a sieve, they did / In a sieve they went to sea . . .' linger delightfully in the memory. Like Carroll, Lear's command of metre and rhyme was impeccable, bringing his musical skills into play. That is one reason why the poems have lasted the test of time. It is clear, for example, exactly how 'The Akond of Swat' should be read, as Lear spells out the rhythm for us. Stress is put on 'sing', 'whistle', 'jabber' and 'talk' in the first line, whereas in the second line he lays stress on every third syllable, starting with '*rid*ing'; the third line is closer to the first where both single syllable words are stressed and so on. It is writing that is very close to music.

Does he sing or whistle, jabber or talk,
And when riding abroad does he gallop or walk,
    or TROT,
    The Akond of Swat?[19]

Lear delighted in playful language in his poems as much as in his letters. In 'The Quangle Wangle's Hat', he created some playful alliterative lists:

On top of the Crumpetty Tree
    The Quangle Wangle sat,
But his face you could not see,
    On account of his Beaver Hat.
For his Hat was a hundred and two feet wide,
With ribbons and bibbons on every side
And bells, and buttons, and loops, and lace,
So that nobody ever could see the face
    Of the Quangle Wangle Quee.[20]

Lear is probably most famous for the limerick, though he is less distinguished here than in his other nonsense. *The History of Sixteen Old Women* was published as early as 1821 and Richard Scrafton Sharpe (1775–1852) produced some very funny limericks in *Anecdotes and Adventures of Fifteen Gentlemen*, 1822, which Lear admired before trying his hand at them himself.

There was an old miser at Reading,
Had a house, and a yard with a shed in;
Twas meant for a cow,
But so small that I vow
The poor creature could scarce get her head in.[21]
                   (Sharpe)

Lear's limericks, whose first and last lines usually repeat, have a rather flat effect.

There was an Old Man of Cape Horn,
Who wished he had never been born;
So he sat on a chair,
Till he died of despair,
That dolorious Man of Cape Horn.[22]
                   (Lear)

Be that as it may, Lear certainly did a great deal to popularize limericks which are, of course, still a well-known form today. Goldthwaite makes the fascinating point in *The Natural History of Make-Believe* that Lear usually avoided young men or old women in his limericks, though there are young ladies and old men a-plenty. Goldthwaite speculates as to whether Lear's fear of ridicule meant he could not make reference to 'young men' in the limericks who could be him. More painfully, perhaps, he could not bear to be playful about old women for fear of that terrible rhyme, so poignant in his own life – 'There was an old woman who lived in a shoe. / She had so many children she didn't know what to do.'

The Book of Nonsense containing only limericks was published in 1846, followed by *More Nonsense* in 1861/2, his finest book, *Nonsense Songs and Stories*, in 1871 and *Laughable Lyrics* in 1877. Lear has never been out of print and you can now buy his poetry as *Complete Nonsense*, in individual volumes, or single poems as picture books for younger children. Many fine artists have illustrated the verse, but it is hard to improve on Lear's own drawings. He was an artist first and foremost and he would probably be amused that it was his poetry for children that secured him a place in posterity. Perhaps that is not so ironic, as it was with the young that this awkward and accomplished man felt most at home. If critics like Kingsley Amis slighted Lear's work, others did not. W. H. Auden[23] understood the man and his verse, as an extract from this moving poem of tribute makes clear. It is simply called, 'Edward Lear':

> How prodigious the welcome was. Flowers took his hat
> And bore him off to introduce him to the tongs;
> The demon's false nose made the table laugh; a cat
> Soon had him waltzing madly, let him squeeze her hand;
> Words pushed him to the piano to sing comic songs;
>
> And children swarmed to him like settlers. He became a land.

Nonsense verse reached its peak with Lear and has been equalled only by Lewis Carroll.

'I weep for you,' the Walrus said – the poetry of Lewis Carroll

Lewis Carroll (1832–1898) was in reality the Reverend Charles Lutwidge Dodgson, Oxford don and mathematics tutor, who produced some of the best nonsense verse ever written in the Alice stories, and some of the most tedious in his book of verse, *Rhyme? and Reason?*[24] Carroll's impact on children's literature as a whole is a profound one, but it is not within my scope to explore his virtues as a writer of fiction. Plenty of others have done so, among them John Lehmann in *Lewis Carroll and the Spirit of Nonsense* who called the *Alice* books 'among the most notable and original books for children ever published'.[25] In this chapter, I consider the nonsense verse, most of which appears in *Alice in Wonderland* and *Alice Through the Looking-Glass*, though some reference will also be made to *The Hunting of the Snark* and the poems in *Sylvie and Bruno*, which are less well known.

Carroll was a shy, scholarly, awkward tutor, brilliant at mathematics and logic, who lived in the same Oxford College (Christ Church) all his adult life. Although he was reserved and often tongue-tied at social occasions, once he became famous he was on familiar terms with some of the leading writers and artists of his day, including John Ruskin, Christina and her brother, Dante Gabriel Rossetti, Alfred Tennyson, John Everett Millais and George MacDonald. Even so, Mark Twain described him as 'the stillest and shyest full-grown man' he had ever met.[26] Carroll's undoubtedly rather stuffy side was tempered by an appetite for spectacle and melodrama. He was an avid pantomime- and theatre-goer, for example, and often attended performances in London and Eastbourne accompanied by one of his 'child friends'. His artistic photographs of children often had them wearing fancy dress in theatrical poses.

Gillian Avery depicts Carroll as 'a once familiar type of Oxford don' in a recent review of a new biography by Morton Cohen. She tells us he was a 'quintessentially Oxford character . . . deeply conservative, obsessional, touchy, pedantic'.[27] But the conventional biographical sketch paints a one-sided picture of Carroll as kindly, entertaining, fond of children and above all, safe. The adjectives on the back cover of his *Selected Letters* also emphasize his suitability for the young – 'best-loved writers . . . delightful nonsense . . . enchanted generations of children . . . bottomless well of humour . . . immortal Wonderland'[28] and so on.

Clichés like these do not help us to understand the writing or the man. The more disconcerting facts are that he liked pretty little girls, but he didn't much care for boys. He had relationships with more than 100 child friends during his lifetime, meeting many of these little girls at the seaside where he spent months most summers, on trains or, like Alice Liddell, they were the daughters of friends and acquaintances. The relationships were pursued through visits to Carroll's rooms, trips to the seaside, outings, visits to the theatre and, of course, through photographic sessions and in letters. Even a sympathetic Carroll scholar like Guido Almansi admits that:

> The devices and manoeuvres used by this shy, Anglican clergyman are astonishingly similar to those of an impenitent seducer . . . he would draw up a careful list of his 'victims' and 'conquests' . . . This unending quest (for love from his little girl friends) with its quarrels, infatuations, and disillusions, constituted Lewis Carroll's tragic destiny.[29]

Carroll was genuinely a keen and gifted amateur photographer; the Rossetti family, Alfred and Hallam Tennyson and Ellen Terry all faced Carroll's camera with memorable results. But he particularly liked to photograph little girls, sometimes in respectable Victorian poses with their mamas, sometimes dressed in picturesque, tattered costumes showing bare chests, legs and feet; latterly, though, what he really wanted to do was to photograph little girls completely naked. Sometimes he asked his child friends to pose or he asked women friends who were artists to find likely models for him. Many of these little girls went to stay with him at his seaside lodgings.

> It was during the month of July 1879 that Lewis Carroll took the largest number of photographs of girls, sometimes lying on a sofa, sometimes on a blanket in the artist's favourite dress of 'nothing' . . . That Lewis Carroll's interest in his tiny girl friends was not entirely *pure* is such an obvious fact that it is hardly worthwhile stating it.

Almansi tells us that 'Carroll was a fetishist with a morbid interest in nudity, and obsessed with articles of clothing.'[30] But only when it pertained to little girls. Carroll did not give much away in his diary or letters to other adults, but he did confess, 'I do *not* admire naked boys. They always seem to me to need clothes, whereas one hardly sees why the lovely forms of girls should *ever* be covered up.'[31]

> He made and secured demands on families usually flattered by his interest in their daughters and who seldom saw harm in his requests. The true test came when he asked if he might photograph the girls naked . . .

writes Donald Thomas, Carroll's biographer –

> He had permission to photograph the Mayhew daughters in their bathing drawers, presumably including 12-year old Ethel and, as a wild hope, 13-year-old Ruth. It was not enough for him. He insisted to Mr Mayhew that there could be no reasonable objection to Ethel at twelve being photographed nude from the back . . . Nor could there be objection to the God-given beauty of nude girls at 12 or 13 before his camera.[32]

One might just about believe that this bachelor took the nude photographs for the sake of art, if there were not the letters to and visits by these little girls to take into account. Superficially the letters are respectable enough, as Carroll had the girls' mamas to think of. There are a few where Carroll offers inducements for a child to visit him alone; more often there is rather pathetic glee when replying to a child's loving message or a fractious tone when the little girls were not affectionate enough. Almansi tells us that in the letters (of which Carroll obsessively made 100,000 cross-references in his files):

Kisses are numbered, sub-divided and distributed according to complex rituals; the value of a letter depends on the childish signature or the amount of affection which is conveyed in it.[33]

The point to remember is that Carroll was not an unfortunate who fell in love with one child named Alice, but someone who pursued a more than friendly acquaintance with several dozen little girls. Donald Thomas describes his current reputation as lying 'somewhere between that of the public creator of Alice and the private admirer of Lolita . . .' going on to suggest that if Carroll 'had behaved in the second half of the twentieth century as he behaved in the second half of the nineteenth, his rooms at Christ Church would surely have been turned over by the Obscene Publications Squad . . .'[34] Carroll must be seen, of course, within the context of late Victorian morality where a predilection for little girls was not unusual. Ruskin shared his weakness. Yet this inscription to a little girl whom he calls 'a dear Child, / in memory of golden summer hours / and whispers of a summer sea'[35] is more suggestive of hopeless romantic love than paedophile intentions.

> Chat on, sweet Maid, and rescue from annoy
>> Hearts that by wiser talk are unbeguiled.
> Ah, happy he who owns that tenderest joy,
>> The heart-love of a child!
>
> Away, fond thoughts, and vex my soul no more!
>> Work claims my wakeful nights, my busy days –
> Albeit bright memories of that sunlit shore
>> Yet haunt my dreaming gaze!

Indeed, the Reverend Dodgson was not in other respects out of time with Victorian morality. Thomas regularly uses the adverb 'prig' to describe the subject of his biography. He was a regular correspondent to newspapers (a sort of 'disgusted' of Christ Church), easily scandalized at small improprieties, fastidious, phobic and moralistic. He considered editing a 'cleaner' version of an already Bowdlerized Shakespeare, for little girls of course. When 'damn me' was included in a Gilbert and Sullivan opera, he wrote to the press that he could not 'find words to convey the pain I felt on seeing those dear children taught to utter such words'. Alexander Woollcott who edited *The Penguin Complete Alice* describes Carroll both as a 'gentle, shrinking celibate' and the great contrast between 'the cautious, prissy pace of the man and the mad, gay gait of the tale he told'.[36]

This fastidious and priggish side sits uneasily with what was certainly an unhealthy attachment to little girls. Carroll wrote himself of the 'blasphemous thoughts, and the unholy thoughts, which torture with their hateful presence the fancy that would fain be pure'.[37] It is important not to paper over unpleasant aspects of Carroll's life, simply because he was such a talented writer; indeed, he often used his stories to encourage children to spend time with him. He certainly used his power as the adult in the relationships to keep his little girls firmly under his control, dropping them with a callous swiftness if they did anything to annoy him. But he also seems to have been able to communicate well with little girls, many of whom continued to feel affection for him once they had grown up. Perhaps his childhood as one of the adored brothers of eight sisters had some bearing on the adult he was to become.

The reason I have laboured this aspect of Carroll's biography is that it seems likely that his 'passion' for little girls was a major source of his inspiration for writing. Almansi helps us put it in perspective:

> Our interest as readers is, or certainly ought to be, not concerned with the vicarious games of probably diseased Eros, but with the vicarious game-playing of all literature.[38]

To that end, let us attend to the poetry.

Carroll's originality lay in his superb verbal wit, his inventive use of language, his interest in words and meanings, his command of prosody and the extravagant ideas, images and other creations of his unusual imagination. It is very hard to pin down exactly what makes the writing so good: 'It is not satire,' said Lehmann, 'though an element of satire may come into it; it is not parody, though an element of parody may come into it; nor is it fantasy . . .'[39] 'Each word becomes mercurial, subject to the most unexpected transformations,' writes Almansi. He goes on:

> Our pleasure as readers also derives in part from our awareness of the plurality of possible ways of handling the text . . . at one level we read his logical paradoxes, his puns, his fascinating nonsense, while at another level we remain fully aware that a quite different reading may be available next door in the nursery . . .[40]

His verse often featured memorable punch-lines, odd juxtapositions and a sure sense of timing. One particular feature of nonsense that Carroll used to splendid effect was to say the most wild and outrageous things, as if they were perfectly natural.

> The sun was shining on the sea,
>   Shining with all its might:
> He did his very best to make
>   The billows smooth and bright –
> And this was odd, because it was
>   The middle of the night.
>
>   . . .

'The time has come,' the Walrus said,
   'To talk of many things:
Of shoes – and ships- and sealing-wax –
   Of cabbages – and kings –
And why the sea is boiling hot –
   And whether pigs have wings.'

   . . .

'I weep for you,' the Walrus said,
   'I deeply sympathise.'
With sobs and tears he sorted out
   Those of the largest size,
Holding his pocket-handkerchief
   Before his streaming eyes.

These extracts from 'The Walrus and the Carpenter'[41] show nonsense logic at work. It sounds almost sensible and yet it is absolutely crazy to match cabbages with kings, to weep with sympathy at the oysters' plight, once you have eaten them all, or to imagine the sun shining in the middle of the night. The verse fairly flows along with Carroll's hand tightly in control of metre and rhyme, adding impact, drive and humour to the whole satisfying experience. Similarly, some of the pleasures of 'The Lobster Quadrille'[42] lie in the rhythm, pace and repetition, as well as in the mad playfulness of the text.

'Will you walk a little faster?' said a whiting to a snail.
'There's a porpoise close behind us, and he's treading on my tail.'
See how eagerly the lobsters and the turtles all advance!
They are waiting on the shingle – will you come and join the dance?
   Will you, won't you, will you, won't you, will you join the dance?
   Will you, won't you, will you, won't you, won't you join the dance?

Another attractive quality to Carroll's poetry is the dextrous precision of his language combined with the ingenious absurdity of the content. A good example is 'The Mad Gardener's Song'[43] where one impossibility is heaped upon another.

He thought he saw a Rattlesnake
   That questioned him in Greek:
He looked again, and found it was
   The Middle of Next Week.
'The one thing I regret,' he said,
   'Is that it cannot speak!'

There was a sadistic side in Carroll's books and letters: in his biography, Derek Hudson talks of the 'ruthless element',[44] Lehmann of the 'oral aggression'[45] in Carroll's writing. The only rhyme or reason to 'Speak Roughly to your little Boy'[46] is Carroll's well-known dislike of aforesaid 'little boys':

> Speak roughly to your little boy
> And beat him when he sneezes:
> He only does it to annoy,
> Because he knows it teases.
>
> *Chorus*
> Wow! Wow! Wow!

Perhaps the pinnacle of this extraordinary writer's talent is most evident in 'Jabberwocky' where Carroll creates a mock-heroic tale in a surreal atmosphere, as strange as anything Dali ever painted. Apparently the opening four lines were written to amuse his family when Carroll was a young man.

> Twas brillig and the slithy toves
>   Did gyre and gimble in the wabe;
> All mimsy were the borogroves,
>   And the mome raths outgrabe.
>
> 'Beware the Jabberwock, my son!
> The Jaws that bite, the claws that catch!
> Beware the Jubjub bird, and shun
> The frumious Bandersnatch!'[47]

Goldthwaite describes 'Jabberwocky' as 'a fragment he retrieved from the past and enlarged into the future, a thought from his youth that he found useful in middle age. It is a puzzle to understand because he designed it to be so; the outward form is a deception. The thing's true nature has been hidden behind a camouflage of verbal misdirection. The poem is actually twice disguised: it is printed in reverse, so that Alice must hold it before a mirror to read it, and the meaning is screened by coinages like 'brillig' and 'fruminous . . .'[48]

Carroll delights in inventive language. Lehmann talks of Carroll's 'portmanteau'[49] words where two meanings are brilliantly packed into one: 'slithy', for example meant lithe and slimy, whereas 'mimsy' referred to being both flimsy and miserable. The poem is visually stunning and it lends itself wonderfully to being read aloud. Although the first stanza is utter nonsense, it is so powerful that readers can create their own wild imaginings. There are moments of pure virtuosity: 'galumphing', for example, is the perfect verb to match the victor's triumphant progress; 'burbled' is a lovely word to describe the Jabberwock as it 'came whiffling through the tulgey wood'; the 'vorpal blade' which went 'snicker-snack!', my 'beamish boy' and 'O frabjous day!' are funny yet convincing.

'The Hunting of the Snark', Carroll's last publication of note, is considered a masterpiece by many, though it is more perplexing and less obviously appealing than the poems in the *Alice* books. Contemporary reviews were mixed; some were negative. *The Atheneum* wondered on 8 April 1876 whether the author 'has merely been inspired by a wild desire to reduce to idiocy as many readers, and more especially reviewers, as possible. At all events, he has published what we may consider to be the most bewildering of modern poems.'[50] *The Spectator* was more straightforward: 'We regret that 'Snark' is a failure.'[51]

This is the poem where Carroll's unhappiness is most evident and he was certainly depressive while he was writing it. Carroll himself called the poem 'An Agony in eight Fits'.[52] However, Martin Gardner's description of the poem as 'existential agony [the Boojum is final, absolute extinction] and the horror of confronting death in a purposeless, Darwinian world'[53] seems to me a little far-fetched. 'The Snark' is certainly a very strange poem and darker than those in his fiction; 'Fit the Fifth' contains some painful imagery and language – 'threatened, dismal, desolate, disgust, a scream shrill and high'[54] – and what might be some autobiographical lines:

> He thought of his childhood, left far far behind –
> That blissful and innocent state –
> The sound so exactly recalled to his mind
> A pencil that squeaks on a slate.'[55]

Edward Guiliano detected 'terror and despair throughout the overtly humorous Snark. This tension between the comic tone and the underlying anxieties is perhaps the poem's most distinguishing and fascinating characteristic.'[56] Morton Cohen mentions the preoccupation with time passing in 'The Snark'; other scholars noted the great number of references to death in the *Alice* books and how Carroll described himself as old at 40. This obsession with time is best exemplified by the White Rabbit (Carroll himself?) anxiously consulting his watch and worrying about being late.

Late or early, Carroll was in many respects a person of his time, yet also sadly out of time. In old age Carroll acknowledged himself as a disappointed man, despite his literary and financial success, often refusing to acknowledge himself as the author of Alice except to his child-friends.

Morton Cohen's assessment of Carroll is sympathetic. His *Selected Letters* and biography tone down the unsavoury side of Carroll's life, emphasizing the loneliness Carroll suffered and his fierce battle with himself to suppress and correct his guilt-ridden urges. Cohen also speculates as to how Carroll's stammer may have played havoc with his self-esteem and confidence. Summing up Carroll's talent, Cohen highlights 'his genius with words, his creative nonsense, his hilarious *dramatis personae*, his way of appealing to ear, eye, head, and heart – they are all elements of his magic.'[57]

Elizabeth Sewell[58] stresses the logic at work in Carroll's nonsense, describing it as 'a self-consistent set of orderly relations . . . having close affinities with logic, mathematics and the analytical processes of the mind' and, interestingly, 'where emotion was excluded'. She contrasts Lear's nonsense: 'simple, concrete, descriptive', with that of Carroll who 'seems to spend much of his time watching the language process itself'.[59] Gillian Avery agrees; replying to her own question as to why the 'Alices' are probably the most quoted texts in English literature, she writes: 'He took over the ruthless spirit and the nonsense of the English nursery rhymes adding his own quirkish humour and his feeling for logical thought, and losing himself in the game.'[60]

F. J. Harvey Darton calls *Alice* 'more than a flare of genius . . . it was the coming to the surface, powerfully and permanently, the first unapologetic, undocumented appearance in print, for readers who sorely needed it, of liberty of thought in children's books.' Darton unerringly points out that Carroll's many imitators 'invent, *but they have not the logic*'[61] (my emphasis). At any rate, as John Carey pointed out in a review of Cohen's biography, Carroll 'made up a story that has changed our culture, has never been out of print, has been translated into virtually every spoken language, and is, with the Bible and Shakespeare, the most widely quoted book in the Western world.'[62] Carroll's originality is embodied in *Alice*, a text that will live as long as any books exist.

Notes

1 Lewis Carroll, from 'The Mock Turtle's Song', *Alice's Adventures in Wonderland*, originally London, 1865. This edition *The Complete Works of Lewis Carroll*, ed. Alexander Woollcott, Nonesuch Press, London, 1989, p. 98.
2 John Lehmann, *Lewis Carroll and the Spirit of Nonsense*, Nottingham Byron Lecture, 1972, University of Nottingham. p. 3.
3 Jean Kenward, 'Just Nonsense', *Books* [Journal of National Book League] No. 363, 1966, pp. 22–26.
4 Vivien Noakes, *Edward Lear: the Life of a Wanderer*, Fontana, London, 1979.
5 John Goldthwaite, *The Natural History of Make-Believe*, Oxford, New York, pp. 33, 36.
6 Brian Alderson, *A Book of Bosh*, Penguin, London, 1975, p. 7.
7 *Edward Lear's Tennyson*, ed. Ruth Pitman, Carcanet, Manchester, 1988.
8 Marianne North, quoted in Noakes, *op. cit.*, p. 112.
9 Alfred, Lord Tennyson quoted in Pitman, *op. cit.*, p. 17.
10 Noakes, *op. cit.*, p. 176.
11 Peter Levi, *Edward Lear: a Biography*, Macmillan, London, 1995.
12 Kingsley Amis, ed. *The New Oxford Book of Light Verse*, Oxford, 1987.
13 Edward Lear, from 'By Way of Preface', *Complete Nonsense*, Wordsworth Editions, Ware, 1994.

14 Edward Strachey, Introduction, *ibid.*, p. 12, 13.
15 Edward Lear, from 'The Nutcracker and the Sugar-Tongs', *ibid.*
16 Edward Lear, from 'The Dong with a Luminous Nose', *ibid.*
17 Edward Lear quoted in Noakes, *op. cit.*, p. 279.
18 The next two extracts which follow come from Edward Lear, *Nonsense Songs and Stories*, 1871, this edition, 1994, *op. cit.*.
19 Edward Lear, from 'The Akond of Swat'.
20 Edward Lear, from 'The Quangle Wangle's Hat'.
21 Richard Scrafton Sharpe, *Anecdotes and Adventures of Fifteen Gentlemen*, quoted in Iona and Peter Opie, *The Oxford Book of Children's Verse*, London, 1973.
22 Edward Lear, *A Book of Nonsense*, London, 1846, this edition 1994, *op. cit.*
23 W. H. Auden, from 'Edward Lear', *W. H. Auden: Collected Poems*, ed. Edward Mendelson, Faber, London, 1976.
24 Lewis Carroll, 'Rhyme? and Reason?' or 'Phantasmagoria' in *Collected Verse of Lewis Carroll*, Macmillan, London, 1932.
25 Lehmann, *op. cit.*, p. 4.
26 Mark Twain, quoted in Goldthwaite, *op. cit.*, p. 97.
27 Gillian Avery, 'Alice and the Road to Wonderland', *Times Educational Supplement*, January 5 1996, p. 31.
28 Morton W. Cohen, ed., *Lewis Carroll: Selected Letters*, Papermac, London, 1979.
29 Guido Almansi, ed. *Lewis Carroll: Photographs and Letters to his Child Friends*, Franco Maria Ricci, Parma, 1975, p. 196.
30 *Ibid.*, p. 25.
31 Lewis Carroll, quoted in Almansi, *ibid.*, p. 195.
32 Donald Thomas, *Lewis Carroll: A Portrait with Background*, John Murray, London, 1996, p. 263.
33 *Ibid.*, p. 20.
34 *Ibid.*, pp. 1, 6.
35 Lewis Carroll, Inscription to a 'Dear Child', *The Hunting of the Snark*, London, 1876, this edition, Woollcott, 1989, *op. cit.*, p. 679.
36 Alexander Woollcott, *The Penguin Complete Alice*, Penguin, Harmondsworth, 1982.
37 Lewis Carroll, quoted in *ibid.*, p. 6.
38 Almansi, *op. cit.*, p. 26.
39 Lehmann, *op. cit.*, p. 4.
40 Almansi, *op. cit.*, pp. 16, 17.
41 Lewis Carroll, from 'The Walrus and the Carpenter', *Alice Through the Looking Glass*, 1871, in Woollcott, 1982, *op. cit.*, pp. 168–9.
42 Lewis Carroll, from 'The Lobster Quadrille' in *Alice's Adventures in Wonderland*, 1865, in *op. cit.*, 1982, p. 98.
43 Lewis Carroll, from 'The Mad Gardener's Song', *Sylvie and Bruno*, in *op. cit.*, pp. 168–9.
44 Derek Hudson, *Lewis Carroll, An Illustrated Biography*, Constable, London, 1954, p. 210.
45 Lehmann, *op. cit.*, p. 7.
46 Lewis Carroll, from 'Speak roughly to your little boy', *Alice's Adventures in Wonderland*, 1865, in Woolcott, 1989, *op. cit.*, p. 62.
47 Lewis Carroll, from 'Jabberwocky', 1871, in Woolcott, 1989, *op. cit.*, p. 140–2.
48 Goldthwaite, *op. cit.*, p. 117.
49 Lehmann, *op. cit.*, p. 8.

50   *The Atheneum*, 8 April 1876, quoted in 'Hark the Snark' by Marton Cohen in *Lewis Carroll: A Celebration* ed. Edward Guiliano, Clarkson Potter Inc. New York, 1982, p. 497.

51   *The Spectator* 40, 22 April, 1876, *ibid.*, p. 527.

52   Lewis Carroll, quoted in Edward Guiliano, 1982, *op. cit.*, p. 124.

53   Martin Gardner, 'Laughter and Despair in *The Hunting of the Snark*', in Guiliano, 1982, *op. cit.*, p. 128.

54   Lewis Carroll, from *The Hunting of the Snark*, London, 1876, this edition, Chatto & Windus, London, 1993, p. 29.

55   Lewis Carroll, *ibid.*

56   Edward Guiliano, 1982, *op. cit.*, p. 123.

57   Morton Cohen, *Lewis Carroll: a Biography*, Papermac, London, 1995, p. 530.

58   Elizabeth Sewell, 'The Nonsense System in Lewis Carroll's Work and in Today's World', in Guiliano *op. cit.*, 1982, p. 60.

59   Elizabeth Sewell, *The Field of Nonsense*, Chatto and Windus, London, p. 18.

60   Gillian Avery, *op. cit.*, p. 31.

61   F. J. Harvey Darton, *Children's Books in England*, revised Brian Alderson, Cambridge University Press, Cambridge, 1932/1982, pp. 260–1.

62   John Carey, quoted on back cover of Cohen 1995, *op. cit.*

CHAPTER 7

'Of the Spontaneous Kind?'

Christina Rossetti's *Sing-Song* and its precursors

I'll nurse you on my knee, my knee,
  My own little son;
I'll rock you, rock you, in my arms,
  My least little one.[1]

Rock on, rock on
My pretty boy.
And you shall be
Your mother's joy.[2]

The first of these extracts is by Christina Rossetti (1830–1894), the second by Jane Johnson (1706–1759). Christina Rossetti was one of the greatest poets of the Victorian period; Jane Johnson, writing more than 100 years earlier, was an obscure middle-class woman who produced stories and poems for her own children with no thought of publication. Unless you happen to know Rossetti's poem, I doubt whether you can tell which is which. The fact that it was easy to find similarities in the writing for children by two such different women living at different times raises some interesting questions about gender, childhood and literature. I want to suggest, for example, that if we explored some of that neglected literature of the eighteenth and nineteenth centuries – namely finding out what women, particularly mothers, were writing for and reading to their children – there might be quite a few alternatives to the received canon.

Women poets

Roger Lonsdale[3] tells us that only two collections of poetry by women were published in the first decade of the eighteenth century; by the end of the century the total reached was 30. It is important to remember that writing for children was the *only* way for many women to get published, so it is no surprise that so many women took to children's literature with a passion and worked so hard at it. Victor Watson suggests in

The Prose and the Passion[4] that children's literature provided a space where affection between adults and children could be openly addressed and that this option was mainly taken up by women. I want to explore how women's voices might be different from those of men in important respects and how we can learn to appreciate their qualities. A key area of research for feminists is to find out more about what women were writing in the private domain, some of it for their children. Exciting new information about this area has come to light through Jane Johnson's *Nursery Library*[5] providing evidence that at least one woman was writing delightful, low key, child-centred texts before Newbery started publishing his little books. How many more Janes were there?

In this chapter, I want to centre on Christina Rossetti's poetry for children and trace my way back to Jane Johnson. The first quotation (above) comes from Christina Rossetti's only collection of poetry for children, *Sing-Song*, although the better-known *Goblin Market*[6] has been marketed and illustrated for the young as well as for adults. By examining some of the poems in *Sing-Song* and considering possible precursors, I want to make a case for viewing this outstanding collection as the culmination of work by a long line of women, demonstrating how children could be the subject matter and audience for poetry. *Sing-Song*, despite its many charms, has been more often out of print than in it: even in Rossetti's centenary year, 1994, it was hard to find a copy. Only generations of editors of anthologies for children have kept the poetry of *Sing-Song* in the public eye since her death.

What Rossetti achieves in the best poems in *Sing-Song* is a lightness of tone, an almost physical expression of affection, playfulness and warmth. A few poems are almost nonsense verse. What some commentators describe as spontaneous or natural or womanly or even slight is actually nursery verse of the highest order, so that it rings like a bell. It *should* be light. Like the text in some of the best picturebooks, it is low key, unobtrusive, merging into the illustrations, deceptively simple. But to do this well is very difficult indeed.

It is worth remembering that Christina Rossetti is one of the few women poets of the nineteenth century to be regularly represented in the children's canon, despite the fact that women were predominant in children's poetry during this period. Despite their numbers and the quality of their writing, they have been largely excluded from influential poetry anthologies. (Some account of this and the reasons behind it are taken up in Chapter 9.) In this context, suffice it to say that Christina Rossetti is the success story, yet her work has been marginalized too. When I checked on *Sing-Song*'s publishing history, I discovered only one mention after its original publication in 1872. There was a new edition in 1893, then a complete blank until 1968 when Dover reissued the original, beautifully illustrated by Arthur Hughes. If this is what happens to Rossetti's only collection for children, what hope is there for other women writers?

'Of the spontaneous kind'

One reason for the neglect (until recently) of Christina Rossetti's poetry may lie with William Rossetti,[7] her beloved brother.

> I have said elsewhere, but may as well repeat it here, that her habits of composition were entirely *of the casual and spontaneous kind*, from her earliest to her latest years. If something came into her head which she found suggestive of verse, she put it into verse. It came to her (I take it) very easily, without meditating a possible subject, and without her making any great difference in the first from the latest form of the verses which embodied it; . . . I question her having ever once deliberated with herself whether or not she would write something or other . . . something impelled her feelings, or came into her head, and her hand obeyed her dictation. (my emphasis).

In her recent biography Jan Marsh[8] tracks the genesis of several poems, showing that some days at least were spent on their composition. So William was not entirely correct in his supposition. And if Rossetti's composition was largely intuitive, what is wrong with that? Many writers describe first drafts as coming from they know not where – the unconscious part of the writing process. William was aware that Christina revised her work: 'but *some* difference, with a view to right and fine detail of execution, she did of course make when needful'.[9] No doubt, Rossetti's modesty and well-known self-disparagement colluded with William's version of her craft, but how easily he slips into that role.

His description of Rossetti's writing process has influenced many subsequent scholars. Walter de la Mare[10] edited a book of her poetry in 1930, entitled *Christina Rossetti: Poems*, where he is both appreciative and condescending, describing her as 'that still rarer thing, a woman of genius':

> It is said that every man of genius shares the hospitality of his heart with a woman and a child. Christina Rossetti was that still rarer thing, a woman of genius.

De la Mare was aware of the quality of her verse, describing *Sing-Song* as 'the simplest, quietest poems for childlike children in the language' and her best poetry for adults as concerned with 'imaginative truth and invariably charged with feeling'. But de la Mare reinforces the apparent spontaneity and what he calls 'naturalness' of her writing:

> It is possible . . . to delight in Christina Rossetti's poems for their pure sensuousness and naturalness . . . And whatever final artistry went to their making, one and all were the outcome of purest impulse . . . and as naturally as

a wild flower out of the half-frozen ground, her lyrics sprang into beauty out of her austerity.[11]

While there is certainly truth in the reference to austerity and a desire on de la Mare's part get to the heart of Rossetti's poetic talent, linking women's poetry with 'pure impulse' and 'naturalness' patronizes and demeans it.

'An amiable facility'

J. D. Symon in a preface to a beautiful edition of Rossetti's *Verses*, privately published when she was a teenager, says this:

> She sang the moment's emotion with a diffuse and amiable facility . . . questions of form never seem to have hindered her spontaneity . . . her first fresh moment of inspiration gives a vision of an unearthly world that was granted in fuller measure to the poet's brother, Dante Gabriel . . . her technical skill was never at any time of the very highest, the girl was mother of the woman . . .[12]

With the benefit of hindsight, it is easy to criticize Symon, but his condescension in the use of words like 'aimiable' and 'spontaneity' make him fair game.

In his preface to *The Poetical Works of Christina Rossetti*, William considers her poetic stature:

> . . . within the range of her subject and thought, and the limits of her executive endeavour, a good one . . . fully conscious as I am of their limitations . . .[13]

That is true of most poets, is it not? Though astute, kindly and loyal, there is still a sense of William's reluctance to recognize his sister's talent in full measure. His view of the capacities of women is conservative even for his day. Here is his assessment of Felicia Hemans, writing a generation before Christina Rossetti. 'One might sum up the weak points in Mrs Hemans' poetry by saying that it is not only "feminine" poetry but also "female" poetry: besides exhibiting the fineness and charm of womanhood, it has the monotone of mere sex.'[14]

Taking the same sort of stance, Arthur Waugh in his review of the 1904 edition of Rossetti's *Poems* for the *Daily Chronicle* writes:

> She was a woman first of all and she was content to remain a woman to the end. Her poetry does not strive or cry: it makes no effort to do anything foreign to its own gentle, tender nature: it accepts the burden of womanhood.[15]

Although this reads ludicrously today, these are the opinions which helped to shape literary assessment of Rossetti and her fellow women writers.

W. H. Auden includes Christina Rossetti in *Nineteenth Century Minor Poets*.[16] In his introduction to *Victorian Verse*, George MacBeth[17] only mentions Rossetti's name in passing. As late as 1970, Elizabeth Jennings described Rossetti as in the 'forefront of minor late nineteenth century poets'. Although Jennings talked of 'the perfection of her lyric ear' and 'her flawless sense of sound', she falls in line with majority critical opinion of the time in stating that 'Christina Rossetti is not a very popular poet today. Her work, to many people, seems extremely dated.'[18] These comments demonstrate how much critics feed on one another. Writing from what feels like the more enlightened standpoint of 1997, I am aware that my views are, of course, only part of a new dogma intent on re-interpreting and re-valuing women writers of the past.

Poetic precursors

In this chapter I consider some of the women poets Rossetti was known to admire, and speculate about others whom she is likely to have read or whose writing shared characteristics with her own, only as they relate to children's poetry. I hope to do these often neglected writers something more like justice.

We know that Christina Rossetti liked Felicia Hemans's (1793–1835) poetry, as Jan Marsh tells us that Hemans was the 'most obvious influence on her juvenile work'.[19] William's present for her fourteenth Christmas was *The Sacred Harp*[20] containing many poems by Hemans which Rossetti described as beautiful. There is some resemblance between the poem she wrote for her mother, aged 11, and Hemans's birthday poem for her son:

> Where sucks the bee now? Summer is flying,
> Leaves round the elm-tree faded are lying;
> Violets are gone from their grassy dell,
> With the cowslip cups, where the fairies dwell;
> The rose from the garden hath passed away -
> Yet happy, fair boy, is thy natal day!
> (Hemans)[21]

> **To my Mother on her Birthday**
>
> Today's your natal day
>   Sweet flowers I bring;
> Mother accept I pray,
>   My offering.

And may you happy live,
    And long us bless
Receiving as you give
    Great happiness.
        (Rossetti)[22]

Hemans, like Rossetti, showed early promise and had a collection of poetry published when she was only 13. Another inspiration for the 'sweet flowers' might have been Charlotte Smith (discussed more fully in Chapter 3) whose books of poetry were highly valued at the end of the eighteenth and early nineteenth century. If Christina Rossetti did not know Charlotte Smith's poetry for adults, and that is unlikely, she might have come across *Conversations Introducing Poetry To Children*, 1804. This contains nature poetry both sensuous and lush, yet full of sadness and disappointment, hallmarks of Rossetti's poetry too.

Queen of fragrance, lovely rose,
Thy soft and silken leaves disclose.
The winter's past, the tempests fly,
Soft gales breathe gently through the sky.
The silver dews and genial showers
Call forth a blooming waste of flowers;
And lo! thy beauties now unclose
Queen of fragrance, lovely rose!
Yet, ah! how soon that bloom is flown!
How soon thy blushing charms are gone!
Today thy crimson buds unveil,
Tomorrow scattered in the gale.
Ah! human bliss as swiftly goes.[23]

Dance little baby

Jane and Ann Taylor's poetry (also considered in Chapters 1, 3 and 4), particularly *Rhymes for the Nursery*, almost certainly influenced Rossetti with their observations of childhood and gentle poems of motherly love. Marsh cites Rossetti's familiarity with Charlotte Yonge's series of articles for *Macmillan's Magazine* about children's literature that appeared around the time *Sing-Song* was published, where Yonge gave credit to the Taylor sisters 'for their astonishing simplicity without puerility'.[24] Indeed, this may be one of the hallmarks of women's voices for the young – simplicity without stupidity. Nursery rhymes share that distinction.

To be a poetess I don't aspire,
From such a title humbly I retire;[25]

Although Jane Taylor professed herself no poetess in this poem written when she was 10, her life gives the lie to that declaration. *Original Poems For Infant Minds*, published with her sister, Ann in 1804, were by two hard-working young women, part of a serious, provincial, literary family whom Leonore Davidoff and Catherine Hall document in their ground-breaking text, *Family Fortunes*.[26]

Before the Taylors' seminal collection, most poetry for children was uninterested in exploring loving relationships between mothers and children. Harvey Darton describes *Original Poems* as awaking the nurseries of England. *Rhymes for the Nursery* was even softer in tone with fewer moral tales in verse and more loving poems to small children. If Christina Rossetti was to make the cradle song her own, it was the Taylor sisters who opened the nursery door seven decades earlier. At last, affection between mother and baby was being openly and tenderly expressed in poetry that was deeply in tune with little children. A noticeable feature of the Taylors' work, which Rossetti also employed to advantage, was the use of loving, inconsequential language – the sort of affectionate, rhythmic talk, often quite close to nonsense, that adults tend to use with babies.

The Baby's Dance

Dance, little baby, dance up high,
Never mind baby, mother is by;
Crow and caper, caper and crow,
There little baby, there you go:
Up to the ceiling, down to the ground,
Backwards and forwards, round and round.
Then dance, little baby, and mother shall sing,
With the merry gay coral, ding, ding, a-ling, ding.
(Ann Taylor)[27]

Such a poem looks commonplace to contemporary readers. But it must have felt like a breath of fresh air to children used to being bossed about by adult authors telling them how to behave. 'The Kind Mamma' is another such example.

Come, dear, and sit upon my knee,
And give me kisses, one, two, three,
And tell me whether you love me,
My baby.[28]

There is a direct line to Rossetti, I think, particularly in the concreteness and physicality of her poems.

> I'll nurse you on my knee, my knee,
>   My own little son;
> I'll rock you, rock you, in my arms,
>   My least little one.[29]
>   (Rossetti)

Certainly, in Rossetti's *Sing-Song* the mother's eyes are always on the baby and she offers unconditional love. 'Love Me' directs our attention to the baby in the mother's arms, looking up into her eyes, as she murmurs sweet nothings. It is very simple, melodious and exquisitely tender.

> Love me, – I love you,
>   Love me, my baby;
> Sing it high, sing it low,
>   Sing it as it may be.
>
> Mother's arms under you,
>   Her eyes above you
> Sing it high, sing it low,
>   Love me, – I love you.[30]

Jan Marsh suggests that this empathy for mothers and babies sprang from her own childhood: 'As the youngest, she was cradled at the breast while the older children played, with that sense of utter security later invoked in her children's verses . . .'[31] Certainly Rossetti's early childhood was a very loving and secure one with Italian parents who were, perhaps, more attentive, demonstrative and affectionate than many English parents of the period. William Rossetti's *Memoir* adds confirmation: 'The children were constantly with their parents; there was no separate nursery, and no rigid line drawn between the big ones and the little ones . . .'[32]

> You are my one, and I have not another;
>   Sleep soft, my darling, my trouble and treasure;
> Sleep warm and soft in the arms of your mother,
>   Dreaming of pretty things, dreaming of pleasure.[33]

On father's knee

William recorded that the baby Christina often sat on her father's knee while he played clapping rhymes with her. It seems likely she drew on her own babyhood when writing *Sing-Song* and the confidence and authenticity came from her experience of adults playing with toddlers using simple, rhythmic language.

Mix a pancake,
Stir a pancake,
　Pop it in the pan;
Fry the pancake,
Toss the pancake, –
　Catch it if you can.[34]

Charles and Mary Lamb (discussed also in Chapter 3) had been influenced by *Original Poems* like a great number of others; they produced *Poetry For Children* in 1809. Charles Lamb wrote to Coleridge:

Our little poems are but humble . . . You must read them remembering they were task work, and perhaps, you will admire the number of subjects, all of children, picked out by an old bachelor and an old maid.[35]

Charles Lamb's apparent modesty is actually quite accurate. The poems appear not to have been written out of conviction, but were, indeed, 'task work' for a particular market by people who did not have much contact with children and they are, therefore, not very distinguished. As usual, Darton's opinion is most acute: (the poems were) 'well within the Moral Tale ring-fence . . . practically none has the real intimacy which a child could . . . keep warm in memory . . . many other arch pieces creak audibly in the mechanism . . .'[36] But they are quite kind and some of them have their moments. One of the most appealing poems in their collection, and one of the most popular at the time, is 'Choosing a Name'. It is written as if in the voice of a child, something rather rare before this date and no mama in sight!

I have got a new-born sister;
I was nigh the first that kiss'd her.
When the nursing woman brought her
To Papa, his infant daughter,
How Papa's dear eyes did glisten! –
She will shortly be to christen:
And Papa has made the offer,
I shall have the naming of her.[37]

The lively tone of this poem recalls one of Rossetti's:

What does the bee do?
　Bring home honey.
And what does Father do?
　Bring home money.

> And what does Mother do?
>   Lay out the money.
> And what does baby do?
>   Eat up the honey.[38]

There is also a sense of playfulness in Lambs's 'The Sister's Expostulation on her Brother Learning Latin'; the title alone says a lot about gender in the nineteenth century. And 'The Reaper's Child', which is typically Romantic in theme, treats tenderly with mothers and babies.

> Shut these odious books up, brother –
> They have made you quite another
> Thing from what you us'd to be –
> Once you lik'd to play with me –
>
> Now you leave me all alone . . .
> (from 'The Sister's Expostulation . . . ')
>
> When you were as young as this field-nursed daughter,
> You were fed in the house, and brought up on the knee;
> So tenderly watched, thy fond mother thought her
> Whole time well bestow'd in nursing of thee.[39]
>   (from 'The Reaper's Child')

As we know from Charles's letters that Mary wrote two-thirds of the poetry (although we don't know which two-thirds were hers) we can claim her as one of the now-forgotten women poets writing for children.

Buds and babies

Rossetti was one of the few poets to write as if a mother were softly addressing a small child, holding it very close and whispering in its ear. It is sad that such sensuous poetry should be written by someone who never had a baby of her own. 'Buds and Babies' may express her feelings on the subject.

> A million buds are born that never blow,
> That sweet with promise lift a pretty head
> To blush and wither on a barren bed
> And leave no fruit to show.

Sweet, unfulfilled. Yet have I understood
One joy, by their fragility made plain:
Nothing was ever beautiful in vain,
Or all in vain was good.[40]

That subject is reminiscent of Dorothy Wordsworth (discussed at length in Chapter 3) who also wrote tender poems to someone else's child.

The days are cold, the nights are long,
The north wind sings a doleful song;
Then hush again upon my breast;
All merry things are now at rest,
  Save thee, my pretty love!

The kitten sleeps upon the hearth,
The crickets long have ceased their mirth;
There's nothing stirring in the house
Save one wee, hungry, nibbling mouse,
  Then why so busy thou?

Nay! start not at that sparkling light;
'Tis but the moon that shines so bright
On the window pane bedropped with rain:
Then little darling, sleep again,
  And wake when it is day![41]

'The Cottager to her Infant' is one of Dorothy Wordsworth's sympathetic observations of the real lives of the poor. Her domestic, informal writing is typical of many women then – modest, unpretentious, honest and admirable for all that. This is a body of work Rossetti would not have known, as Dorothy Wordsworth was not writing for publication. A recent editor of the Grasmere journal describes her thus: 'Dorothy Wordsworth was one of those sweet characters whose only life lies in their complete dedication to a man of genius.'[42] Dorothy Wordsworth was certainly devoted to her brother, but her journal makes plain that she had other interests: her love of nature, her pleasure in reading, her joy in physical exercise, her garden, her satisfaction in domestic pursuits (notwithstanding the hard work involved). Isn't it time such stereotyped views of women were left behind?

Pretty lessons in verse

Rossetti probably was familiar with Sara Coleridge's *Pretty Lessons In Verse For All Good Children*, a rather didactic title as late as 1834, though her intentions are otherwise. Criticizing *Original Poems* for mental depravity, bodily torture and adult sorrow, Coleridge suggested that 'the sentiments . . . are morbid.'[43] Instead, *Pretty Lessons* would focus on 'nothing but what is bright and joyous'. Maybe that is what made them so bland. But the most memorable poem in *Pretty Verse* did have lasting qualities; 'The Months of the Year' is still popular in anthologies today. Rossetti also produced a version:

> January brings the sleet and snow,
> Makes our feet and fingers glow.
>
> February brings the rain,
> Thaws the frozen lake again.
>   (Coleridge)[44]

> January cold desolate;
> February all dripping wet;
> March wind ranges;
> April changes.
>   (Rossetti)[45]

During her childhood, Rossetti became familiar with Mary Howitt's poetry (also mentioned in Chapters 3 and 4) and her translations of Hans Andersen's fairy tales. Howitt was a prolific writer for children, with her husband, William, and one of the most eminent women poets in the 1840s. As a little girl, Christina Rossetti may well have been read poems such as 'Buttercups and Daisies'. Rossetti's poems are infinitely superior in craftmanship as well as in the quality of her imagery, but Howitt can turn a lilting rhyme well enough.

> Buttercups and Daisies –
> O! the pretty flowers!
> Coming ere the spring-time,
> To tell of sunny hours.
> While the trees are leafless,
> While the fields are bare,
> Buttercups and Daisies
> Spring up here and there.[46]
>   (Howitt)

> In the meadow – what in the meadow?
> Bluebells, buttercups, meadowsweet,
>   And fairy rings for the children's feet
>   In the meadow.[46]
>   (Howitt)

Where innocent bright-eyed daisies are,
    With blades of grass between,
Each daisy stands up like a star
    Out of a sky of green.[47]
        (Rossetti)

'Hurt no living thing'

Sing-Song is not entirely composed of cradle songs. Rossetti is, perhaps, the first and best 'green' poet. Her attachment to the less glamorous inhabitants of the animal kingdom is well known.

Hurt no living thing:
    Ladybird, nor butterfly,
Nor moth with dusky wing,
    Nor cricket chirping cheerily,
Nor grasshopper so light of leap,
    Nor dancing gnat, nor beetle fat,
Nor harmless worms that creep.

      *   *   *

Brown and furry
Caterpillar in a hurry,
Take your walk
To the shady leaf, or stalk,
Or what not,
Which may be the chosen spot.
No toad spy you,
Hovering bird of prey pass by you;
Spin and die,
To live again a butterfly.[48]

Christina Rossetti was typical of her time in having what we now consider a somewhat maudlin fascination with death. *Sing-Song* may be a nursery rhyme book, but a goodly handful deal with babies or mothers dying, usually surrounded by angels promising a happy after-life. To some extent this was a reflection of the high infant mortality rate of Victorian Britain.

Baby lies so fast asleep
    That no pain can grieve her;
Put a snowdrop in her hand,
    Kiss her once and leave her.[49]

There are a number of pattern poems in *Sing-Song* that have an educational intention as well as a sense of fun. Rossetti's mother used 'learning rhymes' with her as a child, so there may be echoes from her own nursery days. The fact that she was bilingual probably gave her an edge playing language games.

Here's a puzzle poem:

> A pin has a head, but has no hair;
> A clock has a face, but no mouth there:

A counting poem:

> 1 and 1 are 2 –
> That's for me and you.
> 2 and 2 are 4 –
> That's a couple more.

A sort of riddle:

> No dandelions tell the time,
>   Although they turn to clocks;
> Cat's-cradle does not hold the cat,
>   Nor foxglove fit the fox.

But she was no crude didact. The best riddle is moving and unforgettable:

> What are heavy? sea-sand and sorrow:
> What are brief? today and tomorrow:
> What are frail? spring blossoms and youth:
> What are deep? the ocean and truth.[50]

'In the Bleak Midwinter'

Finally, there is Rossetti's famous carol, 'In the Bleak Midwinter',[51] one of the most beautiful and painful ever written, which was published shortly after *Sing-Song*. It is likely that she would have read *Hymns For Little Children* by Cecil Frances Alexander, published in the 1840s; and she would probably have been familiar with Anna Barbauld's writing as one of the most distinguished authors of the eighteenth century, particularly her *Hymns In Prose For Children*, 1781. Rossetti would also have been aware of the Taylors' *Hymns For Infant Minds*, 1810. (The devotional verse of all three women is discussed in Chapter 1.) Good as they were, none of them could match the exquisite tenderness and yearning of 'In the Bleak Midwinter' which seemed to draw on all her passionate Christian devotion and compassion for the best in human nature. Some commentators have suggested that the poem is about being barren and childless; it is certainly a hymn that dwells on harsh, stark, cold images. It opens with a bleak universe all right for that first Christmas.

> Earth stood hard as iron,
> Water like a stone;

But it does warm up when we get to the stable, the loving mother and those who want to give the special baby a present. You might argue that serenity, for Rossetti, comes with religion; the cold place is the real world. All God's angels 'throng'd the air', the landscape was hard as iron, but the baby's mother recognized that what he needed was the human touch or 'a kiss', as Rossetti had suggested so often in *Sing-Song*. It takes a mother and poor people to bring warmth to the frozen stable in the bleak midwinter by giving the baby all they have – 'my heart'. If this is what women write 'of the spontaneous kind', we certainly have something to be thankful for.

I will end Rossetti's story here. Although Isobel Armstrong[52] states firmly in *Victorian Poetry* that 'in the depth and range of their projects, and in the beauty and boldness of their experiments with language, Tennyson, Browning and Rossetti stand pre-eminent' she is still too often treated as a minor poet by many critics. As for the other women who may have influenced her, their work is hardly known at all today.

Jane Johnson's nursery library

Which brings us back to Jane Johnson and England of the 1740s. What good luck kept this extraordinary (but probably also ordinary) mother's home-produced nursery library of more than 500 pieces together and in good condition, I do not know. Jane Johnson's work uncovers for us some of that secret history of the domestic literacy of women and children in the eighteenth century. Although Jane Johnson was artistically gifted and the little books and cards are special, I suspect she represents an outstanding example of what many women of her period were doing: expressing affection between mothers and children in writing, promoting literacy in an informal setting, and giving scope for their own creativity. If this is typical of what women were privately engaged in with no thought of publication, there is a lot more work to be done on opening up the nursery.

Here are a few snippets of Jane Johnson's verse, which chime like nursery rhymes.

> As John with his rake went out to make hay,
> He met with his sweetheart, and stopped on his way.

> At a house by a steeple,
> Did live many people,
> Who all did love pudding and pie.
> And good bread, and good meat,
> Which they each day did eat,
> And drank small beer when they were dry.
>
>   *   *   *
>
> A duck and a drake
> jumped into the water.
> And all the young ducks
> did paddle in after.
>
>   *   *   *
>
> An eagle flies high,
> But can't touch the sky.[53]

And the link with Rossetti?

> Rock on, rock on
> My pretty boy.
> And you shall be
> Your mother's joy.[54]

The following two extracts are from poems Jane Johnson wrote to her daughter, Barbara. The first is from 'An Invitation to Miss B. J. to Come into the Country' (a new ballad by her Mama, May 1st 1747):

> How fine and sweet it is to see
> The flowers grow on every tree,
> To hear the pretty cuckoo sing
> And welcome in the joyous spring;
> The goldfinch, linnet, and the thrush,
> Now charm our ears from every bush;
> The shrill larks soaring to the sky,
> Most sweetly singing as they fly.
> The nightingale with tuneful song,
> Enchanting warbles all night long;
>
> . . .
>
> Then come Miss Johnson come away,
> No longer in dull London stay.
> But let the country be your choice.
> We'll welcome you with heart and voice.[55]

My point is not that this is great poetry, but that it is a piece of writing, full of personal references and detail of the natural world, which is specifically tailored to the desires of her little girl. In that respect, it is truly child-centred. The second is more formal in language and tone; it is a eulogy on the merits of her young daughter entitled, 'On Miss Barbara Johnson, March 16th 1752'. How many poets have written so seriously of children?

> All sweet and soft of every charm possest
> What can adorn or grace the human breast.
> That soul capacious large extensive wise,
> Without one thought that needs the least disguise.
> Such worth on earth will never more be found,
> When her sweet form is buried underground.[56]

Finally, here is one of Jane Johnson's letters to her son, Robert, just one of many affectionate letters she wrote to all four of her children.

My Dear Robert,
I am sorry you have had such bad weather . . . I heartily wish you a good journey home with your father and I shall be glad to see and hear the pretty account you will give of all you have seen since you left Olney . . . I would have you teach little Benny to be very good and tell him he should pray to God a good many times in a day as you do and say God Bless me and make me a good man. I have sent him and you a few more nuts and raisins, I have nothing else to send you, or I would send it, for I love you dearly and think you one of the most sensible children of your age in the world. Pray give pretty Miss Purvey a kiss for me and tell her she is much in my favour. I have not time to write any more, so I wish you a good night. Past seven o'clock, July 30th 1755.

> On earth who hopes true happiness to see
> Hopes for what never was, nor ne'er will be.
> In heaven, are joys and pleasures ever new,
> And blessings thicker than the morning dew.

(Learn these by heart before you come home.)

And then, tacked on as an afterthought, the sentiment every mother recognizes with a gasp of pain:

'Oh! Robert, live for ever.'[57]

(This chapter appears in a slightly amended form *in Opening the Nursery Door: Reading, Writing & Childhood 1600–1900*, eds M. Hilton, M. Styles and V. Watson, Routledge, 1997, pp. 142–58.)

Notes

1   Christina Rossetti, *Sing-Song*, London, 1872.
2   Jane Johnson, unpublished handmade materials at the Lilly Library, University of Indiana, USA.
3   Roger Lonsdale, *Eighteenth Century Women Poets*, Oxford, 1993, p. xxi.
4   Victor Watson in M. Styles *et al.*, eds, *The Prose and the Passion*, Cassell, London, 1994.
5   Johnson Collection, *op. cit.*, and the Bodleian Library.
6   Christina Rossetti, *Goblin Market*, London, 1862.
7   William Rossetti, *The Poetical Works of Christina Rossetti*, Macmillan, London, 1904, p. lxvii.
8   Jan Marsh, *Christina Rossetti: a Literary Biography*, Jonathan Cape, London, 1995.
9   William Rossetti, *op. cit.*, p. lxviii.
10   Walter de la Mare, ed. *Christina Rossetti: Poems*, part of lecture to Royal Society of Literature, Gregynog Press, Montgomeryshire, 1930, p. xviii
11   *Ibid.*
12   Christina Rossetti, *Verses* ed. J. D. Symon, Eragny Press, London, 1906, p. 15.
13   William Rossetti, *op. cit.*, p. lxxi.
14   William Rossetti, *The Poetical Works of Mrs Hemans*, Ward Lock & Co. London, 1880, p. xxvii.
15   Arthur Waugh, *Daily Chronicle*, 1904, quoted in William Rossetti, *op. cit.*, p. xvii.
16   W. H. Auden, ed. *Nineteenth Century Minor Poets*, Faber, London, 1966.
17   George MacBeth, ed. *Victorian Verse*, Penguin, Harmondsworth, 1969.
18   Elizabeth Jennings, ed. *A Choice of Christina Rossetti's Verse*, Faber, London, 1970, p. 12.
19   Marsh, *op. cit.*, p. 68.
20   *The Sacred Harp*, (anonymous editor) Routledge, London. [The only edition I have been able to view, 1876, does not cite the date of the first edition. It must have been published before 1844.]
21   Hemans, *op. cit.*
22   Christina Rossetti, *Verses*, published privately by G. Polidon [her grandfather), London, 1847.
23   Charlotte Smith, *Conversations Introducing Poetry to Children*, Harris, London, 1804.
24   Charlotte Yonge, Aunt Charlotte's Evenings at Home, *Macmillan's Magazine*, Marcus and Ward, London, 1881.
25   *Jane Taylor: Memoirs, Correspondence and Poetical Remains*, ed. Isaac Taylor, London, 1841, p. 2.
26   Leonore Davidoff and Catherine Hall, *Family Fortunes*, Hutchinson Education, London, 1987.
27   Ann and Jane Taylor, 'The Baby's Dance', *Rhymes for the Nursery*, Darton, London, 1806.
28   Taylor, from 'The Kind Mamma', *ibid.*
29   Christina Rossetti, 1872, *op. cit.*
30   *Ibid.*
31   Marsh, *op. cit.*, p. 1.
32   William Rossetti, 'Memoir of Christina Rossetti' in *The Poetical Works of Christina Rossetti*, Macmillan, London, 1904, p. xiviii.
33   Christina Rossetti, 1872, *op. cit.*

34 *Ibid.*
35 Charles Lamb, Introduction, *Poetry for Children*, 1809, this edition 1872, p. ix.
36 F. J. Harvey Darton, *Children's Books in England*, Cambridge, 1932, p. 193.
37 Charles and Mary Lamb, from 'Choosing a Name', *Poetry for Children*, Godwin, London, 1809.
38 Christina Rossetti, 1872, *op. cit.*
39 Charles and Mary Lamb, from 'The Sister's Expostulation' and 'The Reaper's Child', *op. cit.*
40 Christina Rossetti, from 'Buds and babies', 1872, *op. cit.*
41 Dorothy Wordsworth, 'The Cottager to her Infant', quoted from Iona and Peter Opie eds *The Oxford Book of Children's Verse, Oxford*, 1973.
42 Dorothy Wordsworth, *Home at Grasmere*, ed. Colette Clark, Penguin, Harmondsworth, 1960.
43 Sara Coleridge, *Pretty Lessons in Verse for all Good Children*, London, 1834.
44 Coleridge, from 'The Months of the Year', *ibid.*
45 Christina Rossetti, *op. cit.*
46 Mary Howitt, from 'Buttercups and Daisies', *Sketches from Natural History*, Effingham Wilson, London, 1843.
47 Christina Rossetti, 1872, *op. cit.*
48 *Ibid.*
49 *Ibid.*
50 *Ibid.*
51 Christina Rossetti, from 'In the Bleak Mid-winter', *Christina Rosetti: Poems and Prose*, ed. Jan Marsh, Everyman, London, 1994.
52 Isobel Armstrong, *Victorian Poetry*, Routledge, London, 1993.
53 Jane Johnson, *op. cit.*
54 *Ibid.*
55 *Ibid.*
56 *Ibid.*
57 *Ibid.*

CHAPTER 8

'The Best of Plays' –
A Child's Garden of Verses
The poetry of Robert Louis Stevenson

So you may see, if you will look
Through the windows of this book,
Another child, far, far away,
And in another garden play.[1]

Robert Louis Stevenson is the single poet who gets a chapter to himself in this book, despite writing only one volume of verse for children. The reason for privileging Stevenson in this way is the belief that *A Child's Garden of Verses* is a pivotal collection which changed for ever how children could be written for and about in poetry. H. W. Garrod, during his term of office as Oxford Professor of Poetry (1923–1928), suggested that 'This genre Stevenson created . . . and here his genius for make-believe exercises itself without offence . . .' Garrod went on to say that 'the pretended naturalness of the Child's Garden has no greater element of pretence than accompanies any other attempt at communicating between grown-ups and children.'[2] But there are dissenting views.

Despite his admiration for Stevenson's writing, John Goldthwaite states contentiously that

No one has ever lied up a stereotype [portraying childhood as itself a pleasant land of make-believe) so sweetly or at this artistic level before . . . He enshrined this age for his readers by detailing his own childhood as an habitual daydreamer creeping about behind the furniture, climbing a cherry treee, studying the passing scene through the window of a railway car. The lilting verses are all as beautifully laid out as the toy soldiers parading across his sickbed covers in 'The pleasant land of counterpane'.[3]

Goldthwaite charges Stevenson with dishonesty: admittedly 'a pretty pretense . . . but the seduction is sweet, and generations of parents took Stevenson's book to heart as the gospel truth of who they thought they had been and wanted to see in their own children.'[4] Yet Garrod and many of Stevenson's friends suggest that he was genuinely playful and childlike as a man and that this enabled him to write particularly convincingly for the young. We will return to Stevenson's apparent 'genius for make-believe' elsewhere in this chapter. While generations of critics help to throw light on the poems, in the end they must speak for themselves to the reader as authentic or only a 'pretty pretense'.

'A child's mind'

Nonsense apart, *A Child's Garden of Verses* is the earliest poetry book for children to remain consistently in print since its publication in 1885. Garrod has given us an inkling of its quality in terms of play. Are there other reasons why was it so exceptional and why generations of publishers, purchasers of poetry and, of course, children themselves have chosen to read this book? One factor in its favour is the strength of the poetry. Like cookbooks, many poetry collections are bought because a handful of the content is exceptional. In *A Child's Garden of Verses* many of the poems are outstanding and all are good. Harvey Darton sums up its special appeal: '. . . the substance is in the fabric of a child's mind – the child who was always in Stevenson . . .'[5]

Darton suggests that Stevenson was doing something that no other poet achieved before him, and that few poets have achieved since the publication of *A Child's Garden of Verses*; Stevenson captured, as faithfully as it is possible for an adult to do, what it feels like to be a child. If critical theorists shake their heads in outrage, I can only defend Darton and reply that Stevenson's depiction of childhood comes closer to my own memories of being a child than the work of any other poet. A lifetime's professional contact with children and their poetry has confirmed this view. And children still respond positively to Stevenson's collection, as a visit to any poetry-loving primary classroom will confirm.

Andrew Lang, writing about Stevenson's poetry in the 1890s, said: 'The peculiarity of Mr Stevenson is not only to have been a fantastic child, and to retain, in maturity, that fantasy ripened into imagination: he has also kept up the habit of dramatizing everything, of playing, half consciously, many parts, of making the world "an unsubstantial fairy place".'[6] And therein certainly lies part of the appeal of the poetry.

> And does it not seem hard to you,
> When all the sky is clear and blue,
> And I should like so much to play,
> To have to go to bed by day?
>   (from 'Bed in Summer')

'A child's voice'

It is often forgotten today that in his own time, Stevenson was a revered writer, considered a versatile genius by many and much admired by commentators as dissimilar as Henry James, J. M. Barrie and Gerard Manley Hopkins. Although many of his texts have now been consigned to that marginalized literary corner – the nursery – no such fate was evident in the closing decades of the nineteenth century when eminent Victorians (like the Prime Minister, Gladstone) admitted to staying up half the night to finish *Treasure Island*. Extraordinary that in Frank McLynn's otherwise excellent biography, *A Child's Garden* merits a single paragraph and fails to appear in the index. Neither does any reference to children or play, though McLynn does describe the poems as 'that prime source for his childhood'.[7]

Stevenson had been dabbling with children's poems since 1881 and sent out copies of a version in 1883, entitled *Penny Whistles*, to his friends, Sidney Colvin and William Henley. He changed the title to *A Child's Garden of Verses* which was an immediate success when it was published on 6 March 1885 and went into a second printing three months later. It was published in America in April of the same year. Charles Robinson was the first illustrator and a very fine one. Since then there have been countless editions, translations and illustrated versions. Apparently, Stevenson had no great expectations for his little volume of children's poetry, although it was close to his heart. As he wrote to Edmund Gosse in March 1885:

> there is something nice in the little ragged regiment for all; the blackguards seem to me to smile, to have a kind of childish treble note that sounds in my ear freshly; not song, if you will, but *a child's voice*.[8]

Reminiscences of Stevenson by members of his large circle of friends almost always emphasize the fact that they regarded his as childlike and playful. Here's Edmund Gosse:

> . . . his gaiety . . . a childlike mirth leaped and danced in him; he seemed to skip upon the hills of life. He was simply bubbling with quips or jests . . . his laughter-loving mood was never wholly quenched by ill health, responsibility and the advance of years.[9]

Or Andrew Lang:

> Perhaps the first quality in Mr Stevenson's works . . . which strikes the reader . . . is the survival of the child in him. It was the unextinguished childish passion for playing at things which remained with him.[10]

Cummy

Stevenson was an only child and a sickly one, so he spent a lot of time lonely and cut off from friends of his own age. He did, however, have a nurse, the famous Cummy (Alison Cunningham), to whom *A Child's Garden* is dedicated, who looked after him devotedly and gave him a taste for fantastic stories.

> The angel of my infant life –
> From the sick child, now well and old,
> Take, nurse, this little book you hold!

Cummy was also a religious bigot who frightened the impressionable child half to death with tales of hell-fire and damnation. The themes of sickness, isolation and night-time fears strongly pervade the poetry and we know from the letters and conversations of the adult Stevenson that Cummy was both a comfort to the invalid and a source of religious terror and guilt. Something of this dread is captured in the second section of 'North-West Passage', but Stevenson brings his adult understanding to bear on the vivid remembered imaginings of his childhood experiences.

> All round the house is the jet-black night:
> It stares through the window-pane;
> It crawls in the corners, hiding from the light,
> And it moves with the moving flame.
>
> Now my little heart goes a-beating like a drum,
> With the breath of a Bogie in my hair;
> And all round the candle the crooked shadows come
> And go marching along the stair.
>
> The shadows of the balusters, the shadow of the lamp,
> The shadow of the child that goes to bed –
> All the wicked shadows coming, tramp, tramp, tramp,
> With the black night overhead.

Child's play

Stevenson's description of 'the sorrow and burden of the night' and his experience of 'hideous nightmares'[11] are only hinted at in the poem. Stevenson had the sense to soften painful memories in the poetry and to focus on the imaginative and the playful. In an article entitled, 'R. L. Stevenson and Children's Play',[12] Michael Rosen speculates as to whether 'it is not fanciful to see one aspect of the origins of *A Child's Garden* as an Arcadian relief from the pain of his illness'. Maybe so. Fortunately,

Stevenson also had good times as a child, particularly when he visited his cousins in Colington, on the outskirts of Edinburgh, as Stevenson documents himself.

> When my cousin and I took our porridge of a morning, we had a desire to enliven the course of the meal. He ate his with sugar, and explained it to be a country continually buried under snow. I took mine with milk, and explained it to be a country suffering gradual inundation. You can imagine us exchanging bulletins; how here was an island still submerged, here a valley not yet covered with snow; what inventions were made; how his population lived in cabins on perches and travelled on stilts, and how mine was always in boats . . .[13]

The poet here demonstrates his talent at recollecting and transforming what was probably a mixture of childhood memories, and his own adult construction on these events. In an essay entitled 'Memory and Writing for Children, Especially',[14] Jill Paton Walsh shows us how writers can do that in an insightful account of how genuine memories, family anecdotes, mature reflection and artistic creativity work together in her own work. However, we must be careful in going along with the so-called 'naturalness' of Stevenson's childlike imagination and give proper credit to the adult skill which he employed to make it *seem* so realistic. As Goldthwaite put it more critically, 'A book about childhood can never really be a child's book. Stevenson gave innocence a voice.'[15]

Whatever view is taken, one of the most powerful impressions that comes out of *A Child's Garden of Verses* is the sense of a child's absorption in the world of play and how it is intimately bound up with the imagination. In the article mentioned above, Rosen shows how Stevenson was wrapped up in the twin themes of play and childhood around the same time as he was writing his poetry for children, when he published in succession *Notes on the Movements of Young Children*, 1874, *Child's Play*, 1878, and *Memoirs of Himself*, 1880.[16] Rosen suggests that the ideas he was developing in these prose pieces came to fruition in the poetry. In *Memoirs of Himself*, Stevenson demonstrates that his memories of childhood were far from idealized.

> I have three powerful impressions of my childhood: my sufferings when I was sick, my delights in convalescence at my grandfather's manse of Colinton, and the unnatural activity of my mind after I was in bed at night.

Stevenson draws attention to his 'unnatural' fantasy life as a child which gives further credance to scepticism about the so-called 'natural', child-like writing so many critics credit him with.

Rosen goes on to point out that Stevenson's ideas, though original and distinctive, were part of a growing interest in the empirical study of childhood, promoted by educationalists like Froebel, philosophers like Rousseau and writers like Herbert

Spencer who popularized Schiller's famous observation that 'aesthetic sentiments originate from the play-impulse'.[17] So, Rosen tells us, 'Stevenson's essay and poems on childhood were produced at precisely the moment the issue of play was being formally discussed in Britain for the first time.'[18]

It was in *Child's Play*[19] where Stevenson showed his acute understanding of childhood fantasy:

> We grown people can tell ourselves a story . . . all the while sitting quietly by the fire . . . a child . . . works all with lay figures and stage properties. When his story comes to the fighting, he must rise, get something by way of a sword and have a set-to with a piece of furniture, until he is out of breath. When he comes to ride with the king's pardon, he must bestride a chair . . . lead soldiers, dolls, all toys, in short, are in the category and answer the same end. Nothing can stagger a child's faith; he accepts the clumsiest substitutes and can swallow the most staring incongruities . . . this need for overt action and lay figures testifies to a defect in the child's imagination which prevents him from carrying out his novels in the privacy of his own heart. He does not yet know enough of the world and men. His experience is incomplete . . . He is at the experimental stage; he is not sure how one would feel in certain circumstances; to make sure, he must come as near trying it as his means permit . . . play is all. Making believe is the gist of his whole life . . .

This is one of the finest accounts of children's motivation, indeed, compulsion to play and is undoubtedly the key to the collection. Let me show you some evidence in the poetry.

> We built a ship upon the stairs
> All made of the back-bedroom chairs,
> And filled it full of sofa pillows
> To go a-sailing on the billows.
>
> We took a saw and several nails,
> And water in the nursery pails;
> And Tom said, 'Let us also take
> An apple and a slice of cake';
> Which was enough for Tom and me
> To go a-sailing on, till tea.
>
> We sailed along for days and days,
> And had the very best of plays;
> But Tom fell out and hurt his knee,
> So there was no one left but me.
>   (from 'A Good Play')

Matter of factly, Stevenson states that the stairs and the back-bedroom chairs became the ship, pillows the sea; the fantasy is sustained until one got hurt and the game abandoned. There is no extraneous detail; it is simply told and therein lies its charm and immediacy. Stevenson's addiction to boats and sailing as a child and adult is prevalent in the poems, including this one about playing alone.

> My bed is like a little boat;
>   Nurse helps me in when I embark;
> She girds me in my sailor's coat
>   And starts me in the dark.
>
> At night, I go on board and say
>   Good-night to all my friends on shore;
> I shut my eyes and sail away
>   And see and hear no more.
>
> And sometimes things to bed I take,
>   As prudent sailors have to do:
> Perhaps a slice of wedding-cake,
>   Perhaps a toy or two.
>
> All night across the dark we steer:
>   But when the room returns at last,
> Safe in my room, beside the pier,
>   I find my vesssel fast.
>   ('My Bed is a Boat')

'My Bed is a Boat' is a near-perfect account of how children appear to recognize the boundaries of the fantasy world they create, yet how imagination allows them the escape-route of adventure. For a while the child stays in a sort of 'half-way house' between fantasy and reality – '. . . and say / Good-night to all my friends on shore; / I shut my eyes and sail away / And see and hear no more.' At the same moment, he both knows that he is really in bed *and* imagines that his bed is a boat, 'Safe in my room, beside the pier.' To juxtapose such impossibilities is the prerogative of childhood and it is one with particular appeal to adults.

The contours of childhood

In trying to analyse the lasting appeal of Stevenson's poetry, Cornelia Meigs wrote in 1969:[20]

If we ask why adults also get so much from it, we see that the power of this collection of simple verses lies in the fact that it offers, not a glimpse, but the whole contour of the child's hidden world. It shows the life that a child lives within himself and takes so completely for granted . . . Stevenson has recaptured . . . the whole of that hidden life, and has set these recollections forth in just the terms that children would use, could they put them into words at all.

A Child's Garden made the same sort of impression on E. V. Lucas, a contemporary of Stevenson's, writing one of the earliest essays devoted to poetry for children in 1896:

It stands alone. There is nothing like it, so intimate, so simply truthful, in our language, in any language . . . he has recaptured in maturity the thoughts, ambitions, purposes, hopes, fears, philosophy of the child.[21]

Both Lucas and Meigs could be criticized for taking a Romantic view of childhood for granted and for neglecting the artistic recreation of childhood which Stevenson performs so well. Even so, in Meigs's case, she does try to pinpoint just why these poems resonate for so many children and adults half a dozen generations after they were first written. And Lucas shows us how quickly critical opinion of the late Victorian period recognized Stevenson's particular gifts. As Darton put it:

There are few thoughts in that little 1885 volume . . . that children have not felt, even though here and there the grown-up can be detected using his literary art to express them . . .[22]

A so-called child's voice might well be precious in another writer. Indeed, it is a trap that weaker poets fall into. Goldthwaite lays that charge at Stevenson's door, though he admits he did it with 'unerring panache'.

The land of story books

Lucas went on to note that Stevenson was good at capturing 'the unreason of grown people'. The gardener in the poem of the same title 'does not love to talk' and 'never seems to want to play'.[23] It is there as well in the first verse of 'The Land of Story Books' where the child finds adults and their evening pursuits very dull, mostly because they don't 'play at anything'. It was in this poem that I first noticed connections between Stevenson and the contemporary poet, Michael Rosen, writing 100 years later. Despite apparently jettisoning traditional forms, themes and language, it could be argued that Rosen has a lot in common with Robert Louis Stevenson. The two writers were radicals of a kind and both had mixed feelings about the 'literary establishment' of their own time. They also share at least two important ideas in common about poetry for children – writing 'with a child's voice' in everyday language and the centrality of play. The extracts which follow come from three poems by Stevenson and two from Rosen's first collection.[24]

> At evening when the lamp is lit,
> Around the fire my parents sit;
> They sit at home and talk and sing,
> And do not play at anything.
>
> There, in the night, where none can spy,
> All in my hunter's camp I lie,
> And play at books that I have read
> Till it is time to go to bed.
>   (from 'The Land of Story-Books')

> When at home alone I sit
> And am very tired of it,
> I have just to shut my eyes
> To go sailing through the skies –
> To go sailing far away
> To the pleasant land of play.
>   (from 'The Little Land')

> The shadow of the balusters, the shadow of the lamp,
> The shadow of the child that goes to bed –
> All the wicked shadows coming tramp, tramp, tramp,.
> With the black night overhead.
>   (from 'Shadow-March')

> In the daytime I am Rob Roy and a tiger
> In the daytime I am Marco Polo
>   I chase bears in Bricket Wood
> In the daytime I am the Tower of London
>   nothing gets past me
>   when its my turn
>   in Harrybo's hedge
> In the daytime I am Henry the fifth and Ulysses
>   and I tell stories
>   that go on for a whole week
>   if I want.

At night in the dark
> when I've shut the front room door
> I try and
> get up the stairs across the landing
> into bed and under the pillow
> without breathing once.
>   (Rosen)

Although the diction, metre and form are different, there is a lot of common ground between the two poets. Stevenson suggests the same matter-of-factness as Rosen about the ease with which children apparently enter into fantasy play in everyday settings: 'I have just to shut my eyes / To go sailing through the skies.' 'In the daytime I am Rob Roy ...' They both 'play at books that I have read', though Rosen actually uses more literary and historical references. For both writers, things change when day turns to night: the child's imagined uneasiness about the dark is hinted at in Rosen's final sequence and alluded to more directly in 'Shadow-March'. In both cases, it is the journey out of the living room and upstairs to the bedroom which is associated with fear. Stevenson emphasizes the child's nervousness by using the imagery of '*wicked* shadows' and the repetitive 'tramp, tramp, tramp of the *black* night overhead'; Rosen suggests it with the gulping speed of 'get up the stairs, across the landing, into bed and under the pillow without breathing once'! Both focus on the sensitive child alone. Although there are other people about, they set up situations where night fears have to be coped with by children on their own. They appear to believe that it is only when alone that the child can truly get into that deep imaginative play which both poets are so fascinated by.

In the second set of extracts, both chose to write poems where the coal fire acts as a stimulus for fantasy; again, they present a child feeling alone, though not unhappily so, even when he is surrounded by the family engaged in their own pursuits. In one case, the flames appear to conjure up goblins; in the other it is armies marching. The 'I' child-personas in these poems are presented positively as being independent and reflective with rich imaginative lives. Both poets attempt to speak the language of childhood from the inside out, rather than taking the stance of observing adults (like so many other poets) from the outside in.

I'm alone in the evening
> when the family sits
> reading and sleeping
> and I watch the fire in close
> to see flame goblins
> wriggling out of their caves
> for the evening.
>   (Rosen)

Now in the falling of the gloom
The red fire paints the empty room:
And warmly on the roof it looks,
And flickers on the back of books.

Armies march by tower and spire
Of cities blazing, in the fire;
                    (Stevenson)

Faster than witches

Other attractive features of Stevenson's poetry include satisfying metre and phrasing. This melodious quality makes the verse especially appealing to very young children, though older readers respond to the same qualities in 'From a Railway Carriage'. Here the poet captures both the rhythmic speed of the train and the outlook of the young passenger trying in vain to keep pace with the myriad of impressions racing by the carriage window.

Faster than fairies, faster than witches,
Bridges and houses, hedges and ditches;
And charging along like troops in a battle,
All through the meadows the horses and cattle:
All of the sights of the hill and the plain
Fly as thick as driving rain;
And ever again in the wink of an eye,
Painted stations whistle by.

Although Stevenson experienced isolation and pain as a child, he had the enormous solace of a vivid imagination. In a letter to William Archer who had favourably reviewed *A Child's Garden*, Stevenson wrote on 29th March 1885:

My childhood was in reality a very mixed experience, full of fever, nightmare, insomnia, painful days and interminable nights; and I can speak with less authority of Gardens than of that other 'land of counterpane'. But to what end should we renew these sorrows? The sufferings of life may be handled by the very greatest in their hours of insight; *it is of its pleasures that our common poems should be formed* [my emphasis]; these are the experiences that we should seek to recall or to provoke; and I say with Thoreau, 'What right have I to complain, who have not ceased to wonder?'[25]

Here, perhaps, Stevenson acquits himself of Goldthwaite's charge of dishonesty by admitting the suffering involved in childhood, but he chose to emphasize the happier side. And why not? In life as well as in the poetry Stevenson is never sorry for himself, though he is sometimes a little wistful.

> When I was sick and lay a-bed,
> I had two pillows at my head,
> And all my toys beside me lay
> To keep me happy all the day.
>
> And sometimes for an hour or so
> I watched my leaden soldiers go,
> With different uniforms and drills,
> Among the bed-clothes, through the hills;

'A birdie with a yellow bill'

Stevenson avoids, though occasionally only just, sentimentality in writing for children. He uses diminutives a lot: 'A birdie with a yellow bill', 'with little children saying grace', 'Tiny woods below whose boughs / Shady fairies weave a house', 'Where the little people play', 'For beside the dolly sailor'. Commentators rarely mention his skill as a close observer of nature, though, as Darton put it, 'the child is always, more or less, in an ordinary English garden'.[26] Stevenson describes birds' nests and wild flowers, autumn leaves and digging. Sometimes he roamed into wilder places, like the Highlands of Scotland.

> Down by a shining water well
> I found a very little dell,
> No higher than my head.
> The heather and the gorse about
> In summer bloom were coming out,
> Some yellow and some red.

Despite suffering from poor health and spending a lot of time in bed, Stevenson craved adventure, found it in his life and wrote about it in his books. Goldthwaite likes that side of Stevenson:

> However much Stevenson veered from a child's true perception [sic] from verse to verse, at the centre of the book is a vision of the world and his voice as he tells us about this world he sees is the voice of a man who couldn't wait to be joined with it, and went.[27]

Several poems uncannily anticipate future adventures, such as his somewhat reckless wanderings at sea in the last decade or so of his life. Indeed, Stevenson did end up where 'parrot islands anchored lie' – in Samoa to be precise.

> I should like to rise and go
> Where the golden apples grow; –
> Where below another sky
> Parrot islands anchored lie,
> And, watched by cockatoos and goats,
> Lonely crusoes building boats;
>   ('Travels')

> Where shall we adventure today that we're afloat,
> Wary of the weather and steering by a star?
> Shall it be to Africa, a-steering of the boat,
> To Providence, or Babylon, or off to Malabar?
>   ('Pirate Story')

Thousands of millions of stars

One of Stevenson's greatest gifts was his ability to gaze at the immensity of the world and wonder at it, as children and poets are inclined to do, as if they were seeing it for the first time.

> The lights from the parlour and kitchen shone out
> Through the blinds and the windows and bars;
> And high overhead and all moving about,
> There were thousands of millions of stars.
> There ne'er were such thousands of leaves on a tree,
> Nor of people in church or the park,
> As the crowds of the stars that looked down upon me,
> And that glittered and winked in the dark.
>   ('Escape at Bedtime')

Frank McLynn's recent biography of Stevenson starts with these simple words: 'This book has been written in the firm conviction that Robert Louis Stevenson is Scotland's greatest writer of English prose.'[28] I would want to add 'and poetry for children'. Surely part of Stevenson's genius lies in his ability to write so well for *both audiences* at once and to do so in many different genres. In a reply to Sidney Colvin about the proofs of *A Child's Garden of Verses* on 29 March 1885, Stevenson confided, 'I would as soon call 'em "Rimes for Children" as anything else. I am not proud or particular . . . these are rhymes, jingles; I don't go in for eternity . . .'[29]

For long ago, the truth to say,
He has grown up and gone away,
And it is but a child of air
That lingers in the garden there.[30]

Post-script

Stevenson has been well served by various illustrators in the hundred years or so since *A Child's Garden of Verses* was first published. Charles Robinson's 1895[31] version with exquisite black and white line-drawings have all the hallmarks of art nouveau – flowing lines, decorations of trailing flowers and trees, angelic looking children with gloriously tousled hair. He employs a variety of frames from narrow, rectangular forms, breaking up the page to complex, spiral borders for the poems. Robinson manages to create dramatic tension and intimacy, humour and reflectiveness, demonstrating a feel for childhood in many different guises.

The Dutch artist, Henriette Willebeek Le Mair,[32] produced an enchanting version in 1926 which has been recently reissued. Le Mair's distinctive style uses art deco, though there are still traces of art nouveau and references to William Morris's designs within her paintings. The illustrations are beautifully decorated with flowers, the colours faded mauves, bleached greens, soft pinks, yellows and the distinctive rusty orange of art deco. Her charming, curly-headed children, drawn with great sweetness, look out at the world with eyes of wonder. She goes for escapism into an imagined past of innocence and beauty in a time gone by. One moving picture is of a little boy looking out of a rather grand bedroom window, framed by what could be seen as imprisoning bars, into a luminous purple sky, lit by a line of street-lamps. The image is a haunting one of isolation which perfectly matches Stevenson's painful final lines:

And O! before you hurry by with ladder and with light,
O Leerie, see a little child and nod to him to-night!

Eve Garnett[33] produced exquisite pencil-line illustrations in 1948 which are still in print. The drawings are so faint and delicate, you have to look closely to see them. All three artists evoke an enchanted world of childhood peopled with enchanting children. It is to them that Goldthwaite's complaint that Stevenson started the cult of the beautiful child might be laid, rather than the poems themselves. In fact, the cult of the beautiful child was promoted by artists like Kate Greenaway and later by writers like Rose Fyleman. It was reading one of Greenaway's books of poetry that convinced Stevenson he ought to try out this genre himself. Anyway, surely children's literature is robust enough to keep a valued place for depictions of childhood, idealized though they may be, which these artists provided.

In contrast to Garnett's sensitive and tender drawings comes the artwork of Brian

Wildsmith,[34] 1966, which fairly vibrates with primary colours. His paintings are amusing, attractive and full of interest for the very young. The large hardback edition is a perfect two-lap volume for adults and children to read together. Finally, there is Michael Foreman,[35] whose 1985 volume forced this reader to look with completely new eyes at a familiar text. Some of Foreman's illustrations depict recognizable late twentieth-century children engaged in ordinary childlike pursuits wearing trainers and track-suits. In others, the world of the imagination is explored, often with Foreman's hallmark blue and purple washes with a spot of yellow. But what is so clever and haunting is the 'Everychild' motif which Foreman uses to hold the book together. In one stunning picture, entitled Envoys, a white sheet of paper held by the 'Everychild' is metamorphosized into a dove which flies off, we know not where. There are so many metaphors contained in that single image, doing justice to the multilayered text on which Foreman was working.

Poetry – 'as a child might have written it'

Children's poetry had been placed in a garden for a long time, but Stevenson was the first to locate it there in his very title. I will let Darton, so wise and well informed, offer the final word.

> It *is* a garden, full of natural flowers growing from wind-borne seeds . . . the flowers in such a Garden are not exotic, not forced . . . before the last quarter of the nineteenth century . . . it was not perceived that children were their own spontaneous poets – the makers of their own world of the imagination . . . That has been perceived since . . . But before Stevenson, save for a chance line or two, hardly a verse had been written as a child, given word-skill, might have written it . . .[36]

Notes

1 Robert Louis Stevenson, from 'To Any Reader', A *Child's Garden of Verses*, Longman & Green, London, 1885. All the references to Stevenson's poetry in this chapter refer to this collection, unless otherwise indicated.

2 H. W. Garrod, *The Profession of Poetry*, London, 1929, p. 184.

3 John Goldthwaite, *The Natural History of Make-Believe*, Oxford, New York, 1996, p. 28.

4 *Ibid.*, p. 31.

5 F. J. Harvey Darton, *Children's Books in England*, Cambridge University Press, 1932, p. 314.

6 Andrew Lang, *Essays in Little*, Henry & Co., London, 1891, p. 25.

7 Frank McLynn, *Robert Louis Stevenson: A Biography*, Pimlico, London, 1994, p. 213.

8 Robert Louis Stevenson, Letter to Edmund Gosse, March 1885, in ed. Sidney Colvin, *Robert Louis Stevenson Letters to his Family and Friends*, Vol. 1, Methuen, London, p. 353.

9 Edmund Gosse, *Critical Kit-Kats*, Heinemann, London, 1913, p. 279.

10   Andrew Lang [i], *Essays in Little, op. cit.*, p. 24 [ii] *Adventures Among Books*, Longmans, Green & Co., London, 1905, p. 53.

11   R. L. Stevenson, *Memoirs of Himself*, 1880, Edinburgh, 1925, p. 220.

12   Michael Rosen, 'R. L. Stevenson and Children's Play', *Children's Literature in Education*, Vol. 26, No. 1, March 1995, p. 55.

13   R. L. Stevenson, 'Child's Play', *Cornhill Magazine*, Sept. 1878, this edition, *R. L. Stevenson. Essays and Poems* ed Claire Harman, J. M. Dent, 1992, p. 59.

14   Jill Paton Walsh, 'Memory and Writing for Children, Especially', *The Prose and the Passion*, eds M. Styles, E. Bearne, V. Watson, Cassell, London, 1984.

15   Goldthwaite, *op. cit.*, p.28.

16   R. L. Stevenson, 'Notes on the Movements of Young Children', 1874, see *The Works of R.L.S.* Vol 22, London, 1912; *Child's Play, op. cit., Memoirs, op. cit.*

17   Rosen, *op. cit.*, p. 58.

18   Rosen, *ibid.*, p. 57.

19   R. L. Stevenson, 'Child's Play', Harman, ed., *op. cit.*, p. 56.

20   Cornelia Meigs, *A Critical History of Children's Literature*, Macmillan, Canada, 1969, p. 270.

21   E. V. Lucas, 'Some Notes on Poetry for Children', *Fortnightly Review*, Vol. LX, ed. W. Courtney, Chapman & Hall, London, 1896, p. 393.

22   Darton, *op. cit.*, p. 314.

23   Lucas, *op. cit.*, p. 394.

24   Michael Rosen, *Mind Your Own Business*, Andre Deutsch, London, 1974.

25   Stevenson, a letter to William Archer, 29 March 1885, in B. Booth and E. Mehew, eds *The Letters of R. L. Stevenson*, p. 97.

26   Darton, *op. cit.*, p. 314.

27   Goldthwaite, *op. cit.*, p. 31.

28   McLynn, *op. cit.*, p. 1.

29   Stevenson letter to Sidney Colvin, Oct 1883, *op. cit.*, p. 285.

30   R. L. Stevenson, 'To any Reader', 1885, *op. cit.*

31   R. L. Stevenson, *A Child's Garden of Verses*, illustrated by Charles Robinson, Bodley Head, London, 1985.

32   R. L. Stevenson, *A Child's Garden of Verses*, illustrated by Henriette Willebeek le Mair, 1926.

33   R. L. Stevenson, *A Child's Garden of Verses*, illustrated by Eve Garnett, Puffin, London, 1948.

34   R. L. Stevenson, *A Child's Garden of Verses*, illustrated by Brian Wildsmith, Oxford, 1966/92.

35   R. L. Stevenson, *A Child's Garden of Verses*, illustrated by Michael Foreman, Gollancz, London, 1985.

36   Darton, *op. cit.*, pp. 314–54.

CHAPTER 9

'From the Best Poets'?

How the canon of poetry for children is constructed

'From the best poets' is the sub-title to Coventry Patmore's highly regarded anthology of poetry, *The Children's Garland*, which was published in 1862. Patmore, like many anthologists of the past and present, was a poet himself and he explains the reasons for his selection of poetry in his preface – a convention many anthologists feel the need to do. He writes:

> I have excluded nearly all verse written expressly for children and most of the poetry written about children for grown people . . . this volume will, I hope, be found to contain nearly all the genuine poetry in our language fitted to please children.[1]

Thus Patmore introduces several of the ideas I want to deal with in this chapter on anthologizing poetry for children: the extraordinary exclusion from anthologies of nearly all *verse written expressly for children*; the notion of 'genuine' poetry which ought to be included in a good anthology; the concern to 'please children'.

Now pleasing children is a difficult idea to grapple with, particularly when the time-scale I deal with in this book covers three centuries, during which the notion of children or 'childhood' has been constructed in many different ways and is constantly evolving. Untangling what might be meant by 'pleasing' one young person, let alone children in their infinite variety, is also tricky. Sales figures and regularity of new editions are helpful indicators, but we must not forget that it is adults, by and large, who buy children's poetry – and write, sell, publish and teach it. And adults are often dismissive of children's taste. Indeed, one of my guiding principles in writing this book has been to take as much account as I can of what evidence there is about what children choose to read with pleasure. More importantly, there is Patmore's extraordinary determination to avoid poetry written specifically for children. This exclusion is even more perplexing when one learns that it was commonplace: Patmore, as we shall see, was by no means alone in taking such a stance.

To help us grapple with this issue, it might be instructive to ask some questions. What did Patmore actually select for children? What did he mean by 'genuine' poetry?

Did all the poetry written for children at that time somehow fail to be 'genuine'? What did he think would please children? Why was he so firm about excluding poetry written with children in mind?

I want to bring E. V. Lucas (1868–1938), writing 30 years later, into this discussion. Lucas was another distinguished anthologist with a wide knowledge of and interest in children's poetry. In one of the earliest essays dealing seriously with poetry for children (1896), he takes Patmore's *The Children's Garland* to task:

> As a collection of poems about childhood each in its own way is delightful, although even then not satisfactory. It is as vehicles for the entertainment of young readers that they are so sadly to seek . . .[2]

Lucas's view of childhood was as a time of 'fun and irresponsibility' where literature 'should amuse and delight from first page to last'. Do we seem to have a champion for children's poets? Not quite; in the Introduction to Lucas's own anthology, *A Book of Verses for Children*, he writes:

> When you feel . . . that these pages no longer satisfy, then you must turn to the better thing. You must understand that there is a kind of poetry that is finer than anything here, poetry to which this book is only a stepping stone.[3]

In the end, Lucas wants children to read the same sort of poetry as that anthologized by Patmore, but not until they are older. This is the classic example of the golden staircase metaphor: start with easy accessible things on the lower rungs and gradually progress to the higher steps where you will encounter 'real' poetry. Could this be poetry for adults written in language children can understand on topics they might be interested in? Nature, perhaps, some narrative verse, simple forms, universal sentiments? And does that not lead to poetry predominantly written, as the cliché goes, by dead, white, university educated, middle-class men? One of the motivations for writing this book is to challenge these assumptions, take children's poetry out of its ghetto, and to declare loudly that *this is good poetry for everyone*. Not only do I take issue with Lucas and Patmore who held, after all, the conventional views of their day, but I want to open the debate with many contemporary anthologists and critics who still seek to marginalize poetry written expressly for children.

My argument is that Patmore and Lucas, despite their disagreements, held views about poetry and children in common which also had currency with most anthologists of influence who preceeded them and with many who have succeeded them. They believe in a canon of great or 'genuine' poetry which children must read, sooner or later. They believe that what is written with children in mind is inferior to what is written by 'great' poets for adults. They want to please young readers, but that does not necessitate being interested in what they actually choose to read. Despite the protestations of many anthologists that they are guided by their own personal preferences, clear patterns and continuities of editing poetry for children have developed over time.

Here is John Rowe Townsend: 'If an editor doesn't please himself he doesn't intend to please anyone . . . an anthology is a personal thing: that is what gives it its flavour.'[4] This may be true, but the established canon of poetry for children which has emerged over time marginalizes the very poetry actually written for young readers. The main reason for this has been the role played by editors of anthologies for children, many of whom, while believing they were making unique and fresh collections, have actually been strongly influenced by a tradition of anthologizing from the so-called 'best poets'.

Let me tell you the story and show my evidence.

Early anthologizing

We have already encountered (in Chapter 4) one of the earliest, if not the first, poetry anthology for children, *Mother Goose's Melody*,[5] 1760, a delightful chapbook compilation of nursery rhymes, plus a selection of Shakespeare's songs. The contemporary reader immediately recognizes at least two familiar features of the poetry anthology – nursery rhymes and poems by Shakespeare. It does not seem surprising that as soon as anthologies started to be published for children, nursery rhymes were considered suitable material with their lively rhymes, humour, melody, enjoyable repetitions and simple forms, though they were not actually widely considered respectable until the middle of the nineteenth century. However, the successful children's publishers of the eighteenth century believed, like Patmore and Lucas 100 years later, that giving pleasure to children in their reading (as well as instruction) was desirable and commercially advantageous. So a trend began in the mid-eighteenth century for attractive compilations of nursery rhymes which is still in evidence as Mother Goose collections are a mainstay of children's bookshops today.

As for Shakespeare 'that sweet songster', the same extracts were chosen in *Mother Goose's Melody* that anthologists have drawn on ever since 'Where the bee sucks', 'When icicles hang by the wall', 'Under the greenwood tree', 'Ye spotted snakes' . . .[6] Lucy Aikin did not select any nursery rhymes in *Poetry For Children*, 1801, but she did include two Shakespeare poems. Since then Shakespeare has had a consistent place in anthologies for children, including many new books coming on the market in the late twentieth century. As I write, a new, handsomely illustrated book of Shakespeare's poetry, *Something Rich and Strange*,[7] is doing good trade in the shops. So drawing on the work of William Shakespeare in poetry books for children has been well-established practice for nearly 250 years.

That set me wondering about other poets writing for adults. Who gets anthologized for the young, and why? Which poets pass that test of time? In order to make the investigation manageable, I decided to concentrate on a handful of poets who fulfilled the criteria described in the list below.

1. They were included in the Opies' *Oxford Book Of Children's Verse*,[8] a historical landmark of poetry for children, and/or Lucy Aiken's *Poetry for Children*, 1801,[9] because it was one of earliest selections for children and because she included a wide cross-section of the poets of her time.
2. They were widely anthologized for children for some time after their deaths.
3. They were considered by many to be fine poets, either in their day or by posterity.
4. Their main poetic output was for adults rather than children.

In my choice of poets I tried to span the most popular genres and to be representative of the overall output of published poetry. I also tried to select equal numbers of men and women, but there were not enough published women poets to fulfil my stated criteria. In the end I chose Robert Burns, John Clare, William Cowper, Oliver Goldsmith, Felicia Hemans, Thomas Hood, Alexander Pope, Alfred Tennyson and William Wordsworth who straddle between them the eighteenth and nineteenth centuries. Felicia Hemans did write for children occasionally, but her main output was for adults.

I then set about choosing some key anthologies, from the nineteenth century to the present day, in order to trace the representation of my chosen poets. I added a number of large, mainstream anthologies of poetry for children by well-qualified editors published more recently. My rough rule of thumb has been (a) poetry for children aged roughly between 6 and 12 and (b) one or two anthologies per decade. I believe my sample contains most of what would be widely regarded as the influential anthologies of my chosen period. I included poetry books intended for school use and those for sale to the general reader, though the latter predominate.

It is as well to underline certain principles regarding the anthologizing of poetry. Most editors compiling large, general anthologies select a personal collection of poems which they believe to be good for their chosen age group, sometimes by theme, sometimes by other criteria. In almost every case, editors try to include the poets and poems they most admire. If a poet is neglected, it is either because the editor does not know of her/his existence, lack of space or because the exclusion is intentional. There will, no doubt, be some chance omissions, but if general trends are indicated, then there are probably reasons for them.

Table 9.1 *Anthologies for children from 1801 to 1995*

Title	Editor
Poetry For Children, 1801	Lucy Aikin
First Book Of Poetry, 1820	W. F. Mylius
Poetry For Children, 1825	Lucy Aikin
The Children's Harp, 1850	unknown
The Golden Treasury of Songs and Lyrics, 1861	Francis T. Palgrave
The Children's Garland, 1862	Coventry Patmore
Easy Rhymes And Simple Poems, 1864	unknown
Child Life, 1874	John Greenleaf Whittier
Poetry For The Young, 1883	unknown
Blue Poetry Book, 1892	Andrew Lang
A Book of Verses for Children, 1897	Edward Lucas
Poems Every Child should Know, 1904	Mary Burt
Another Book of Verses for Children, 1907	E. V. Lucas
The Golden Staircase, 1910	Louey Chisholm
Come Hither, 1923	Walter de la Mare
Tom Tiddler's Ground, 1931	Walter de la Mare
A Poetry Book for Boys And Girls, 1933	Guy Pocock
A Puffin Book of Verse, 1953	Eleanor Graham
The Faber Book of Children's Verse, 1953	Janet Adam Smith
This Way Delight, 1957	Herbert Read
The Cherry Tree, 1959	Geoffrey Grigson
The Dragon Book of Verse, 1977	Harrison & Stuart-Clark
A New Treasury of Poetry, 1990	Neil Philip
Classic Poems to Read Aloud, 1995	James Berry

Table 9.2 *British poets writing for adults represented in key anthologies for young readers from 1801–1995 (Note: The date given below each poet's name is the date of first publication of a book of poetry likely to be used by anthologists for children. The dates in the left-hand column represent the poetry anthologies.)*

	Burns 1780	Clare 1820	Cowper 1782	Golds 1760	Hemans 1834	Hood 1825	Pope 1730	Tennyson 1842	W'worth 1798
Aikin 1801		x	*	*	x	x	*	x	
Aikin 1825			*	*	x	x	*	x	
Mylius 1820	*	x	*	*	x	x	*	x	
Harp 1850	*		*		*				*
Palgrave 1861	*	*	*	*		*	*	*	*
Patmore 1862			*	*	x			*	*
Easy 1864				*	*			*	*
Whittier 1874			*		*	*		*	*
Young 1883	*		*		*	*			*

	Burns 1780	Clare 1820	Cowper 1782	Golds 1760	Hemans 1834	Hood 1825	Pope 1730	Tennyson 1842	W'worth 1798
Lang 1892	*		*	*		*			*
Lucas 1897	*		*	*		*			
Lucas 1907						*		*	*
Burt 1904	*			*		*		*	*
de la Mare 1923	*	*	*	*	*	*	*	*	*
de la Mare 1931	*		*			*		*	*
Pocock 1933		*							*
Graham 1953		*	*						*
Smith 1953	*	*	*	*				*	*
Read 1957		*						*	*
Grigson 1959	*	*	*			*			*
Dragon 1977	*	*		*			*	*	*
Philip 1990	*	*		*		*		*	*
Berry 1995	*		*	*	*		*	*	*

* = at least one poem included in anthology
x = couldn't be included in anthology because writing at a later date.

What can we make of the pattern that emerges? The most obvious point is that poets who write for adults are very popular in anthologies for the young. Some poets quickly get incorporated into the children's canon and maintain their popularity right up to the present day: Wordsworth, Tennyson and Burns share that distinction. Some poets are popular for a while, then disappear from view. Whereas Cowper has fallen out of favour since the 1960s, Goldsmith and Pope seem to go in and out of fashion. But in my final anthology representative of 1995, all but two of the poets (Clare and Hood) are included; and they feature in Philip's *New Treasury* of 1990. One might wonder if Pope's poetry would seem dated for the young, yet he is included in nine out of 24 anthologies.

Lucy Aikin drew extensively on Cowper, Shakespeare and Pope in the first edition of *Poetry For Children*, but in the 1825 edition she cut down on Pope and brought in Wordsworth. She did *not* choose to include popular children's poets like Ann and Jane Taylor, William Roscoe or Elizabeth Turner and she drops Isaac Watts after the first edition. She does not offer any clues as to the reasoning behind the selection in her Introduction, which is liberal and enlightened about both children and poetry. Whatever her reasons, Lucy Aikin preferred to draw from what she presumably considered to be the best poetry of her day that was accessible to children. *And that is what anthologists have done ever since.*

How then do the poets fare who *are* well known for writing for children in the same anthologies? Was I right in believing that this poetry was under-represented? This time I chose children's poets who were popular in their day and who fulfilled the criteria outlined above: Mary Howitt, Edward Lear, A. A. Milne, William Roscoe, R. L. Stevenson, Jane Taylor and Isaac Watts. I added four more poets whose work was or is equally well known for children and adults – Anna Barbauld, Charlotte Smith, Christina Rossetti and William Blake.

Table 9.3 *British poets writing for children represented in key anthologies for young readers from 1801 to 1995. (Note: The date given below each poet's name is the date of first publication of a book of poetry likely to be used by anthologists for children.)*

	Howitt 1834	Lear 1846	Milne 1923	Roscoe 1809	Stevenson 1885	Taylor 1804	Watts 1715
Aikin 1801	x	x	x	x	x	x	x
Aikin 1825	x	x	x		x		x
Mylius 1820	x	x	x		x		
Harp 1850	*		x		x		
Palgrave 1861			x		x		
Patmore 1862			x		x		
Easy 1864			x		x	*	*
Whittier 1874	*	*	x			*	
Young 1883	*		x		x	*	*
Lang 1892							
Lucas 1897	*	*	x	*	*	*	
Lucas 1907			x		*	*	
Burt 1904	*		x		*	*	*
de la Mare 1923	*		x		*		*
de la Mare 1931	*				*	*	
Pocock 1933					*		
Graham 1953		*			*	*	*
Smith 1953		*			*	*	*
Read 1957							
Grigson 1959		*					
Dragon 1977					*		
Philip 1990		*			*		
Berry 1995		*	*		*		

What conclusions can we draw? Poets writing for children are half as likely to be included in anthologies as those writing for adults. The poor representation of some poets is remarkable. Milne remains popular in early-years classrooms today, yet only one out of ten possible editors chose to include him. Although Lear and Stevenson are well represented, Lear is ignored in 14 out of 21 and Stevenson in four out of 15 poetry books. Compare that with the representation of Wordsworth or Tennyson in Table 9.2. Of course, many will argue that Wordsworth and Tennyson are anthologized for children simply because they wrote some of the best poetry ever written. Best poetry *for whom*?

None of our children's poets was included in Andrew Lang's influential *Blue Poetry Book*[10]. Sixteen editors chose to include only two or fewer of our representative children's poets in their anthologies. Women poets writing for children do better in this table than the last. Mary Howitt and Jane Taylor fare pretty well until this century; William Roscoe hardly survives his lifetime, though Isaac Watts lasted right up to 1953 and is still occasionally anthologized today.

Table 9.4 *British poets writing for children and adults represented in key anthologies from 1801 to 1995.*

	Barbauld 1782	Blake 1789	Smith 1804	Rossetti 1872
Aikin 1801	*		x	x
Aikin 1825	*		*	x
Mylius 1820	*		*	x
Harp 1850				
Palgrave 1861	*	*		x
Patmore 1862	*	*	*	x
Easy 1864	*			x
Whittier 1874		*		
Young 1883		*	*	
Lang 1892		*		
Lucas 1897		*		*
Lucas 1907	*	*	*	
Burt 1904	*			
de la Mare 1923		*		*
de la Mare 1931		*		*
Pocock 1933		*		
Graham 1953		*		*
Smith 1953		*		
Read 1957		*		*
Grigson 1959		*		
Dragon 1977		*		*
Philip 1990		*		*
Berry 1995		*		*

Once Blake's poetry was well known and widely circulated, he solidly maintained his place in children's anthologies. Not so, Rossetti who is excluded (10 omissions) more often than she is included (she is selected in eight texts). There is neither rhyme nor reason for this neglect and it certainly cannot be justified on any grounds to do with the quality of the poetry. Barbauld and Smith are even more poorly represented. As relatively few women were able to get published at all, it would appear that because of the marginalized status of poetry written for children, they suffer a double disadvantage. The neglect of women poets from anthologies is a sad part of this tale.

This evidence seems to confirm my suspicions that children's poets are less likely to gain a place in anthologies for the young than poets writing for adults. The editor of *The Children's Harp* (1850) brings us up full square with the main thesis of this chapter:

> So far as possible, we have taken our specimens from standard writers, who, with the true sublimity of genius, have often, amid their loftiest flights, poured forth simpler melodies than *meaner bards can command* when handling the lute with a *purposed view to meet the infantile capacity*.[11] [my emphasis]

Meaner bards seems to imply those who write for children. It is amusing with hindsight to read editors' introductions to poetry anthologies, as so many seem to believe that others have got it wrong while they hold the key to selecting just the right poetry for children. In fact, most of them share the same prejudices and, indeed, feed off one another's choices. John Greenleaf Whittier was a fine selector of poetry for the young, but his preface is revealing when he describes the limitations of poetry anthologies: '. . . noticing in nearly all of them much that seemed lacking in literary merit'. He sought to combine 'simplicity with a certain degree of literary excellence, without on the one hand descending to silliness, or, on the other, rising above the average comprehension of childhood'.[12]

Thus poetry written specifically for a young audience gets marginalized by influential editors and a tradition becomes established where adult poetry by the so-called 'great' poets is considered preferable to writing directed at children. And it is still happening today. Here is Angela Huth, author of *Island of the Children*, writing her introduction in 1987.

> The discovery that there was a certain scarcity of modern poetry for children . . . came to me when searching for new poems to entertain my daughter, Eugenie. I had been reading her poetry from a very young age, and found with surprising swiftness we were running out of material. What was plainly missing was a rich anthology of contemporary poetry written . . . by disparate modern poets . . . I hope their efforts [i.e. the poets included in her anthology] will delight many a poetry-starved child in the future.[13]

Such comments are insulting to the many talented poets writing today and show ignorance on the part of the editor. Huth subscribes to a form of elitism quite in keeping with the well-established tradition of editing poetry for children. Here is Robert Hull being slightly condescending about Brian Patten's *Puffin Book of 20th Century Verse*.[14] 'Brian Patten's volume is a book of good poems for children written in the twentieth century, and that's about it.'[15] What else should it be? Or Anthea Bell discussing Prelutsky's *The Walker Book Of Poetry For Children*:[16] 'If I am lukewarm . . .

it is because I feel that Prelutsky has been compiling down . . . He draws largely on specifically children's poets . . .'[17] Or Neil Philip in his introduction to *A New Treasury Of Poetry* 1990:

> I have also been cautious with poems written specially for children, preferring on the whole work which makes itself available to a young reader without any sense of talking or writing down. Of course, some poets have written marvellously for children . . . [18]

Or consider Gillian Avery's comments in her *Everyman Anthology of Poetry for Children*, 1994, where she talks of avoiding: 'poems deliberately aimed at youth which – with the exception of nonsense – tend to be worthy and dull, if not arch and fey'.[19] But does it follow that poetry written for children will talk down or be dull and fey?

How does this prejudice on the part of editors affect the representation of women? Coventry Patmore declares that *A Children's Garland* is only from 'the best poets' and *Poems Every Child Should Know* is a selection from 'the best poems of all time'.[20] Both excluded most women. Although the latter purports to deal with poems *every child* should know, the introduction is addressed exclusively to boys. Other editors do likewise. I could only identify for certain three women in Lang's *Blue Poetry Book* which contains about 100 poems, and only six out of 170 entries in Geoffrey Grigson's otherwise magnificent *The Cherry Tree* (1959) are not by men.[21] Yet this is not inevitable. The editors, of whom I am one, of *Mother Gave A Shout*,[22] an anthology of women poets writing for children, declared that their only problem in selection lay in deciding what to leave out. Nor have editors of the calibre of Carol Ann Duffy,[23] or Wendy Cope[24] had any difficulty in finding excellent poetry by women in similarly focused anthologies. There is no scarcity of good poetry written by women, now or in the past.

It is *not* natural for anthologists to select poems written mainly by men for other adults in poetry books for children. A tradition has developed in anthologizing for children which needs to be challenged. Traditional often means conservative, sticking with the 'tried and tested' rather than appreciating what is new, unusual, different or risky. When you combine this conservatism with nostalgia for some idealized past, often associated with adults' interest in children's poetry, then it is easy to see why anthologies for young readers fall into this pattern. There are unrecognized and unexamined historical continuities in anthologizing for children that most editors seem unaware of, and too little understanding about the poetry children actually like and choose to read. It is not surprising that black British poetry, which was developing in innovative and exciting ways in the early 1980s, took a long time to get any place in the canon and is still under-represented. It surely is time to open up the canon particularly to show what women and poets from other parts of the world can write for children. This does not mean discarding the poetry from the past, but appreciating its value alongside new and changing voices. There is a great heritage of children's poetry in Britain and some of it is by women and working-class people and black writers, and of course, those who choose to concentrate on writing for the young.

Notes

1   Coventry Patmore, ed. *The Children's Garland*, Macmillan, London, 1862.
2   E. V. Lucas, ed. 'Some Notes on Poetry for Children', *Fortnightly Review*, Vol LX, Chapman & Hall, London, 1986, p. 391.
3   E. V. Lucas, ed. *A Book of Verses for Children*, Grant Richards, London, 1897, this edition, 1904
4   John Rowe Townsend, ed. *Modern Poetry*, OUP, London, 1973, p. 212.
5   *Mother Goose's Melody*, Marshall, London, 1760.
6   *Ibid.*
7   *Something Rich and Strange*, ed. Gina Pollinger, Kingfisher, London,1995.
8   Iona and Peter Opie, *The Oxford Book of Children's Verse*, 1973.
9   Lucy Aikin, *Poetry for Children*, London, 1801.
10   Andrew Lang, ed., *The Blue Poetry Book*, Longmans, Green & Co., 1891.
11   *The Children's Harp*, London, 1850.
12   John Greenleaf Whittier, ed. *Child Life: A Collection of Poems*, Nisbet & Co., London, 1874, p. vii.
13   Angela Huth, ed. *Island of the Children*, Orchard Books, London, 1987.
14   Brian Patten, *The Puffin Book of Twentieth Century Verse*, Penguin, London, 1991.
15   Robert Hull, 'A Jostle of Poetries', *Books for Keeps*, January 1992 No. 72, London, p. 21.
16   Jack Prelutsky, ed. *The Walker Book of Poetry for Children*, Walker, London, 1984.
17   Anthea Bell, *The Signal Poetry Award*, 47, May 1985, p. 82.
18   Neil Philip, ed. *A New Treasury of Poetry*, Blackie, London, 1990, p. 15.
19   Gillian Avery, ed. *Everyman Anthology of Poetry for Children*, David Campbell Publications, London, 1994.
20   Mary Burt, ed. *Poems Every Child Should Know*, Doubleday, London, 1904.
21   Geoffrey Grigson, ed. *The Cherry Tree*, Phoenix House, London, 1959.
22   Susanna Steele and Morag Styles, eds *Mother Gave a Shout: Poems by Women and Girls*, A&C Black, London, 1988.
23   Carol Ann Duffy, ed. *I Wouldn't Thank you for a Valentine*, Viking, London, 1992.
24   Wendy Cope, ed. *Is That the New Moon?*, Collins, London, 1989.

CHAPTER 10

Song and Story

Narrative and lyric verse for children

And out of my mind a story shall come,
Old, and lovely and wise.[1]

In this chapter I want to consider some of the best-known and most anthologized songs, ballads and narrative poems, mostly from the nineteenth century, which appeal to young and old alike. These are the poems that contain lines that many people can recite by heart, verse that forms the 'furniture of the mind' as Isaac Watts put it in 1715.[2] The best-loved exponents of narrative verse, such as Browning, Coleridge and Tennyson, were essentially poets for adults, yet particular poems of theirs have been regularly selected for children's anthologies. One reason for this is that the poems told such good stories that children have been willing to surmount difficulties of language or understanding in order to savour the pleasures of a satisfying narrative. Barbara Hardy's much-quoted description of narrative as 'a primary act of mind' is very much to the fore in this chapter:

> My argument is that narrative . . . [is] a primary act of mind transferred to art from life . . . what concerns me here are the qualities which narrative fiction shares with that inner and outer storytelling that plays a major role in our sleeping and waking lives. For we dream in narrative . . . remember, anticipate, hope, despair, gossip, learn, hate, love by narrative. In order really to live, we make up stories about ourselves and others, about the personal as well as the social past and future.'[3]

The other feature that most of these poems share is that they use rhyme combined with a strong, compelling metre. These are the poems many of us learned at school with relative ease and which were regularly recited in traditional poetry lessons. Today we might call this verse a kind of mantra to comfort or keep us company on lonely walks, on dark nights, or in difficult circumstances. In *Shout, Whisper and Sing*, Beverly Matthias talks of this poetry as the kind 'to be whispered while waiting at airports and stations' or 'to shout aloud when walking'.[4] It is also the poetry collected in anthologies of 'classic' verse from Palgrave's *Golden Treasury*[5] of 1861 to James Berry's *Classic Poems to Read Aloud*,[6] 1996.

In his book about the nightmare experience of being a hostage, Terry Waite quoted from the Bible, Kipling and Byron's chilling 'The Prisoner of Chillon': 'All was blank, and bleak, and grey / It was not night, it was not day . . .'[7] Brian Keenan found reassurance in Blake:

> . . . I raged and raged and tried to remember those convoluted chapters of the Book of Revelation. There in those apocalyptic words, I found enough violence of expression to condemn these men. Exhausted from my ranting I would try to recall that hymn by William Blake:
>
>> Bring me my Bow of burning gold:
>> Bring me my Arrow of desire:
>> Bring me my Spear: O clouds unfold![8]

When human beings have lost almost everything – their freedom, their dignity, chained like animals, blindfolded and in pain – one of the resources that is left is the comfort afforded by poetry which they know by heart. And it is on those poems that I want to concentrate in this chapter.

If there was space, I would draw on the Bible, Shakespeare, Homer and other ancient texts; as there is not, I invite the reader to take this opportunity to revisit charismatic figures like 'Hiawatha', 'The Ancient Mariner', 'The Lady of Shalott' and 'The Pied Piper of Hamelin', whose deeds are so well known that they are almost as much a part of English/American culture as Lord Nelson or McDonald's. The old ballads by unknown bards are some of the best of them, but I will concentrate on poems whose parentage is known. Older readers may get a whiff of nostalgia, as the poetry of their schooldays is recalled.

Mad dogs and drowned cats

My story starts, unusually for children's verse, with odes and elegies of the eighteenth century by Oliver Goldsmith (1730–1774) and Thomas Gray (1716–1771). Young people encounter Gray through his 'Elegy Written in a Country Churchyard'. Its tone of introspection and its themes hold marginal interest for children these days, but many young readers respond to its music and language.

> The curfew tolls the knell of parting day,
> The lowing herd wind slowly o'er the lea,
> The ploughman homeward plods his weary way,
> And leaves the world to darkness and to me.[9]

Gray's 'Ode on the Death of a Favourite Cat Drowned in a Tub of Gold Fishes' is more likely to set infant pulses alight. So does Goldsmith's 'Elegy on the Death of a

Mad Dog' which was included in more than one recent anthology for children. Both use a mock heroic style to tell their amusing tales.

> Good people all, of every sort,
>   Give ear unto my song;
> And if you find it wondrous short,
>   It cannot hold you long.[10]
>   (Gray)

> But soon a wonder came to light,
> That show'd the rogues they lied,
> The man recover'd of the bite,
> The dog it was that died.[11]
>   (Goldsmith)

Staying in the eighteenth century, William Cowper, whom we met in an earlier chapter, wrote one of the earliest comic narratives, 'John Gilpin' published in 1748. Essentially, it is an amusing tale of a hard-working shopkeeper, rather mean with his money, who takes his family out for a rare day-trip which goes disastrously wrong, partly because his horse has a mind of its own.

> Away went Gilpin, and away
> Went postboy at his heels,
> The postboy's horse right glad to miss
> The rumbling of the wheels.

> Six gentlemen upon the road
> Thus seeing Gilpin fly,
> With postboy scampering in the rear,
> They rais'd a hue and cry . . .

> 'Stop thief! – stop thief! – a highwayman!'
> Not one of them was mute;
> And all and each that passed that way
> Did join in the pursuit.[12]

The poem, like the story, fairly rolls along; in its time, it was one of a smallish number which children could read for pure light relief with the approval of their elders.

Towards the end of the eighteenth century came one of the finest and most enduringly popular narrative poems of all time, 'The Rime of the Ancient Mariner'.

'Water, water, everywhere'

Its author, Samuel Taylor Coleridge (1772–1834) could certainly tell a good tale, though he did not usually write with children in mind. One of the few times he directly addresses the young is in the much-quoted poem he wrote for his own son, 'Answer to a Child's Question', which begins like this:

> Do you ask what the birds say? The sparrow, the dove,
> The linnet and thrush say, 'I love and I love!'
> In the winter they're silent – the wind is so strong;
> What it says, I don't know, but it sings a loud song.[13]

But it is 'The Ancient Mariner' (spelled Ancyent Marinere in the original version) which comes to mind when Coleridge's name is mentioned: it was first published in *Lyrical Ballads*, 1798, and has been selected for children ever since. Coleridge's lengthy poem certainly needs some mediation by adults for most children, but it works because it is a compelling story with a supernatural sub-plot in a dramatic setting, told in rhythmic, mainly four-line, rhyming stanzas. One of the sections most young readers remember is when the ship is becalmed.

> Day after day, day after day,
> We stuck, nor breath nor motion;
> As idle as a painted ship
> Upon a painted ocean.

> Water, water, every where
> And all the boards did shrink;
> Water, water, every where,
> Nor any drop to drink.[14]

The poem is vivid and gory enough, peopled by ghosts and phantoms as it is, to compete with modern horror stories once children can penetrate the language. Most are horrified by the injustice of killing the albatross and can be slow to feel compassion for the tortured mariner. When they are old enough to understand something of suffering and retribution, many children are deeply moved by the morality and spirituality of the tale.

Stirring tales

Coleridge's 'Kubla Khan' holds similar appeal for children, this time with added exotica.

In Xanadu did Kubla Khan
A stately pleasure-dome decree:
Where Alph, the sacred river, ran
Through caverns measureless to man
Down to a sunless sea.[15]

Even if children do not understand all the words, the music of the language can be appreciated. It shows that when well-crafted poems have strong narrative drive, arresting characters or vivid imagery, the difficulties for younger readers can be surmounted. This is something shared by all the nineteenth-century narratives which follow. Byron, Keats and Shelley all told memorable yarns. In Lord Byron's case (1788–1824), 'The Destruction of Sennacherib' was a great favourite for its declamatory language and sumptious description.

The Assyrian came down like the wolf on the fold,
And his cohorts were gleaming in purple and gold;
And the sheen of his spears was like stars on the sea,
When the blue wave rolls nightly on deep Galilea.[16]

Byron's subject matter was often radical and heroic (and sometimes epic), full of classical and historical references – 'The Eve of Waterloo', 'The Dying Gladiator', 'Don Juan', for example. As for sheer romance, you cannot beat 'So, We'll Go No More a-Roving' or 'She walks in beauty'.

Though the night was made for loving,
    And the day returns too soon,
Yet we'll go no more a-roving
    By the light of the moon.[17]
        ('So, we'll go no more a-roving')

She walks in beauty, like the night
    Of cloudless climes and starry skies;
And all that's best of dark and bright
    Meet in her aspect and her eyes:[18]
        ('She walks in beauty')

Too many children have turned their backs on Percy Bysshe Shelley (1792–1822) by encountering poems too early with little resonance for youth. One of the exceptions is 'Ozymandius'. It does not seem to matter whether they understand it or not; this fragment stirs the imagination and the language reverberates in the mind.

> I met a traveller from an antique land
> Who said: Two vast and trunkless legs of stone
> Stand in the desert . . . Near them on the sand,
> Half sunk, a shattered visage lies, whose frown
> And wrinkled lip, and sneer of cold command
> Tell that its sculptor well those passions read
> Which yet survive, stamped on these lifeless things,
> The hand that mocked them, and the heart that fed.[19]

In similarly exotic vein is John Keats's 'On First Looking into Chapman's Homer'. The title might sound dry, but the poem breathes life from its opening to its closing lines:

> Much have I travelled in the realms of gold,
>   And many goodly states and kingdoms seen;
> Or like stout Cortez, when with eagle eyes
>   He stared at the Pacific – and all his men
> Looked at each other with a wild surmise –
>   Silent, upon a peak in Darien,[20]

Keats's outstanding ballad, 'La Belle Dame Sans Merci', is that exquisite mixture of tune and tale. Once heard, it lingers in the memory, like the unfortunate Knight.

> 'O what can ail thee knight-at-arms,
>   Alone and palely loitering?
> The sedge has withered from the lake,
>   And no birds sing.'[21]

Spinning yarns

Keats included 'There was a Naughty Boy' in a letter to his younger sister, Fanny, after quoting Meg Merrilies and telling her that 'since I scribbled the Song we have walked through a beautiful country to Kirkudbright – at which place I will write you a song about myself . . . '[22] It is unusual in form with its long thin shape and is full of inconsequential nonsense and playful language.

> There was a naughty Boy
>   A naughty boy was he
> He would not stop at home
>   He could not quiet be –

He took
In his knapsack
A book
Full of vowels
And a shirt
With some towels . . .[23]

We stay in the early years of the nineteenth century with Robert Southey (1774–1843), James Leigh Hunt (1784–1859), Thomas Campbell (1777–1844) and Charles Wolfe (1791–1823). Their narrative verse was sure to be included in anthologies for children for the next 150 years with rousing poems like 'The Inchcape Rock', 'Abou Ben Adhem', 'Lord Ullin's Daughter' and 'The Burial of Sir John Moore after Corunna'. Here is a verse or two from the beginning of each poem which quickly draws the young reader in with promise of excitement and high drama told in dramatic language with a powerful rhythm. I remember them all from my schooldays.

No stir in the air, no stir in the sea,
The ship was still as she could be;
Her sail from heaven received no motion;
Her keel was steady in the ocean.

The Abbot of Aberbrothok
Had placed the Bell on the Inchcape Rock;
On a buoy in the storm it floated and swung,
And over the waves its warning rung.[24]
            ('The Inchcape Rock')

Abou Ben Adhem (may his tribe increase)
Awoke one night from a deep dream of peace,
And saw within the moonlight in his room,
Making it rich, and like a lily in bloom,
An angel writing in a book of gold . . .[25]
            ('Abou Ben Adhem')

A chieftain to the Highlands bound
    Cries, 'Boatman, do not tarry!
And I'll give thee a silver pound
    To row us o'er the ferry.'[26]
            ('Lord Ullin's Daughter')

Not a drum was heard, not a funeral note,
    As his corse to the rampart we hurried;
Not a soldier discharged his farewell shot
    O'er the grave where our hero we buried.

We buried him darkly at dead of night,
    The sods with our bayonets turning,
By the struggling moonbeam's misty light
    And the lanthorn dimly burning.[27]
('The Burial of Sir John Moore after Corunna')

'The Pied Piper'

Jumping ahead to the Victorian period brings us to a rich source of narrative poetry. In *Victorian Verse* George MacBeth describes it as 'the great age of fiction in English poetry'. He goes on to suggest that the hypocrisy and reluctance for realism in the Victorian age (T. S. Eliot thought it 'pompous, shallow and fundamentally dishonest'[28]) gave rise to an 'immense development of purely imaginative writing, a literature springing from, and dependent upon, a willingness to invent situations which were not real or true'.[29] Although MacBeth's thesis does not take proper account of poets like Christina Rossetti, he was certainly right in his assessment of the Victorian period as the golden age of epic verse narratives, as the poets who follow will demonstrate.

Robert Browning (1812–1889) is described by the Opies as 'a poet almost from birth . . . [attempting] in his poetry to represent on the highest intellectual level the complexity of human nature'.[30] He is also famous for his elopement and marriage to a poet of equal stature, Elizabeth Barrett Browning. Many pupils still study 'My Last Duchess' and 'Oh to be in England / Now that April's there . . .' ('Home Thoughts from Abroad') at school these days, but little of the rest of Browning's poetry features in most syllabuses, except perhaps extracts from 'How They Brought the Good News from Ghent to Aix'.

I sprang to the stirrup, and Joris, and he;
I galloped, Dirck galloped, we galloped all three;
'Good speed!' cried the watch, as the gate-bolts undrew;
'Speed!' echoed the wall to us galloping through;
Behind shut the postern, the lights sank to rest,
And into the midnight we galloped abreast.[31]

However, Browning's celebrated narrative poem, 'The Pied Piper of Hamelin', which was published in 1842, assures him a place in the children's canon. Based on a popular German legend, it was written for the son of William Macready, the well-known Victorian actor. This was Browning's only serious attempt to write a poem for the young and it is still in print today, a testament to its enduring appeal. He employs a winning combination of wit, spellbinding storytelling and dramatic tension, employed with a varied rolling metre and ever-changing rhyme-scheme.

> Rats!
> They fought the dogs and killed the cats,
> And bit the babies in the cradles,
> And ate the cheeses out of the vats,
> And licked the soup from the cooks' own ladles,
> Split open the legs of salted sprats,
> Made nests inside men's Sunday hats . . .
> . . .
> Into the street the Piper stept,
> Smiling first a little smile,
> As if he knew what magic slept
> In his quiet pipe the while;
> Then like a musical adept,
> To blow the pipe his lips he wrinkled,
> And green and blue his sharp eyes twinkled,
> Like a candle-flame where salt is sprinkled;
> . . .
> And the grumbling grew to a mighty rumbling;
> And out of the houses the rats came tumbling.
> Great rats, small rats, lean rats, brawny rats,
> Brown rats, black rats, grey rats, tawny rats,
> Grave old plodders, gay young friskers,
> Fathers, mothers, uncles, cousins,
> Cocking tails and pricking whiskers,
> Families by tens and dozens . . .[32]

Browning's predominantly amusing tale turns into tragedy at the end when the harshest of sentences comes down on the heads of the town and its mean-spirited Mayor. 'The Pied Piper' has deservedly featured in numerous versions, many of them lavishly illustrated, in the century and a half since it was first written.

'The Cry of the Children'

Elizabeth Barrett Browning's (1806–1861) best-known poetry, such as *Sonnets from the Portuguese*, is not suitable for children. She could certainly tell a good story: *Aurora Leigh* is a novel-length prose poem, innovatory in form and theme and popular in the Victorian period. Elizabeth Barrett Browning was also interested in political and social issues, including the plight of the poor and child labour. 'The Cry of the Children' is an indictment of child exploitation.

> O my sisters! children small,
> Blue-eyed, wailing through the city,
> Our own babies cry in them all,
> Let us take them into pity.[33]

Unfortunately, in her personal life she was as thoughtless of the children of the poor as most other women of her class, demanding that her maid's child remain in Britain with relatives while she accompanied her mistress abroad. Margaret Forster, Barrett Browning's biographer, declared:

Nowhere in Elizabeth's correspondence at the time did she express any compassion for [her maid] Wilson's agony. The mother who adored her own child and had been overwhelmed by the violence of maternal feeling, and the poet who was about to publish a poem full of the tenderness of women for children and a defence of the exploited working-class girl, both seemed untouched by her own maid's anguish.[34]

Barrett Browning's 'Romance of the Swan's Nest' and other poems like it were often cited in books of children's poetry in the nineteenth century.

> Little Ellie sits alone
> Mid the beeches of a meadow
> By a stream-side on the grass;
> And the trees are showering down
> Doubles of their leaves in shadow
> On her golden hair and face.[35]

Emily Brontë (1818–1848) wrote some spellbinding poems as well as the novel she is famous for, *Wuthering Heights*. The menacing atmosphere, gloomy landscape and mysterious, heightened emotions are also features of her beguiling lyric poetry. Take 'Song':

> The night is darkening round me,
> The wild winds coldly blow;
> But a truant spell has bound me
> And I cannot, cannot go.

The giant trees are bending
Their bare boughs weighed with snow,
And the storm is fast descending
And yet I cannot go.

Clouds beyond clouds above me,
Wastes beyond wastes below;
But nothing drear can move me;
I will not, cannot go.[36]

If Felicia Hemans is recognized at all these days, it tends to be as the author of 'Casabianca', which has been parodied so often, it is hard to do the poem justice and read it seriously. It is as good a heroic poem as Kipling ever wrote and, if melodramatic in tone, also moving. As the single mother of five boys herself, Hemans is likely to have empathized with the sad tale, based on a true story of her day. If it sounds a little sentimental now, it also does that unusual thing – treats a child as a hero.

The boy stood on the burning deck
    Whence all but he had fled;
The flame that lit the battle's wreck
    Shone round him o'er the dead.

. . .

Yet beautiful and bright he stood,
    As born to rule the storm –
A creature of heroic blood,
    A proud, though child-like form.

There came a burst of thunder-sound –
    The boy – oh! where was he?
Ask of the winds that far around
    With fragments strewed the sea! –

With mast, and helm, and pennon fair,
    That well had borne their part;
But the noblest thing which perished there
    Was that young faithful heart![37]

Charles Kingsley (1819–1875) also took an interest in children and is, indeed, best known for *The Water Babies* (1863) and other fiction, but he also wrote poetry which was popular in nineteenth-century children's anthologies. Those who have not encountered Kingsley's famous story since childhood have probably forgotten the harshness and didacticism embedded within this appealing tale: here is a lighter section from 'Young and Old' which readers of an older generation may have stored away in their memory banks.

> When all the world is young, lad,
> And all the trees are green;
> And every goose a swan, lad,
> And every lass a queen;
> Then hey for boot and horse, lad,
> And round the world away;
> Young blood must have its course, lad,
> And every dog his day.[38]

'The Lady of Shalott'

The most famous Victorian of them all is Alfred, Lord Tennyson (1809–1892) who was immensely popular with a wide range of readers in his day, not just the literati. George MacBeth calls him 'the most accomplished verse technician of his age' and the 'most consistently successful writer of symbolist narrative in the nineteenth century . . .'[39] A quiet, retiring poet with a penchant for long poems based on romantic and classical literature, Tennyson is best known in children's verse for the haunting (in both senses) 'Lady of Shalott' and poems such as 'The Lotus Eaters', 'Morte D'Arthur' and 'The Brook'.

> I come from haunts of coot and hern,
> I make a sudden sally,
> And sparkle out among the fern,
> To bicker down a valley.
>
> By thirty hills I hurry down
> Or slip between the ridges,
> By twenty thorps, a little town,
> And half a hundred bridges.[40]

The tongue-twister qualities of 'The City Child' are less well known, but many children used to relish the rhythm of the flower names recited aloud.

> Dainty little maiden, whither would you wander?
> Whither from this pretty home, the home where mother dwells?
> 'Far and far away,' said the dainty little maiden,
> 'All among the gardens, auriculas, anemones,
> Roses and lilies and Canterbury-bells.'[41]

Other children meet Tennyson in anthologies where poems like 'The Eagle' ('He clasps the crag with crooked hands; / Close to the sun in lonely lands, / Ringed with the azure world he stands'), 'When Cats Run Home' ('Alone and warming his five wits / The white owl in the belfry sits'), 'Sweet and Low' ('Sweet and low, sweet and low, / Wind of the western sea'), 'The Charge of the Light Brigade' or 'Mariana' are regularly selected, though less often of late in the case of the latter two. 'Mariana' is exceptional for dramatic language, tunefulness and powerful balladry. In 'The Charge of the Light Brigade' the reader is hurled along with that famous charge:

> She only said, 'My life is dreary,
>   He cometh not,' she said;
> She said, 'I am aweary, aweary,
>   I would that I were dead.'[42]
>   ('Mariana')

> Half a league, half a league
> Half a league onward,
> All in the valley of Death
> Rode the six hundred.[43]
> ('The Charge of the Light Brigade')

The Lady of Shalott utters similar sentiments to Mariana before she made her doomed atttempt at freedom. It is a fine, romantic tale which provides the perfect vehicle for Tennyson's lyrical gifts, particularly in the moving conclusion. This is one of the most popular poems of all time.

> Who is this? and what is here?
> And in the lighted palace near
> Died the sound of royal cheer;
> And they crossed themselves for fear,
>   All the knights at Camelot.
> But Lancelot mused a little space;
> He said, 'She has a lovely face;
> God in his mercy lend her grace,
>   The Lady of Shalott.'[44]

The Highwayman came riding

The gifted illustrator, Charles Keeping, produced an enthralling version of 'The Lady of Shalott' in 1986, creating powerful images in swirling pen and pencil strokes mixed with soft chalk and printed in black and sepia. Keeping's strong, atmospheric drawings match the rhythms of the poem and combine period detail with the shadowy fantasy of an old, old tale. Keeping did not believe in compromising for the young, so when he illustrated Alfred Noyes's (1880–1958) 'The Highwayman' in equally vivid style in 1981, he brought a terrifying realism to the ballad.

> Let's be honest, these guys came and they probably raped the girl too. When I read something I get feelings about it – I can't keep that out of my work. I may not show a rape, but that's in my mind.[45]

Noyes himself earns his place in children's literature with the tense melodrama of the poem.

> The wind was a torrent of darkness among the gusty trees,
> The moon was a ghostly galleon tossed upon cloudy seas.
> The road was a ribbon of moonlight over the purple moor . . .
> And the highwayman came riding –
> Riding – riding –
> The highwayman came riding, up to the old inn-door.[46]

'Dover Beach'

Matthew Arnold (1822–1888), son of the Thomas Arnold who wrote *Tom Brown's Schooldays*, also took to education (his father was headmaster of Rugby) and spent his professional life as an Inspector for Schools. Poems like 'The Scholar Gypsy', once popular, have gone out of vogue, but 'Dover Beach' and 'The Forsaken Merman' are still much quoted. In the case of 'Dover Beach', it is the ringing final lines that people tend to remember; knowing that Arnold wrote it on his honeymoon casts a romantic light on the poem. As for 'The Forsaken Merman', the repetitive refrain 'let us away, let us away' still carries many 'dear' children to that wild seashore.

> Ah, love, let us be true
> To one another! for the world, which seems
> To lie before us like a land of dreams,
> So various, so beautiful, so new,
> Hath really neither joy, nor love, nor light,
> Nor certitude, nor peace, nor help for pain;
> And we are here as on a darkling plain
> Swept with confused alarms of struggle and flight,
> Where ignorant armies clash by night.[47]
>   ('Dover Beach')

> Come, dear children, let us away;
>   Down and away below.
> Now my brothers call from the bay;

Now the great winds shorewards blow;
Now the salt tides seawards flow;
Now the wild white horses play,
Champ and chafe and toss in the spray.
Children dear, let us away.
   This way, this way.[48]
        ('The Forsaken Merman')

'Hiawatha'

During the Victorian period Henry Wadsworth Longfellow (1807–1882), Professor of French and Spanish at Harvard, was the most popular American poet of his day. He could have slipped into the annals of childhood with a single, narrative poem, 'The Song of Hiawatha', published in 1855. In the nineteenth century many of his other poems were a regular feature in poetry books, such as 'Rain in Summer' and 'The Wreck of the Hesperus', another dramatic tale.

It was the schooner Hesperus,
   That sail'd the wintry sea;
And the skipper had taken his little daughter,
   To bear him company.

Blue were her eyes as the fairy-flax,
   Her cheeks like the dawn of day,
And her bosom white as the hawthorn buds,
   That ope in the month of May.[49]

The reader instantly knows that something dreadful will happen to the father or the daughter or both and is compelled to read on. But it is 'The Song of Hiawatha' that everyone knows. Less accomplished technically than 'The Pied Piper' or 'The Lady of Shalott', it featured a maddeningly repetitive rhythm which can easily be parodied and ridiculed. But it is also a poem with widespread appeal. Longfellow drew on Native American traditions in 'Hiawatha', especially their knowledge of and respect for the animal kingdom and it can be seen as a song of admiration for a dying way of life.

Then Iagoo, the great boaster,
He the marvellous story-teller,
He the traveller and the talker,
He the friend of old Nokomis,
Made a bow for Hiawatha;
From a branch of ash he made it,
From an oak bough made the arrows,

> Tipped with flint, and winged with feathers,
> And the cord he made of deer-skin.
>   Then he said to Hiawatha:
> 'Go, my son, into the forest,
> Where the red deer herd together,
> Kill for us a famous roebuck,
> Kill for us a deer with antlers!'
>   Forth into the forest straightway
> All alone walked Hiawatha
> Proudly, with his bows and arrows;
> And the birds sang round him, o'er him . . .'[50]

The National Theatre's lively production in London round about 1980 may have given the poem a new lease of life, where they used a wonderfully insistent drumming to enhance the natural rhythms of the verse. Errol le Cain's delightful picture book version of 1986 is also a tribute to Native American culture.

Father Christmas, a raven and nobody

A more modest achievement, but of equal longevity, was the narrative poem by Longfellow's compatriot, Clement Clarke Moore (1779–1863), who entered the history books with 'A Visit from St Nicholas', now usually known as 'The Night Before Christmas', published in 1823. There have been numerous illlustrated versions of the poem in Britain and America right up to the 1990s.

> Twas the night before Christmas, when all through the house
> Not a creature was stirring, not even a mouse;
> The stockings were hung by the chimney with care,
> In hopes that St Nicholas soon would be there.[51]

Moore's rotund, jolly St Nicholas who fills the poem with his reindeers and sleigh packed with toys, and who slides down chimneys to fill up children's stockings, may have a lot to do with what has become the enduring Western imagery associated with Christmas. No doubt Moore's illlustrators share that responsiblity with him; they include W. W. Denslow, 1902 (who also did *The Wizard of Oz*) and Arthur Rackham, 1931. This enduringly popular poem by the Professor of Hebrew and Greek at the Protestant Seminary of New York has been translated into most European languages.

A much darker American poet is the journalist and literary editor, Edgar Allan Poe (1809–1849) whose Gothic imagination appeals to those who like a horror story. In *Poetics of Influence*, Harold Bloom tells us that Poe wanted to be the American

Coleridge or Shelley, but ended up as the American Lear. The opening of 'The Raven' is typical of his verse; and like any good storyteller, Poe raises questions which urgently require an answer.

> Once upon a midnight dreary, while I pondered, weak and weary,
> Over many a quaint and curious volume of forgotten lore,
>   While I nodded, nearly napping, suddenly there came a tapping
> As of some one gently rapping, rapping at my chamber door.
> 'Tis some visitor,' I muttered, 'tapping at my chamber door –
>   Only this and nothing more.'[52]

One of the most distinctive American voices of the nineteenth century belongs to Emily Dickinson (1830–1886), the outstanding but reclusive Amherst poet, most of whose work was published after her death. Her poetry is often collected for children because of her apparently naive style.

> I'm nobody, who are you?
> Are you nobody too?
> Then there's a pair of us.
> Don't tell – they'd banish us you know.[53]

'If you can dream . . .'

Crossing the threshold into the twentieth century leads us to four poets who straddle the nineteenth century as well – Rudyard Kipling, Hilaire Belloc, William Butler Yeats and Harold Munro. Yeats and Monro are typical poets of this chapter writing exclusively for adults, but whose poems come up again and again in poetry books for children. It is the lyrical quality in the poetry which is to the fore and both poets employ rich visual imagery. 'The Lake Isle of Innisfree' and 'The Song of Wandering Angus' come up in children's anthologies again and again.

> I went out to the hazel wood,
> Because a fire was in my head,
> And cut and peeled a hazel wand,
> And hooked a berry to a thread,
> And when white moths were on the wing,
> And moth-like stars were flickering out.
> I dropped the berry in a stream
> And caught a little silver trout.[54]

How delicately the poet takes the reader through the simple processes of fashioning a fishing rod impelled by the 'fire' in his head, creating as he does an unforgettably luminous nightscape. The lyric is so strong that the reader would know it was a song without that word in the title. Sharing many qualities in common, it is the element of magic and mystery surrounding Harold Monro's 'Overheard on a Saltmarsh' which makes it one of the most popular poems for children of all time. The voice and form of the poem are quite unusual. This is how it ends.

> Better than any man's fair daughter,
> Your green glass beads on a silver ring.
>
> Hush, I stole them out of the moon.
>
> Give me your beads, I want them.
>
> No.
>
> I will howl in a deep lagoon
> For your green beads, I love them so.
> Give them me. Give them.
>
> No.[55]

Hilaire Belloc has been well represented in Chapter 5, but he requires a mention here for his captivating narrative, 'Tarantella', with its stange, amusing and deeply compelling opening.

> Do you remember an Inn,
> Miranda?
> Do you remember an Inn?
> And the tedding and the spreading
> of the straws for a bedding,
> And the fleas that tease in the High Pyranees,
> And the wine that tasted of the tar?
> And the cheers and the jeers of the young muleteers
> (Under the dark of the vine verandah)?[56]

Rudyard Kipling (1865–1936) spent his early childhood in India, then was left by his parents in England for many years to the not-so-tender mercies of prep school and indifferent Scottish relatives. Kipling gives us a hint of the pain he suffered as a child in his aptly titled autobiography, *Something of Myself*. He also shared something of his childhood reading tastes which included *Aunt Judy's Magazine*, the stories of Mrs Ewing and, of course, *Robinson Crusoe*.

I set up in business alone as a trader with savages . . . in a mildewy basement room where I stood my solitary confinements. My apparatus was a coconut shell strung on a red cord, a tin trunk, and a piece of packing-case which kept off any other world . . . The magic, you see, lies in the ring or fence that you take refuge in.[57]

That is almost as good as Stevenson on the magic of children's play. Kipling wrote some playful verse for C. R. L. Fletcher's *History of England*, 1911, such as 'The River's Tale':

> And life was gay, and the world was new,
> And I was a mile across at Kew!
> But the Roman came with a heavy hand,
> And bridged and roaded and ruled the land,
> And the Roman left and the Danes blew in –
> And that's where your history books begin![58]

One of the most famous children's authors in the world in his own time, Kipling is known now for his patriotic, bombastic verse and for those classics of children's literature, the *Just So Stories* and *The Jungle Book*. If there is a slick, simplistic and sentimental side to Kipling's writing, there is also evidence of an original imagination at work. Peter Keating in *Kipling the Poet* discusses the educative impulse in his writing: '[it] is moral and patriotic rather than religious, and his method usually rests on a trust in the child-reader's imagination to interpret the subtle meanings and rhythms of the poems, and to relate them to the prose stories . . . '[59] Although Kipling did not write much poetry specifically for the young (most of it was included within his fictional works), his verse struck a chord with adults and children alike and Kipling has retained his popularity ever since. *I Remember, I Remember*, sub-titled 'Famous People's Favourite Childhood Poems', cites Kipling more often than any other poet. Margaret Thatcher, for example, chose 'The Glory of the Garden', which concludes:

> Oh, Adam was a gardener, and God who made him sees
> That half a proper gardener's work is done upon his knees,
> So when your work is finished, you can wash your hands and pray
> For the Glory of the garden, that it may not pass away![60]

This seems to me the worst side of Kipling – easily digested sentiments in verse that is close to doggerel. Kipling certainly favoured a public poetry; no exploration of inner life for him. His style can be hectoring, his content facile, yet lines from Kipling's verse have passed into the vernacular. The nation's favourite poem declared on National Poetry Day, 1995, was 'If', from one of Kipling's children's books, *Rewards and Fairies*.

> If you can dream – and not make dreams your master;
> If you can think – and not make thoughts your aim:
> If you can meet with Triumph and Disaster
> And treat those two imposters just the same.[61]

Many poetry devotees were very disappointed: how could such a dated, sexist, much parodied poem be selected with the whole world of poetry to choose from? Further reflection shows why. It is a poem which many people learned at school and remembered, because of the striking, if simple, rhythm and the sentiments about decency and integrity. It is probably a deeply reassuring poem for many, even in this rather different era. If you behave honourably, do your best and act from principle rather than expediency, it will probably come out all right in the end. If it doesn't, you can hold on to your self-respect. In uncertain times, Kipling's decent, old-fashioned virtues seem to hold wide appeal.

Puck of Pook's Hill contains several of his most popular poems. The best of them, perhaps, is 'The Way Through the Woods' for its delicate language and mood of regret and uncertainty, not traits normally associated with Kipling.

> They shut the road through the woods
> Seventy years ago.
> Weather and rain have undone it again,
> And now you would never know
> There was once a road through the woods
> Before they planted the trees.[62]

A more limited but similarly patriotic poet was Henry Newbolt (1862–1938) who is remembered for stirring poems like 'Drake's Drum' with its insistent metre. Newbolt's patronizing attempt at working-class sailors' dialect is forced and crude, but the tune stays in one's head, like it or not.

> Drake he's in his hammock an' a thousand mile away,
> (Capten, art tha sleepin' there below?),
> Slung atween the round shot in Nombre Dios Bay,
> An' dreamin' arl the time o' Plymouth Hoe.
> Yarnder lumes the Island, yarnder lie the ships,
> Wi' sailor lads a dancin heel-an-toe,
> An' the shore-lights flashin', an the night-tide dashin',
> He sees et arl so plainly as he saw et long ago.[63]

'I must go down to the seas again'

John Masefield (1878–1967) was writing at a time when poetry for children was dominated by Walter de la Mare who was immensely talented at lyric and narrative verse; he features in Chapter 11. Masefield's poetry was standard fare for learning by heart, particularly his sea shanties, for children like me at primary school in the 1950s. He was also the author of popular stories for children like *The Box of Delights*, serialized on television and radio. His poetry has not lasted so well, except for two poems, 'Sea Fever' and 'Cargoes'. The opening refrain of the former is part of the culture – 'I must go down to the seas again, to the lonely sea and the sky'; although 'Cargoes' is dated, it still carries a punch with its declamatory tone, ringing alliterations and forceful rhythm.

> Dirty British coaster with a salt-caked smoke stack
> Butting through the Channel in the mad March days,
> With a cargo of Tyne coal, Road-rail, pig-lead,
> Firewood, iron-ware, and cheap tin trays.[64]

Those were the days! Masefield is associated with the good old British virtues which can deter readers today and, like most of his fellow Georgian writers, his poetry is out of fashion.

Born in Herefordshire, Masefield had a hard early life, losing both parents by the age of 12, starting out in a wealthy family which suddenly became impoverished, in the care of neglectful relatives from whom he could not wait to escape and, consequently, living rough in America and contracting tuberculosis before he reached the age of 20. Despite suffering agonies of sea-sickness, Masefield found solace on the sea, though he was always clear that he would become a writer. He became Poet Laureate in 1930.

Macavity

T. S. Eliot (1888–1965) is still considered one of the finest and most influential poets of the twentieth century and is not usually associated with humour, storytelling or light verse. *Old Possum's Book of Practical Cats* is the single Eliot publication which is suitable for younger children (though individual poems like 'The Coming of the Magi' are regularly anthologized) and then only insofar as it is funny, fairly easy to understand and features lively tales about various eccentric cats. Eliot was lucky in two outstanding illustrators of *Old Possum*, first published in 1939 – Nicolas Bentley and Edward Gorey – both versions remarkably still in print. The best-known poem features Macavity, that resourceful and endearing pussy-cat.

Ezra Pound nicknamed Eliot 'Old Possum' and Eliot apparently used to call himself by that name in letters to friends. The book, it seems, was inspired by his godson, Tom Faber; he is one of several children we have to thank for getting their elders to write for the young. Eliot was also known to love cats and was a keen observer of their habits. The poems are close to songs, so it is not surprising that Andrew Lloyd Webber should feature them in a musical which opened in London in 1981. 'Cats' is still drawing huge audiences 16 years later, which will not do the original poems any harm. It also shows that *Old Possum* is for adults rather than children.

G. K. Chesterton (1874–1936) was guaranteed a place in children's poetry books until recently. Now his work appears a bit old-fashioned, but poems like 'The Donkey', a little sentimental no doubt, will surely live on. The skilful alliterative opening strikes a dramatic note:

> When fishes flew and forests walked
> And figs grew upon thorn . . .[65]

Two other nature poets stand out in the first decades of this century and neither of them wrote for children – Thomas Hardy (1840–1928) and Edward Thomas (1878–1917). Hardy's forte is the atmospheric recreation of a particular place at a particular moment in time and the emotions associated with it. 'Snow in the Suburbs' and 'Weathers' are representative of the kind of poems by Hardy chosen for children. Both use metre impeccably.

> This is the weather the cuckoo likes,
>   And so do I;
> When showers betumble the chestnut spikes,
>   And nestlings fly:
> And the little brown nightingale bills his best,
> And they sit outside at 'The Traveller's Rest',
> And maids come forth sprig-muslin drest,
> And citizens dream of the south and west,
>   And so do I.[66]

Thomas, friend to de la Mare when he was penniless and unknown, wrote some memorable poems that many people can quote and which often get selected for children – 'Adlestrop', 'Thaw' and 'Snow' are good examples. Thomas was one of several gifted poets who died before his time in the First World War. A fine nature poet with a quirky eye for human nature, Thomas was the kind of poet who could describe a perfectly ordinary scene on an ordinary journey so that it lives in the memory. One reading of 'Adlestrop' and you know you are in the presence of poetry.

> Yes, I remember Adlestrop –
> The name, because one afternoon
> Of heat the express-train drew up there
> Unwontedly. It was late June.
>
> The steam hissed. Someone cleared his throat.
> No one left and no one came
> On the bare platform. What I saw
> Was Adelstrop – only the name.
> ('Adlestrop')[67]

One recent poem that I feel fairly sure will gain 'classic' status in the future is Alan Brownjohn's 'We're going to see the Rabbit'. Although the poem is only about 20 years old, it is much anthologized and has been included in *The New Oxford Book of Verse*. It is interesting that my single representation of contemporary poetry in this chapter is 'green' – a stinging indictment of the way our society treats the environment and the inhabitants of the animal kingdom.

> We are going to see the rabbit,
> We are going to see the rabbit,
> Which rabbit? people say.
> Which rabbit? ask the children.
> Which rabbit?
> The only rabbit in England,
> Sitting behind a barbed-wire fence
> Under the floodlights, neon lights,
> Sodium lights,
> Nibbling the grass
> On the only patch of grass
> In England . . .[68]

Thus ends a chapter which focuses on favourite, easy-listening, narrative poems or those with a melodious, lyric quality. Few of these poems make the reader work hard or offer serious challenge; in truth, they are poems that conjure up vivid images, tell grand tales and delight the ear. But this is the very poetry which regularly features on programmes like *Poetry Please* where viewers send in their requests. This is the poetry which adults and children share. This is the poetry which excludes few and makes many people feel that verse has a place in their lives. On these grounds alone it earns its place in this book. Those of us who love poetry and long for it to have the widest possible audience should be grateful for poems which, indeed, please so many and link us to the poetry of the past. One can only speculate about which of the poems of the later twentieth century may win such universal approval.

Notes

1　Walter de la Mare, from 'Listen!', *Collected Rhymes and Verses*, Faber, London, 1944/89.
2　Isaac Watts, *Divine Songs attempted in easy language for the use of Children*, London, 1715, facsimile ed. J. H. P. Pafford, OUP, London, 1971, p. 146.
3　Barbara Handy, 'Narrative as a Primary Act of Mind', *The Cool Web*, ed. M. Meek *et. al.*, Bodley Head, London, 1977, p. 12.
4　Beverley Matthias, ed. *Shout, Whisper, Sing, 101 Poems to be Read Aloud*, Bodley Head, London, 1989, p.9.
5　Francis Palgrave, ed. *The Golden Treasury of Songs and Lyrics*, 1862, this edition, Macmillan, London, 1931.
6　James Berry, ed. *Classic Poems to Read Aloud*, Kingfisher, London, 1995.
7　George Gordon Noel, Lord Byron from 'The Prisoner of Chillon', quoted in Terry Waite, *Taken on Trust*, Hodder, London, 1993, p. 181.
8　William Blake, from 'Jerusalem', quoted in Brian Keenan, *An Evil Cradling*, Hutchinson, London, 1992, p. 215.
9　Thomas Gray, from 'Elegy Written in a Country Churchyard', quoted in *The New Oxford Book of English Verse*, ed. Helen Gardner, London, 1972, p. 442.
10　Thomas Gray from 'Ode on the Death of a Favourite Cat Drowned in a Tub of Gold Fishes', *ibid.*, p. 441.
11　Oliver Goldsmith, from 'Elegy on the Death of a Mad Dog', quoted in Coventry Patmore ed. *The Children's Garland*, Macmillan, London, 1862.
12　William Cowper, from 'John Gilpin', quoted in Patmore, *ibid.*
13　Samuel Taylor Coleridge, from 'Answer to a Child's Questions', quoted in Patmore, *ibid.*
14　Samuel Taylor Coleridge, from 'The Rime of the Ancient Mariner', 1798, quoted in Gardner, *op. cit.*, p. 529.
15　Samuel Taylor Coleridge, from 'Kubla Khan', *ibid.*, p. 544.
16　George Gordon Noel, Lord Byron, from 'The Destruction of Sennacherib', quoted in Patmore, *op. cit.*
17　George Gordon Noel, Lord Byron, from 'So we'll go no more a rovin', quoted in Gardner, *op. cit.*, p. 573.
18　George Gordon Noel, Lord Byron, from 'She Walks in Beauty', quoted in Gardner, *op. cit.*, p. 563.
19　Percy Bysshe Shelley from 'Ozymandius', *ibid.*, p. 580.
20　John Keats from 'On First Looking into Chapman's Homer', *ibid.*, p. 602.
21　John Keats from 'La Belle Dame Sans Merci', *ibid.*, p. 613.
22　John Keats in a letter to Fanny Keats 2–5 July 1818, *The Letters of John Keats*, ed. Robert Gittings, Oxford, 1970, p. 112.
23　*ibid.*, pp. 112–3
24　Robert Southey from 'The Inchcape Rock', quoted in Patmore, *op. cit.*
25　James Leigh Hunt from 'Abou Ben Adhem' quoted in Gardner, *op. cit.*, p. 559.

26 Thomas Campbell, from 'Lord Ullin's Daughter', quoted in Patmore, *op. cit.*

27 Charles Wolfe, from 'The Burial of Sir John Moore after Corunna', quoted in Gardner, *op. cit.*, p. 579.

28 T. S. Eliot quoted in George MacBeth ed. *Victorian Verse*, 1969/87, Penguin, London, p. 19.

29 George MacBeth, *ibid.,* p. 18, 24.

30 Iona and Peter Opie eds. *The Oxford Book of Children's Verse*, Oxford,1973/93, p. 356.

31 Robert Browning from 'How they brought the good news from Ghent to Aix', quoted in Palgrave, *op. cit.*

32 Robert Browning from 'The Pied Piper of Hamelin', quoted in Opie, *op. cit.*

33 Elizabeth Barrett Browning from 'The Cry of the Children', quoted in *The Brownings for the Young*, ed. F. G. Kenyon, London, 1896.

34 Margaret Forster, *Elizabeth Barrett Browning*, Chatto and Windus, London, 1988, p. 315.

35 Elizabeth Browning from 'Romance of the Swan's Nest', quoted in Patmore, *op. cit.*

36 Emily Brontë, 'Song', quoted in *Nineteenth Century Minor Poets*, ed. W.H. Auden, Faber, London, 1966.

37 Felicia Hemans from 'Casabianca', quoted in Patmore, *op. cit.*

38 Charles Kingsley from 'Young and Old', quoted in Opie, *op. cit.*

39 MacBeth, *op. cit.* p.21.

40 Alfred Lord Tennyson, from 'The Brook', quoted in Patmore, *op. cit.*

41 Tennyson, from 'The City Child', *ibid.*

42 Tennyson, from 'Mariana', quoted in Gardner, *op. cit.*, p. 634.

43 Tennyson, from 'The Charge of the Light Brigade', quoted in Patmore, *op. cit.*

44 Tennyson, from 'The Lady of Shalott', quoted in Gardner, *op. cit.*, pp. 641/2.

45 Charles Keeping in *The Books for Keeps Guide to Poetry 0-16*, eds. M. Styles and P. Triggs, London, 1988, p. 19.

46 Alfred Noyes, *The Highwayman*, quoted in *The New Dragon Book of Verse*, ed. M. Harrison and C. Stuart-Clark, Oxford, 1977.

47 Matthew Arnold, from 'Dover Beach', quoted in Gardner, *op. cit.*, p. 703.

48 Matthew Arnold, from 'The Forsaken Merman', quoted in *I Remember, I Remember: famous peoples' favourite childhood poems*, ed. Rob Farrow, Bodley Head, 1993.

49 Henry Wadsworth Longfellow, from 'The Wreck of the Hesperus', quoted in *The Oxford Book of Children's Verse in America*, ed. Donald Hall, Oxford University Press, New York, 1985.

50 Longfellow from 'The Song of Hiawatha', J. M. Dent, London, 1992.

51 Clement Clarke Moore, from 'A Visit from St Nicholas' quoted in Opie, *op. cit.*, p. 154.

52 Edgar Allan Poe, from 'The Raven', quoted in Hall, *op. cit.*

53 Emily Dickinson, from 'I'm nobody', quoted in Hall, *op. cit.*

54 W. B. Yeats, from 'The Song of Wandering Angus', quoted in Farrow, *op. cit.*

55 Harold Monro, from *Overheard on a Saltmarsh*, quoted in Neil Philip, ed., *The New Oxford Book of Children's Verse*, Oxford, 1996.

56 Hilaire Belloc from 'Tarantella', quoted in *The Oxford Treasury of Classic Poems*, ed. M. Harrison and C. Stuart-Clark, Oxford, 1996.

57 Rudyard Kipling, *Something of Myself*, Penguin, London, 1936/78.

58 Kipling, quoted in *Kipling the Poet*, Peter Keating, Secker and Warburg, London, 1994, p. 177.

59 *Ibid.,* 1994, p. 168.

60 Kipling, from 'The Glory of the Garden', quoted in Farrow, *op. cit.*

61 Kipling, from 'If', quoted in Farrow, *op. cit.*

62   Kipling from 'The Way Through the Woods', quoted in Farrow, *op. cit.*
63   Henry Newbolt, from 'Drake's Drum', quoted in Farrow, *op. cit.*
64   John Masefield from 'Cargoes', quoted in Farrow, *op. cit.*
65   G. K. Chesterton, from 'The Donkey', quoted in ed. Harrison and Stuart-Clark, *op. cit.*
66   Thomas Hardy from 'Weathers', quoted in *A New Treasury of Poetry*, ed. Neil Philip, Blackie, London, 1990.
67   Edward Thomas from 'Adlestrop', quoted in Farrow, *op. cit.*
68   Alan Brownjohn from 'We Are Going to See the Rabbit', quoted in *New Dragon*, *op. cit.*

For quick and easy reference I have located most of the poems quoted in this chapter in well-known anthologies.

CHAPTER 11

The Travellers

Poetry for children in the first half of the twentieth century

That is the farthest thing I can remember.
It won't mean much to you. It does to me.
Then I grew up, you see.[1]

This chapter deals with the period from the beginning of the twentieth century until the advent of a new movement in poetry for children which emerged in the 1970s. De la Mare's debut, *Songs of Childhood*, was published in 1902 after which many lively voices appeared, like those of Eleanor Farjeon, James Reeves and A. A. Milne, who are still well known today. Some others, who were popular for two decades after the Second World War, have fallen out of favour. In this chapter I make an assessment of the key poets within this period and outline changing perceptions about poetry and childhood along the way. We have not yet moved out into the street: the location for this poetry remains firmly in the garden.

Songs of Childhood

Walter de la Mare (1873–1956) is probably the most significant poet for children of all time writing in the Romantic tradition. His best-known collections include *The Listeners and Other Poems*, 1912, and *Peacock Pie*, 1913, though his adult work also contained many poems which could be enjoyed by children and were later brought together in *Collected Rhymes and Verses*, 1944. Also a successful writer of fiction, his *Collected Stories for Children* appeared in 1947.

In *Biographia Literaria*,[2] Samuel Taylor Coleridge says that

> to carry on the feelings of childhood into the powers of manhood; to combine the child's sense of wonder and novelty with the appearances, which everyday life . . . rendered familiar with sun and moon and stars throughout the year . . . this is the character and privilege of genius, and one of the marks which distinguish genius from talent.

If Coleridge is right, then de la Mare has the stamp of genius about him. John Keats's famous statement about poetry and the imagination also applies to de la Mare: 'I am certain of nothing but the holiness of the Heart's affections and the truth of Imagination – What the Imagination seizes as Beauty must be truth . . .'[3] Theresa Whistler, who wrote a recent biography of de la Mare and, indeed, knew him and his family well, confirms it:

> He felt strongly as Keats that what the imagination seizes as Beauty *must* be truth . . . the Romantic movement stirred more profound feelings in him than any other of the Nineties poetry . . . he lived by a romantic reality he could discover in the commonplace and familiar.[4]

As a man, de la Mare was child-like. If Robert Louis Stevenson was an adult who was closely in touch with his own childhood, de la Mare was a man who never grew out of his. Whistler writes:

> What moved the child will move the heart's imagination to the end. At least this is true of artists whose vision is essentially childlike . . . He not only kept, spontaneously, the childlike vision, but also continued deliberately to exercise the special faculties of childhood – day-dreaming, make-believe, questioning that takes nothing for granted . . . The greater part of all he wrote is either the recreation of experience through the eyes of childhood, or else the absorbed lifelong investigation of how such eyes work.[5]

Edward Thomas, friend and fellow poet, also recognized this quality in de la Mare, and confided his opinion to Eleanor Farjeon.

> Thomas always loved the homely and direct enchantments best, and disliked anything that smacked of artifice and deliberate decoration . . . There was a realness he looked for . . . and found in de la Mare's poems – truth to childhood, truth to the human heart when romance genuinely moves it, and truth to his own vision of Englishness.[6]

This may account, in some part, for what is lacking as well as what is strong in de la Mare's work. While he could tell romantic tales, paint beautiful pictures of the natural world and catch a tiny detail or moment in time like no one else, there is, perhaps, a softness in his work which, while attractive, makes readers like me long for something more bracing. Whistler puts her finger on it:

> One could say that his *view* of childhood, in relation to the whole of life, was exaggerated, and to that extent was partly distorted and tinged with the

sentimental; whereas his *vision* of it – childhood considered in itself alone – is one of unsurpassed insight.[7]

Whistler goes on to suggest that the creed on which de la Mare's life was based was that childhood holds the key to life and that age brought stupidity, not greater wisdom. When he met Katherine Mansfield, part of their affinity came from their shared belief and value in their child-selves. And Whistler tells us that what he prized about his own four children: '. . . were the morning-new responses, uninfluenced by adult standards, revealing life from a vantage point more fortunate than acquired wisdom can put in its place'.[8]

John Bayley says something similar in an article entitled 'The Child in Walter de la Mare':

Childhood, for de la Mare, is a state of acceptance – acceptance of power and evil, joy and woe, the real and the feigned, the natural and the supernatural – inhabiting the same dimension. Because, in consciousness, we never leave the childhood world, there is no special enclave for children.[9]

It is no surprise that De la Mare's first book of poetry is called *Songs of Childhood*; he returned to that theme in 1935 with *Early One Morning*,[10] an anthology of writing about childhood, though it could be said he never really left it.

My own mixed feelings about de la Mare's poetry are probably evident by now. On the one hand, one cannot deny the charm and delicacy of his poetry which is crafted with meticulous care. His depiction of people is often well observed, kind and appreciative. Few have rivalled his evocation of nature or his melodious voice. And yet . . . what gets in the way of the undoubted pleasure readers gain from reading de la Mare is, perhaps, the avoidance of anything rough or unpleasant, the idealistic tone, the lack of any grit, at times the blandness. Theresa Whistler seems to share these reservations, despite her admiration and affection for the man and his work: 'Sometimes . . . the prose seemed exhausting and blood-thinning, sometimes in verse, the sentiment dated . . .' And yet: 'it stands time and trouble, it carries the tang of authentic experience – however elusive, fantastic, fine-spun and minor-keyed the stuff in which de la Mare may deal'.[11]

Indeed, Whistler's impressive balancing-act shows de la Mare's limitations and strengths, achieving that difficult goal of writing an honest yet fair biography about a person she was fond of. Reading de la Mare's life throws up few surprises; you can read him in the poems – a man with great lyrical talent and a rich imaginative life who was for the most part kind, decent, unadventurous and predictable. Like many other poets, he toiled away for years in a 'day job' he hated before achieving success and devoting himself entirely to his writing.

'Is there anybody there?'

> 'Is there anybody there?' said the Traveller,
> Knocking on the moonlit door;
> And his horse in the silence champed the grasses
> Of the forest's ferny floor:
> And a bird flew up out of the turret,
> Above the Traveller's head:
> And he smote upon the door again a second time;
> 'Is there anybody there?' he said.[12]
>   ('The Listeners')

Why is it so good? Perfect harmony of metre, rhyme and content; clever repetition and alliteration; memorable imagery – 'moonlit door', 'forest's ferny floor', the horse who 'champed the grasses' . . . and the sense of uneasiness – questions to be answered. 'What's up?' asks the reader, hooked from the very first line. It is a strong opening, combining powerful storytelling with lyrical language, all of it working together seamlessly. De la Mare was a master storyteller in verse, including ballads of romance and adventure, such as 'The Englishman' ('I met a sailor in the woods, / A silver ring wore he, / His hair hung black, his eyes shone blue, / And thus he said to me: . .); to little tales of mystery, such as 'Five Eyes' or 'Some one' ('Some one came knocking / At my wee, small door; / Some one came knocking, / I'm sure – sure –sure;'). Then there are stories of creatures, often small ones, and strange or enchanting, but certainly not realistic, folk like John Mouldy, Old Tillie Turveycombe, Miss Cherry, Miss T and Poor Miss 7.

W. H. Auden was an admirer of de la Mare's poetry: 'As a revelation of the wonders of the English Language, de la Mare's poems for children are unrivalled . . . They include . . . his greatest "pure" lyrics . . . and their rhythms are as subtle as they are varied.'[13] But in the statement which follows, I think Auden is wrong: '. . . de la Mare's descriptions of birds, beasts, and natural phenomena are always sharp and accurate, and he never prettifies experience . . .'[14]

It is not hard to find examples of de la Mare's outstanding ability to depict nature, but to say that he never prettifies experience is simply not true. Take the well-known Nicholas Nye,[15] de la Mare's endearing donkey. His observations are appealing and he wins the reader's sympathy with ease, but surely this *is* experience prettified.

> Nicholas Nye was lean and grey,
> Lame of a leg and old,
>   . . .
> Alone with his shadow he'd drowse in the meadow,
> Lazily swinging his tail,
>   . . .

And once in a while: he'd smile . . .
Would Nicholas Nye.

. . .

Bony and ownerless, widowed and worn,
Knobbly-kneed, lonely and grey.

De la Mare is anthropomorphic and sentimental in this poem. Nicholas Nye is 'widowed', 'lonely' and seems to smile. He engages our emotion by making us feel for the donkey as if he were human. However, any unpleasant realism about a typical old donkey (smelly, fly-ridden, moth-eaten are adjectives that come to mind) is avoided. Compare this poem with Ted Hughes's donkey in *What is the Truth?*, admittedly 50 years on, and the differences become glaringly apparent.

And his quite small body, tough and tight and useful,
Like traveller's luggage,
A thing specially made for hard use, with no trimmings,
Nearly ugly. Made to outlast its owner.[16]

In the same way, de la Mare's people are sometimes clichéd and even patronized: there's a 'poor old Widow in her weeds' ('A Widow's Weeds'); 'Tiny and cheerful, / And neat as can be' ('Miss T'); 'Black as a chimney is his face, / And ivory white his teeth' ('Sooeep'); 'Wrinkled with age, and drenched with dew, / Old Ned, the shepherd goes' (Nod). Vivid portraitures, yes, but stereotypes rather than realistic individuals.

'Myself, and me alone'

One of de la Mare's gifts was to write with a tremendous eye for detail. As he said himself:

our deepest, sharpest emotions are concerned, not so much with our knowledge . . . or with generalities, but with the particular, with what is most personal to us, with the self within, its dreams and visions, its half-hidden desires, instincts and passions.[17]

Take the peerless 'Silver', that poem of lyrical description which begins :

Slowly, silently, now the moon
Walks the night in her silver shoon;
This way, and that, she peers, and sees
Silver fruit upon silver trees;[18]

'Silver' shows up another of de la Mare's talents – his almost flawless command of metre and rhyme. Whistler tells us that de la Mare had 'the gift of improvisation to counterbalance the fastidious conscious craftsman in his nature'.[19] He also had a passion for the miniature which he indulged to the full in his novel, *Memoirs of a Midget*, 1921. Whistler suggests that he took 'the same satisfaction in tininess for its own sake that children have . . .'[20] This is demonstrated well in 'The Fly', which has echoes of Isaac Watts:

> How large unto the tiny fly
> Must little things appear! –
> A rosebud like a feather bed,
> Its prickle like a spear.[21]

In 'Seeds', de la Mare makes the reader imagine the seed with 'pygmy / Shoots of green' pushing against an enormous weight to see the light of day.

> At least a cherry-stone
> In size,
> Which that mere sprout
> Has heaved away,
> To bask in sunshine,
> See the Day.[22]

For a gorgeous holiday from everyday life, de la Mare is rarely excelled. 'Tartary'[23] is one of the best:

> If I were Lord of Tartary,
>   Myself, and me alone,
> My bed should be of ivory,
>   Of beaten gold my throne;
> And in my court should peacocks flaunt,
> And in my forests tigers haunt,
> And in my pools great fishes slant
>   Their fins athwart the sun.

There have been some superb pairings of artists and poets in this history, but Walter de la Mare with Edward Ardizzone must be one of the most compatible partnerships of all time. Ardizzone is a subtle illustrator and his drawings are suggestive; they hint at moods and feelings rather than making them explicit, the perfect complement for de la Mare's verse. Ardizzone can also be amusing, is very sympathetic in his treatment of people, especially small ones, and is good at animals, landscapes and interiors. It was an inspired collaboration, as good as Milne and Shepard, Rossetti and Hughes, Carroll and Tenniel, and much later, Causley and Keeping, Rosen and Blake.

Come Hither

De la Mare was extremely knowledgeable about most branches of poetry, as a glance at his anthologies will confirm. As well as providing a wonderful selection of poetry from the distant past and the oral tradition, alongside more typical poetry of the nineteenth and twentieth centuries, *Come Hither* (1923)[24] is a ground-breaking anthology which comes with pages of information, advice and wisdom about multifarious aspects of poetry. Like the *Oxford Book of Children's Verse*, it is more of a compilation of children's poetry and writing about it for older readers, than an anthology for children themselves. De la Mare must have been aware of this, even in the rather different climate of the 1920s, because he suggests that *Come Hither* is for 'the young of all ages'. It contained nearly 500 poems for a start! Whistler says:

> He wanted it to transcend the ordinary anthology, to have real unity, and to be a true introduction to poetry. The result was a completely original kind of book, personal and creative . . . The relation between childhood and poetry that the book posits is at once serious and radiantly spontaneous, and can have an effect for life on those who meet it young.[25]

Auden was one such reader: he loved the 'unofficial poetry' in it. *Come Hither* opens with 'The Story of the Book' and ends with the words: 'I set off at a sharp walk on the journey that has not yet come to an end.'[26] De la Mare's work will always be worth pausing for as young people make their personal journeys into literature.

When We Were Very Young

> *So now I am six I'm as clever as clever,*
> *So I think I'll be six for ever and ever.*[27]

Alan Alexander Milne (1882–1956) was probably the most successful poet ever to write for very young children. He made his living as a journalist, humorist, playwright and regular contributor to *Punch*. Editor of *Granta* while at Cambridge University, Milne's skill for children's verse was just a small part of his extensive writerly output. A contemporary of de la Mare and Eleanor Farjeon, Milne's two collections, *When We Were Very Young* and *Now We Are Six* appeared in 1924 and 1927 respectively to mostly rave reviews and massive sales. He began writing poetry for children in response to a request from Rose Fyleman (author of many fairy books and poems) to contribute to

The Merry-Go-Round, a new children's magazine in 1923. The poem in question was 'The Dormouse and the Doctor', and soon Milne was busy adding others, some of which first appeared in the magazine, *Punch*. Milne was friendly with E. V. Lucas, then Chair of Methuen, who put him in touch with Ernest Shepard; the rest is history. One of the most enduring and fruitful collaborations in children's literature had begun.

Milne often talked to friends about his own happy childhood with a father he adored and a brother, Ken, with whom he shared many adventures. Humphrey Carpenter suggests that Milne's

> highly developed memory for his own childhood can be attributed to his sharing of them, and later the adult recollections of them, with his brother, Ken, and that Milne's most deeply-felt emotion was nostalgia for his own happy childhood.[28]

Christopher Milne confirms this view:

> Some people are good with children. Others are not. It is a gift. You either have it or you don't. My father didn't . . . It was precisely because he was *not* able to play with his small son that his longings sought and found satisfaction in another direction. He wrote about him instead.[29]

Whatever the truth of the origins of Milne's impulse to write for children, what cannot be denied is that his poetry appeals both to the many adults who continue to buy his books as well as the children who receive them.

Of course, Milne had and has his critics. Some commentators have a problem with what now seems a rather precious upper middle-class world of nannies and nurseries. There is sometimes a veneer of sentimentality and, occasionally, adult knowingness in Milne's work which almost spoils the verse. Some contemporary critics were hard on the poetry, too. John Drinkwater in the *Sunday Times* of 1924 was appreciative as well as critical, praising the poems to do with children, but rejecting 'the stuff which seems to have strayed in from any book of bad poetry for children "into an extremely good one"'[30]: 'Twinkletoes', 'Water Lilies' and 'Spring Morning' were apparently some of the 'bad' poems in question. At any rate, the poetry was instantly successful in America as well as Britain where Milne was unlucky to be reviewed by Dorothy Parker. Using expressions like 'sedulous cuteness' she goes for the literary jugular:

> But I too have a very strong feeling about the whimsicality of Milne. I'm feeling it this very minute. It's in my stomach . . . Of Milne's recent verse, I speak in a minority amounting to solitude. I think it is affected, commonplace, bad.[31]

Writing after Milne's death and more than 30 years after the books were published, Geoffrey Grigson was one of his sternest critics. Having taken Milne to task for the class-ridden exclusiveness of his verse, he declares:

> Children, in my experience . . . have found the poems nauseating, and fascinating. In fact, they were poems by a parent for other parents . . . The innocence of *When We Were very Young* . . . chimes with the last tinkle of a romantic innocence which by the Twenties had devolved to whimsy . . . Would it be too ponderous to say as well that they were poems for a class of middle to top people who had lost their intellectual and cultural nerve . . .[32]

and so on. If you read the whole article, Grigson seems to be using Milne as the vehicle for a tirade against class and English society in general during the 1920s. While I sympathize with many of the points Grigson is making about class, I believe he misses what is strong in Milne. Grigson is also wrong in saying that most children dislike the poems, as under-seven-year-olds in infant classes up and down the country will testify.

Milne certainly presents a privileged middle-class world, but then so did many other poets of his time. To put it in perspective, nannies are mentioned fewer than ten times in the two books of verse. Milne is sometimes arch (worse in the prefaces than in the poems) and his effort to speak 'in a child's voice' does sometimes sound affected. But, having said that, the poetry still appeals to huge numbers of children today and it *is* extremely well written. These important facts cannot be ignored in assessing Milne's work.

One of his most loved and loathed poems, depending on your point of view, is 'Vespers'. The image of a little boy kneeling 'at the foot of the bed, / Droops on the little hands little gold head' fits perfectly with an idealized notion of childhood favoured by many. Others find it a despicably sentimental portrait in the 'Beautiful Child' vogue which was popular in the 1920s. Humphrey Carpenter suggests that both responses miss the substance of 'Vespers'.

> But the point of the poem is that Christopher Robin is *not* praying. He occasionally repeats one of the formulas he has been taught: '*God bless Mummy. I know that's right.*' But immediately he is distracted by something of real interest . . . The poem is in fact veiled ridicule of the whole business of formal prayers . . . against which Milne rails in his autobiography . . . Christopher Robin . . . is no angel. Milne does not believe that 'Heaven lies about us in our infancy'; the child in 'Vespers', far from having an unsullied perception of the divine, cannot turn his attention from the mundane to the spiritual.[33]

> *God bless Mummy.* I know that's right.
> Wasn't it fun in the bath to-night?
> The cold's so cold, and the hot's so hot.
> Oh! *God bless Daddy* – I quite forgot.
>
> If I open my fingers a little bit more,
> I can see Nanny's dressing-gown on the door.
> It's a beautiful blue, but it hasn't a hood.
> Oh! *God bless Nanny and make her good.*[34]

Milne was a superb writer of light verse; he was open and honest about his intentions. Speaking of *When We Were Very Young* he said:

> It is not the work of a poet becoming playful, nor of a lover of children expressing his love, nor of a prose-writer knocking together a few jingles for the little ones, it is the work of a light-verse writer taking his job seriously, even though he is taking it into the nursery.[35]

And one of the reasons his poetry has lasted the test of time is because of Milne's sure command of metre and rhyme, a sense of humour and verses that sing. Ann Thwaite quotes Milne's own account of the genesis of the poems in her excellent biography: 'There are three ways in which a writer knows about people: by remembering, by noticing, and by imagining.'[36] Thwaite goes on to point out some of Milne's other qualities that are often ignored by critics.

> The children in the poems are always wanting to break free from the constraints that are constantly being imposed on all children, from whatever social background . . . It is not a bland world. The menaces and uncertainties of real life are there all right, but perfectly adjusted to a small child's understanding . . . the child in the poems is protected by his own egoism, is perfectly in control.[37]

'The King's Breakfast'

To begin to appreciate the poems, let us consider the range of his work. First of all, Milne wrote some delightful nonsense in the two books of verse.

> Once upon a time there were three little foxes
> Who didn't wear stockings, and they didn't wear sockses,
> But they all had handkerchiefs to blow their noses,
> And they kept their handkerchiefs in cardboard boxes.[38]

*   *   *

If I were a bear,
    And a big bear too,
I shouldn't much care
    If it froze or snew;[39]

*　　*　　*

There were Two little Bears who lived in a Wood,
And one of them was Bad and the other was Good.
Good Bear learnt his Twice Times One –
But Bad Bear left all his buttons undone.[40]

Milne also produced some comic masterpieces; he may have learned this craft as a regular contributor to *Punch*. 'Bad Sir Brian Botany' ('Sir Brian had a battleaxe with great big knobs on;/ He went among the villagers and blipped them on the head'), 'Disobedience' and 'The Dormouse and the Doctor' are prime examples.

There was once a Dormouse who lived in a bed
Of delphiniums (blue) and geraniums (red),
And all the day long he'd a wonderful view
Of geraniums (red) and delphiniums (blue).[41]

Perhaps, best of all, is 'The King's Breakfast', an outstanding comic poem whose careful line-breaks and rhythms add to the glorious sense of fun.

The King asked
The Queen, and
The Queen asked
The Dairymaid:
'Could we have some butter for
The Royal slice of bread?'
The Queen asked
The Dairymaid,
The Dairymaid
Said, 'Certainly,
I'll go and tell
The cow
Now
Before she goes to bed.'[42]

'Halfway down the stairs'

Milne also shows empathy for the vulnerability of children, as well as respect for the way they resist adult niceties. There is a sense of wistfulness in some of the poems when the child is alone, but too much should not be made of this, as a lot of the emotion comes from Shepard's sensitive illustrations. Milne only gives us a hint of loneliness; it is Shepard's images which are charged with feeling in poems like 'Come Out With Me' ('If I'm a little darling, why won't they come and see?'), 'Binker' ('But Binker's always Binker, and is certain to be there'), 'Halfway Down' ('Halfway down the stairs / Is a chair / Where I sit') , 'The Wrong House' ('But nobody listened to it, / Nobody/ Liked it, / Nobody wanted it at all') and 'Solitude':

> I have a house where I go,
> Where nobody ever says 'No'
> Where no one says anything – so
> There is no one but me.[43]

At other times the child alone is, like Stevenson's, in a fantasy world of play where the imagination has free rein. Indeed, Milne might have intended direct homage to Stevenson in 'If I Were King', 'The Island', 'Swing Song' and 'Nursery Chairs'. He also had a deft feel for the nursery jingle, that little child-centred scrap of rhythmic chanting, such as 'Busy', 'Shoes and Stockings', 'Corner of the Street' , or these two:

> John had
> Great Big
> Waterproof
> Boots on;[44]
> (from 'Happiness')

> Christopher Robin goes,
> Hoppity, hoppity,
> Hoppity, hoppity, hop.
>   (from 'Hoppity')

In a few poems, he almost seems to anticipate the introspective realism that characterizes poetry being written for children in the late twentieth century: there is 'Growing Up', 'Journey's End', 'A Thought' and 'In the Dark':

> I think to myself,
> I play to myself,
> And nobody knows what I say to myself;
> Here I am in the dark alone,
> What is it going to be?[45]

In still others that hardly get noticed by most readers, there are affectionate dealings with animals (beetles, mice, puppies, cats, cows, rabbits . . .) and references to nature. See, for example, 'Wind on the Hill', 'Summer Afternoon', 'The Mirror; or Daffodowndilly': 'She wore her yellow sun-bonnet, / She wore her greenest gown.'

'Have you been a good girl, Jane?'

Milne is also very good at catching exchanges between adults and children:

> 'Have you been a good girl, Jane?'
> I never did, I never did, I never did like 'Now take care, dear!'
> 'Has anybody seen my mouse?'
> 'What is the matter with Mary Jane?'
> 'You must never go down to the end of the town,
> if you don't go down with me.'

These small bullies are hard to dislike, particularly James James / Morrison Morrison and those winsome yet determined little girls – Anne, Elizabeth Ann, Mary Jane and Emmeline.

Milne's books still sell in large numbers. No doubt, adult nostalgia as well as good marketing by Methuen has contributed to the success of these texts, but Milne has successfully stood the test of time because the poetry is so successful with its primary audience. No one has created a more secure, amusing and comforting world for the very young in better verse than Milne. And, as Thwaite confirms, 'They work both for children and for adults who can see through the class trappings to what is actually there.'[46] As for Ernest Shepard's drawings, it almost seems an affront to consider anyone else illustrating these poems.

Something I Remember

Eleanor Farjeon (1881–1965) was contemporary with de la Mare whom she knew and admired; de la Mare, in turn, selected a good number of her poems for his anthologies. Like de la Mare, Farjeon was someone who retained childlike qualities into adulthood. A plain, shy, awkward girl in company, she preferred life at home with her three brothers and her books to the social world outside. Coming from a privileged and idiosyncratic background, Farjeon received no formal schooling, but was educated at home. Her parents encouraged her to write and this she most cetainly did, becoming a prolific author and making a lifetime's living from her pen.

Anne Harvey describes her as 'singing songs before she could write . . . and as soon as she could guide a pencil she began to write them down. Words were always a delight to her . . .'[47] As an adult, Farjeon always took a special pleasure in being with children, as her niece, Annabel Farjeon, recounts in the preface to *Invitation to a Mouse*, 1981.

'My aunt Eleanor's child friends were multitudinous. I well remember from the age of five the excited alarm of those crowded and noisy parties.' She goes on to recount feasts with wobbling jellies and iced, animal biscuits, energetic games, music, dancing, tug-of-war, and candle-lit Christmas trees groaning with presents. 'Eleanor was far fuller of the milk of human kindness than anyone I have ever met.'[48] And it showed in the poetry.

Farjeon's first collection, *Nursery Rhymes of London Town*, appeared in 1916 and she kept on publishing until well into old age. She was a good storyteller with a sweet, lyrical voice and a child-centred vision of the world. Some of her books are written with her brother, Herbert, such as *Kings and Queens*. She was a religious writer, too, and her hymns for children are mentioned in Chapter 1. *The Children's Bells*, 1957, contains Farjeon's personal selection gleaned from her many books of verse. Anne Harvey chose her own favourites in *Something I Remember*, 1987.

The range of Farjeon's work is rarely recognized in critical texts and she is usually described as lightweight in a literary sense. Humphrey Carpenter, for example, says of Farjeon's verse: 'Her poetry is slight, but always technically deft.'[49] Another way of looking at it is that lightness of touch is part of Farjeon's appeal. Sometimes she goes further: in its simple and melodic profundity, the ending of 'The Night Will Never Stay' could almost be Rossetti.

> Though you bind it with the blowing wind
> And buckle it with the moon,
> The night will slip away
> Like sorrow or a tune.[50]

Lively narratives include 'Mrs Malone' and 'City-Under-Water', where you can almost hear Maureen's lilting Irish accent.

> Next day I told my Mother, and I told my Maureen too,
> I'd seen City-Under-Water. Mother said it wasn't true.
> I'd had a dream. But *Maureen* said, sure, did I think because
> I'd dreamed about a thing it wasn't true? Indeed it was.[51]

Like many other children's poets Farjeon wrote about cats particularly well. She loved them in real life, too; Harvey describes all the local strays gravitating towards Farjeon's home! In her poems we meet among others a golden cat and a kitten, but the one children inevitably go for is 'Cat!' where the reader chases after the cat at a brisk old pace.

Cat!
Scat!
Atter her, atter her,
Sleeky flatterer,
Spitfire chatterer,
Scatter her, scatter her
Off her mat!
Wuff!
Wuff!
Treat her rough!
Git her, git her,
Whiskery spitter!
Catch her, catch her,
Green-eyed scratcher![52]

. . . and so on.

One of Farjeon's finest poems, 'It Was Long Ago', sounds that note of regret so many poets express, when something infinitely precious about chidhood is left behind.

And that is almost all I can remember,
The house, the mountain, the grey cat on her knee,
Her red shawl, and the tree,

And the taste of berries, the feel of the sun I remember,
And the smell of everything that used to be
So long ago,

Till the heat on the road outside again I remember,
And how the long dusty road seemed to have for me
No end, you know.

That is the farthest thing I can remember.
It won't mean much to you. It does to me.
Then I grew up, you see.[53]

As an old woman, Farjeon confided to her niece that:

In my youth I dreamed of being a 'real' poet, but halfway through my life that dream died, and whatever figments of it remained went into writing songs and verses for children.[54]

Many of us will be glad she did. It is disappointing to learn that, as I write, there is no Farjeon poetry in print, though she is still widely anthologized today. It is reassuring to know that the major annual British award for services to children's literature bears Eleanor Farjeon's name.

'The sea is a hungry dog'

James Reeves (1909–1978) was a well-known writer, critic and broadcaster whose work was divided between youthful and adult audiences, and for fiction as well as poetry. Reeves's *Complete Poems for Children*, 1973, is not quite complete, but the collection pulls together most of his verse for the young, including 'The Wandering Moon', 1950, and 'The Blackbird in the Lilac', 1952. Reeves also wrote three well-informed books about children and poetry for teachers and others. Blessed with Edward Ardizzone as his illustrator, he was very popular in children's poetry until the middle of this century. Although lines like 'The sea is a hungry dog' and 'Slowly the tide creeps up the sand' may still be familiar to children today, Reeves has not been so much in favour of late. He shares many of the same qualities as de la Mare and Farjeon; like them his poetry may be on the tame side for the more robust taste of children in the late 1990s. His verse is full of delicate observations, the storyteller's taste for the strange and romantic and an almost childlike yearning at the wonder of the world. An extract from 'Little Fan' shows how adept he was at creating a mysterious narrative:

> I don't like the looks of little Fan, mother,
> You'd best go and close the door.
> Watch now, or she'll be gone for ever
> To the rocks by the brown sandy shore.[55]

'The Sea' includes one of the most telling extended metaphors in the business:

> The sea is a hungry dog,
> Giant and grey.
> He rolls on the beach all day.
> With his clashing teeth and shaggy jaws
> Hour upon hour he gnaws
> The rumbling, tumbling stones,
> And 'Bones, bones, bones!'
> The giant sea-dog moans,
> Licking his greasy paws.[56]

Reeves was also the author of some splendid nonsense, entitled, *Prefabulous Animiles*, 1957: 'Along the valley of the Ump / Gallops the fearful Hippocrump. / His hide is leathery and thick; / His eyelids open with a Click! / His mouth he closes with a Clack! / He has three humps upon his back'[57] memorably brought to life by Ardizzone's extraordinary imagination.

Currently unfashionable and mostly out of print are poets of the same generation as Reeves, publishing for children between the 1950s and the early 1970s. Unfortunately, space does not permit a full appreciation of these poets, so I offer readers a little taste in the hope that they will go back for more.

Ian Serraillier, for example, comes to mind, though he is better known for adaptations of Greek myths and outstanding children's novels such as *The Silver Sword*. His poetry usually features a conversational style and sensitively touches corners of a child's world, as in the rescue of a beloved pet in the first extract and the discovery of a field-mouse in the second.

> So tired and wet
> And still it lies.
> I stroke its head,
> It opens its eyes,
> It wags its tail,
> So tired and wet.
> I call its name,
> For it's my pet,
> Not his or hers
> Or yours, but mine –
> And up it gets,
> And up it gets!
> (from 'The Rescue')[58]

> We found a mouse in the chalk quarry today
> In a circle of stones and empty oil drums
> By the fag ends of a fire. There had been
> A picnic there; he must have been after the crumbs.
> (from 'Anne and the Field Mouse')[59]

E. V. Rieu was one of the select four to feature in *A Puffin Quartet of Poets* which was in most primary classrooms until the late 1960s. I can still quote Rieu's 'Sir Smashem Uppe' from memory more than 40 years after learning it at school! It was just so satisfying when the accident-prone hero broke up all the furniture and the best china, too.

> Good afternoon, Sir Smashem Uppe!
> We're having tea: do take a cup!
> Sugar and milk ? Now let me see –
> Two lumps I think: Good Gracious me!
> The silly thing slipped off your knee.
> Pray don't apologise, old chap:
> A very trivial mishap!
> So clumsy of you? How absurd
> My dear Sir Smashem, not a word![60]

Rieu's verse may seem a little dated in the late twentieth century; so does the poetry of John Walsh, but it is a kinder, more reassuring world that he presents in 'The Truants'. Walsh's poetry was popular in schools during the 1960s and 1970s. So was the work of Phoebe Hesketh who also wrote a poem about a truant, where she likens real learning to education through nature, as the Romantics did before her.

> They call him dunce, and yet he can discern
> Each mouse-brown bird,
> And call its name and whistle back its call,
> And spy among the fern
> Delicate movement of a furred
> Fugitive creature hiding from the day.
> Discovered secrets magnify his play
> Into a vocation.
> . . .
>
> Back in the classroom he can never find
> Answers to the dusty questions, yet could teach,
> Deeper than knowledge,
> Geometry of twigs
> Scratched on a sunlit wall;
> History in stones,
> Seasons told by the fields' calendar –
> Living languages of Spring and Fall.[61]

'Warning to Children'

Robert Graves is highly regarded for his adult verse and fiction; *I, Claudius* and *Goodbye to All That* may be the best known of the latter. His considerable body of poetry has recently been reissued by Carcanet in a new edition of several volumes, a tribute afforded to a minority of poets. Graves also wrote several books of poetry for younger readers and his adult work is sometimes scavenged for them. The enigmatic 'Warning to Children', which begins like this, is a great favourite in anthologies.

> Children, if you dare to think
> Of the greatness, rareness, muchness,
> Fewness, of this precious only
> Endless world in which you say
> You live . . . [62]

Graves is also the author of popular ditties such as 'I have a little cough, sir'; a great admirer of traditional nursery rhymes, he wrote some good examples himself. 'The Mirror' is typical:

> Mirror mirror tell me
> Am I pretty or plain?
> Or am I downright ugly,
> And ugly to remain?
>
> Shall I marry a gentleman?
> Shall I marry a clown?
> Or shall I marry
> Old Knives and Scissors
> Shouting through the town?[63]

'You got to take me like I am'

There are other poets whose writing, while primarily directed at adults, features regularly in the children's canon. In Britain the work of Edmund Blunden, W. H. Davies (b. 1871), Elizabeth Jennings, Dylan Thomas, D. H. Lawrence, R. S. Thomas and others fall into this category and some of their more accessible poems are quite well known to young readers who encounter them in anthologies. The same is true in the period under discussion for the following American poets, including those living a generation or two earlier: Elizabeth Coatsworth (b. 1893), E. E. Cummings (b. 1894), Rachel Field (b. 1894), Randall Jarrell, Vachel Lindsay (b. 1879), Myra Cohn Livingstone, Edna St Vincent Millay (b. 1892), Theodore Roethke, Elizabeth Madox Roberts (b. 1881), William Jay Smith, May Swenson, John Updike, William Carlos Williams and others. I would like to have paid proper tribute to some of these poets, but space does not permit.

Robert Frost and Carl Sandburg made selections of their poems for children, entitled *You Come Too*, 1959, and *Wind Song*, 1960, respectively. Emily Dickinson and Langston Hughes have had their work mediated for children by editors – *A Letter to the World*, 1968 and *Don't You Turn Back*, 1969, respectively. While most readers will be familiar with the distinctive and distinguished poems of Frost and Dickinson, the public and private faces of American poetry, Carl Sandburg and Langston Hughes may be less well known. Both poets were radical, loathing injustice and speaking up for the 'have-nots'. Sandburg tells his reader she must choose the 'single clenched fist lifted and ready' or 'the open hand held out and waiting . . . For we meet by one or the other'.[64] Affectionately known as the Poet Laureate of Harlem, Langston Hughes gave a voice to black American experience. Often tender and lyrical, sometimes wry and ironic, Hughes writes of love, song, dance, the blues, racism, indeed of life in all its pain and its joy. As he wrote mainly short poems in a musical, everyday language, much of his work is appropriate for children.

> My old mule,
> He's got a grin on his face.
> He's been a mule for so long
> He's forgot about his race.
>
> I'm like that old mule –
> Black – and don't give a damn!
> You got to take me
> Like I am.[65]

Another popular American poet, David McCord (1897–1996), was born before Langston Hughes, but was still publishing until quite recently. His many collections include *One at a Time* and *Far and Few*, both published in 1952. Superficially light and low key, Neil Philip rates his poetry as highly as the work of James Reeves. Writing about 'Father and I in the Woods', Philip admires: 'The perfect harmony of form, style and subject. The elegant restraint of the language and the delicate stepping quality of the rhythm, are inseparable from the meaning of the words.'[66]

> 'Words,'
> My father used to say,
> 'Scare birds.'
>
> So be:
> It's sky and brook and bird
> And tree.[67]

'The pain will go, in time'

Russell Hoban is a distinguished American novelist who has lived in Britain for many years and has at least one classic story for children to his credit, *The Mouse and his Child*. He is also the author of some of the best picture books ever written about an endearing but wilful little badger called Frances. Don't imagine anything too cosy; Hoban is a challenging writer and in books for young children he is never bland. Apart from some songs from the Frances books, there is *The Pedalling Man*, 1968, and *The Last of Wallendas and Other Poems*. Often amusing, it is full of surprises and the poems demand a thoughtful response of the reader. An extract from 'Small, Smaller' is typical:

> I thought that I knew all there was to know
> Of being small, until I saw once, black against the snow,
> A shrew, trapped in my footprint, jump and fall
> And jump again and fall, the hole too deep, the walls too tall.[68]

Although Vernon Scannell is contemporary with Robert Graves and Edmund Blunden, unlike them he turned his attention to writing for children when he was much older. Three delightful poetry books for children were published by Scannell between 1988 and 1992, all of which are undeservedly out of print as I write. Scannell combines strong narrative ability, a nice sense of fun and an accomplished mastery of poetic technique. In 'Growing Pain', for example, the little five-year-old boy does not understand the source of his suffering:

> 'A girl at school called Jessica,
> She hurts –' he touched himself between
> The heart and the stomach – 'she has been
> Aching here and I can see her.'
> Nothing I had read or heard
> Instructed me in what to do.
> I covered him and stroked his head.
> 'The pain will go, in time,' I said.[69]

Scannell is most famous for earlier poems like 'The Apple-Raid', the searing honesty of 'A Case of Murder' and 'Hide and Seek' which ends on an almost existential note: 'The darkening garden watches. Nothing stirs. / The bushes hold their breath; the sun is gone. / Yes, here you are. But where are they who sought you?' The concluding sentiments of 'Poem on Bread' are typical Scannell straight-talking.

If you can't read, then eat: it tastes quite good.
If you do neither, all that I can say
Is he who needs no poetry or bread
Is really in a devilish bad way.[70]

'The ghost of a man'

Leonard Clark published the last of his many books for children, *The Corn Growing*, as late as 1981, the year he died. For all its qualities, particularly the poems rooted in Clark's beloved countryside, it feels like a book which was out of its time. A wise anthologist in his day, his own poems rarely find a place in current books of verse. Clark was one of that admirable breed of School Inspectors who loved literature and promoted it widely all his life. He had a hand in the Writers in Schools scheme which has done so much good work for children's poetry in the last 30 years. Clark was friendly with and influenced by de la Mare.

The poets featured in this chapter mostly write about a world that has gone. Poetry for children has moved out of the nursery into busy streets, populated by voices from many different cultures. The security that came with much of the poetry of the past has been replaced by greater diversity relating to a wider world-view. If we have lost some certainties, there is now a much greater willingness on the part of poets to take risks and make waves. Childhood as it is constructed in poetry has undergone a revolution; the concluding chapter of this book will address these changes. Before that we need to look at two outstanding poets of the second half of the twentieth century – Charles Causley and Ted Hughes.

Notes

1   Eleanor Farjeon, from 'It was long ago', *Something I Remember, Selected Poems for Children* by Eleanor Farjeon, ed. Anne Harvey, Penguin, London, 1987.
2   Samuel Taylor Coleridge, *Biographia Literaria*, 1817, p. 11.
3   *John Keats, Letters,* ed. Robert Gittings, Oxford, 1970, p. 36–7.
4   Theresa Whistler, *Imagination of the Heart; the life of Walter de la Mare*, Duckworth, London, 1993, pp. 62, 69, 200.
5   *Ibid.*, pp. 10–11.
6   Edward Thomas, *The Green Roads: Poems for Young Readers,* 'Introduction', Eleanor Farjeon, p. 154.
7   Whistler, *op. cit.*, p. 294.
8   *Ibid.*, p. 163.
9   John Bayley, 'The Child in Walter de la Mare', *Children and their Books*, ed. G. Avery and J. Briggs, Oxford, 1989, p. 340.
10   Walter de la Mare, *Early One Morning*, Faber, London, 1935.
11   Whistler, *op. cit.*, p. x.

12   Walter de la Mare, from 'The Listeners', *The Listeners and Other Poems*, 1912, this edition, Walter de la Mare, *Collected Rhymes and Verses*, Faber, London, 1970.

13   W. H. Auden, ed., *A Choice of de la Mare's Verse*, Faber, 1963, p. 19.

14   *Ibid.*

15   Walter de la Mare, from 'Nicholas Nye', *op. cit.*, 1970.

16   Ted Hughes, *What is the Truth?*, Faber, London, 1984, pp. 56.

17   Walter de la Mare, ed. *Christina Rossetti, Poems*, Gregynog Press, Newtown, Montgomeryshire, 1930, p. ix.

18   Walter de la Mare, from 'Silver', 1913, *op. cit.*, 1970.

19   Whistler, *op. cit.*, p. 75.

20   Whistler, *op. cit.*, p. 303.

21   Walter de la Mare, from 'The Fly', *op. cit.*, 1970.

22   Walter de la Mare, from 'Seeds', *ibid.*

23   Walter de la Mare, from 'Tartary', *ibid.*

24   Walter de la Mare, *Come Hither*, Constable & Co., London, 1923.

25   Whistler, *op. cit.*

26   De la Mare, 1923, *op. cit.*, p. xxxi.

27   A. A. Milne, *Now We Are Six*, Methuen, London, 1927.

28   Humphrey Carpenter, *Secret Gardens, 'The Golden Age of Children's Literature*, George Allen & Unwin, London 1985.

29   Christopher Milne, quoted in Carpenter, *ibid.*, p 201.

30   Ann Thwaite, *A. A. Milne, His Life*, Faber, London, 1990, quoting John Drinkwater, p. 264.

31   Dorothy Parker quoted in Thwaite, *ibid.*, p.332.

32   Geoffrey Grigson, *The Contrary View*, 1974, quoted *ibid.*

33   Humphrey Carpenter, *op. cit.*, pp. 196-7.

34   A. A. Milne, from 'Vespers', *When We Were Very Young*, Methuen, London, 1924.

35   Thwaite, *op. cit.*, p 248.

36   Thwaite, *ibid.*, p. 249.

37   Thwaite *ibid.*, p. 267.

38   Milne, from 'The Three Foxes', 1924, *op. cit.*

39   Milne, from 'Furry Bear', 1927, *op. cit.*

40   Milne, from 'Twice Times', *ibid.*

41   Milne, from 'The Dormouse and the Doctor', 1924, *op. cit.*

42   Milne, from 'The King's Breakfast', *ibid.*

43   Milne, 'Solitude', 1927, *op. cit.*

44   Milne, from 'Happiness', 'Hoppity', 1924, *op. cit.*

45   Milne, from 'In the Dark', 1927, *op. cit.*

46   Thwaite, *op. cit.*, p. 267.

47   Anne Harvey, *Something I Remember: Selected Poems for Children* by Eleanor Farjeon, Puffin,London, 1989.

48   Annabel Farjeon, ed. *Invitation to a Mouse*, Hodder & Stoughton, London, 1981.

49   Humphrey Carpenter and Mari Pritchard, *The Oxford Companion to Children's Literature*, 1984, p. 183.

50   Eleanor Farjeon, from 'The Night will Never Stay', Harvey, 1987, *op. cit.*

51   Farjeon, from 'City-Under-Water', *op. cit.*, 1986.

52   Farjeon, from 'Cat!', *ibid.*

53   Farjeon, 'It Was Long Ago', Harvey, 1987, *op. cit.*

54   Farjeon, quoted 1986, *op. cit.*

55   James Reeves, from 'Little Fan', *James Reeves Complete Poems for Children*, Heinemann, London, 1973.
56   James Reeves, from 'The Sea', *ibid.*
57   James Reeves, *ibid.*
58   Ian Serraillier, from 'The Rescue', *I'll Tell You a Tale,* Puffin Books, London, 1973.
59   Ian Serraillier, from 'Anne and the Field-Mouse', *Happily Ever After,* Oxford University Press, 1963.
60   E. V. Rieu, *Cuckoo Calling: a book of verse for younger people,* London, 1933.
61   Phoebe Hesketh, 'Truant', quoted in *A Puffin Sextet of Poets,* ed. Anne Harvey, Penguin, London, 1989.
62   *Robert Graves, Collected Poems*, Oxford, 1975.
63   *Ibid.*
64   Carl Sandburg, see *Complete Poems: Carl Sandburg,* New York, 1950.
65   *Langston Hughes, Selected Poems*, Alfred A. Knopf Inc., New York, 1959.
66   Neil Philip, ed. *The New Oxford Book of Children's Verse*, Oxford, 1996, p. xxxi.
67   David McCord, 'Father and I in the Woods', quoted in *ibid.*
68   Russell Hoban, 'Small, Smaller', *ibid.*
69   Vernon Scannell, *Love Shouts and Whispers*, Hutchinson, London, 1990.
70   Vernon Scannell, *New and Collected Poems*, Robson Books, London, 1980.

CHAPTER 12

'What is the Truth?'

The poetry of
Charles Causley and Ted Hughes

Who is that child I see wandering, wandering
Down by the side of the quivering stream?
Why does he seem not to hear, though I call to him?
Where does he come from, and what is his name?[1]

Two of the most significant poets for the young in the second half of the twentieth century are Charles Causley and Ted Hughes. As poets they are quite different from one another, though both are equally esteemed with many honours to their credit; both have reached retirement age and both are writing as well as ever. I have given these two poets a chapter to themselves not only because they are extremely good at what they do, but also because their work does not lie within any conventional sub-genres of children's poetry. Each has a unique voice and style which is quite simply, out on its own. In the case of Causley, we see many continuities with the past, particularly in his use of traditional rhyme and metre, themes and settings, ballads and songs. But what Causley does with these familiar ingredients is entirely original. Hughes usually favours a free verse which is powerful, vigorous and striking. It is difficult not to be stirred by Hughes's poetry (even those who do not like his work, invariably react strongly to it), whereas Causley more often beguiles with his musical touch. However, the challenge they offer young readers and the respect they show for their audience is entirely shared.

Early in the Morning – the poetry of Charles Causley

Clive Wilmer writes of Charles Causley:

> He is a *maker* of songs in the grand Old English sense of the word: a craftsman who sees his job as the production of well-wrought artifacts . . . most of his poems, even if not actually meant to be sung, are in song form: they are ballads, chants, carols, riddles, shanties and nursery rhymes.[2]

The quotation comes from *Poets Talking*, a book of interviews with poets, most of whom do not write for children. Causley makes no such distinction: 'I don't concern myself about the audience at all. It's no good thinking about the reader over your shoulder . . .'[3] As he spent most of his working life as a primary teacher after a spell in the Navy, Causley clearly understands children well and their taste in poetry.

> I never went to school with a heavy heart. I used to set off feeling like a nineteenth-century explorer with a butterfly net . . . as if I was going into undiscovered territory . . . if you get kids on your side they'll die for you . . . they're heroic . . . I love the way they go flat out at things . . . they're economically unsound, physically small . . . and they're often badly treated by adults who fail to understand them . . .[4]

Perhaps one of the reasons why Causley's poetry is so good is that he combines sound knowledge of children with exceptional musical and literary talent. This modest, down-to-earth man with a passion for learning and a nice sense of irony is one of the finest poets for children of all time.

Figgie Hobbin is the first of a number of outstanding collections by Causley, much of whose writing is located in his home town of Launceston and the surrounding countryside. Not markedly different from the poetry that had gone before in form, prosody or theme, it has a strength and honesty that was new, plus sharp technical skill and a musician's ear exercised in ballads that are unequalled in children's poetry. He is a difficult poet to pin down, as his work has so many subtle hallmarks. There is the ring of the storyteller, the instinct for melodious language, often a hint of something sinister that is left unexplained. His work is rooted in folklore, often from his native Cornwall, steeped in the oral tradition and the ancient magic of words.

Pick up *Figgie Hobbin*, 1970, and you are lured inside by predominantly amusing narratives in the first half of the book, featuring extraordinary characters like Riley, Mr Pennycomequick, Colonel Fazackerley, Sal Scratch, Reverend Sabine Baring-Gould and King Foo Foo. Wonderful as they are, and probably the poems children like best alongside playful romps such as 'As I Went Down Zig Zag', Causley can crank into a higher gear, as he shows later in the book. 'I Saw a Jolly Hunter', for example, is both funny and challenging. It begins on a familiar comic note, but there is steel in the final verse.

> I saw a jolly hunter
>   With a jolly gun
> Walking in the country
>   In the jolly sun.
>
>   . . .

Bang went the jolly gun.
   Hunter jolly dead.
Jolly hare got clean away.
   Jolly good, I said.[5]

'Timothy Winters' is both a compassionate and angry poem of everyday child abuse:

The Welfare Worker lies awake
But the law's as tricky as a ten-foot snake,
So Timothy Winters drinks his cup
And slowly goes on growing up.

At Morning Prayers the Master helves
For children less fortunate than ourselves,
And the loudest response in the school is when
Timothy Winters roars 'Amen!'[6]

An animal is treated as an object of ridicule and made to perform unnatural acts in 'My Mother Saw a Dancing Bear'. Without striking a didactic note, Causley shows the reader that mindless cruelty is involved in taking an animal out of its natural habitat, let alone exploitation by human beings who should know better.

They paid a penny for the dance,
But what they saw was not the show;
Only, in bruin's aching eyes,
Far-distant forests, and the snow.[7]

'Tell Me, Tell Me, Sarah Jane'

Figgie Hobbin also includes some memorable ballads, most of which are either connected to the history or folklore of Cornwall or tell tales of the sea, like 'Tell me, Tell Me Sarah Jane'.

Mother, I hear the water
Beneath the headland pinned,
And I can see the sea-gull
Sliding down the wind.
   I taste the salt upon my tongue
   As sweet as sweet can be.

Tell me, my dear, whose voice you hear?

It is the sea, the sea.[8]

Later collections also feature some glorious ballads, such as 'On St Catherine's Day' in *Jack The Treacle Eater*, 1987, reminiscent of Blake's 'Holy Thursday' in attitude and theme. Here is the beginning and the end.

> We are the Workhouse children,
> Maids dressed in white,
> Our gowns are trimmed with ribbon,
> With flowers our hair is bright.
>
> . . .
>
> Though the Workhouse wall is broken,
> With truest eye and clear
> Watch for the Workhouse children,
> For we are always here.[9]

'His iron hand in mine'

Jack the Treacle Eater won the Kurt Maschler Award in 1988. 'Tavistock Goose Fair' is the saddest poem in it, one of Causley's many unobtrusive visits to his own childhood. It begins matter of factly:

> The day my father took me to the Fair
> Was just before he died of the First War.

He goes on to recreate the fun of that day out with his father by using period detail (the roundabout playing 'Valencia', farthings painted as gold guineas, geese with their heads sticking out of wicker pens . . .) then comes the final verse with its understated emotion:

> Today, I hardly remember my father's face;
> Only the shine of his boot-and-legging leather
> The day we walked the yellow October weather;
> Only the way he strode at a soldier's pace,
> The way he stood like a soldier of the line;
> Only the feel of his iron hand in mine.[10]

All the other stanzas are four lines long with an a,b,a,b rhyme-scheme. Part of the impact of the final stanza comes from the extra two lines, the rhyme-scheme changing to a,b,b, a, c,c, the alternate openings of each line – 'Today,' 'The day', 'The way' – and the repetition of 'Only the' three times over. The implicit recognition of the enormity of the loss of his father is what charges the poem with feeling much more effectively than any direct reference to it would do. As for sentimentality, Causley does not know the meaning of the word.

'Here is a childhood book'

No one tells a better tale in verse than Causley. *Early in the Morning*, 1986, is for a slightly younger age group: the cover of the hardback original had birds singing on a telegraph wire, the perfect pictorial image for what are essentially songs. *The Young Man of Cury*, 1991, includes some humorous ditties like this one about a bride who can't be bothered getting up for her wedding.

> Rise up, Jenny.
> Hear the ringing tower.
> Take your veil, your white gown
> And the orange flower.
> 'Not today,' said Jenny.[11]

But Causley is not always so benign and he has always liked asking questions in his poems. 'Why?' relates to Guy Fawkes and makes us shudder at the macabre annual ritual. Causley does not supply any neat answer and the last line is just plain chilling. Discussing how he achieves the aura of mystery in some of his poems, Causley mentions 'the thin dividing line between ecstasy and terror . . . The great problem is to achieve these resonances and hints and suggestions and reverberations, and it's an endlessly difficult and endlessly fascinating task to get the thing to work somehow or other.'[12]

> Why do you take my hand, Susanna,
> As the pointing flames jump high?
> It's only a bundle of sacking and straw.
> Nobody's going to die.[13]

Causley is probably unique in a triple publishing coup: *Figgie Hobbin* was reissued with a few extra poems 20 years after its original publication in 1990; Causley's *Selected Poems*, 1994, *Going to the Fair*, and *Collected Poems*, 1996, are *both* for children. I don't think any other living poet has a volume of selected poems for children to his credit, let alone a 'Collected' as well. Causley aptly deserves that distinction for a number of reasons. The first is that he has served his time as a poet for children for more than 25 years. Secondly, as Causley does not separate his poetry into rigidly adult and juvenile genres, it is fitting that the honour of Selected and Collected Poems, normally reserved for adult poetry, should be bestowed on him. Finally, it is a tribute to the versatility of Causley's work. He is a genuinely popular poet, who can 'sing both high and low'.[14] The *Collected Poems* offers a fresh reading from Causley's organization of material: interestingly, 'Who?' is the final poem in the book.

> Who is that child I see wandering, wandering
> Down by the side of the quivering stream?
> Why does he seem not to hear, though I call to him?
> Where does he come from, and what is his name?[15]

Causley has another claim to distinction in the world of children's books as a gifted anthologist. Not for him the predictable assortment of familiar names; Causley searches long and deep in original sources and brings up pearls. The Puffin Books of *Salt Sea* and *Magic Verse* are exemplary selections of poetry from many times and places. As he puts it: 'All poetry is magic. It is a spell against insensitivity, failure of imagination, ignorance and barbarism.'[16] Another Charles illustrated some of these anthologies and *Jack the Treacle Eater*, namely Charles Keeping, who serves the poetry well with his evocative swirling pencil style of artwork, always profound, always original, and by turn dazzling, morbid, earthy, tortured, tender, rumbustious, capturing the changing mood of the poetry.

Michael Foreman was the charming illustrator of *Early in the Morning* and *The Young Man of Cury*. In the latter, there are delicate blue washes with just a touch of yellow and purple, familiar hallmarks of Foreman's work, combined with skilful pencil drawings and luminously colourful spreads. *Figgie Hobbin* was reissued with lavish illustrations by Gerald Rose who is equally at home depicting the granite figure of Mary, Mary Magdalene on Launceston Church, knights in armour, evocative landscapes and seascapes, or wild and wonderful people and animals engaged in crazy antics. His illustration for the final poem perfectly matches the note of regret and reverie in Causley's recurrent theme, the loss of childhood.

> Why do I see him at sunrise and sunset
> Taking, in old-fashioned clothes, the same track?
> Why, when he walks, does he cast not a shadow
> Though the sun rises and falls at his back?[17]

The *Collected Poems* would have been a challenge to any artist; John Lawrence took up the baton, travelling to Cornwall to meet Causley before starting work. The collaboration worked superbly – exquisite black and white drawings of animals doing impossible things that make you laugh; pretty little vignettes dotted around the poems; references to Launceston and its history; some poems receiving only a delicate scratch or two from the artist's pen. Lawrence works unobtrusively fitting his drawings into the spaces betweeen the poems, seamlessly tapping into Causley's blend of real memory, storytelling, lyric and lore. In providing him with four outstanding artists, Causley has been well served by his publishers. It is more than repaid in Causley's ability to challenge as well as delight young readers ensuring him a special niche in the annals of children's poetry.

What is the Truth? – the poetry of Ted Hughes

Ted Hughes is *the* nature poet of the twentieth century for adults and children alike. He turns his back on the Romantic tradition and strikes out on his own by making his readers face realities about the animal word – cruelty, harshness, sex and death, as well as beauty and instinct and awe. Hughes does not compromise for the young: he gives them the real thing, nothing held back, but delivered with what he calls 'affection'.

> Writing for children one has a very definite context of communication. Adult readers are looking for support for their defences on the whole . . . One can communicate with children in a simple and whole way – not because they're innocent, but because they're not yet defensive. Providing one moves with affection . . .[18]

Hughes's poetry titles include *Under the North Star*, 1981, and *Moon-Whales*, 1988; he is also the author of several books of fiction such as the outstanding, *The Iron Man. Poetry in the Making*, 1967, recently reissued, is an excellent book about reading and writing poetry, and was based on some innovative schools radio programmes featuring his work, produced in the 1960s. This classic text is addressed to children, but avidly read by teachers who want to learn more about using poetry in the classroom. Hughes has been Poet Laureate since 1984 and is widely regarded as a distinguished poet, critic and anthologist for adults as well as children.

The finest of his titles for children, *What is the Truth?*[19] 1984, is an extraordinary display of poetic virtuosity. In 1995 Faber reissued Hughes's nature poetry in four attractive volumes: as well as *Truth*, there is *The Thought-Fox*, *A March Calf* and *The Iron Wolf*. The two former are excellent for teenage readers, but *The Iron Wolf* is also suitable for children of primary age. Hughes is at his gentlest in this book, though the animals are brought stunningly alive in a mystical as well as realistic landscape. The language of Snow-shoe Hare, for example, is straightforward, but the image of the hare he presents is arresting and unusual.

> In his popping eyes
> The whole crowded heaven struggles softly.
>
> Glassy mountains, breathless, brittle forests
> Are frosty aerials
> Balanced in his ears.
>
> And his nose bobs wilder
> And his heart thuds harder
>
> Tethered there, so hotly
> To his crouching shadow.[20]

Hughes can be amusing and endearing, too. 'Cat' is an affectionate portrait of the comfort that comes from stroking a purring cat after a hard day in town. Even here, Hughes does not let the reader forget that a cat's roots are wild, as the first and last two verses show.

> You need your Cat.
> When you slump down
> All tired and flat
> With too much town
>
> . . .
>
> For into your hands
> Will flow the powers
> Of the beasts who ignore
> These ways of ours
>
> And you'll be refreshed
> Through the Cat on your lap
> With a Leopard's yawn
> And a Tiger's nap.[21]

'Thrush' starts conventionally enough, then Hughes employs a stunning metaphor lifting the poem out of the realms of the everyday.

> The speckled Thrush
> With a cheerful shout
> Dips his beak in the dark
> And lifts the sun out.

At the end of the poem the thrush sings . . . 'Rejoice! / Then he scoops up some dew / And washes his voice.'[22]

What is the Truth? is Hughes's masterpiece for children, though it is not an easy book for young readers. For one thing, it is sometimes difficult to tell where the poems begin and end and the prose sections are, deliberately I think, not well demarcated from the poetry. Many of the poems are long and demanding. Hughes sometimes revisits a single animal over and over again from different perspectives. The language is often rich and complex, like the ideas Hughes is exploring. All the poems basically seek to establish the truth about the nature of certain common animals, birds and insects and, to some extent, their relationship with human beings. The overarching device which holds the book together is described by Margaret Meek as a '. . . modern Aesop in a village where God and his son go to visit mankind and ask a few simple questions. "In their sleep they will say what they truly know."'[23] But the real heart of the book lies in the poems.

This poetic *tour de force* is matched by the brilliance and originality of R. J. Lloyd's artistry. Many of his birds, insects and animals who often look out disconcertingly at the reader are both naturalistic and iconographic, set in a landscape underneath the moon or the sun, adding to the elemental flavour of his depiction. Lloyd never lets us forget that this book is about God's affinity with the animal kingdom. The animals are distinctive, themselves in every sense; and like the poetry, they seek to show their instinctive nature. Lloyd is pre-eminent as an artist, but in the smaller format reissue Lisa Flather does a very good job of the illustrations, providing sympathy, charm and a fresh perspective on the poems.

Early in the book Hughes introduces the reader to a specific badger, then badgers in general through several poems, one of which comes late in the book. At first we meet 'Bess my badger'[24] in a poem which is a forceful denunciation of keeping wild beasts in captivity.

> Trudging to-fro, to-fro, in her tight cage,
> Her nose brushed by the mesh, this way, that way,
> All night, every night, keeping pace
>
> With the badgers out in the woods. She was
> Learning to be a prisoner.

Hughes's language keeps pace with the badger rhythmically stalking its lonely cage. When the badger is returned to the wild, Hughes tellingly presents his view of people as 'Big noisy monkeys, addicted to diesel and daylight.'[25] Then, placing the badger as king of the animal kingdom with all the dignity and majesty that confers:

> But the badger's fort was dug when the whole land was oak.
> His face is his ancient coat of arms, and he wears the same grey cloak.
>
> As if time had not passed at all, as if there were no such thing,
> As if there were only the one night-kingdom and its Badger King.[26]

We meet badger one last time. Hughes begins in affectionate mode employing the sort of snuffling language one imagines badgers might use if they could speak, and almost without any punctutation at all.

> Main thing about badgers is hating daylight.
> Funny kind of chap snore all day
> In his black hole – sort of root
> A ball of roots a potato or a bulb maybe
> A whiskery bulb he loves bulbs he'll do a lot to get a good bulb
> Worms beetles things full of night
> Keeping himself filled up with night.[27]

As this extract shows, Hughes shies away from conventional expectations of poetry, deviating from other nature poets today, changing style, diction and form as he pleases, leaving the reader to pick up nuances and fill gaps in the text. This poem ends in the vernacular and folk tradition:

> Kill a badger kill your granny. Kill a badger never see
> The moon in your sleep. And so it is.
> They disappear under their hill but they work a lot
>   inside people.

This short sequence demonstrates Hughes's ability to work across a range of registers. On another occasion he gives us a cow observing its mucky natural functions –

> A cowclap is an honest job
> A black meringue for the flies.[28]

Then we get the cold scrutiny of the fly itself:

> He knows his job is dangerous, wading in the drains
> Under cows' tails, in pigs' eye-corners
> And between the leaky broken toes
> Of the farm buildings.[29]

or the wonder at the new-born –

> Suddenly he's here – a warm heap
> Of ashes and embers, fondled by small draughts.
> A star dived from outer space – flared
> And burned out in the straw
> Now something is stirring in the smoulder
> We call it a foal.[30]

Hughes explores the sensuousness of worms in the final poem. What other poet writing for children could we imagine saying this?

> They were big blue-nosed lobworms who stretched to embrace
> From their separate dug-outs, in that dreadful place
> O they twisted together like two loving tongues
> And they had not a care for the world and its wrongs.[31]

Hughes can be funny: swallows have a 'chirruppy chicken-sweet expression, / With goo-goo starlet wide-apart eyes'; 'The Rat the Rat the Ratatat / The house's poltergeist, shaped like a shuttle / Who longs to join the family'. Instead of pretty little lambs we get:

> His fleece is for Scab. For Ticks. For Keds. And for Itch-mites. And
>
> Then his back end for maggots.
> The blow-fly is Beelzebub.

And

> Brain – what looks just like brainlessness
> Is a one-track genius
> For roaming, for searching out new pastures,
> Always somebody's else's

Finally,

> Sheep is a machine
> Of problems
> For turning the Shepherd grey as a sheep.[32]

The sequence of four poems on sheep, which need to be read in full to be appreciated, is extraordinarily inventive, full of unexpected metaphors, yet as knowledgeable about sheep as a shepherd would be. This is one of the secrets of Hughes's success as a nature poet – the fact that he has loved and worked with animals for most of his life and sees them without sentimentality as a farmer does.

The next is a donkey, so different from de la Mare's 'Nicolas Nye' (see Chapter 11) as to be almost unrecognizable as the same animal. Hughes and de la Mare both feel compassion for the donkey, but Hughes is as determined to scrutinize what he sees with searing honesty as de la Mare, writing 50 years earlier, was to wear rose-tinted spectacles. With Hughes's donkey, nature poetry for children comes of age. Here is the beginning and ending of the poem:

> My donkey
> Is an ancient colour. He's the colour
> Of a prehistoric desert
> Where great prehistoric suns have sunk and burned out
> To a bluish powder.
>
> He stood there through it all, head hanging.

He's the colour
Of a hearth-full of ashes, next morning,
Tinged with rusty pink.
. . .
But mostly he's comical – and that's what I like.
I like the joke he seems.
Always just about to tell me. And the laugh,
The rusty, pump-house engine that cranks up laughter
From some long ago, far-off, laughter-less desert –

The dry, hideous guffaw
That makes his great teeth nearly fall out.[33]

Perhaps the poem that shows Hughes at full stretch is 'The Fly'. It would be hard to view the common fly with disdain after reading this poem which almost scorches the reader with its brilliant extended metaphor of the fly as the Sanitary Inspector.

In his black boiler suit, with his gas-mask,
His oxygen pack,
his crampons,
He can get anywhere, explore any wreckage,
Find the lost –
Whatever dies – just leave it to him.
He'll move in
With his team of gentle undertakers,
In their pneumatic clothing, afraid of nothing,
Little white michelin men,
They hoover up the rot, the stink, and the goo.

The ending takes your breath away and shows the originality of Hughes's imagination at its peak.

But this is his duty.
Just let him be. Let him rest on the wall there,
Scrubbing the back of his neck. This is his rest-minute.

Once he's clean, he's a gem.

A freshly barbered sultan, royally armoured
in dusky rainbow metals.

A knight on a dark horse.[34]

Neil Philip writes of Hughes's 'authority of rhythm, of tone, of observed and felt experience' in his article which accompanied the Signal Award for *What is the Truth?* Philip goes on to discuss the penultimate sequence of poems about a fox who gets shot and killed, describing its 'lithe muscularity' and 'its delicate balance between stillness and movement, its stunningly compact and vivid imagery'.[35] The way Hughes conveys the experience, particularly from the animal's point of view, is nothing short of masterful:

> Somebody is struggling with something.
> An elegant gentleman, beautifully dressed,
> Is struggling there, tangled with something,
> And biting at something
> With his flashing mouth. It is himself
> He is tangled with . . .
>
> . . . He is desperate
> To get himself up on his feet,
> And if he could catch the broken pain
> In his teeth, and pull it out of his shoulder,
> He still has some hope, because
> The long brown grass is the same
> As it was before, and the trees
> have not changed in any way,
> And the sky continues the same . . .[36]

It must be clear by now that Hughes places his nature poetry in the real farm or countryside. The natural world it may be, but far removed from the 'garden' of children's poetry we have been exploring elsewhere in the book. Hughes's poetry makes few concessions and only a small percentage of young readers will find their way to him without skilled teacher intervention. Jill Pirrie[37] is an inspirational teacher who has used Hughes's poetry successfully in her outstanding work with young people. In an essay on Hughes, she reminds us of his own comments about writing and children.

> I find a common wavelength . . . between the self I was then and the self I am now . . . [children] will accept plastic toys, if that's all they're given, but their true driving passion is to get possesssion of the codes of adult reality – of the real world.'[38]

His work is inevitably too uncompromising for some tastes, particularly those who hold idealized views of childhood. Neil Philip puts it well when he writes of Hughes as a poet:

. . . working at his full power. Confidence is its hallmark: confidence to take the time to say what he has to say, confidence to sustain a line . . . confidence to modulate between reverent intensity and irreverent fun. Confidence in the writing, and confidence in the reader.[39]

Ted Hughes offers those young readers who can manage it poetry of power and potency, presenting a stirring and often mythic vision of the world that has echoes, perhaps, of William Blake.

While Causley and Hughes were publishing their outstanding work a new genre had been developing simultaneously. Some commentators believe it threatens to engulf and swallow up the best of children's poetry. John Rowe Townsend calls this informal, riotous, insistently cheeky new material 'urchin verse'.[40] Children's poetry has burst out of the garden into the street all right, causing havoc in its wake. Like the Pied Piper, the children follow along, laughing and shouting with pleasure. But what of the adults left behind?

Notes

1   Charles Causley, from 'Who?', *Figgie Hobbin,* Macmillan, London, 1970/90.
2   Clive Wilmer, *Poets Talking,* Carcanet, Manchester, 1994, pp. 63, 68.
3   Charles Causley in Wilmer, *ibid.*, p.69.
4   Charles Causley quoted by Morag Styles, *The Best of Books for Keeps,* ed. Chris Powling, Bodley Head, London, 1995, p. 103.
5   Charles Causley, from 'I Saw a Jolly Hunter', 1970/90, *op. cit.*
6   Charles Causley, from 'Timothy Winters', *Collected Poems for Children,* Macmillan, London, 1996.
7   Causley, from 'My Mother Saw a Dancing Bear', *ibid.*
8   Causley, from 'Tell Me, Tell Me, Sarah Jane', *ibid.*
9   Charles Causley, 'On St Catherine's Day', *Jack the Treacle Eater,* Macmillan, London, 1987.
10 Charles Causley, 'Tavistock Goose Fair', *ibid.*
11 Charles Causley, *The Young Man of Cury,* Macmillan, London, 1991.
12 Causley quoted in Styles, *op. cit.*, p. 102.
13 Causley, from 'Why?', 1987, *op. cit.*
14 From a review in *The Times,* quoted on the cover of the first edition of *Going to the Fair, op. cit.*
15 Charles Causley, from 'Who?', *Collected Poems for Children,* Macmillan, 1996.
16 Charles Causley, Introduction to *The Puffin Book of Magic Verse,* quoted by Morag Styles, in Powling, *op. cit.*, p.102.
17 Causley, from 'Who?',1996, *op. cit.*
18 Ted Hughes quoted in Lissa Paul, *Signal,* 49, 1986, p.55.
19 Ted Hughes, *What is the Truth?* Faber, London, 1984.
20 Ted Hughes, from 'The Snow-shoe Hare', *The Iron Wolf,* Faber, London, 1995.
21 Hughes, from 'Cat', *ibid.*
22 Hughes, from 'Thrush', *ibid.*

23   Margaret Meek in *School Librarian*, 1984, quoted on back cover of first edition of *What is the Truth?*, *op. cit.*

24   Hughes, 1984, *op. cit.*, p.13.

25   *Ibid.*, p.14.

26   *Ibid.*, p.15.

27   *Ibid.*, p.60.

28   *Ibid.*, p.22.

29   *Ibid.*, p.70.

30   *Ibid.*, p.17.

31   *Ibid.*, p.119.

32   *Ibid.*, p. 39.

33   *Ibid.*, p.56.

34   *Ibid.*, p.70.

35   Neil Philip, *The Signal Poetry Award*, 47, May 1995, p.71.

36   Hughes, *op. cit.*, p.73.

37   Poems written by Jill Pirrie's pupils and an account of her approach can be found in *On Common Ground*, World Wide Fund for Nature, 1994; also Jill Pirrie edited *Apple Fire*, an anthology of poetry by children at Halesworth Middle School, Suffolk, 1995.

38   Jill Pirrie quoting Hughes in an unpublished essay for *The Cambridge Guide to Children's Books*, ed. Victor Watson, (forthcoming).

CHAPTER 13

The Street and Other Landmarks

In defence of 'urchin verse'

I've had this shirt
that's covered in dirt
for years and years and years.[1]

When I started teaching in 1970, most children greeted the suggestion that they read or write poetry with reluctance or hostility. It did not take long, of course, to show them the pleasures it offered, but one got used to the experience of having to 'break children in' to poetry. This is no longer the case; most primary classrooms welcome poetry in the curriculum and most pupils have a healthy appetite for verse.

For the last 25 years or so, children's poetry has been flourishing in terms of the number of new publications, buoyant sales and interest in schools, particularly at primary level. The poetry section of any good children's bookshop is bursting with new titles, collections and anthologies, often lavishly illustrated. Many well-regarded poets choose to spend at least part of their time writing for the young; performances of children's poetry in schools, libraries and theatres are commonplace. Scores of poets visit schools regularly, and writing workshops which focus on poetry for teachers and children are widespread. In my 30 years of professional interest in poetry and the young, I have been able to witness the easy delight so many children take in the verse being written for them now. The poetry seems to speak to children in their own language with directness and power.

'Urchin verse'

John Rowe Townsend[2] coined the term 'urchin verse' in *Written for Children*, his book on the history of children's literature, to describe the unofficial school of poetry which grew up in the 1970s. Townsend: '[it is about] family life in the raw, with its backchat, fury and muddle, and instead of woods and meadows are disused railway lines, building sites and junkheaps'.

(I am not totally happy with the term 'urchin verse', but since no one has come up with a better alternative, it can serve as a useful catch-all for the poetry I am going to discuss.) The first publication in this genre, *Mind Your Own Business* by Michael

Rosen, 1974, blasted onto the decorous world of children's publishing, taking many by surprise with its sheer cheek, its down-to-earth, yet comical tone, its flouting of conventions, as well as the original way in which it tapped into contemporary childhood. As for young readers, they couldn't get their hands on it quickly enough. The quotation from the *School Librarian*[3] on the first paperback edition says it all: 'Here, at last, is a real book of poems for modern children.' The publishers cleverly teamed Michael Rosen with the talented illustrator, Quentin Blake, whose comic style perfectly matched the informality of Rosen's writing: a vibrant new partnership between words and pictures had begun.

Gone were nicely brought up children; instead, they were fighting about trivia, bonding with their friends, contradicting grown-ups, getting the better of their teachers. Gone were romantic descriptions of beautiful countryside. If animals are around in urchin verse they are likely to be scruffy mongrels lifting their legs at lamp-posts, parrots shouting rude remarks, or the subjects of straight talking about humans as carnivores. The location has moved from the garden or the natural world or magic space to everyday houses, streets and the school playground.

Before *Mind Your Own Business*, poetry for children had largely ignored working-class, urban and black experience, so change was long overdue. Now the ordinary ups and downs of most children's lives became the subject matter for poetry, replacing what, with some notable exceptions, had been a somewhat idealized, middle-class world of childhood that was depicted in children's verse for nearly 300 years. A similar shift had taken place about a decade earlier in fiction for children which started to feature realistic working-class characters living in council estates in cities, rather than upper-middle-class heroes and heroines in grand country houses with servants to do their bidding. But if poetry was slower off the mark, the new trend has proved to be long lasting. *Mind Your Own Business* was followed in quick succession by a series of similar collections for children, illustrated by some of the finest artists of the day. A long line of voices has continued working in this genre ever since. The reference points for this 'new wave' are city streets instead of countryside, realism has replaced magic, and the emphasis has changed from regular metre and rhyme to free verse and the vernacular. Titles are often provocative and firmly urban – *The New Kid on the Block, Wouldn't You Like To Know, Salford Road, I Din Do Nuttin, Rabbiting On*, etc.

Despite the great appeal to children and to many teachers who see its potential in the classroom, 'urchin verse' exists in a somewhat hostile critical climate. One complaint is that it is superficial in theme; another that it is badly written; a third that humour and triviality have taken over serious concerns. I believe that such judgements are wrong on all those counts except, of course, in the case of writers lacking in talent, but they exist, unfortunately, in every branch of poetry and fiction.[4]

What then is the value of 'urchin verse'? First of all, it speaks directly to a great number of children who choose to read it. At best, it casts an entertaining, witty, yet honest eye on the world, dealing sharply and responsibly with some of the most significant issues of the day. This means that challenging topics such as death, divorce, violence, war, the environment and child abuse are seriously tackled by poets who are well known for their light-heartedness and fun. In order to communicate with children and engage with their everyday lives some, though not all, of the poets who might be described as 'urban versifiers', have used vernacular language and experimental forms of free verse in their writing. This is a discontinuity with the past and many commentators on children's poetry do not like it. They argue that by trying too hard to get on children's 'wavelengths' and by replacing the heightened language, regular metre and expected subject matter of traditional poetry with free verse, commonplace content and the vernacular, writers have abandoned what is most distinctive about children's poetry. Or, more crudely, many of the people writing for children today are not real poets. The rest of this chapter is devoted to the background for this debate, as well as introducing the reader to 'urchin verse' itself.

'Populist' or 'heritage' poetry?

The annual Signal Award for a book of children's poetry is the only prize of its kind and is a flag-waver for the promotion of current verse for children. Most of the regular, substantial discussion of children's poetry comes within the wrappers of *Signal* magazine. But in her review of ten years of the Signal Poetry Award, Nancy Chambers[5] made a distinction between what she calls 'populist' and 'heritage' poetry:

> . . . the adult poetry-reading public has to begin somewhere, and this is the great weakness of the Verse-for-Kids school of writing . . . An unleavened diet of pop poetry in the first 11 years leaves no one in any condition to proceed to the real thing . . . Already we have one, if not two, generations of adults unable to approach poety without fear and suspicion (not because they don't like it but because they have never read any), branding anything halfway literate as elitist.

In the same article, Neil Philip[6] sums up what he sees as the characterisitcs of the populist school of poetry:

> . . . more boisterous, less reflective, less recognizably 'poetry' in the English tradition. The focus is on shared not unique experience, on the rhythms of speech not the patterns of prosody, on school not home . . . The shift from nursery to classroom inevitably encourages immediately accessible work such as that of McGough, Rosen and Ahlberg. We must be careful, though, that 'accessible' doesn't come to mean 'disposable'.

Those associated with *Signal* and its annual poetry award have a long and honourable tradition of supporting writers for children and promoting the cause of intellectual and morally serious regard for children's books. In spite of these admirable virtues, there is a problem with the way children's poetry is sometimes discussed. An extract from the review which follows is a good example of what I mean. After scrutinizing dozens of poetry books, including Allan Ahlberg's *Please Mrs Butler*, Adrian Mitchell's *Nothingmas Day*, some wonderful anthologies such as Charles Causley's *The Sun, Dancing* and Helen Nicoll's *Poems for Seven and Under*, all now widely considered classics of their kind, Anthea Bell[7] says this. '*What is the Truth?* is real poetry by a real poet, generous in scope and in achievement: an obvious candidate for the Signal Poetry Award.' Quite true. She goes on:

On this year's showing, I still don't know what's to be done in the way of real poetry for the children who can't tackle Hughes, or aren't offered his work. But as Aidan Chambers pointed out, joining us at the end of the discussion meeting, given that good little bunch of Puffin paperbacks, and the new Ted Hughes, one has the makings of a poetry bookshelf. That was decidedly a cheering way to look at poetry publications for children in 1984.

I want to take issue with these views. First of all, categories like 'populist' or 'heritage' do not stand up to scrutiny. There is no easy distinction between two such groupings, even if you could put every poet in one or the other category. Who decides what is 'the real thing' and why have *Signal* given the award on numerous occasions to poets who fall into the 'populist' category – Rosen, Owen, Ahlberg, McGough, Kay and Gross, for example? Children certainly can't make these distinctions, so they are not particularly helpful. Isn't it more worthwhile to consider what is distinctive and valuable about different poets than to erect false barriers which work against constructive debate?

Any discussion of children's poetry must take account of young readers, yet many reviewers seem more interested in children's poetry that appeals to adult sensibilities than to a youthful audience. In *The Narrator's Voice*, Barbara Wall suggests that contemporary fiction for children uses 'a voice concerned more genuinely and specifically with child readers': this is equally relevant to poetry. 'The challenge', continues Wall, 'is a stiff one: to adjust language, concepts and tone to the understanding of the child without loss of significance or dignity.'[8] But is this not exactly what current poets for children have achieved? Margaret Meek thinks it is:

what delights children is the double audienced appeal of, say, *Please Mrs Butler* – children's voices, yet not children's voices, but certainly children's verses . . . contemporary poets see the centrality of learning to play with words as ways of endowing children with poetic potential.[9]

In this chapter I start with the premise that contemporary children's poets have done a fine job of opening doors into poetry which had previously been shut for many people. In the process, I want to consider what is distinctive and new about modern poetry for children, while attempting to convince the reader that there are still continuities with the past. All these ideas need contextualizing.

Children's poetry does not exist in a vacuum; it is part of a post-modern world where poetry, like the other arts, is interested in exploring the limits of taste, pulling away from notions of universality, asking questions about the nature of art itself. That is not new, but the present era is one where artists are prone to destabilize our apparently orderly world with disturbing, fragmented and unexpected perspectives. Visit an art gallery and you might see Damien Hirst's dead calf in formaldehyde or a naked woman in a glass box looking at visitors looking at her. Go to a Pina Bausch production of contemporary dance and no one dances; but the dancers do and say provocative things which make the audience question rather more than 'What is dance?' New ideas are always unsettling for many; just think of reactions to Mozart in his day or Impressionism in the late nineteenth century.

The shock of the new describes more than modern architecture. In the same way, modern children's poetry could be described as conducting a dialogue with what has gone before. In the process, romantic notions of children's poetry have been superseded by the realization that there is not one single version of childhood, but many. Contemporary poets offer us diversity of perspectives which include attempts to see the world from one particular nine-year-old's point of view. A sense of wonder has to compete with gritty realism and 'grunge'. All the certainties and niceties are being questioned. It is a chaotic and confusing world for literary critics, especially those who are not closely involved with children and their preferences in reading. But those who spend time regularly with young readers, watching their responses to poetry, interacting with them as writers and listening to what they say, are much more optimistic about the future.

The language really spoken by children

Many literary critics are people who have felt attuned to poetry all their lives; and many have educational backgrounds which make them confident at dealing with literature. So it is natural for them to fall into the trap of using their own experience as touchstones for other people's. 'If only English was taught the way it used to be,' they lament, 'then children would appreciate decent poetry.' But that is a fallacy. There never was a golden age when large numbers of the population eagerly read 'quality' poetry, even if we could retrieve it. Most people did not have the privilege of finding poetry an essential part of their lives, though they might have encountered it in popular forms and songs through chapbooks, the oral tradition, the hymns they sang at church and the Music Hall, as I have documented elsewhere. Adrian

Mitchell[10] was being combative when he said that 'most people ignore most poetry because most poetry ignores most people', but there was a lot of truth in that statement when it was written in the 1960s.

It certainly is not true now and maybe that is one of the reasons why poetry is enjoying a modest boom in sales as I write. There are probably more children who read poetry for pleasure now than at any other time. Modern children's poetry has been massively successful in pleasing its young audience. Further research may reveal whether or not the result is lasting. But it seems likely that the encouraging sales in poetry titles at present must be due in part to younger people who first encountered poetry through the work of contemporary poets, when they were at school. And what children read has an effect on the adults around them. As Ted Hughes[11] put it:

So in writing for children, it seems to me there's an attractive possibility – of finding, in some way, on some wavelength of imagery and feeling, a lingua franca – a style of communication for which children are the specific audience, but *which adults can overhear.* (my emphasis)

In fact, I like to think that some adults may have lost their fear of poetry through the good offices of their children's books of verse.

Let us pay tribute to poets today for using *the words really spoken*, not by men as in Wordsworth's famous remark, but *by children*. Such poetry appears to be simple because it uses ordinary words in apparently ordinary ways, it is easy to understand, it is invariably on the side of the child whose domestic and school life it explores, and the content is often carried by the natural rhythms of speech. But I ask the reader to review the qualities which are shared by Bunyan's rough verse with its insistence on everyday objects as the subject matter for poetry, Rossetti's sublime but essentially simple rhymes in *Sing-Song*, Blake's 'Cradle Song', all those lullabies by women typified by the Taylor sisters, Lear's nonsense, Milne's nursery jingles, Causley's ballads, and nursery rhymes themselves. The true voice of the nursery *is* unpretentious. It seems to be slight, precisely because it is so close to speech or song. It is, in fact, *light*, what Geoffrey Grigson[12] called 'the best *game* of words which has ever been invented' in his introduction to *The Cherry Tree* (my emphasis).

Nowadays poets use colloquial language more than ever before. It is easy to construe it negatively as slang, especially as poems often centre on arguments, dares, jokes, cheeky remarks, advert ditties, nags, snatches of pop songs, playground chants . . . The language is no longer uniformly standard English, but draws on regional dialect, Creole and the idiom of the street. Verse-forms with regular metre are still regularly used, but varieties of free verse are also common and there is plenty of experiment with form. Humour has become more robust and the subject matter very open. Almost anything can now be tackled in poetry – bad behaviour from child protagonists is more likely than good; unmentionable topics like farting, burping, wetting your pants or picking spots have become fair game. This is the aspect that many critics loathe, calling it the 'nose-picking school of poetry'. It is certainly not the side of urchin verse which adults find appealing, precisely because we are grown up and have left those aspects of childhood behind. That, of course, is what makes it so attractive to so many children, and the fact that so much of it is funny, anti-propriety and subversive. So it draws many children into poetry who might be less attracted initially to traditional verse.

Some commentators say it isn't poetry at all. Rosen[13] mocks them in *There's A Poet Behind You* – 'Is it a poem? Is it a story? Is it a film? Is it a banana?' Urchin verse is certainly unsettling for those holding rarefied notions of poetry. It is not rich in obvious metaphor and it pokes fun at any target it cares to take on. But we must be careful not to exaggerate: 'urchin verse' is extremely varied. All the poets writing within this genre have different emphases, different styles of writing, different forms, diverse viewpoints. Earlier reviewers often failed to read these texts carefully enough: if they had done so, they would have noticed the quieter, more reflective moments and the willingness to grapple with challenging issues which could always be found amidst the horse-play. Has quality really been sacrificed in an attempt to appeal to children? Not, I think, by the poets who do it well and who respect their young readership. A more legitimate concern of some critics is whether children and their teachers devote all their time to 'urchin verse' to the exclusion of other kinds of poetry. To displace traditional forms of poetry and poets who do not fall into this category would certainly be a mistake and should be resisted. The poetry curriculum should be both balanced and wide-ranging.

Isn't there a connection between 'urchin verse' and the sort of material the Opies spent their lives studying and making respectable in pioneering books like *The Lore and Language of Schoolchildren*? For scholars of the oral tradition, the Opies's *I Saw Esau* is a supreme achievement, yet it is full of rude, crude, disrespectful and not at all respectable verse. The logic of valuing the poetry of today for its use of the idiom and backchat of childhood seems to have escaped many critics. It is not the kind of poetry that lends itself to literary criticism, though I suspect that the scholars of the future will document how poetry of the late twentieth century drew splendidly on the vernacular and tuned sensitively into children's lives to develop a new and thriving genre. They might also notice that poetry started to sell well in the shops about this time too.

The Poet's Tongue

Seamus Heaney,[14] recipient of the Nobel Prize for Literature, says something similar in *Preoccupations*:

. . . words as bearers of history and mystery began to invite me. Maybe it began very early when my mother used to recite lists of affixes, and Latin roots . . . rhymes that formed part of her schooling . . . the exotic listing on the wireless dial . . . Maybe it was stirred by the beautiful sprung rhythms of the old BBC weather forecaster or the gorgeous and inane phraseology of the catechism; or with the litany of the Blessed Virgin that was part of the enforced poetry in our household . . . I still recall them with ease, and can delight in them as verbal music . . . means that they were bedding the ear with a kind of linguistic hard-core that could be built on some day.

Heaney writes prose like a poet: the notion of everyday language, which also happens to be poetic, as 'verbal music' which 'beds the ear' with what is tuneful in the cadences of speech, is persuasive. Similarly, Les Murray[15] who won the T. S. Eliot Award for Poetry in 1996, described the Australian country town where he grew up as 'full of the wild poetry of malice and gossip and wit and that sort of thing — nicknaming and casual little remarks . . .' Both of these distinguished poets underline the fact that poetry is rooted in ordinary things and ordinary speech; being poetry, it moves it into a higher plane.

In *The Poet's Tongue*, W. H. Auden[16] tells us that the best definition for poetry is 'memorable speech' and the first few entries in this ground-breaking anthology include a folk song, a nursery rhyme, a sea shanty ('Casey Jones! Got another papa! / Casey Jones, on the Salt Lake Line! / Casey Jones! Got another papa!/ Got another papa on the Salt Lake Line!'), an anonymous dialect poem, an extract from an eighteenth-century broadsheet and a Christmas carol, side by side with Keats, Shelley and Emily Dickinson who were, in turn, criticized in their own day for taking liberties of various kinds with poetry. Auden's passionate declaration for memorable speech is still relevant:

Memorable speech then. About what? Birth, death . . . the abysses of hatred and fear, the awards and miseries of desire, the unjust walking the earth and the just scratching miserably for food like hens, triumphs, earthquakes, deserts of boredom and featureless anxiety . . . the gratifications and terrors of childhood . . . Yes, all of these, but not these only. Everything that we remember no matter how trivial: the mark on the wall, the joke at luncheon, word games . . . are equally the subject of poetry . . . Those, in Mr Spender's words, who try to put poetry on a pedestal only succeed in putting it on the shelf . . . In compiling an anthology . . . one must overcome the prejudice that poetry is uplifted . . . [be] free from the bias of great names and literary influences . . . [it is] a human activity, independent of period and unconfined in subject.[17]

This is the spirit in which we should consider the work of contemporary poets for children – with open minds and as free as possible from prejudice. Let me show the way and introduce the reader to four of the main players within this apparently disreputable genre.

Mind Your Own Business

> I've had this shirt
> that's covered in dirt
> for years and years and years.
>
> It used to be red
> but I wore it in bed
> and it went grey
> cos I wore it all day
> for years and years and years.
>
> The arms fell off
> in the Monday wash
> and you can see my vest
> through the holes in the chest
> for years and years and years.
>
> As my shirt falls apart
> I'll keep the bits
> in a biscuit tin
> on the mantelpiece
> for years and years and years.[18]

Thus begins the second poem in *Mind Your Own Business*, Michael Rosen's first publication. The poem is about hanging onto something you feel comfortable wearing, although it is almost falling apart. Is it a suitable subject for poetry? I think so. First of all, the poem is easy to understand, it is written in the first person and deals with something everyone can relate to. The underlying theme of feeling at home with what is familiar can be applied to more than favourite items of clothing. The human desire to horde things we value and hang on to mementoes is also suggested. As for the form, Rosen uses some rhyme and repetition, and breaks his poem into lines to follow the natural cadences of speech, providing a semi-regular rhythm. The language is everyday in keeping with the content. The overall tone and lack of title makes it very informal and direct. This poem invites identification for the reader with the shirt-wearer; no one is excluded, unless they choose to be. These features are characteristic of Rosen's poetry as a whole and 'urchin verse' in general.

Rosen is one of the best-selling and most influential of modern poets for children, promoting his work widely through broadcasting, journalism, teaching, performances and the prolific number of his own collections and anthologies. Some critics have been much too quick to label Rosen as a *mere* humorist, though he is certainly extremely funny and most inventive in his comic writing. In fact, his poems cover different moods and forms: his free verse includes many kinds of imaginative word play, the dramatic monologue, extended comic narrative and question-and-answer poems. Here is an extract from the latter about a parent counting while a child finds her shoes to go out in.

> If you don't put your shoes on before I count fifteen
> then we won't go to the woods to climb the chestnut
> One
> > *But I can't find them*
> Two
> > *I can't*
> They're under the sofa three
> > *No*
> > *O yes*
> Four, five, six
> > *Stop – they've got knots they've got knots*
> You should untie the laces when you take your shoes off seven
> > *Will you do one shoe while I do the other then?*
> Eight but that would be cheating
> > *Please*
> All right[19]

This poem is an amusing and authentic account of how resourceful and irritating children can be, and how adults use threats and promises in dealing with them. But there is warmth and security, too; the reader, like the child in question, knows that the grown-up will take her out in the end and will help her get her shoes on, even though she is old enough to do it herself. Rosen captures real conversations most skilfully, though in post-modernist fashion, he expects the reader to jump straight into the poem without bothering to provide typographical devices, a title, speakers' names or speech marks to indicate who is saying what. At other times, Rosen does use descriptive language, like this one about two cats out at night:

> The beads in their eyes stole some of
> our kitchen light
> and spilt it on the path . . .

and sat still thawing their patches
like two warm loaves . . .[20]

Rumbustious behaviour is always prevalent in Rosen's work, so it is all too easy to miss the quieter poems that deal with feelings, including sadness. A child missing his mother asks:

and can we have grilled tomatoes
Spanish onions and roast potatoes
and will you sing me 'I'll never more roam'
when I'm in bed, when you've come home.[21]

What is not said is as important as what is said. The specificity of Spanish onions and roast potatoes gives a concreteness to the poem, and the longing in the child's voice is only too clear. This serious and tender side of Rosen has always been interspersed with the madness and hilarity. I can't think of a poem that catches more truthfully the way children deal with tragedy than 'Harrybo'. The ending reveals embarrassed children who desperately want to be kind to a stricken friend, but don't yet have the words or the culture in which to express sympathy about the death of Harrybo's grandad. The final line carries the weight of the children's grief, resonating with feeling.

                . . .
        Dave said
        My hamster died as well
        So everyone said
        Shhhh . . .
        And Dave said
        I was only saying
        And I said
        My gran gave me a red shoe horn
        Rodge said
        I got a pair of trainers for Christmas
        And Harrybo said
        You can get ones without any laces
        And we all said
        Yeah, that's right, Harrybo, you can.
        Any other day we'd've said
        Of course you can, we know that, you fool
        But that day
        we said
        Yeah, that's right Harrybo, yeah, you can.[22]

Perhaps the most popular poems of all within Rosen's *oeuvre* are those that relate to one of his sons, Eddie, when he was a baby. Part of the appeal must lie in the authenticity of a two year old throwing a 'wobbly', refusing to have his nappy changed, demanding another set of cards to open the day after his birthday or covering his father's hairbrush with soggy breakfast cereal! Brian Morse writes appreciatively about his pupils' reactions to Rosen's poetry: '. . . my class of six- and seven-year-olds are still demanding rereadings . . . [of] all the baby-Eddie poems . . . six months after they first heard them, and greeting me "Nappy, nappy, nappy" in the morning . . . Rosen's skill is to put children in touch with themselves.'[23]

In his Introduction to *The New Oxford Book of Children's Verse*, Neil Philip reminds us of Rosen's own perspective on why children seem to like his poetry. 'I see them using my writing like a catalyst, tuning in to its small hurts, jokes and fantasies of everyday life as a means to explore their own.'[24]

Please Mrs Butler

Allan Ahlberg works in an older tradition but his poetry also strikes a chord with the young. Better known as an extremely popular and best-selling author of stories and picture books for children, Ahlberg's first poetry book of 1984, *Please Mrs Butler*,[25] is one of the most successful collections for children of all time.

> Please Mrs Butler
> This boy Derek Drew
> Keeps copying my work, Miss.
> What shall I do?
>
> Lock yourself in the cupboard, dear.
> Run away to sea.
> Do whatever you can, my flower.
>   But, *don't ask me!*

These are poems about school life. The keenest point of view in Ahlberg's work is that of the teacher he once was, a kind one who appreciates his pupils, even when they are infuriating. Children love the title poem 'Please Mrs Butler'; while it is funny and well observed, it does suffer a little from metaphorically winking at the adult reader over the head of the child. Poems like 'The Cane'[26] are more honest. In it Ahlberg catches perfectly the friendly relationship between primary teachers and their classes, contrasted nicely with the severity of schooling in the past, and all with an admirably light touch.

Other children
left their seats and crowded round
the teacher's desk.

Other hands
went out. Making kites was soon
forgotten.

My turn next!
He's had one go already!
That's not fair!

Soon the teacher,
to save himself from the crush,
called a halt.

(It was
either that or use the cane
for real.)

Reluctantly,
the children did as they were told
and sat down.

If you behave
yourselves, the teacher said,
I'll cane you later.

Heard It in the Playground, companion volume to *Please Mrs Butler*, is a Signal Award winner, praised by Jan Mark[27] for 'the excitement of rhythm, rhyme, antiphon, assonance and word play . . . the experience of form and structure . . . that a line can be made to scan without inversion . . .' Her fellow-judge, Peter Holding,[28] called it 'public poetry – almost every poem is made to be spoken, sung, chanted aloud . . .' Ahlberg sounds a different note when he branches out in *The Mighty Slide* with his considerable storytelling skills to the fore. Fritz Wegner was illustrator for the first two volumes; his art work is so low key that it would be easy not to notice the excellent job he does of matching, complementing and enhancing Ahlberg's poetry.

Two's Company

Jackie Kay won the Signal Award for her first children's poetry book, *Two's Company*;[29] its sequel, *Three Has Gone*,[30] 1994, is in similar vein. Kay achieved equally quick success in her adult poetry and the same characteristics are evident in her writing for both audiences – honesty, a droll sense of humour, acute observations of people, true-to-life situations. Some of the poems are inspired by Jackie Kay's little son, Matthew; others are memories of her own Scottish childhood, holidays abroad, particular places, capturing moments of the daily routine. The poems share a concreteness and authenticity which speaks to older and younger readers alike. Kay usually writes in standard English in varying forms of free verse; when she uses dialect, it is Scots.

All this would have been impressive enough, but in *Two's Company* Kay does something quite adventurous which no other poet had tried for children before in quite that way. Sprinkled throughout the book are poems written from the standpoint of Carla Johnson, a little girl who lives two different lives at the divided homes of her divorced parents. As Carla also has a rich fantasy life, the reader can almost enter someone else's head. Kay touches on her sadness, but very delicately, and intersperses it with humour and Carla's wonderful imaginings. None of this is easy to put into children's poetry, so Kay's achievement in her first book is remarkable. We meet Carla in the first poem, where she tells us:

> People don't understand: there are two Carla Johnsons.
> The one with wings and the one with hands.
> The one who flies and the one who flops exams.[31]

In other poems, Kay lets the fantasy world predominate.

> Whilst I was doing the dinner dishes
> Carla Johnson flew past the moon
> twice, in different skies,
> and landed in Toronto five hours behind
> the Greenwich mean Time. Autumn.
>
> All rust and yellow and glowing orange.
> Trees ahead of ours, lit like halloween lanterns.[32]

Carla doesn't need conventional transport in order to travel.

> She believes, all she needs, she believes
> Is her kiwi fruit and tangerine wings,
> a glass of water, before and after,
> and a small fruit of the season – maybe
> a mango, a black fig or a papaya.[33]

In poems like 'Big Hole' and 'Duncan Gets Expelled', Kay tackles racist cruelty from Carla's point of view – the shame, puzzlement and hurt of a small child who doesn't quite understand what it is all about. Fighting the developers, hanging on to woodland, how we ruin our environment also feature in poems; so do new baby brothers, latchkey children and the Rottweiler next door. The final poem returns to the central theme, exploring the feeling of being literally split in half, experienced by some children with divorced parents. Kay does it so gracefully in 'Two of Everything' that you could miss its profound message.

> My friend Shola said to me that she said to her mum:
> 'It's not fair, Carla (that's me) has two of everything:
>
> Carla has two bedrooms,
> two sets of toys, two telephones,
>
> two wardrobes, two door mats
> two mummies, two cats
>
> two water purifiers, two kitchens
> two environmentally friendly squeezies.'
>
> My friend Shola said to me that she said to her mum:
> 'Why can't you and Dad get divorced?'
>
> But the thing Shola doesn't even realize yet,
> is that there are two of me.[34]

'Nothingmas Day'

Adrian Mitchell has been a champion of children's poetry and a regular visitor to schools for about 20 years, plying his 'Secrets of Poetry' in classrooms up and down the land. He has great respect for young writers. Once he took 30 ten year olds on a flying expedition while the author looked on: the children's concentration and willingness to 'suspend disbelief' were quite remarkable; so were the poems which followed. To help children compose Mitchell provides them with a model in language they can understand, echoing Wordsworth's famous remarks about writing poetry and making them laugh too.

> I always carry three pens. One to write with. One not to lend to my daughters. And one to leak in my pocket. And a notebook and postcards. *I scribble down ideas for poems, stories and plays while they're hot.* Scribble, scribble, as much of the poem as I can get down. Later on, *I work on that scribble in a cool way*, taking out the words that aren't needed, seeing if the muddle of my first ideas can be turned into a poem that works.[35] (my emphasis)

Even simpler is the advice offered in 'Secret Three'.

> Don't write about Autumn
> Because that's the season –
>   Write your poems
>   For a real reason.[36]

Mitchell has been entertaining adult audiences for even longer with many titles to his credit, including a *Collected* and a *Selected Poems*. There are several distinctive elements to Mitchell's poetry. Writing for adults he sometimes favours a political voice, condemning social injustice and passionately anti-war. He was well known in the 1960s for campaigning against the Vietnam War and his pacifist convictions are often aired in his poems. Anger at the miseries caused by small cruelties at school, bullying and pupil disaffection are all tackled in his poetry.

> I don't hit em
> They can do you for that
>
> I stick my hands in my pockets
> And stare at them
>
> And while I stare at them
> I think about sick
>
> They call it dumb insolence
>
> They don't like it
> But they can't do you for it.[37]

Mitchell also writes tenderly of love, children, friends, dogs; his poems often employ rhythm so skilfully that readers find themselves tapping out the beat. Mitchell's sense of humour is never far away, even when he is making a serious point. Elephant poems and pictures are his trademark of peace, though he sometimes adds an amusing touch. In 'An Infant Elephant Speaks', the poem is shorter than the title: 'I got a rusk / Stuck on my tusk'. 'Give Us a Brake' combines word play with an echo of a traditional rhyme, 'Piggy on the Railway'.

> The runaway train knocked the buffers flat:
> 'Hey!' said the Stationmaster. 'That's enough of that.
> I've been forty-two years at this station
> And I've never seen such bufferation.'[38]

'Nothingmas Day' works playfully, contradicting all the reader's expectations about Christmas.

> At school Miss Whatnot taught them how to write No Thank You Letters.
>
> Home they burrowed for Nothingmas Dinner.
> The table was not groaning under all manner of
>   NO TURKEY
>   NO SPICED HAM
>   NO SPROUTS
>   NO CRANBERRY JELLY SAUCE
>   NO NOT NOWT[39]

Mitchell's special gift lies in his extraordinary imagination and he still manages to look out at the world with eyes of wonder like his great hero, William Blake.

> Why are the seas so full of tears?
> Because I've wept so many thousand years.
> Why do you weep as you dance through space?
> Because I am the Mother of the Human Race.
>   (from 'Song in Space')[40]

John Lawrence's woodcuts for the original edition of 'Nothingmas Day' are the perfect foil for Mitchell's poems, which can be dreamy and ethereal or strong and uncompromising. Also an accomplished anthologist, *The Orchard Book of Poems*, 1993, makes for lively and unpredictable reading.

Contemporary American verse

The list of British poets I have reluctantly neglected in this chapter includes Gerard Benson, Wendy Cope, Helen Dunmore, Richard Edwards, Mick Gowar, Philip Gross, Adrian Henri, Libby Houston, John Mole, Judith Nicholls, Brian Patten and Matthew Sweeney, all of whom deserve proper attention and some of whose poetry falls into the category of 'urchin verse'. Others are considered in earlier chapters.

Some of their American counterparts are Harry Behn, John Ciardi, Eloise Greenfield, Mary Ann Hoberman, Eve Merriam, Jack Prelutsky, Nancy Willard and Charlotte Zolotow. American poetry tends to be more well-mannered and less provocative than that which we are used to in Britain. It does these poets less than justice to say that their style tends to favour amusing, thoughtful and reflective accounts of children's lives (black and white) mostly in the context of the home. Others use fantasy or strike an exuberant note; for example, there is Shel Silverstein (considered in Chapter 5) and Karla Kuskin. Siv Widerberg and Nikki Giovanni's feminist poetry is anything but tame; they examine girls' experience in bracing and original ways.

> and they always said 'all those B's
> what a good student you are'
> and she would smile and say thank you
>
> they said: you will make a fine woman some day'
> and she would smile and go her way
>
> because she knew[41]
> (Giovanni: 'Mattie Lou at Twelve')

'Urchin verse' in Britain with its egalitarian credentials is still thriving in all its diversity, 25 years on. Many poets divide their time between two audiences, children and adults. You can count on the fingers of one hand those who do not regularly write for both readerships – apart from pure humorists, Michael Rosen, Judith Nicholls and Allan Ahlberg are the only names that come to mind. John Mole warns of the dangers in deliberately setting out to write for children, though he goes on to say that 'to write for a particular child whose wavelength you happen to be on . . . is another matter'.[42] Others find that shift in gear refreshing and liberating. Adrian Henri began writing for the young after a stint as Writer in Residence at an Arts Centre. 'A part of my mind that was closed off before has opened up. Now I've a whole new area of subject matter. Almost all my poems start from observing some small thing.'[43]

Kit Wright talks of welcoming the chance to work in a vein distinctive from his adult writing: 'I think in a different way for each with a different audience in mind.'[44] Roger McGough found that his own children provided ideas for writing and reintroduced him to his own childhood. He likes to keep the two audiences distinct, concentrating on writing either for the young or for adults, one at a time. That so many gifted poets choose to write for children as well as adults is, I think, unique to Britain and means that all their knowledge, skill and passion for poetry is being transmitted to the young.

I want to conclude this chapter on an upbeat note. What we have now is a positive climate for poetry with children reading, reciting, performing and listening to a wider range than ever before. Most children are not afraid of poetry and many like writing it themselves. The work of gifted teachers like Jill Pirrie show that children who are not specially privileged can write wonderful poetry. A recent initiative from the Arvon Foundation offers a subsidized place on a writing course for teachers in training. All this is exciting and promising. But, a cautionary note – we must encourage publishing houses, in their rush to get new titles out, to be able to recognize which of their current collections and backlist need to be truly valued and kept in print. Nor ought there to be any complacency about literature when schools are struggling to find enough money to buy books and libraries are closing. There is still much to achieve. Just the same, I believe that poetry for children has never been healthier.

Notes

1   Michael Rosen, *Mind Your Own Business*, Andre Deutsch, London, 1974.
2   John Rowe Townsend, *Written for Children*, Penguin, 1974/ 1987, p. 303.
3   Review in *School Librarian* quoted on paperback cover of *Mind Your Own Business* by Michael Rosen, *op. cit.*
4   There is plenty of badly written 'urchin verse', as there is plenty of crudely written fiction.
5   Nancy Chambers, *Signal* 59, 1989, pp. 94–7.
6   Neil Philip, *ibid.*
7   Anthea Bell, The Signal Poetry Award, *Signal* 47, May, 1985, pp. 84–5.
8   Barbara Wall, *The Narrator's Voice: the dilemma of children's fiction*, Macmillan, London, 1991, pp. 9, 18.
9   Margaret Meek in a letter to the author, April, 1996.
10   Adrian Mitchell, dedication page, *Poems*, Jonathon Cape, London, 1964.
11   Ted Hughes, quoted in Lissa Paul, *Inside the Lurking-Glass with Ted Hughes*, Signal 49, 1986, p. 55.
12   Geoffrey Grigson, *The Cherry Tree*, Phoenix House, London, 1959, p. ix.
13   Michael Rosen quoted in *There's a Poet Behind You*, eds Helen Cook and Morag Styles, A & C Black, London, 1988, p.89.
14   Seamus Heaney, *Preoccupations: Selected Prose 1968–1978*, Faber, London, 1980, p. 45.
15   Les Murray, quoted in Clive Wilmer, ed. *Poets Talking*, Carcanet, Manchester, 1994, p. 105.
16   W. H. Auden, & John Garrett, eds *The Poet's Tongue*, G. Bell & Sons Ltd., 1936, p. v.
17   *Ibid.*
18   Michael Rosen, 'I've had this shirt', *Mind Your Own Business,* Andre Deutsch (Scholastic), London, 1947.
19   *Ibid.*
20   *Ibid.*
21   *Ibid.*
22   Michael Rosen, from 'Harrybo', *The Hypnotizer*, Andre Deutsch, London, 1988.
23   Brian Morse, *Signal* 1986, quoted by Neil Philip, ed. *The New Oxford Book of Children's Verse*, 1996, p. xxxiii .
24   Michael Rosen, 'Memorable Speech', *Times Educational Supplement*, 1984, quoted in *op. cit.,* Neil Philip, 1996, p. xxxiii.
25   Allan Ahlberg, *Please Mrs Butler*, Puffin, London, 1984.
26   Ahlberg, from 'The Cane', *ibid.*
27   Jan Mark, *Signal* 62, 1990, pp.87, 96.
28   Peter Holding, *ibid.*
29   Jackie Kay, *Two's Company*, Blackie, London, 1992.
30   Jackie Kay, *Three Has Gone*, Blackie, London, 1994.
31   Kay, from 'Two Carla Johnsons', *Two's Company*, *op. cit.*
32   Kay, from 'Two Niagaras', *ibid.*
33   Kay, from 'Carla's Kisses', *ibid.*

34 Kay, from 'Two of Everything', *Ibid.*

35 Adrian Mitchell, quoted in *There's a Poet Behind You*, eds. Helen Cook and Morag Styles, A & C Black, London, 1988, p.34.

36 Adrian Mitchell, from *The Thirteen Secrets of Poetry*, Simon & Schuster, Hemel Hempstead, 1993.

37 Adrian Mitchell, from 'Dumb Insolence', *All My Own Stuff*, Simon & Schuster, Hemel Hempstead, 1994.

38 Adrian Mitchell, 'Give us a Break', *Nothingmas Day*, Allison & Busby, London, 1984.

39 Mitchell, from 'Nothingmas Day', *ibid.*

40 Mitchell, from 'Song in Space', *ibid.*

41 Nikki Giovanni, from 'Mattie Lou at Twelve', *Spin a Soft Black Song*, Hill and Wang, New York, 1985.

42 John Mole, 'Questions of Poetry', *Signal* 74, p. 89.

43 Adrian Henri, quoted by Morag Styles in *Poetry 0-16*, eds. M.Styles & P. Triggs, Books for Keeps, London, 1988, p. 47.

44 Kit Wright, quoted by Morag Styles in *Poetry 0-16*, *ibid.*, p.31.

CHAPTER 14

Epilogue

Caribbean poetry in the late twentieth century

Bring me now where the warm wind blows,
where the grasses sigh,
where the sweet-tongue'd blossom flowers;

where the showers
fan soft like a fisherman's net
thrown through the sweeted air.[1]

In the 1980s another exciting trend was developing in children's poetry. Black writers with their roots in the Caribbean, who were either born in Britain or who came here to live, began to make an impact on poetry for children. In the Caribbean itself, immensely popular poets like Louise Bennett were not only writing, performing and collecting dialect poetry, but contributing to (in her case, Jamaican) a flowering of nationalism and pride in Caribbean culture. Before that many parts of the Caribbean had been dominated by English culture and practices, including English literature. The distinguished Barbadian poet and academic Edward Kamau Brathwaite came to the forefront of a movement that properly valued and celebrated African-Caribbean culture, including the use of Creole in oral and written form and giving it status with the title of Nation Language.

Some of the poetry which grew out of this movement was angry; poets were facing the horrors of their history of slavery and challenging the relics of colonialism. Many people of Caribbean origin who had been encouraged to come to Britain after the war found a cold welcome and the realities of racism. The poetry which came out of this experience from writers like Linton Kwesi Johnson and Benjamin Zepaniah was uncompromising and tough. 'Dis policeman keeps on kicking me to death' screamed Zepaniah about the experience of African-Caribbean young men in London. *Inglan Is a Bitch* roared the title of one of Linton Kwesi Johnson's collections.

w'en mi jus' some to landan toun
mi use to work pan di andahgroun

but workin' pan di andahgroun
y'u don't get fi know your way aroun'

Inglan is a bitch
dere's no escapin' it
Inglan is a bitch
dere's no runnin' whey fram it[2]

This poetry was powerful, vibrant, committed and topical, speaking with the authentic voice of black youth and often brilliantly performed. In the same way that the Beat poets of the 1960s made a strong impact on society, so did these young black British poets. Their following, largely from the African-Caribbean community at first, rapidly spread to encompass both a much wider poetry-reading public and youth culture.

Out of this lively 'melting pot' some poets emerged with an interest in reaching children as well as adult audiences and speaking with a gentler voice. What began for some as a desire to educate black (and white) pupils about their cultural heritage in the Caribbean, developed into a new poetry for children which took account of black experience in Britain and gave a focus for writing about West Indian life, too. In the late 1990s there are now many gifted Caribbean British poets published in Britain. Many of these poets are electrifying performers (John Agard, Valerie Bloom, Benjamin Zephaniah, to name but three), but it is important not to put Caribbean poetry in a performance ghetto; their work demands attention because it is good poetry. And it is worth remembering that although some Caribbean poetry is, of course, written in a very appealing form of Creole, rich in rhythm, wit and vitality, a great many distinguished black British poets choose to write some or all of the time in standard English.

However, it is certainly true that some Caribbean poetry lends itself to performance and comes alive when it is read aloud. Who can hear 'Wha Me Mudder Do' (particularly if Grace Nichols is performing it) or Benjamin Zephaniah's 'Over De Moon' and not want to join in?

Mek me tell you wha me mudder do
wha me mudder do
wha me mudder do

Me mudder beat hammer
Me mudder turn screw
she paint chair red
then she paint it blue.
          (Grace Nichols)

Dere's a man on de moon
He has a spaceship,
Dere's a man on de moon
  An we payed fe it,
Dere's a man on de moon
His mission ain't done,
Dere's a man on de moon
He's after de Sun.[3]
  (Benjamin Zephaniah)

Another strong feature of Caribbean poetry lies in its links with music, particularly in terms of dub and rap. There is now a direct relationship between popular music and poetry, as those who listen to contemporary groups will know. The quality of Bob Marley's lyrics are now widely recognized and his place in the classroom can be justified as a poet, alongside his obvious musical credentials. As teenagers are often addicted to popular music, but not very interested in poetry, Caribbean verse can be used to pull both strands together. The promotion of Caribbean poetry in schools has been a small but significant phenomenon of the last ten years. Of the many fine poets I could discuss, I will focus on four – John Agard, James Berry, Grace Nichols and Benjamin Zephaniah.

Come on into my Tropical Garden

When *Come on into my Tropical Garden* was published in 1988, a significant new player had joined the ranks of those writing poetry for the young. According to Aidan Chambers, Grace Nichols's voice was vigorous, energetic, amenable and conversational.

> She enjoys and handles strong rhythms well. She is at home with everyday subject matter . . . She enjoys the play of words and is not afraid of naivity, which yet she controls so well that she is never embarassing or twee.[4]

An award-winning adult poet and novelist, Nichols has also written fiction for children and collected and composed (with John Agard) Guyanese nursery rhymes. Her poetry can be lyrical, conversational, physical, tender; Nichols has a terrific sense of fun, but though she can also be deadly serious, she is always warm and has a sure sense of her audience. Here she writes convincingly about the equal measure of attraction and terror which jumbie (ghost) stories inspire in children:

Then is when
I does feel a dread

Then is when
I does jump into me bed

Then is when
I does cover up
from me feet to me head

Then is when
I does wish I didn't listen
to no stupid jumbie story

Then is when
I does wish I did read
me book instead.[5]

Grace Nichols can write about Dilberta, biggest of the elephants at London Zoo as 'the walking-whale of the earth kingdom' or the Great Womb-Moon – 'Time was a millennium / In my mother's belly'.[6] She can also take a simple bit of daily routine to express that special affection between a child and her granny.

Granny Granny please comb my hair
you always take your time
you always take such care

You put me on a cushion
between your knees
you rub a little coconut oil
parting gentle as a breeze.[7]

Whether it's that 'Rat on Ararat / He isn't thin, he isn't fat' or 'Wha Me Mudder Do', no one can rap it and zap it with quite the energy, vitality and rhythm of Nichols. She also offers children understanding of their view of the world and a positive sense of worth:

Give yourself a hug –
a big big hug

And keep on singing,
'Only one in a million like me
Only one in a million-billion-thrillion-zillion
like me.'[8]

'Come and join de poetry band'

John Agard has lived in Britain since 1977, but it was his Guyanese childhood which strongly shaped the writer and performer he was to become. Agard worked for the Commonwealth Institute for several years, travelling all over the country to many different schools, festivals and libraries, so he knows his youthful audience well. His range spans new versions of nursery rhymes, Caribbean proverbs, well-chosen anthologies as well as poetry collections for adult and juvenile readers. His poetry for children, written both in dialect and standard English, is rhythmic and playful, bursting with energy and fun. Here is an invitation it is hard to refuse: a truly democratic poem, offering every reader a part so long as you 'take yu pen in yu hand . . . or just shout de poem out!'

> Come on everybody
> come and join de poetry band
> dis is poetry carnival
> dis is poetry bacchanal
> when inspiration call
> take yu pen in yu hand
> if you dont have a pen
> take yu pencil in yu hand
> if you dont have a pencil
> what the hell
> so long de feeling start to swell
> just shout de poem out.
>
> Words jumpin off de page
> tell me if Ah seein right
> words like birds
> jumpin out a cage
> take a look down de street
> words shakin dey waist
> words shakin dey bum
> words wit black skin
> words wit white skin
> words wit brown skin
> words wit no skin at all
> words huggin up words
> an sayin I want to be a poem today
> rhyme or no rhyme[9]

This extract is a good example of performance poetry at its best. Apart from the sheer vitality, witty rhymes and lively rhythms, Agard is both irreverent about poetry ('words shakin dey bum') and pays homage to it – words are likened to birds breaking free from the confines of cages, an imaginative and fitting metaphor. There is also a firm but positive racial message in the poem which truly lives with the spoken voice: 'this poem wants you to say it out loud and to shake your waist'[10] as the poet says himself.

Agard often pushes at the boundaries of how experience can be constituted in language. He tackles racial prejudice in his poetry, though he tends to shame the reader through irony rather than anger. In *I Din Do Nuttin*, which is for under-eights, Dilroy asks his mother why the little boy on his birthday card isn't black like him: 'Why de boy on de card so white?'[11] The point is not laboured, but it is effective just the same. Although laughter features in the title of another collection, Agard's philosophical side comes through.

> We are born. We grow up.
> We laugh. We cry.
> Then when the egg
> inside us stops beating,
> it's quite simple. We die.[12]

Agard's most recent book at the time of writing is *Get Back, Pimple*, where he grapples with some of the issues that affect young people. Speaking directly in language that draws them in, he celebrates music, dance, exams, clothes, skate-boards, make-up and money through poems which tease, challenge or amuse. Take 'Half-Caste':[13]

> explain yuself
> wha yu mean
> when yu say half-caste
> yu mean when light an shadow
> mix in de sky
> is a half-caste weather
> well in dat case
> england weather
> nearly always half-caste
> in fact some o dem cloud
> half-caste till dem overcast . . .

Agard's poetry should not be underestimated because it is approachable. This is a clever poem with an extended pun beautifully played out, all the while turning racist language on its head. There is also a streak of wild abandon in Agard which does what John Mole[14] requires of poetry – surprising the reader. 'You think you are on familiar ground when all of a sudden a particular phrase, a twist of syntax, a chance rhyme or a pivotal line-break takes you where you have never been before.' The geography teacher who threatens to 'dance on the globe / in a rainbow robe' and is also 'a million dreaming degrees / beyond the equator'[15] does just that. Agard is capable of playing with serious subjects – unjust immigration policies and the history of slavery, for example – by imagining a wonderfully anarchic limbo dancer with 'nothing to declare': 'And when limbo dancer revealed ankles / bruised with the memory of chains / it meant nothing to them / So limbo dancer bent over backwards / & danced.'[16] Agard is a gifted performer and writer who gets better with every book. Interested in all the arts, his poetry is good at crossing artificial boundaries between music, dance, painting and words.

When I Dance

When I Dance, 1988, won James Berry the Signal Prize for his first volume of poetry for children. He was already highly regarded as a poet with many awards to his credit and chose to spend time in schools and classrooms over a long period, taking a particular interest in the progress of children of African-Caribbean origin. Not every talented poet is able to write successfully for the young, but Berry is one of those who can. The title poem and several others explore the uniqueness of the individual as convincingly as any Romantic poet.

> Only one of me
> and nobody can get a second one
> from a photocopy machine.[17]
> (from 'Only One of Me')

> It is that when I dance
> I gather up all my senses
> Well into hearing and feeling,
> With body's flexible posures
> Telling their poetry in movement
> And I celebrate all rhythms.[18]
> (from 'When I Dance')

Sometimes Berry uses the rhythms of speech to write about music, dance, games, food, heat or carnival in Caribbean Nation Language, as in 'Sunny Market Song' ('Buy quatty wo't' noh, gal – / Buy quatty wo't') and 'Mek Drum Talk, Man',[19] with its pulsating beat:

Wake the people out-a they trance.
Tell people come dance.

> Lawks O, slap the drum, slap it Buddy.
> Slap it like yu mad somebody –
> budoom-abudoom-abudoom-a ba dap,
> budoom-abudoom-abudoom-a ba dap.

He conjures up raps that sing and lyrical evocations of time and place in standard English as well as dialect, in haiku, riddles, free verse and verse forms. At other times, he is interested in making the rhythm and the content work together for humorous effect.

> My sista is younga than me.
> My sista outsmart five-foot three.
> My sista is own car repairer
> and yu nah catch me doin judo with her.

> > I say I wohn get a complex
> > I wohn get a complex.
> > Then I see the muscles my sista flex.[20]

Berry makes excellent use of the oral tradition of Jamaica with riddle poems and proverbs which are incredibly funny. The need to take care before you insult someone is economically expressed in 'Noh cuss alligator "long-mout" till yu cross riber'; more serious, but still witty, is his reference to slavery . . . 'Cow wha belang a butcher neber say him bery-well.' Berry's poetry is located in a different cultural context from most British writers, offering diversity of outlook, yet made accessible through the poet's skill and kindness. His is not a harsh voice. Take the 'Jamaican Toad', tenderly looked out for:

> the sea is full of more than I know
> moon is bright like night time sun
> night is dark like all eyes shut

> > Mind – mind yu not harmed
> > somody know bout yu
> > somody know bout yu.[21]

Berry's letter poem from YOUR SPeCiAL-BiG-pUPPY-DOg is funny and perceptive :

> You know I'm so big
> I'll soon become a person.
> You know I want to know more
> of all that you know. Yet
> you leave the house, so, so often.
> And not one quarrel between us.
> Why don't you come home
> ten times a day?[22]

Though he doesn't avoid painful subjects, including facing up to racism ('Holding my first identity card / stamped "Negro"'), Berry is essentially an optimist and the overall mood is positive. He is particularly good at opening out some of the contradictory feelings of black children who have come to live in Britain.

> Mum walked everywhere, at my age.
> Dad rode a donkey.
> Now I take a bus
> or catch an underground train.
>   (from 'Mum Dad and Me')

> Rooms echo my voice. I see
> I was not a migrant bird. I am
> a transplanted sapling, here
>   blossoming.[23]
> (from 'Black Kid in a New Place')

His new collection, *Playing a Dazzler*,[24] 1996, gives equal weight to the experience of black youngsters growing up in Britain. The urgency to bring to life for others his affection for and memories of Jamaica, the land of his birth, seems undiminished. But Berry's interest is in the human condition and his compassion for foibles and awkwardness on the one hand, and admiration for the uniqueness of each individual, on the other, is apparent in both books. These are poems for everyone.

> You bash drums playing a dazzler;
> I worry a trumpet swaying with it.
>
> You write poems with line-end rhymes;
> I write poems with rhymes nowhere or anywhere.[25]

'Don't worry, Be happy'

One of the best-selling Caribbean poets for children is Benjamin Zephaniah whose very successful *Talking Turkeys*, 1994 was followed by *Funky Chickens*, 1996. Both books are inventively designed for younger readers. Their overall flavour is extremely likeable with Zephaniah's face smiling out at the reader in various guises. Funky it is with raps, hip-hop, epics, shape poems, rhymes and word play of every description. Zephaniah's enjoyment of language is evident and although his work is very oral, he includes a number of poems which look at writing from many different perspectives. Another favourite topic is the Queen:

> Dis ting is serious
> Do it for all of us
> Save our asparagus,
> God save
> Our
> Green.[26]

There are also serious moments in Zephaniah's poetry too and he is not afraid to expose the sensitive side of himself or to make a point about racism, as in 'Walking Black Home' which ends:

> Sometimes it's hard
> To get a taxi
> When you're **Black**.[27]

Zephaniah wants the reader to think about injustice, the environment and poverty, as well as celebrating love, Vegan food and messages like – 'Don't worry / Be happy'. He refers to Martin Luther King, the poor, pollution, the need to understand and appreciate difference and to live co-operatively together. *Funky Chickens* is dedicated to Danny, Zephaniah's adored cat, who was kicked to death by a teenage gang.

> What kind of world do we live in today,
> When our future adults
> Treat life this way.[28]

Thoughtful, tender, humane and humorous, Zephaniah 'struts his stuff' through the pages of his two engaging collections.

A Caribbean Dozen

A Caribbean Dozen,[29] edited by John Agard and Grace Nichols, came out to critical acclaim in 1994. The dozen in the title refers to the 13 poets who are featured in this book in keeping with the market tradition of a little bit extra or 'mek up' thrown in by generous vendors at Caribbean markets. The 13 poets represent some of the varied vernacular voices within African-Caribbean verse who have provided such a joyful extension of the English language. The body of Caribbean poetry in standard English has helped to widen the range of poetry available to adults and children alike. In terms of young readers, recent moves to make English literature more traditional may be a backward step, when it has taken so long to get poetry from other cultures established within the curriculum. But with so many talented poets of Caribbean origin publishing widely today, there are encouraging signs of the vitality of this poetry with the public at large. I am confident that Caribbean verse is here to stay.

Notes

1   Edward Kamau Brathwaite from 'Didn't he ramble', *The Arrivants*, Oxford, 1974.
2   Linton Kwesi Johnson, from *Inglan Is a Bitch*, Race Today Publications, London, 1980.
3   Grace Nicols, from 'Wha Me Mudder Do', *Come on into my Tropical Garden*, A & C Black, London, 1988; Benjamin Zepaniah, from 'Over de Moon', *Talking Turkeys*, Viking, London, 1994.
4   Aidan Chambers, 'The Signal Poetry Award', *Signal* 59 p. 86.
5   Nichols, from 'I Like to Stay Up', *op. cit.*
6   Grace Nichols, *Give Yourself a Hug*, A & C Black, London, 1994.
7   Nichols, from 'Granny Granny Please Comb My Hair', 1988, *op. cit.*
8   Nichols, from *Give Yourself a Hug*, 1994, *op. cit.*
9   John Agard from 'Poetry Jump-Up' in Morag Styles ed. *You'll Love This Stuff*, Cambridge, 1986.
10 John Agard quoted in M. Styles & H. Cook, eds *There's a Poet Behind You*, A & C Black, London, 1988, p. 114.
11 John Agard, from 'Happy Birthday, Dilroy!', *I Din do Nuttin*, Bodley Head, London, 1988.
12 John Agard, from 'A Clown's Conclusions', *Laughter is an Egg*, Viking, London, 1988.
13 John Agard, from 'Half-Caste', *Get Back, Pimple*, Viking, London, 1995.
14 John Mole, 'The Signal Poetry Award', *Signal* 74, 1994, p.8 6.
15 John Agard, from 'What the Geography Teacher Said When Asked: What Er We Avin For Geography Miss?' *Get Back Pimple*, Penguin, 1996.
16 John Agard, from 'Limbo Dances' at 'Immigration', *ibid.*
17 James Berry, from 'Only One of Me', *When I Dance*, Hamish Hamilton, London, 1988.
18 James Berry, from 'When I Dance', *ibid.*
19 James Berry, from 'Mek Drum Talk Man', *ibid.*
20 James Berry, from 'Hisa Big Brodda Dread, Na!, *ibid.*
21 James Berry, from 'Jamaican Toad', *ibid.*
22 James Berry, from 'Scribbled Notes Picked up by Owners', *ibid.*

23   James Berry, from 'Mum Dad and Me', and 'Black Kid in a New Place', *ibid.*
24   James Berry, from 'Playing a Dazzler', *Playing a Dazzler*, Hamish Hamilton, London, 1996.
25   *Ibid.*
26   Benjamin Zephaniah, *Funky Chickens*, Viking/Penguin, London, 1996.
27   Benjamin Zephaniah, from 'Walking Back Home', *ibid.*
28   Benjamin Zephaniah, from 'Danny Lives On', *ibid.*
29   John Agard, Grace Nichols, eds *A Caribbean Dozen*, Walker Books, London, 1995.

Subject Index

Index of Names